Theatres and Encyclopedias in Early Modern Europe

In early modern Europe, before a "theatre" was a playhouse, it was an encyclopedia. In this book William N. West explores what "theatre" meant to medieval and Renaissance writers and critics, and places Renaissance drama, for the first time, within the powerfully influential context of the encyclopedic writings which were being produced at the time. Recent criticism has recognized that the culture of early modern Europe was a theatre culture, fascinated by performance of all kinds, but it was also an encyclopedic culture, obsessed with collecting and sorting knowledge. Early encyclopedias presented themselves as textual theatres, in which everything knowable could be represented in concrete, visible form. Medieval and Renaissance plays, similarly, took encyclopedic themes as their topics: the mysteries of nature, universal history, the world of learning. But instead of transmitting authorized knowledge quickly and unambiguously, as it was supposed to, the theatre created a situation in which ordinary experience could become a communicable source of authority.

By the mid seventeenth century, the theatre had become the model for the reformation of the encyclopedia and the encyclopedia for the theatre, as knowledge itself came to be seen as a kind of performance. West covers a wide range of works, from the canonical encyclopedic texts of the Middle Ages and Renaissance to Marlowe's *Doctor Faustus*, Jonson's *The Alchemist*, and Bacon's *Novum Organum*, and provides a fascinating picture of the cultural and intellectual life of the period.

WILLIAM N. WEST has taught at the University of California at Berkeley, Stanford University, the University of Nevada, Reno, and is currently Assistant Professor of English at the University of Colorado at Boulder. He has published on encyclopedism, the arts of memory, symbolic economies, and the epistemology of early modern performance. He is currently working on a book about the significance of confusion and misunderstanding in early modern drama.

Cambridge Studies in Renaissance Literature and Culture

General editor
STEPHEN ORGEL
Jackson Eli Reynolds Professor of Humanities, Stanford University

Editorial board
Anne Barton, *University of Cambridge*
Jonathan Dollimore, *University of York*
Marjorie Garber, *Harvard University*
Jonathan Goldberg, *Johns Hopkins University*
Peter Holland, *University of Notre Dame*
Kate McLuskie, *University of Southampton*
Nancy Vickers, *Bryn Mawr College*

Since the 1970s there has been a broad and vital reinterpretation of the nature of literary texts, a move away from formalism to a sense of literature as an aspect of social, economic, political, and cultural history. While the earliest New Historical work was criticized for a narrow and anecdotal view of history, it also served as an important stimulus for post-structuralist, feminist, Marxist, and psychoanalytical work, which in turn has increasingly informed and redirected it. Recent writing on the nature of representation, the historical construction of gender and of the concept of identity itself, on theatre as a political and economic phenomenon, and on the ideologies of art generally, reveals the breadth of the field. Cambridge Studies in Renaissance Literature and Culture is designed to offer historically oriented studies of Renaissance literature and theatre which make use of the insights afforded by theoretical perspectives. The view of history envisioned is above all a view of our own history, a reading of the Renaissance for and from our own time.

Recent titles include

38. Ann Jones and Peter Stallybrass, *Renaissance Clothing and the Materials of Memory*

39. Robert Weimann, *Author's Pen and Actor's Voice: Playing and Writing in Shakespeare's Theatre*

40. Barbara Fuchs, *Mimesis and Empire: The New World, Islam, and European Identities*

41. Wendy Wall, *Staging Domesticity: Household Works and English Identity in Early Modern Drama*

42. Valerie Traub, *The Renaissance of Lesbianism in Early Modern England*

43. Joe Loewenstein, *Ben Jonson and Possessive Authorship*

A complete list of books in the series is given at the end of the volume

Theatres and Encyclopedias in Early Modern Europe

William N. West
University of Colorado at Boulder

PUBLISHED BY THE PRESS SYNDICATE OF THE UNIVERSITY OF CAMBRIDGE
The Pitt Building, Trumpington Street, Cambridge, United Kingdom

CAMBRIDGE UNIVERSITY PRESS
The Edinburgh Building, Cambridge, CB2 2RU, UK
40 West 20th Street, New York, NY 10011-4211, USA
477 Williamstown Road, Port Melbourne, VIC 3207, Australia
Ruiz de Alarcón 13, 28014 Madrid, Spain
Dock House, The Waterfront, Cape Town 8001, South Africa

http://www.cambridge.org

© William N. West 2002

This book is in copyright. Subject to statutory exception
and to the provisions of relevant collective licensing agreements,
no reproduction of any part may take place without
the written permission of Cambridge University Press.

First published 2002

Printed in the United Kingdom at the University Press, Cambridge

Typeset in Times 10/12 pt.   *System* QuarkXPress™   [TB]

A catalogue record for this book is available from the British Library

ISBN 0 521 80914 2 hardback

"But one who tries every study indifferently, and who goes at his task of learning gladly and cannot get enough of it, him we shall justly call the lover of wisdom (*philosophon*), shall we not?"

Then Glaukon said, "You will then be giving the name to a numerous and strange band, for all the lovers of spectacles (*philotheamones*) seem to me to be the sort that delight in learning something, and those who love to listen to things are very strange to be reckoned among the lovers of wisdom. They would not go willingly to a serious debate or any such entertainment, but as if they had farmed out their ears to listen to every chorus in the land, they run about to all the Dionysiac festivals, never missing one, either in the towns or in the country. Are we to call all these, then, and those who like to learn something, and all the practitioners of minor arts, lovers of wisdom (*philosophous*)?"

"Not at all," I said, "but they are like lovers of wisdom (*homoious men philosophois*)."

"The true lovers of wisdom, then," he asked, "whom do you mean?"

(*Tous de alêthinous, ephê, tinas legeis?*)

"The lovers of the spectacle of truth," I said.

(*Tous tês alêtheias, ên d' egô, philotheamonas.*)   Plato, *Republic* V, 475c–e

Contents

List of illustrations	*page* x
Acknowledgments	xiii
Note on texts	xv
Introduction: Circles of learning	1
1 The space of the encyclopedia	14
2 The idea of a theatre	43
3 Tricks of vision, truths of discourse: Illustration, *ars combinatoria*, and authority	79
4 Holding the mirror up to nature?: The humanist theatre beside itself	111
5 The show of learning and the performance of knowledge: Humors, *Epigrams*, and "an universal store"	143
6 Francis Bacon's theatre of Orpheus: "Literate experience" and experimental science	193
Notes	224
Bibliography	274
Index	291

Illustrations

1	Temple of Juno, from Vergil, *Opera*, ed. Sebastian Brant (Strassburg: Iohannis Grieninger, 1502). Reproduced by permission of the Huntington Library, San Marino, CA.	*page* 20
2	"Theatrum," from Terence, [*Comoediae*], ed. Sebastian Brant (Strassburg: J. Grüninger, 1496). Reproduced by permission of the Huntington Library, San Marino, CA.	21
3	Three-headed Philosophy, frontispiece from Gregor Reisch, *Margarita Philosophica* (1503). Reproduced by permission of the Huntington Library, San Marino, CA.	25
4	"Tower of learning," from Gregor Reisch, *Margarita Philosophica* (1503). Reproduced by permission of the Huntington Library, San Marino, CA.	26
5	Title page, from Theodor Zwinger, *Theatrum Vitae Humanae*, 4 vols. (Basel: Frobenius, 1571). Reproduced courtesy of the John M. Wing Foundation on the History of Printing, The Newberry Library, Chicago, IL.	54
6	Calliopius as judge, from Vat. Lat. 3305 (tenth century CE). © Bibliotheca Apostolica Vaticana, Rome.	60
7	Calliopius as an actor, from Terence, *Andria*, in *Comoediae*, ed. Jodocus Badius Ascensius (Lyons: [Johannes] Wechsel, 1493). Reproduced courtesy of the John M. Wing Foundation on the History of Printing, The Newberry Library, Chicago, IL.	61
8	Calliopius as an actor, from Terence, *Heauton Timoroumenos*, in *Comoediae*, ed. Jodocus Badius Ascensius (Lyons: [Johannes] Wechsel, 1493). Reproduced courtesy of the John M. Wing Foundation on the History of Printing, The Newberry Library, Chicago, IL.	62
9	Terence as a lecturer, from Terence, *Comoediae* (Venice: Simon Bevilacqua, 1496). Reproduced courtesy of the John M. Wing Foundation on the History of Printing, The Newberry Library, Chicago, IL.	65

List of illustrations   xi

10 Terentian actor, from Terence, *Comoediae* (Venice: Simon
    Bevilacqua, 1496). Reproduced courtesy of the John M. Wing
    Foundation on the History of Printing, The Newberry Library,
    Chicago, IL.   66
11 Guido Iuvenalis, frontispiece from Terence, *Comoediae*,
    ed. Jodocus Badius Ascensius (Lyons: [Johannes] Wechsel,
    1493). Reproduced courtesy of the John M. Wing Foundation
    on the History of Printing, The Newberry Library,
    Chicago, IL.   67
12 "Theatrum," from Terence, *Comoediae*, ed. Jodocus Badius
    Ascensius (Lyons: [Johannes] Wechsel, 1493). Reproduced
    courtesy of the John M. Wing Foundation on the History of
    Printing, The Newberry Library, Chicago, IL.   68
13 *Gorgo*, from Giulio Camillo, *L'Idea del Theatro dell'Eccelente
    M. Giulio Camillo* (Florence: Lorenzo Torrentino, 1550).
    Reproduced by permission of the Folger Shakespeare Library,
    Washington, DC.   88
14 Animals, from Bartholomaeus Anglicus, *De Proprietatibus
    Rerum*, ed. Wynkyn de Worde (London: Wynkyn de
    Worde, 1495). Reproduced courtesy of the John M. Wing
    Foundation on the History of Printing, The Newberry Library,
    Chicago, IL.   103
15 Dogs, from Conrad Gessner, *Historiae Animalium*, vol. I
    (Frankfurt: Bibliopolium Camberiano, 1603). Reproduced by
    permission of the Huntington Library, San Marino, CA.   104
16 Lynx, from Conrad Gessner, *Historiae Animalium*, vol. I
    (Frankfurt: Bibliopolium Camberiano, 1603). Reproduced by
    permission of the Huntington Library, San Marino, CA.   107
17 Lynxes, from Conrad Gessner, *Historiae Animalium*, vol. I
    (Frankfurt: Bibliopolium Camberiano, 1603). Reproduced by
    permission of the Huntington Library, San Marino, CA.   108
18 Fictional sea monsters, from Conrad Gessner, *Historiae
    Animalium*, vol. IV (Zurich: Christophoros Froscherus, 1558).
    Reproduced by permission of the Huntington Library,
    San Marino, CA.   109
19 Hammerhead shark, from Conrad Gessner, *Historiae
    Animalium*, vol. IV (Zurich: Christophoros Froscherus, 1558).
    Reproduced by permission of the Huntington Library,
    San Marino, CA.   110
20 Illustration from Terence, *Andria*, in [*Comoediae*], ed.
    Sebastian Brant (Strassburg: J. Grüninger, 1496). Reproduced
    by permission of the Huntington Library, San Marino, CA.   148

xii List of illustrations

21 Illustration from Terence, *Andria*, in [*Comoediae*], ed.
    Sebastian Brant (Strassburg: J. Grüninger, 1496). Reproduced by
    permission of the Huntington Library, San Marino, CA.   149
22 Illustration from Terence, *Andria*, in [*Comoediae*], ed.
    Sebastian Brant (Strassburg: J. Grüninger, 1496). Reproduced by
    permission of the Huntington Library, San Marino, CA.   150

Acknowledgments

No person alone can make an encyclopedia, a theatre, or, as I have been discovering, a book. I am happy to say that my understanding of how knowledge is created by the sharing of information socially has deepened empirically as well as theoretically over the course of this project. At times it seemed as if I must have buttonholed everyone I knew at least once with some of these ideas, but in particular I am grateful to the leads, stray thoughts, moral encouragement, and intellectual and personal generosity of Elizabeth Allen, Albert Ascoli, Shadi Bartsch, Erin Carlston, Jennifer Colbert, Jody Enders, Bettina Gockel, Anthony Grafton, Tim Hampton, Stephen Hartnett, Bill Ingram, Giuseppe Mazzotta, Kathy McCarthy, Stephen Mullaney, Alex Nagel, Catherine Paul, Jim Porter, David Quint, Catrien Santing, Mike Schoenfeldt, Betsy Sears, Jeremy Smith, Terri Tinkle, and J. B. Voorbij. Some of them may not even know how much their contributions helped me in putting a shape to my ideas or in inspiring me to set them down on paper, but all of them have become part of this venture.

My parents provided not only a place of retreat but went so far as to proofread several entire drafts, while my sisters offered me examples of the best side of academics – equal parts engagement, passion, and discipline. I was delighted when David Bevington stepped from behind his anonymity as a reader for Cambridge University Press to take credit for his exacting and unfailingly helpful comments. Most of them I simply stole wholesale, with no acknowledgment of their tremendous help other than this, and I recognize that the ones I stubbornly ignored, I do so at my peril. Robert Weimann, whose knowledge of early theatre is encyclopedic, has been encouraging, helpful, and inspirational throughout, and my thinking on theatre owes much to his work. Lisa Manter has been both receptive and demanding of my ideas here, and knew which stance was called for when. Rose Bell's tireless copy-editing tied up all the loose ends that I had left during my writing; her work gave me the luxury of concentrating on saying what I wanted to say. Leonard Barkan has proven as indispensable to the process of turning this into a book as he was directing it as a dissertation, so that I can still write of him now what I wrote in my acknowledgments then: I could not have written this without him. Stephen Orgel, as series editor and one-time colleague, and Vicki Cooper, my editor at Cambridge, shepherded me patiently through the long process of revision and were kind enough to pretend to believe me when I told them how long it would take me to finish. My daughter Amelia has kept me going by letting me tell stories of another kind.

I owe another sort of debt to the people I worked with while working on this book. *Theatres and Encyclopedias* took shape while I circulated among several institutions in one-year positions, a process that was sometimes grueling but that wonderful colleagues and students made invigorating. They provided a continual reminder of the pleasures and virtues of persisting in that course, and I am grateful to all of them, both for the chance to try out some of these ideas in classrooms and hallways, and the opportunity on occasion to escape from them into teaching. I have been lucky in all my colleagues at Berkeley, Stanford, Reno, and Colorado, but in particular in three of my chairs at Berkeley, each of whom managed to find, at different moments of crisis but always at the last minute, work for me in their departments that let me keep teaching and thus keep writing: Janet Adelman of English, Judith Butler of Rhetoric, and Ralph Hexter of Comparative Literature. Without the practical support they provided, I would not have had the resources to finish this book, or indeed to continue in the profession of teaching at all.

An early version of chapters 1 and 2 appeared in *Renaissance Drama* as "The Idea of a Theatre: Humanist Ideology and the Imaginary Stage in Early Modern Europe" (n. s. 28 [1997]), and a section of chapter 5 was published as "Public Knowledge at Private Parties: Vives, Jonson, and the Circulation of the Circle of Knowledge," in *Pre-Modern Encyclopaedic Texts: Proceedings of the Second COMERS Congress* (ed. Peter Binkley, Leiden: E. J. Brill [1997]). I began the research on this project with support from the W. M. Keck Foundation and Andrew W. Mellon Foundation at the Huntington Library, San Marino, CA; I completed the manuscript on a Short-Term Fellowship at the Folger Shakespeare Library, Washington, DC, and as Audrey Lumsden-Kouvel Fellow at the Newberry Library, Chicago. I can imagine no better circle of knowledge than that joining these three wonderful libraries.

Note on texts

Where it is relevant to my discussion, I have included the approximate date of appearance of works and plays in parentheses after the title. For written works, this is the date of composition or widespread circulation, as far as can be ascertained; for plays, it is the approximate date of performance. In either case, this date can differ significantly from the date of publication or the dates of the texts I cite in the Bibliography.

I have standardized English spelling throughout the text, but somewhat idiosyncratically. I have not modernized Middle English, although this has meant making some risky judgment calls, because it seemed too close to rewriting. I have also felt free to leave non-standard spelling in texts when it seemed to me to pun or suggest layers of meaning, e.g., Jonson's "Laborinth" (presumably because one must "labor in't") for Labyrinth.

Where possible, I have quoted from published translations, although some of them I have silently modified. When I have used my own translation for a work that has a modern translation in the Bibliography, I have noted it in the appropriate footnote. Translations from works with no published translation are my own.

Introduction: Circles of learning

> Great movements begin with ideas in people's heads.
> —Isaiah Berlin, *The Crooked Timber of Humanity*

The culture of early modern Europe was a theatre culture, fascinated by ostentation, performance, pretense, and pretentiousness of all kinds. But it was also an encyclopedia culture, obsessed with collecting and sorting information, diligently reducing knowledge to the possession of discrete facts, driven by the desire to map the world's order and to construct a universal theory of everything.[1] The articulation of these two institutions – the ideas and the practices of theatre and the encyclopedia – upon and against each other in fifteenth-, sixteenth-, and seventeenth-century Europe is the topic of this book.

Public theatre and encyclopedic texts seem in some ways to be almost antithetical objects. What can private readership and public spectatorship, knowledge and appearance, surface show and deep truth have to do with one another? They were each, in different ways, circles of learning, the literal meaning of *encyclopedia* and the meaning that seemed to inhere in the theatre's distinctive "wooden O." Each made a claim, at least initially, to represent the manifold of the world in literally or metaphorically circular form – that is, with completeness, perfect symmetry, and self-containment. In early modern Europe, the ideas of these two institutions were used to define one another. Compendious textual "Theatres," with running metaphors of audiences and actors demonstrating the theatricality of the book, or performed dramas that took the moral universe as their theme, suggest a conceptual link between these two seemingly distant sources of knowledge and authority. What they share – at least what they were imagined to share – was a conception of knowledge as the ordered representation of everything. This order was seen as difficult to grasp and sometimes even deceptive, but not as dynamic. That is, however mysterious it might be, it was stable; its order was the order of a structure of atomized elements arranged in a static relation to one another rather than as a changing vector or varying pattern. It was imagined as *spatialized* and *visual*, *objective* in the sense that it existed independently of its knowers. The encyclopedia as the repository of the elements that made up the world and the theatre as their place of display were thus linked. During the course of the sixteenth century, as actual theatres were built in England and Europe, the kind of knowledge associated with them changed. Instead of mimicking the static visuality of the encyclopedia, the theatre revealed itself as a space of duplicity and equivocation where word and spectacle, or indeed all different kinds of discourse, could be placed in uneasy conjunction. In the seventeenth century, the encyclopedia followed suit, revising its earlier self-representation as a frozen echo of the world to a more fluid one, evolving eventually into ideas of experimentalism and the possibility of quantifying and organizing human action. To put timeless knowledge into play within the human realm of events was in a sense to perform it, to understand by acting. Between experimental science and the disciplines of authority, between encyclopedia and theatre, there developed in early modern Europe a different standard of knowing that I call the performance of knowledge.

Before a theatre was a real space in which to enact plays, the theatre was an idea built around a word that referred to an object that no longer existed except in texts, in which its attributes, functions, and powers changed. Roughly the same period that saw the construction of the first physical theatres in Italy and England also saw the development of a new proper term for the universal texts that previously had been given titles like *speculum*, *thesaurus*, and of course *theatrum*. The word "encyclopedia" was newly coined by fifteenth-century humanists who misread it from their texts of Pliny and Quintilian, while the term "theatre," for the first time since the fall of the Roman Empire, referred to an actual physical structure. "Encyclopedia" and "theatre" were thus both, in different ways, as new to the fifteenth century as the objects they described. One of the dominant ideas about the nature of the theatre in the sixteenth century was that it resembled that other new, still mysterious and imperfectly defined object, the encyclopedia. Early modern encyclopedias presented themselves as textual theatres, where all knowledge was represented as objectified and displayed as if on stage. Medieval and early modern plays, similarly, often took encyclopedic themes as their topics – the mysteries of nature, universal history, the world of learning. Just as medieval drama often belies or at least complicates its supposedly didactic aims, though, the early encyclopedia approached the universal knowledge it depicted with a sense of playfulness and skepticism missing in later versions, from its great eighteenth-century descendant, the *Encyclopédie* of Diderot and D'Alembert, to the present web-based *Britannica*. Both early modern theatre and encyclopedia show a marked awareness of the impossibility of their projects – namely, that the representing thing and the represented thing should become one in the representation – and this sense of impossibility in each is the basis for their unstable relations to one another. In their combination of these two conflicting tendencies between showing and knowing, displaying and hoarding, encyclopedia and theatre outlined – *within* each of their separate discourses and practices as well as *between* them – a transitional form of knowledge between the more familiar modern form and its medieval precursors.

In his *Image of Governaunce* (1541), a treatise on the ideal management of the state, Thomas Elyot proposed an educational system that combined theatre and encyclopedia into a unified whole. The wise emperor of Elyot's text constructs

a new library, garnishing it as well with most principal works in every science, as also with the images of the authors . . . . which library was divided into sundry galleries, according to divers sciences, all builded round in the form of a circle, and being separate with walls one from another.[2]

The library's circular shape echoes that of the theatre, while the clear divisions between fields of study – the quadrivium of Geometry, Astronomy, Arithmetic, and Music – show it to be firmly within the encyclopedic tradition of the liberal arts. The theatre's circle and the contents of human learning are the two components from which the idea of the encyclopedia is generated – the Greek *enkuklios paideia* becomes, through a jarringly literal translation into Latin, the *orbis disciplinae*, or the circle of learning, or, as Elyot defined it in his *Dictionary* (1538), "the circle or course of all doctrines" (s.v. "Encyclios, & Encyclia").[3]

The library, though, is only half of Elyot's complete educational system. It is complemented by an actual theatre building: "Many would report to the common houses called *Theatres*, and purposing some matter of philosophy, would there dispute openly" (*Image*, 42r–v). This theatre is not the theatre of Shakespeare, Marlowe, Alleyn, Burbage, the playwrights and entrepreneurs of the generation after Elyot, nor even that of Elyot's contemporaries, like John Bale or Nicholas Udall, who sought to harness the power of theatrical performance to the pedagogical ends of Protestantism and Tudor rule. There is no suggestion in Elyot's text that he even considers contemporary drama when he mentions his theatre. Instead of providing entertainment, Elyot's "common houses called *Theatres*" provide the opportunity for the students to keep up their skill in the arts of the trivium, Grammar, Rhetoric, and Logic, "disput[ing] openly" their philosophical topics. In contrast to the private contemplation of the library, Elyot's theatre provides a public forum for public skills.[4] Together the theatre and the encyclopedic library form a single system for a complete humanist education in the liberal arts. For Elyot, the areas of the theatre and the library are contiguous and complementary; they have different objects but the same didactic goal (*Image*, 41r–42v). In fact, the circularity of the library and the vivid statues and images with which it is decorated mark it as a kind of asymptotic ideal for the theatre as a perfectly legible spectacle of knowledge. The encyclopedic theatre is a practical ordering of space that enables it to hold knowledge and to mark it as meaningful, so that a later reader might draw the collected wisdom forth at his leisure. For Elyot and for his peers, there is no tension between the two seemingly unlike conceptions of theatre and encyclopedia, with his theatre being no more based on feigning than his encyclopedic library. Elyot's library, like his imaginary theatre, is rather a space of exposition than production, where the statues and images, like the theatrical disputants, display their cases "openly," apparently without the possibilities of dramatic recognition or reversal.

For Elyot, the theatre is also subject to the same authority as an encyclopedic work, which is the authority of the prince to control the meaning of things: "teaching representeth the authority of the prince." When Dionysios, the tyrant of Syracuse, was expelled from his city he fled to Italy and became a schoolmaster, and thus was able to gloat that, "although Sicilians had exiled him, yet in despite of them all he reigned, noting thereby the authority that he had over his scholars."[5] The prince also controls the meanings disseminated in the theatre, which makes theatre as useful as any other pedagogical tool for the production of knowledge. Even when theatre is not meant to be strictly didactic, its reception remains for Elyot under the prince's control; it makes up, after all, part of the apparatus of the perfect educational system in *The Image of Governaunce*. As emperor, Elyot tells us, Nero required attendance at his own theatrical performances, and relied on his imperial power to enforce the appreciation of the audience. Anyone who slept or seemed bored was struck in the face by one of Nero's slaves,

Or if anyone were perceived to be absent, or were seen to laugh at the folly of the emperor, he was forth with accused as it were of misprision. Whereby the emperor found occasion to commit him to prison, or put him to tortures. (*Governour*, 23r)

Nero enforces a particular kind of enjoyment with as much authority as Elyot's own king enforced religious orthodoxy. To misprise, to refuse the meaning offered by the prince or even to fail to respect its intent, is both epistemological failure and civil disobedience. In a sense, no distinction is made between teaching and entertainment, though not in a realization of the Horatian requirement that art be "dulce et utile."[6] What entertains in this example does not necessarily teach anything except the extent of the prince's authority to monitor all interpretive activity. The encyclopedia and the theatre are conceptually identical – not merely similar, but in fact versions of the same idea. Together they present a controlled, organized expression of reality.

The shifting relations between encyclopedia and theatre depicted by Elyot are typical in their implicitness and mobility of those in the Renaissance. It is impossible to argue for a single sustained relation between them; what is striking is how frequently there seems to be *some* relation, so that the mention of one form will draw in a discussion of the other, whether the relation is one of likeness, opposition, synecdoche (the theatre is the vehicle in which the encyclopedia is displayed and the encyclopedia is the depiction of the greater *theatrum mundi*), analogy (the theatrical relation of audience and actor suggests a structure for the relation of philosopher to truth), or something less clearly

Introduction: Circles of learning

defined. During this period theatre and encyclopedia serve as Other to each other, as terms and things that hover between an objective reality and an equally important figurative valence. Since each is equally universal and equally capable of encompassing any term that is opposed to it, although usually in different ways, they provide each other with an unassimilable – or rather, semi-assimilable, since they are always in conjunction, but no more – difference that lets each pretend to a kind of positive existence. One way to determine what is theatrical is to set it against a spectacle that is whole, accurate, or complete; one way to define an encyclopedia is to show that it is not feigned, superficial, or merely pleasurable like the spectacles of the theatre.

The connection of theatre and knowledge has a long history prior to the Renaissance. It was in part by drawing on the history of this relation between being and pretending that Renaissance culture developed its own understanding of the relation of the two categories, working with late antique encyclopedic writers like Martianus Capella, Macrobius, Isidore, and the Augustine of *The City of God*, medieval compilers like Vincent of Beauvais and Bartholomaeus Anglicus, and the newer conceptions of the encyclopedia advanced by Angelo Poliziano and Guillaume Budé. As it developed in humanist culture, the unique role of the encyclopedia was to educate the self in ethics, the total field of human relations. Quite accidentally, the public theatre proved to offer the same education – not by showing a true content, but through its complex negotiations of desire, authority, vision, language, and cultural and physical structures. But the idea that not only do seeming and being stand in a particularly significant relation to one another, but that that relation has a practical analogy in the relation of the theatre to the total knowledge provided by philosophy, goes back to Plato's *Republic*, when Sokrates is questioning his interlocutor Glaukon about the nature of philosophy in the passage that serves as this book's epigraph (*Republic* V, 475c–e). Plato links the lover of wisdom (*philosophos*) and the lover of dramatic spectacle (*philotheamones*) as both opposites and, strangely, as doubles. While Glaukon distinguishes absolutely the eager and careless love of novelty and spectacle of the lovers of theatre from the serious inquiry of the lovers of wisdom, at least etymologically all that separates the spectators (*philotheamones*) from the philosophers (*philosophoi*) is the change in suffixes from *-theamones*, "watchers," to *-sophoi*, "wise men." The distinction is in fact still less clear cut. More than merely in the words, the *philotheamones*, "lovers of spectacle," provide a physical, sensible model for the philosophers who here seem so elusive to Glaukon. Those who love to look, whom Glaukon finds so out of place among the philosophers, are *like* the lovers of wisdom (*homoious men philosophois*) who have also lost their place in society. The lovers of spectacle may be out of place among the philosophers, but the philosophers are *atopoi*, placeless, too, perhaps because they delight in the process of learning rather than in its goal, wisdom, and take in indiscriminately the show of truth and what only looks like it. The philosopher differs from the playgoer only in that he looks at the truth uncovered and visible (*alêtheia*); he too is a kind of "spectator of truth." While Plato sets up a distinction between these two viewers, the analogy suggests that a philosopher is not simply an onlooker of an unsuspecting reality, but one towards whom reality is directed as if in performance.

The implications of this passage about the complex relation between viewer and spectacle shape how theatre and philosophy are seen by readers and writers in Europe over the next two millennia. First, there is a separation, at least physical and perhaps psychological or ontological, of the roles of spectator and performer. Second, on both sides of the stage there is an awareness of the tacit rules that govern the performance and allow it to proceed. Finally, there is a residue of extradramatic reality that inheres in every performance, making even its feigning not the opposite of knowing, but something more like its declension. Although in one sense opposites of each other, spectation in the theatre and investigation of truth in the world are connected by a flexible bond of likeness, contrary but polar, so that they are both opposed and linked to each other.

This relation of congruence between seeming and knowing appears antithetical to some of the most powerful and productive tenets of philosophy as it develops in Europe: that appearances deceive, that truth is hidden from the casual glance and buried deep within things, that the labor of knowing is not the same as the pleasure of watching a drama. Knowledge and drama brush continually against each other, even serve to define each other, but the culture in which knowledge and spectacle are equal is always represented as one that is alien to the definer: oral instead of literate, "primitive" or decadent rather than modern, with all the allusive relations that these terms imply.[7] But the ascription of difference in Plato and in the unspoken traditions of European thinking relies on another sameness, as Plato says a *likeness*, that leads from drama – in Greek, an action – to knowledge and back again to action by way of the theatre – from the Greek word for a place of looking. This counter-tradition that delight in what is feigned has a bearing on the knowledge of what is true is just as old and august as the more familiar one that opposes pleasant deception and knowledge. Aristotle, in the opening chapters of *Metaphysics*, remarks that "The lover of tales (*philomuthos*) is in some sense a lover of true knowledge, because a myth is composed of wonders" (I, 2. 10, 982b). Aquinas' comment on this passage is even more direct, although no more clear about the relation than Aristotle or Plato: "The lover of tales is some kind of lover of wisdom" (*philosophus aliqualiter est philomythes*). The Aristotelian linkage is more concerned with the fictional plot than with its display, but the idea that links what is played as in a theatre with what is in reality remains a shaping one.

Plato's two most important translators in the Renaissance, Marsilio Ficino and Johannes Serranus, pass over without comment the section of the *Republic*

Introduction: Circles of learning

in which Sokrates tentatively likens the philosophers and the playgoers. If anything, they weaken the homology of *philotheamones* and *philosophoi*, and the one between the *philotheamones* of plays and the *alêtheias philotheamones*, by translating the first as "qui spectaculorum avidi sunt" and the second as "veritatis inspiciendae cupidos."[8] Serranus almost pointedly leaves Ficino's words for the cluster of *philotheamones* unchanged. He is rarely this generous to his predecessor's Latin translations of the Greek; it is as if perhaps he is unsure of having understood it this time himself. In general, though, Serranus seems to be particularly at pains to point out the gross incongruity of the playfulness of the theatre and the serious business of philosophy. When in the *Laws* Plato stoops to discussing the appropriate penalties for those who cheat in theatrical competitions, Serranus sneers in a rare marginal note, "Plato ought to be more careful about being so concerned about the theatre in these matters."[9]

Serranus' translation of the works of Plato was the most highly visible one for writers and readers in early modern England and indeed throughout Europe.[10] His preoccupation with distancing Platonic philosophy from its stagy likenesses thus has the effect of driving the connection between these two positions into the center of neo-Platonic thought in the later Renaissance. In the introductory epistle, Serranus proposes a series of interpretive strategies by which he will be able to separate "true Philosophy from the philosophic buskin (*cothurno philosophico*), the true use of Philosophy from its abuse."[11] What this suggests that he fears is not *Philosophia cothurnata*, the costuming of philosophy, but the donning of philosophic costume, *cothurnus philosophicus* – the way that what should be the kernel of wisdom can suddenly be worn on the outside as a disguise, with no immediate signal given that it is any less legitimately philosophy. What he argues against is not false philosophy, but the abuse of a philosophy that is presumably true by, specifically, its display as a spectacle.

But Serranus slips the players he has expelled from his *Republic* back into his own philosophy. He returns obsessively to his theatrical metaphor throughout his introduction, undermining the distinction he establishes between true philosophy and its mimic counterpart each time he asserts it. Queen Elizabeth I, the dedicatee of his volumes, he says, is fortunate to have had a front-row seat for the tragedies that sweep Europe, just as if they were tragic spectacles, rather than taking part in them.[12] Part of Serranus' dedication to the first volume is also a defense of philosophy against its real or imagined critics; Serranus assures the reader that he has prepared for this defense because "I was not ignorant that I would incur the diverse judgments of men when I made my entrance in so famous a theatre . . ."[13] It is hard to say whether the theatre here is the (good) arena of legitimate academic give-and-take or the (bad) broils of bean-counting scholasticism; before we imagine that the word can imply only the latter, we should recall that the reception of Serranus' translation was favorable enough that it provides us with the Stephanus numbers still in use today. The spectacles of academic debate are also legitimated by the larger spectacle that contains them. One of Serranus' defenses of studying pagan philosophy is that "it gives pleasure to track down causes and the effects of causes in this theatre of the Universe."[14] Whether the theatre of learned society is philosophical or spectacular, the theatre of the Universe must be a philosophical one if Serranus' defense is to make sense; while *effects* may be ascribed to the deceptive appearances of a theatre of the world, *causes* cannot be.

As he begins his argument for the seriousness and utility of philosophy, Serranus takes on the same tones that his rough contemporaries in England will take in defending the theatre:

nor in a matter of such importance do we lack solid reasons, by which it is agreed that we have hardly played at working (*ludere operam*) in this affair, but that a task both pleasing to God and useful to the Church has fallen to us . . . . In this defense of my project, I am witness that it was proposed to me to satisfy good and learned men, not rash fools (*improbis momis*), for whom it is easy enough to carp (*mômeisthai*), but not so easy in fact either to imitate (*mimeisthai*) or to correct what they find fault with.[15]

Serranus is alluding to a saying attributed to another famous compiler, the painter Zeuxis. In another story, recorded by Pliny, Zeuxis inscribes under the painting of an athlete that had attracted criticism, "One may more easily mock (*mômêsetai*) than imitate (*mimêsetai*) this."[16] *Momi* are wielders of shallow and brutal criticism and the frequent targets of apotropaic gestures by humanists and some of their favorite classical authors; they appear in Lucian's *How to Write History* and Erasmus' *Praise of Folly*.[17] On the one hand, then, the readers are told not to be like the ignorant clown of the theatre who ridicules what he cannot improve or understand. The alternative, though, is equally theatrical – the understanding philosopher will be not so much an interpreter as a mimic, one who participates in *mimêsis*.[18] Even more definitively than Plato's analogical relationship between the lover of wisdom and the lover of spectacle, Serranus' involved text implicates, without offering a means of untangling them, three different images of philosophical investigation: the pursuit of knowledge as vision of truth, its pursuit as spectacle, and the imitative performance of drama. The reader can respond as a good actor or spectator or as a bad actor or spectator – but his response is always figured in terms of some role that he would have in relation to a play, an enactment of one kind or another.

This might seem to be only another skirmish in the old quarrel between philosophy and poetry, albeit a poetry exclusively imagined as dramatic, but Serranus closes his defense with a gesture that forces us to reappraise philosophy, too, in a narrower scope. Serranus sympathizes with the impression that Plato is difficult and disorderly, and in his text and translation he offers a new ordering of the dialogues (which, like the pagination of this edition, remains standard today), changing their traditional grouping by tetralogies into one that is thematic (*Opera* [1578], **. iiiiv). This new arrangement, together with Serranus' commentary, reveals

an organization of universal learning (*universae doctrinae syntagma*) composed from the very words of Plato and woven together similarly, so that for complete and absolute learning nothing will be seen to be lacking.[19]

Serranus further asserts that with proper care for organization, it can be shown that Plato and Aristotle are not in opposition, and further, that there is nothing in Aristotle that Plato had not at least alluded to first. This, Serranus promises, is his next project:

One thing remains, but very necessary in our judgment: that we will show to you, reader, a *summa* of universal learning (*universae doctrinae summam*) gathered out of various places and put together, in a single body, so to speak, and illustrated indeed by the application of examples, by comparison of Aristotle and other authors; that whatever has been variously scattered and dispersed (*variè disiecta atque disseminata*) may be brought back opportunely into a single whole, with individual elements called back to their groups, and with their use indicated.[20]

For Serranus, Plato contains all knowledge already; what is needed is an effort of organizing and arranging the discrete elements of his works, illustrating and expanding on them with reference to other writers, to reveal this "complete and absolute knowledge" in all its clarity and totality. Serranus never seems to have written this work, which would have been a kind of Platonic encyclopedia. Since it promised to indicate the proper use of what it contained, it no doubt would have definitively answered the question of how to tell "true Philosophy from the philosophic buskin, the true use of Philosophy from its abuse." Serranus' final answer to the problem of spectacular, theatrical philosophy comes in the form of the promise of an encyclopedia.

During the Renaissance, the likeness of theatre and encyclopedia became visible precisely because for the first time it was being called into question. Earlier treatments had not felt this as strongly as a tension – the encyclopedia's project was seductive but also impossible, and treatments were therefore both ironized and serious in a way that is difficult to characterize systematically. Such a text could both contain useful information organized into a world-system that described the order of things *and* treat its knowledge with a playfulness that continuously mocked its own pretensions. We are currently undergoing a similar shift from the concept of objectified knowledge as commodity to one that incorporates many of the ideas of knowledge as performance banished by the thinkers of the Enlightenment. The period of the museum-as-archive, where knowledge is stockpiled and which one visited to observe the noteworthy objects of the past, is ending. Instead, attendance increases in the museums-as-experience, for instance at the Holocaust Museum in Washington or the

Viking Village in York, where the claim is that you do not look at a collection from the outside, but experience it – its "sights, sounds and smells," as the brochure from the Viking Village proclaims – from within. We remain interested in objects, but more than ever we desire intercourse with them instead of distanced gazing. Our problem – at least as we cast it – becomes one of devising the means by which such objects can speak for themselves and address us, can offer themselves up to us free from mediation. For an answer we turn to generally representative space, a space that itself means nothing because it is separated from the "real world" but which for the same reason can be given any number of forms. This space is the space of the encyclopedia, the circle of learning of the theatre as it was originally conceived, and we turn to it now because we feel that we can no longer experience the real itself, but must somehow remake and refind it. But such spaces with their earnest commitment to fidelity, or at least to faithful copying, trivialize the real. When New York or Paris or Venice is realized as a casino in Las Vegas (or Siena in Reno) instead of as a city with its history, its residents living and dead, there is necessarily some attenuation of what constitutes a place or even an experience. Such experiences reduce experience to the expected and even the stereotyped. They are, in a sense, abstract theories posing as experiences. The same transition occurs between encyclopedia and theatre in the early modern period and is interrupted by the process of the Enlightenment. Both encyclopedia and theatre begin by offering themselves as kinds of displays for their passive viewers. As they develop in practice, though, the theatre is realized as an experience, not a spectacle, while the encyclopedia remains a closed collection of elements.

Thomas Elyot and Johannes Serranus introduce a historical period within which the relation of theatre and encyclopedia changed from an imaginary one, based on the ideas about two non-existent objects that were assigned similar characteristics, to a real one. In early modern Europe the idea of the theatre preceded the material theatre, shaping its subsequent history even as actual theatres broke down the assumptions surrounding them.[21] The concepts that developed around the word "theatre" in the late Middle Ages and early Renaissance crucially shaped the development of physical theatre buildings in the fifteenth and sixteenth centuries.[22] Unlike the materialist understanding, though, this placement of the idea before its manifestation is not a misrecognition of material elements as mental ones, but the analysis of the development of mental concepts in the absence of their real equivalents so that they apply a shaping pressure to their eventual realizations. It remains, in other words, materialist, but a kind of materialist intellectual history rather than the ideal materialism that Michel Foucault criticized when he observed that the physical arrangement of space alone is not enough to determine the discursive formations that are connected with it.[23] Taken in this light, the epigraph from Isaiah Berlin becomes non-trivial – that the weight of ideas, of mental concepts and expectations, can exert force on the material world in ways analogous to material changes in it. During the period of the sixteenth and seventeenth centuries, actual theatres and actual encyclopedias were produced for the first time. In this period, the theatre changed from being a part of the encyclopedia which was a part of the world to being a part of the world but not of static knowledge. The physical, textual, visible, and performative objects and practices that followed on their ideological pre-conceptions also altered them irremediably.

The result was ultimately a division of the discourses and concepts of theatre and encyclopedia. For a while, though, as the ideas of each of these objects were permeated by the uses to which they were set and the resistances and pressures of materially inflected practices, their coextensiveness gave rise to what we may call an early modern epistemology of performance. This epistemology formed a bridge between the experimental science of the seventeenth century and earlier forms of knowledge that were grounded in the mastery of traditional authorities. In their earlier, imaginary forms, *theatre* and *encyclopedia* shared a conception that centered on the undistorted display of objects of knowledge before passive spectators. In practice, their supposedly spectatorial knowledge changed over the sixteenth century to a knowledge that was conceived of as performative, as relying on and shaped in its presentation rather than simply offering a faithful representation of a truth housed elsewhere. The performative conception of knowledge likens the activity of the spectator to that of the actor in producing meaning from the world she or he both replicates and observes. Later encyclopedias adopted some of the flexibility, ambiguity, and experiential knowledge that the theatre had proven it could explore. This tension and jointure marks the subsequent histories of both encyclopedia and theatre, the one representing itself as an accurate description of what is real that, for better or worse, falls back on the techniques of play and performance, the other represented as having, in its pretending – at some times and in some circumstances – the power to show the spectacle of truth. The early modern theatre not only opens up a new realm of existence – human experience – to intelligibility, it does so in a new way. By the seventeenth century, the encyclopedia begins to learn from its double the theatre how to standardize and measure experience, how experience itself can be regulated and commodified, how thought can be turned into a form of production. We stand well before the beginnings of the social sciences still, but they have, through the interplay of encyclopedia and theatre, become imaginable.

This book traces an old path from the ideal to the real, from theory to practice, on its way to a middle ground which it calls performance – practice that does not set itself in opposition to theory but that takes as its basis the intermediate space of theatrics. It would, perhaps, be possible to offer a history of the relations between the encyclopedia and the theatre as a rigorous and logically self-consistent exploration and development of several distinct ideas – of the changing conception of the *topoi*, for instance, and of the minute shifts between one treatment and another. Such a treatment, though, would remain theoretical, and exclude much of the inconsistency, confusion, and vagueness of the practices associated with these concepts. To produce that kind of intellectual history would be a very different project from what I want to do here. In theory, the connection between theatre, encyclopedia, and the establishment of a space for experiment might be produced as a set of logical steps responding to each other and to larger cultural conditions. Practice, though, can be fuzzy and inconsistent; it can leave things unspoken, overlook contradictions, make countless small adjustments in the use of something that never coalesce into an orderly, directional narrative. If there seems to be little logic in the clustering of ideas and actions that I offer here, it is because they are governed not by *logos* but by *praxis* – although in many cases it is the praxis of logos, the labor of scholars at work making theories. Theories are themselves always practices, if not the practices that they theorize, and words always have effects, if not always the ones they claim. Johannes Kepler once responded to Robert Fludd's criticism that Kepler's books failed to capture the grandeur of the cosmos: "I have compared my diagrams to your pictures; I admit that my book is not the equal of your ornate one; . . . I have excused this defect with the explanation that I was *doing mathematics*."[24] To recognize that Renaissance thinkers like Fludd may *not* be "doing mathematics" is to see that an evaluation of their work in strictly logical terms may hide some of the inconsistency, analogical thinking, and muddiness that lets it work.[25]

In my attempt to recognize a persistent, though fluid, idea from ancient Rome into the early modern period, I have taken core samples from the works of many thinkers and from many encyclopedic texts, reassembling and interpreting them. In giving them a shape I have at some times and to some extent dehistoricized them in the same way as these works tend to dehistoricize their sources, and so I am doing what I diagnose. My first two chapters explain what significance the ideas of encyclopedia and theatre possessed before their realizations in the sixteenth century, posing the twin ideals of vision and of space that they share. The third chapter addresses a third factor in both forms, the fantasy of a combinatory system that could produce an infinity of texts or knowledge by the application of a finite number of rules of combination to a finite set of elements. I also look more closely at two sixteenth-century encyclopedic texts, one of which tries to establish its accuracy on an absolute linguistic systematization, while the other puts into practice the theatrical bias in favor of vision. The fourth chapter looks at what happened to humanist notions of theatre when they encountered the performance practices of Shakespeare and Kyd. The theatre, praised as a pedagogical device long before actual examples were built, turned out to provide a very different sort of education than its backers had foreseen; instead of transmitting authorized knowledge quickly and unambiguously, it created a situation in which common experience could become a communicable source of authority. The fifth and sixth chapters examine two particular responses to the practice of the theatre and encyclopedia. In these two concluding chapters, I look at the careers of Ben Jonson and Francis Bacon, whose writings are markedly broad, varied, and incomplete, but who each insisted that the body of his work was part of a single, unified life-project. In Jonson and Bacon, the resistance to fragmentation and the desire to totalize are explicitly cast as contests between the theatre and the encyclopedia, in which one form becomes the model for the reformation of the other. Jonson and his humanist models shifted the congruence that was initially imagined between theatres and encyclopedias into an ideal of the ethical encyclopedia – learned individuals so perfectly centered in their knowledge that they could meet any situation by drawing on their stored wisdom, in a sense enacting or performing it. But Jonson also explores what it means for knowledge to exist not as reflection but as performance, particularly in *The Alchemist*. Bacon similarly has a double project. Explicitly antitheatrical – he expels what he calls the "Idols of the Theatre" from his encyclopedic *De Augmentis Scientiarum*, a projected guide to the renewal of learning through the use of experiment that served as an inspiration for the scientific revolution – Bacon nonetheless describes the experimental investigations he hopes for as literal stagings of the drama of nature.

1   The space of the encyclopedia

> Wisdom has but one book in which all the sciences are treated and which is taught to all the people. He has had all of the sciences pictured on all of the walls and on the outworks, both inside and out.
> —Tommaso Campanella, *The City of the Sun* (1602)[1]

Despite their great historical and cultural range, almost coextensive with that of the European literatures themselves, encyclopedic writings share certain consistencies that are more than merely generic. Fundamentally, they are reference works, compiled and organized to reflect some reality to which by definition they are secondary.[2] All encyclopedias, in this sense, are imagined to be created equal; their form, we believe, should disappear in the shadow cast by the strong light of their object, the whole of the real world. The forms taken by encyclopedic texts have changed from Hesiod to Aristotle, from Martianus Capella to Vincent of Beauvais to Guillaume Budé to Diderot and D'Alembert, to Joyce, Eco, and the most recent web-based edition of the *Britannica*. Insofar, though, as they all tend towards one goal – literal reference, in the sense of *bearing* their users *back* to the substratum of a reality, to things themselves, conceived as univocal – there can be only one encyclopedia and no encyclopedia but *the* encyclopedia. It is thus no error to speak of *the* encyclopedia, because one of the markers that lets us define encyclopedism as a genre is the persistence of the claim that it is a singular entity.[3] In this chapter I will outline some of the consistent features of the encyclopedia that are not definitionally motivated, in particular its irony and spatiality, and conclude with a discussion of how the encyclopedia was related logically to the idea of theatre.

What is an encyclopedia, in particular an early modern one? After a fierce debate conducted in sign language, the hero of *Pantagruel* says of his opponent, a travelling English scholar – whether in praise or abuse is hard to determine – "I can assure you that he has opened for me the true well (*puys*) and abyss of the encyclopedia."[4] As perhaps the earliest occurrence of the word "encyclopedia" in French, the passage is a *locus classicus* in the history of the term, although it is not at all clear what object or idea Rabelais meant by it.[5] The word itself poses a series of questions, not the least of which is its intelligibility to readers not acquainted with its use in Latin, where, by 1535 when *Pantagruel* was published, it had been in use for perhaps a generation.[6] The encyclopedia is, or includes, a "vray puys et abisme," but *puys* means either "well" or "hillock,"[7] and so Pantagruel's encyclopedia is defined in part by a word that means two opposite things. In either case, *puys* is also opposed to *abisme*: it is either the hill that inverts the bottomless pit just as it does the well, or it is the life-giving fountain of commonplaces as opposed to the swallowing void. Instead of being in a relation of simple inversion, as *hill* and *abyss* are, the two meanings in the second pairing are in one sense identical. What differentiates them is their particular relation to the viewer. Standing on the edge of a water-filled shaft and dipping a bucket into it, one makes use of a well; falling into it, one finds it to be an abyss.

I begin with Rabelais' allegory of encyclopedism as, alternately, and often in the same form, a spring of truth and a pit of error because one of the functions of the encyclopedia is to combine different fields of analysis and coordinate them – theory and practice, active and passive, subject and object, any number of apparently contradictory categories. Whatever else it is, including an allegory, Pantagruel's encyclopedia is something that contains and coordinates contraries, both those that are opposite objectively, such as *hill* and *well*, and those that are subjectively opposite, *well* and *abyss*. Just as fictions have had the most interesting things to say in the twentieth century about encyclopedic tendencies as particular practices, the encyclopedic fictions of the Renaissance like those of Rabelais or Robert Burton often express the double functions of encyclopedic texts – culturally bound versus timeless and eternal, serious versus parodic – more openly than traditional reference works, although such works also offer critiques of their own form. Thomas Elyot in *The Book Named the Governour* (1531) likewise combines two unlikely senses in his definition: "a heap of all manner of learning, which of some is called the world of science and of other the circle of doctrine, which is in one word of Greek *Encyclopedia*" (*Governour*, 48v). Is Elyot's imagined encyclopedia an orderly circle or a messy (but perhaps still circular) heap? In the context of this etymological point of origin, we should also note the fictionality of the two examples from my introduction. Elyot never builds his library and Johannes Serranus never completes his index to Plato and Aristotle; Rabelais is never called upon to expound Pantagruel's new learning and Burton's proffered cures for melancholy are also part of its genesis. The concept of the circle of learning, whether encyclopedia, theatre, or something in between, is as problematic as it is attractive.

The encyclopedia as an object, or the idea of an object, is first fashioned in the Greek-reading humanist circles surrounding Angelo Poliziano in the 1480s. It derives from mistranscriptions of the Greek phrase *enkuklios paideia* in the Latin manuscripts of Pliny and Quintilian.[8] This origin in error did not prevent attempts in the early modern period to write real encyclopedias as well. Not long after its first appearance as an idea, books were being published using the word as a title.

In 1508, Gregor Reisch's *Margarita Philosophica* used Κυκλωπαιδεια as a subtitle, and a few years after Rabelais' reference, Paul Skalich de Lika entitled his text of universal knowledge *Encyclopaedia* (1559), apparently the first book so named. The list of contents of his work seems to support both senses of Pantagruel's description, a universal source and inescapable trap. De Lika's outline for his volume – not a particularly large one – claimed for its contents

> the whole Encyclopedia, of sacred as well as of secular studies: of Philosophy, of course, [both] supernatural, which is called Metaphysics and First Philosophy; [and] natural, from which are born Medicine, then the study which treats of the soul, and the four Mathematical sciences, which are also called doctrinal, Arithmetic, Music, Geometry, and Spherics (with their footmen, so to speak, Calculation, Geodesy, Proportion, Astrology, Optics, and Mechanics). Similarly of Morals, Economics, and Politics; of the Rational arts, whence Grammar, History, Dialectic, Rhetoric, and Poetics emerge. Finally, of that holy and inexpressible symbol of sacred letters, which I usually call symbolic Philosophy.[9]

This collection, more heap than circle, is a lot to cover in one volume, even without trying to unify it into an ordered whole, but encyclopedic works consistently make the claim to contain everything that is necessary or knowable, even the "vray puys et abisme." Pierre Gregoire, a French encyclopedist and another participant in the early modern boom in encyclopedic writings, succinctly articulates this fantasy at the end of a similar swarm of disciplines in *Syntaxes Artis Mirabilis* (1578): "Whoever possesses our labors (*lucubrationes*) will need no other books, or certainly very few, for learning the Encyclopedia of disciplines."[10]

The capaciousness of the word "encyclopedia" in the sixteenth century and its almost utopian claims for comprehensiveness, compression, and speed of access, similar in tone and content to modern ones for the World Wide Web, are in part a result of its newness; like the word "theatrum," "encyclopedia" was a sign for which a referent had to be imagined before it could be realized. From its beginnings, the term was unstable, implying a great deal about totality and mastery but difficult to pin down or even to evaluate as serious or satirical. Although composed of Greek elements – *enkuklios* means "general" or "everyday" and derives from the root *kuklos*, "circle," while *paideia* means "education" or "training" – it is in fact not the product of any Greek-*speaking* culture, but rather of one that *read* Greek voraciously, early modern humanist Europe. What "encyclopedia" meant by the early sixteenth century is nothing like the original Greek sense of *enkuklios paideia*. *Paideia* was the training a young man received to form him into a citizen of his community. *Enkuklios* means ordinary, common, literally "what is in circulation," and so the original sense of the phrase was something like "general education." By Plato's time it meant an elite education in a variety of liberal arts.[11] Before Plato, some intellectual historians have speculated, the circularity of the phrase may have been more prominent, referring to the civically supported training in making the strophic motions of the tragic chorus, and the word *enkuklios* may have originally applied to the circle of choral dancers.[12] Still more of a reach into the word's prehistory is the idea that even those circling dances took their shape – and their metaphoric completeness – from the wheeling of the stars in their regular revolutions over the earth. This origin for the word begs the question of the later universality that attaches to it. Even if this origin is based on a false history of the phrase, it carried an indisputable weight in the formation of the ideas that were joined to it, the more so when they are products of reading the Greek phrase and interpreting it to fit different historical circumstances. Whether or not an ancient Athenian would have heard a literal circle in *enkuklios paideia*, a humanist who had laboriously acquired Greek as a dead language certainly did, as countless translations of the phrase as a "circle of doctrine" (Elyot, *Governour*, 48v) or "erudition circulaire" (Budé, *L'institution du prince*),[13] or even Quintilian's *orbis doctrinae* (I, 10. 1), attest. In a discussion of Augustine's intellectual training, Henri Marrou acknowledges that already by Hellenistic times the curriculum was thought of as somehow circular.[14]

The single link that binds this complex of various and often speculative meanings is space, the empty, enclosed arc of the circle. Giuseppe Mazzotta has characterized the medieval encyclopedia as "a logical space, a framework within which the entities of the world are interpreted and classified," (*Dante's Vision*, 5) but the titles of early encyclopedic works – *hortus, thesaurus, mansio* (also a term for the "houses" marking particular locations on a medieval or early Renaissance stage), *arca*, even *speculum* and *convivio* – show that the space was more than merely a logical convention. The most common ideal space, however, was circular, a round *speculum* or *theatrum* whose shape echoed that of the world and seemed also to encompass everything within it. The encyclopedia is thus not thought of as a continuous form unrolling in a single line across time, but as a simultaneous juxtaposition of elements in imaginary space. Arranged like courses at a feast in Dante's *Convivio* (c.1295) or jewels in a strongbox in Hugh Plat's *Jewell House of Art and Nature* (1594), the encyclopedia is atemporal and antinarrative.

The word "encyclopedia" itself is in part the product of this spatial conception. Early printed editions of Quintilian and Pliny, where the term originates, show an array of variant readings, ranging from other plausible ones such as *tas idiopaedeias*, "of a private or individual education," to the farfetched *peripetias chieplocas*, "Aristotelian handtext" (less generously, "crossbraidings of reversal"), to the nonsensical *ciecyclopedias*, until at last finding in *encyclopaedia* a consensus among manuscript readings, etymology, and suitability to the humanist understanding of what the new word represented.[15] The individual tailoring implied by *idiopaideias* is rapidly replaced by a word which suggests universality, and the speed with which a consensus was established on *encyclopaedia* once the word emerges suggests that the *kuklos* that is audible within it played a significant role in its formation.[16]

With the fusion of the two words into a single, more apparently objective noun, the "common knowledge" of *enkuklios paideia* becomes the *orbis disciplinarum* of *enkuklopaideia*, and the implication, stressed in early works like Martianus Capella's *De Nuptiis* (fifth century CE) or later ones like Campanella's *Città del Sol* (1602) that there is a very literal *universitas scientiarum* – that in some conceptual way the knowledge of things, and the order of things themselves, turn inward to form a complete, interrelated (in the sense of judiciously divided, so that each element has its distinct place), and self-contained circle. The association of the concrete shape of the circle with the encyclopedia predates the name encyclopedia itself. Early encyclopedic works often include a self-representation which is enclosed and circular. In a tenth-century manuscript of the *Hortus Deliciarum* ("Garden of Delights"), the Liberal Arts are represented within a closed circular space.[17] The painted walls surrounding the garden in the *Romance de la Rose*, the garden of Dante's good pagans, Chaucer's House of Fame, Campanella's City of the Sun described in the epigraph, and even Shakespeare's Globe are literary examples of spatial representations of encyclopedic totalities. This image of a literal circle of learning persists and even increases in frequency during the Renaissance. Erasmus could slide easily from the figurative circle of learning to an actual geometric one:

> to complete (*absolvere*) the circle is to offer back a thing perfect in all its measures and all its parts. Whence is said both *cyclopaideia*, which perfects (*absolverit*) as an orb of all the disciplines, and *encyclopaideia*. The metaphor is taken from the mathematicians, among whom the circular figure is judged the most perfect and most absolute (*absolutissima*) . . .[18]

In each of these examples, the encyclopedia is imagined as an empty place in which knowledge is discovered as it plays out a scene detached from its viewer. It is experienced not as a temporally distanced subjective re-enactment, as in a memory, but as something spatially distanced and objective; the perfection that makes the circle of knowledge *absolutissimus* also shuts the viewer outside it, where it can be viewed but not disturbed.

What brought forth this order in the encyclopedia was a knowing looking called *contemplatio*.[19] What was meant by *contemplatio*, though, was not only the detached and passive observation implied by its English cognate, "contemplation." According to the Roman etymologist Varro, the word *contemplatio* comes from the ritual practice of demarcating a space in the world within which the ordinary rules of action are suspended and replaced by observation and interpretation:

> Whatever place the eyes had gazed on (*intuiti*) was originally called a *templum*, from "to gaze" (*tueri*). . . . On the earth, *templum* is the name given to a place delimited by certain formulaic words for the purposes of augury or the taking of the auspices . . .

Varro then describes how the augur would specify the boundaries of his *templum*. Once these were established, a bird flying outside the boundary could be safely ignored; within the *templum*, though, anything that appeared had to be interpreted as a sign:

> In making this *templum*, it is evident that the trees are set as boundaries, and that within them the regions are set where the eyes are to view, that is, we are to gaze (*tueamur*), from which was said *templum* and *contemplare* . . .[20]

Necessarily prior to any passive scrutiny that "contemplation" suggests, in fact what makes the scrutiny possible at all, is an active delimitation of a space in which the observation will take place and which will allow it to be meaningful. In Varro's etymology, *templum*, derived from *tueri*, "to gaze," becomes a Latin calque of the Greek *theatron*, "a place of seeing." This tradition linking the two begins to explain the frequent appearance in medieval literature of altars in descriptions of theatres and of visual displays in temples, like the fifteenth-century illustrated edition of Vergil which shows the temple of Juno in Carthage with Aeneas and Achates standing outside it. The composition echoes an image of a theatre in an earlier work by the same printer. With its hexagonal sides and faces peering out of windows, the encyclopedic Tower of Learning in Reisch's *Margarita Philosophica* mimics both these earlier illustrations (Figures 1 and 2; see also Figure 4).

What links *templum* and *theatrum* and the act designated as *contemplatio* is not only the centrality of vision to all three, but the importance of the viewer's prior intervention into what he will later view in order to set aside a space in which signs can appear – a space which, in fact, *allows* these signs to be meaningful when they are observed passively and interpreted or understood. To *contemplate* nature is to delimit a restricted space, within which the whole of nature can then reappear and reveal its secret logic. This, in essence, is the project of the encyclopedia – to re-present every thing that exists in a (more) manageable form for detached study and manipulation. The sensual display of exotic objects in an early modern museum or cabinet of curiosities presents the viewer with what Steven Mullaney calls "things on holiday," detaching them from their context and setting them into a neutrally valent space in which any virtual context can be produced, or none.[21] The encyclopedia posed as a similarly empty space in which its wonderful things, released from the contexts in which they had been produced, were free and available to the viewer's gaze. Like theatres, encyclopedias rely on a border of some kind that distances them from the world they refer to, while simultaneously making that reference possible. For Varro, the ritual that establishes the space of the *templum* does not determine what appears inside it, but designates it so that what appears within it becomes worthy of attention and significant. As Varro's account suggests, and as the historical development of theatres in Italy and England confirms, it was construction of the circle and the delimitation of

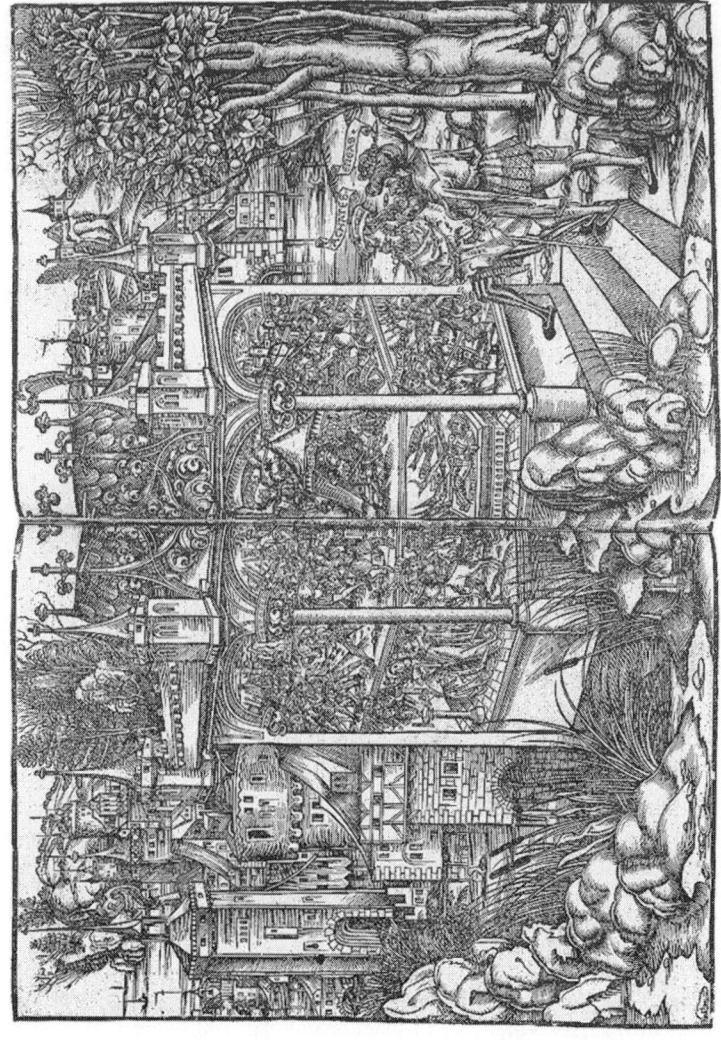

Fig. 1 Temple of Juno, from Vergil, *Opera*, ed. Sebastian Brant (Strassburg: Iohannis Grieninger, 1502).

The space of the encyclopedia 21

Fig. 2 "Theatrum," from Terence, [*Comoediae*], ed. Sebastian Brant (Strassburg: J. Grüninger, 1496).

space, real or mental, that made possible the spectacular encyclopedic show within it, in fact what made it spectacular at all. What is produced in the encyclopedia is space itself, as Varro describes the establishment of a *templum*, a neutral space that is devoid of all the physical and social features that mark the spaces of the real world. Once the space is established, according to the encyclopedist's logic, the things within it will manifest their own order – invisible in the realm of actuality because of the confusion that it exists in – to the experience of the viewer.

The encyclopedia as it was imagined in early modern Europe was thus not a space where knowledge was produced, but where it was preserved or discovered – the library as the resting place of truth rather than the laboratory as its delivery room.[22] Gian Biagio Conte discusses Pliny's *Natural History* as a work of consolidation, in which already established knowledge can be arranged and ordered.[23] Conte's remark captures the detached, referential character of encyclopedic texts – they do not create, but instead seek to reflect a reality that can be fully perceived only in their uniquely neutral textual space. In the neutral space of the encyclopedia, knowledge can be found, rehearsed, authorized, but not made; its origin lies outside it.[24] It brackets the parts played by economics, personal authority, and other tactical and accidental considerations and takes as its object science ready-made[25] – complete, atemporal, authorized by a truth outside it rather than by those things that we, from within that viewpoint, call contingent. In an encyclopedic text, rule precedes action; furthermore, action must be completely reducible to a finite set of rules that can then be externalized. Encyclopedias do not deny the existence of action under mental structures such as knack, *habitus*, or *empeiria*, but they recognize it as alien to their own function, which is to record the unchanging and timeless. Hugh of St. Victor distinguishes the properly encyclopedic topic of *ratio* from the *actus* that it supports and makes possible: "the theory (*ratio*) of agriculture is for the philosopher, its management (*administratio*) for the rustic ..." This division means that the world of practice is exactly reproduced in a realm of theory that is distinct from it but mirrors it: "now you see for what reason we determine that philosophy is diffused through all human acts, so that it is necessary that there be as many parts of philosophy as there are varieties of things to which it must pertain."[26]

The physical delimitation of things into spaces as a way of ordering and managing them does not address how these limits are to be placed nor what can be contained within them. The claim made by texts like Hugh of St. Victor's or Pliny's, even if it was immediately called into question by ironizing compilers like Burton or Rabelais, was that the encyclopedic order reflected reality in some way. From another perspective, though – one not alien to premodern encyclopedists themselves – this claim was simply bad faith. Within the traceless, mutable area of the encyclopedia, the compiler can re-establish the strictures he desires, consciously or not; the encyclopedia allows him the pleasure of finding what he assumed would be there anyway. The principal shift between the earlier and later spatializations is less the change from a vocal to a visual conception, as Walter Ong has suggested, than a progressive blurring of the activity by which that space is established.[27] Jürgen Henningsen argues that the encyclopedia is an attempt to reconcile the objective demands of a field of study – its own rules, as it were – with subjective demands for order, symmetry, totality, and so on ("'Enzyklopädie,'" 297, 303). In a similar vein, Gian Biagio Conte argues that Pliny the Elder's work is doubly organized: first and explicitly as an account of the order of things as they are in themselves, but also implicitly in conformity with an anthropocentric final cause, human usefulness.[28] The possibility of an encyclopedia relies on a conception of knowledge that locates it in a space external to any user, or use, of it – *a* knowledge because the form the encyclopedic text takes demands that knowledge be broken into its elements, although the goal of humanist encyclopedic texts is precisely the non-fragmented, unformalized wisdom of *prudentia*, which cannot be divided from an acting subject. When narrativity and temporality are represented in such texts as spatial extension, the ethical poles of human action reverse, making the encyclopedia the Barthesian readerly text *par excellence*.[29] *Habitus est dispositio* – what is internal and the result of accommodation and habit over time is represented as external posture; what derives from a context is taken out of its dialogic relation with that context and established as an autonomous object. Active, passive; subjective, objective – like the words *contemplatio* or *puys*, encyclopedias must balance contradictions within themselves. To do so, they tend to hide the contradictions by embracing them within a shared imaginary or real space.

This duplicity of origin holds true for most Renaissance versions of the encyclopedia, which often conflate their order with the naturally given order (even the label "*the* natural order" belies some of the prejudices of these works). But that is part of the encyclopedic text's function as a reference work – it is meant to reproduce the world without becoming involved in it, hence its delimitation of a separate space, hence its emphasis on vision, the noblest sense both because it is both the most accurate and because it requires no physical contact. World and encyclopedia are distinguished so that the world can be approached again with sureness in interpreting signs or any other action. This opening between an object and its meaning is necessary to allow the encyclopedia to emerge as a volume of text in which the signs correspond to things in the world referentially without being confused with them, but this opening also swallows the encyclopedic text into a theatrical practice, no longer as a mere metaphor but as an active staging that shapes the world by holding itself in part aloof from it. Robert Burton describes himself as "myself a theatre" ("*ipse mihi theatrum*"), but then clarifies that he is not the performer but the audience, "a mere spectator of other men's fortunes and adventures, and how they act their parts, which methinks are as diversely presented unto me, as from a common theatre or scene."[30] The encyclopedic space is effective because it insists on no perspective; it is Nagel's "view from nowhere," instantly and completely visible to its external spectator. What allows for this perfect reproduction is its perfect separation from the world that contains it.[31]

This separation is the encyclopedia's advantage over reality; possibilities can be scrutinized without their possible ill effects spilling into the world, because in this ideology action follows contemplation rather than being concurrent with it. In the space of the encyclopedia action *becomes* contemplation. Action can be perilous, and the spectation of nature provides a safe space for working out right courses of action by setting up a buffer of theory around that of practice. Pierre Gregoire in part explains the usefulness of his abstract encyclopedic art in terms of its relative safety; it leads eventually to action (Gregoire was in fact a professor of law), but avoids both the dangers and the delays of immediate practice: "while life may be short, art is long; and not only in medicine, as Hippocrates used to say, is experience dangerous, but also particularly in all human actions."[32] What permits this distance is the way the encyclopedia itself renders the world conceivable as a whole and at the same time – as part of the same process, in fact – reduces it to signs that can be safely viewed, interpreted, or admired without actually absorbing the viewer. The circle of learning is no different from the charmed circle that protects the conjuror from demons – it enables a kind of summoning and detaining of reality without granting it the power to harm. In the encyclopedia, though, at the same time the user loses his power to intervene in reality, making of the world a kind of spectacle.

The practical negotiation of this doubled vision – the encyclopedia as somehow both acting and watching, ordering and contemplating – is suggested in the *Margarita Philosophica* (*The Philosophic Pearl*, 1503) of the Carthusian prior Gregor Reisch. Reisch intended his book to be an elementary guide to everything that one might need to know.[33] By reading over 1,500 pages of dialogue between the aptly if predictably named characters Discipulus and Magister (Student and Teacher), a diligent student, Reisch claimed, could be spared the time and expense of attending university.[34] As an emblem of its contents, the volume is prefaced by the woodcut image of a circle, within which dwells Philosophy, a tall woman with three faces for the three branches of philosophical knowledge, Natural, Rational, and Moral (Figure 3). Around her stand figures of the Liberal Arts, holding various objects to identify them. Outside this circle of knowledge sit the human representatives of wisdom, Aristotle and Seneca, gazing in admiringly and hoping, perhaps, to gain admittance. Appropriately above the circle of worldly knowledge is Divine Philosophy, attended by Augustine and other Church Fathers.

The first section of Reisch's universal volume begins with another woodcut image, representing, like the first woodcut, the entire body of knowledge (Figure 4). This image is a circular tower with figures peering out of its windows and porches. Both images are illustrations of the contents of Reisch's book, but they are also, in a sense, pictures of his thought. But although Reisch's pictures represent the same object[35] – Reisch's, and potentially the reader's, knowledge – they display the architecture of Reisch's mind in two different ways. Reisch's first image for his book shows Philosophy whole and at a glance. It is the kind of image that someone trained in the arts of memory

Fig. 3 Three-headed Philosophy, frontispiece from Gregor Reisch, *Margarita Philosophica* (1503).

might plausibly have kept in his memory storehouse, a diagram showing the parts of Philosophy in vivid and easily recollectable form. It makes no attempt to refer to actual space through perspective or any other way. Instead, the image occupies a space different from that of the viewer and is meant to be scanned rather than entered, so that the viewer does not see the drawing in his or her own spatio-temporal terms, but as an alien, abstracted field, perfectly

Fig. 4 "Tower of learning," from Gregor Reisch, *Margarita Philosophica* (1503).

visible but equally inaccessible in all its parts. Even a knower of Aristotle's or Seneca's stature must remain outside the circular limit that separates them from the mystical bodies of knowledge themselves, although these can be freely and completely viewed.

In the second image, on the other hand, the undistorted circle of knowledge of the first image has become a circular tower, pulled out of true by the perspectival position of the viewer in a space that fictionally extends beyond the border of the image. It is as if the first picture had adopted a view of knowledge from directly overhead, while in the second the viewer has slid to one side and down, taking a position in space continuous with the represented space and turning the circle of knowledge into a tower that can be entered. Its contents are no longer instantly, completely, and equally visible; instead the crude perspective of the image suggests that, like an actual space, it cannot be grasped instantaneously but must be traversed in a sequence, as if the viewer were crossing it physically. The tower's contents reflect this shift to temporality as well. Instead of the allegorical figures of the Liberal Arts, the different branches of knowledge are represented by historical human figures who remain partially hidden by the tower's walls. Labels below the figures identify them as the writers of texts frequently used by students of the liberal arts: Donatus, known to a millennium of schoolboys as an editor of Terence and therefore as the gateway to formal education, appears just inside the door on the lowest level, with Priscian, the grammarian, near the door. Higher up are more advanced *auctores* who provided the texts that older students used: Cicero for rhetoric, Euclid for geometry, Ptolemy for astronomy, Peter Lombard and theology at the summit. Outside the base of the tower, as if to make the narrativity of the process of knowledge still more clear, a boy with a tablet stands behind a large female figure, labeled Grammatice, who gestures towards the door. The boy is about to enter and begin his climb under the guidance of Grammar.

In contrast to the diagrammatic first image, which served as a kind of visual table of contents, in this second image Reisch shows how his text is to be used – how allegory, in fact, becomes history, or how the authority of Philosophy and the Liberal Arts is transformed into personal experience.[36] Reisch casts the act of reading his encyclopedic text as entering and moving through an imaginary space filled with a shared set of authoritative figures and texts – knowledge is mediated and represented metonymically, by its exemplary practitioners, rather than appearing allegorically and as a whole. To read, to learn, is to move through a series of stepped levels, to pass through a space until one transcends it and achieves, at the end of space, the masterful "view from nowhere." The first image presents such a view without a viewpoint; the second maps the course that one follows to reach it. In this literal change in perspective, Reisch's second woodcut signals a shift, whether intended or not, from the idealization of thought as a still and coherent space to its realization, its being-made-real, as the temporality of thinking.

Reisch's text, or Elyot's educational system of an encyclopedic library and a theatre, like humanist education in general, were meant to prepare their users for action. To stop at observation and never proceed to action is to remain merely within the realm, as Reisch described it, of the theatre. Philosophy must be lived as well as written, and those who philosophize but do not act ethically with their knowledge are like *histriones* "who, when they act poems on stage enter often as kings or as powerful men, though they are neither kings nor powerful, nor even perhaps freeborn."[37] Reading an encyclopedic text, it was imagined, allowed its user to familiarize himself with the world's structure free from risk.[38] It was a way of setting physics and other non-theoretical arts (in Aristotle's terms) into a form of *theoria*, extending the reach of the exact observational sciences into the sublunary realm of action and change. Later encyclopedic texts of the Renaissance, notably those of the theatre, prefigure much later models of the social sciences in their application of *theoria* to prudential arts, and the *Encyclopédie* of Diderot and D'Alembert remains famous for its attempts to include the practical arts within the sphere of knowledge. Before any worldly objects could be set into the circle of the encyclopedia, they had to be abstracted from their real existence, codified and ordered. Writers like Elyot used the figures of the encyclopedia and the theatre to impose an order on the world, while other writers like Giulio Camillo went much farther in claiming the order of the encyclopedic text not as the writer's arbitrary imposition, but as literally reflective of the world itself. But they show a varying degree of interest in the two visions of knowledge represented by Reisch – knowledge as reflection and knowledge as narrative, knowledge as possession and knowledge as action – or as performance.

The encyclopedia's border and the theatrical distance it established with its reader are in place not only because reality is a threat. They are there because the contemplation of reality is also so absorbing. When Varro's *contemplatio* cut out its *templum* from the whole of the world, the result was to render the newly founded space an object of fascination. In the strangely diffuse dialogue of Skalich de Lika's *Encyclopaedia*, Philomusus (meaning "Lover of the Muses") tells Epistemon ("Knower"), whom he is trying to convince to be his teacher, that he has come to him "for no other reason . . . than burning desire (*desiderium*) and leisure for contemplation (*contemplandi ocium*)."[39] The dialogue form in which this and so many works are set points to an additional characteristic of encyclopedic writings. This wonder is to be shared; it should fashion both a world of information and a community to inhabit it. Thus in his dedication Skalich de Lika mentions the innate need of men to know and to communicate their knowledge as a motive for writing his *Encyclopaedia*. The love of knowledge (*scientiae cupiditatem*) and desire for community is so great "that none can doubt that we seize these things drawn on by no advantage" other than the sheer desire to see, to hear, to learn "the acquaintance of things either hidden or exposed to wonder (*aut occultarum aut admirabilium*)."[40] Desire is both inexplicable (because it is treated as axiomatic) and irresistible. Varro's *contemplatio* is the initiation of augury, which is itself a practice devised to help one to prepare for action.

But it is also the emergence of the wonderful from the ordinary – from birds and trees, truth. At the heart of every encyclopedic effort is this desire to marvel, what Conte calls "the will to astonish and the capacity for astonishment,"[41] elegantly combining in the reflexive verb *stupirsi* both the agency of the wonderer and his passivity before the object that he sets before himself. The Roman encyclopedist Pliny the Elder, who is cited by Renaissance encyclopedists perhaps more than any other predecessor as both a positive and a negative example, links this desire for wonder to human inadequacy.[42] Unlike all other animals, man is born helpless and needs to acquire *disciplina* (*Natural History* VII, 1). But what makes him helpless at birth also reveals the world to him as a chain of wonders:

> What is not a wonder when it first comes to our attention? How many things come to pass that earlier were judged not to be possible? Truly, the force and majesty of the nature of things lacks credence at every moment (*in omnibus momentis*) if one embraces its parts and not the whole in one's spirit.[43]

Pliny recognizes that it is human ignorance that renders the world constantly (*in omnibus momentis*) surprising; fragmented by time and the partial perspective of humankind, the world reveals itself as marvel after marvel rather than as a single comprehensible whole.

Aristotle is the first theorizer of this desire practiced and exemplified by Pliny, in his famous observation in *Metaphysics* I: "It is through wonder that men now begin and originally began to philosophize."[44] Aristotle immediately distances the desire to philosophize from any practical (*poiêtikê*) science; it is obvious, he says, that the first philosophers pursued science for the sake of knowledge itself and not for any immediate practical purpose.[45] This sounds very close to Pliny's position; the search for knowledge is not rational or practical, occasioned by specific needs and difficulties, but is entailed by the universal human conditions of ignorance and amazement. For Aristotle, though, philosophy only *begins* in wonder; it also leaves wonder behind. By giving his desire for wonder a purpose, or at least an end, Aristotle has already gone beyond Pliny's sense of the purely marvelous. For Pliny, nature is everything in the world worthy of memory, prior to any consideration of its usefulness. This catholicity of interest challenges the purposefulness that Elyot or Serranus or Reisch claim for their encyclopedic texts. In spite of being reference works, encyclopedic writings contain a strongly utopian bent towards a potentially timeless suspension of disbelief and practical interest in the sheer sense of wonder – and pleasure – at the things of the world.

Wonder and the desire for it alone, prior to any application of it to the progress of knowledge through philosophy, to moralizations, or to other practical purposes, connect encyclopedic writings from Herakleitos to Eco, however sincere the belief in the possibility of knowledge or however ironized it becomes. Vincent of Beauvais, for instance, explains in his preface to the thirteenth-century *Speculum Maius*, called the *Apologia Actoris*, that the work is intended for other Dominicans, interpreters of Scripture, and the learned, then surprisingly he adds another category:

> but also for others, who, laboring under a kind of curiosity of knowing unfamiliar things (*curiositate quadam sciendi incognita laborantes*), perhaps are delighted by the awareness of such things (*talium noticia*)...[46]

This *curiositas* is what makes of the contemplative space of the encyclopedia a theatre of learning – a desire to know unrooted in any practical concerns, a hopefulness that charges the ordinary, in its new context, with meaning. Vincent has no explanation for such *curiositas*, and, surprisingly, no condemnation of it either. Knowing itself has a kind of attraction apart from any purpose or organization attached to it, and indeed prior to both. In the "Prohemium" to his edition of John of Trevisa's translation of Bartholomaeus Anglicus' *De Proprietatibus Rerum* (1495), located inexplicably at the end of the volume, the printer Wynkyn de Worde links world and book as the parallel and equal objects of this desire to know:

> For in this worlde to reken every thynge
> Plesure to man there is none comparable
> As is to rede and understondynge
> In bokes of wysdom they ben so dilectable.[47]

As Stephen Greenblatt has remarked on European reactions to the New World, wonder is in a sense pre-ethical – it is one of the forces that shapes ethics, action, belief, and so on, but the shock of the truly new and strange may properly come, or be hoped to come, outside of the fields of ordinary practices.[48] Greenblatt suggests that in the context of early modern Europe, this sense of wonder quickly converts into a desire to dominate or conquer. For learned men of the Renaissance – or Romans, for that matter – knowledge was both intimately linked to *imperium* and distinct from it. Pliny writes his encyclopedia for the Roman emperor; more famously, and recounted in dozens of medieval and Renaissance sources, is Aristotle's tutelage of Alexander and his use of Alexander's resources to carry out his researches throughout the world.[49] To see with Greenblatt or Aristotle something in wonder prior to ethics is not to ignore or forget Varro's lesson of preparing a ground for the wonderful. Before there can be augury, there must be *contemplatio* – the entempling of the world into significant and insignificant. But this activity, alone of encyclopedic activities, is represented as productive rather than conservative or reflective. The point of these stories of scholars and emperors is to distance wonder from power and *praxis* while at the same time acknowledging their connection. The ruler provides an example of titanic, conquering will, asserting himself in the face of worldly resistance. The scholar, in contrast, is completely submerged in the desire to know, in the texts he has read, in the fascinating objects he gathers. Pliny, for instance, does not assume responsibility for the facts he enumerates, but refers the reader to his index for the sources of his information. It is not until Marlowe writes a Faustus on the model of his Tamburlaine that these figures of scholar and emperor begin to coalesce and it is acknowledged that the scholar, like the emperor, can segment the manifold world that confronts both of them. Even for Galileo, the self-fashioning scholar looks ridiculous compared to the disciplined follower of knowledge and power, or of knowledge-as-power.[50]

Pliny the Elder serves both as a model for the Renaissance idea of the scholar and as a source of amazement at the thoroughness of his self-effacement. In his preface, not only does he remove his own labor from consideration (however ironically), he also removes the labor of the audience by assuring Titus Vespasian, the emperor's son and the dedicatee of the *Natural History*, that he has included a detailed table of contents of the volumes "so that you will not have to take the trouble to read them."[51] Taking the model of contemplative teacher and active, worldly student to its extreme, Pliny's work effectively isolates itself completely from any realm but the study and any perusal but its author's. But Pliny the Elder also becomes, in the letters of his nephew and namesake Pliny the Younger, a figure of a different sort of power than an imperial one: he becomes prodigious, a source of wonder in himself – physically immense and preternaturally relentless in his pursuit of information, an example of the active desire for marvels who "read nothing which he would not excerpt," and also the object of that desire; appropriately, since his work "is no less various than nature itself," mixing marvelous human effort with nature's marvels.[52] Pliny the Younger recounts stories of his uncle's encyclopedic drive with his own sense of wonder, but also with an exemplary intention – his uncle's life and death model an ideal, if nearly incredible, relation of labor and admiration to a whole world. In one letter, Pliny the Younger goes on at length describing his uncle's obsession with conserving time in which to write – taking a litter rather than walking so that he could dictate to a slave, being read to at all hours of the day except during his bath ("and by bath I mean his actual immersion, for while he was being rubbed down and dried he had a book read to him"), berating a friend who asked a slave to reread a passage, thus wasting the time in which at least ten more lines could have been read (Letter 3. 5). In a letter to the historian Tacitus, Pliny the Younger recounts how his uncle met his death in the eruption of Vesuvius that destroyed Pompeii when he led a ship to shore to investigate the disaster, making him into what Umberto Eco describes as "a paramount example of scientific holocaust,"[53] a researcher so single-minded in his pursuit of knowledge that he eliminates himself altogether. But Pliny the encyclopedist is also a figure of ridiculous excess, one who cannot set limits at all. He dies at Pompeii in part because he insists on spending the night in a villa near the eruption to study it, and in part because he is asthmatic – he snores loudly enough to be heard through doors – and is what his nephew coyly calls "ample of body." This self-erasure is the consequence threatened by limitless, consuming *curiositas* – it is as if Pliny the Elder had allowed his fascination to consume him literally.

In the Renaissance, Pliny the Elder becomes the emblem of the desire to see the world whole and to grasp it instantly, conclusively, and (marvelously) selflessly. In the formulation of Conrad Gessner, the Swiss polymath and author of a book reviewing every Latin, Greek, or Hebrew book ever written, Pliny's desire is a model of selflessness: "There is, said Pliny, much more merit in having persevered for the love of the work . . . and not for the sake of one's ego."[54] Juan Luis Vives, too, finds Pliny not only an example for Vives' own philological activity, but an object of wonder in his own right: "In general things there is learning, just as in singulars there is pleasure; the first is of the mind, the latter of the senses. By this token Pliny delights more, Aristotle teaches more."[55] Aristotle's rules for comprehending give way in Pliny, in an undoing of the move from wonder to philosophy he recounts in *Metaphysics*, to an emphasis on particulars themselves, bright astonishing shards of information about the wonderful world. Aristotle moves on towards philosophy, and learning as a practical skill, but Pliny represents learning as pleasure, or, better, learning as its own pure and endless *telos*, as unstinting activity – an uncalculated, aneconomic expenditure of effort.

In spite of his own pleasures, Pliny the Elder is oddly at pains in the preface to the *Natural History* to stress the superficial unpleasantness of his work. It contains none of the elements in which pleasure is usually thought to consist:

> it does not allow of digressions, nor of speeches, or dialogues, nor marvelous accidents or unusual occurrences – matters enjoyable (*iucunda*) to relate or pleasant (*blanda*) to read. A barren subject (*sterilis materia*) – the nature of things, or in other words, life, is narrated; and that in its most sordid part, and employing either rustic terms or foreign, downright barbarian, words that must be introduced by an apology. (Preface, §§12–13)

Even taking into account the obligatory obsequiousness of a dedicatory preface, Pliny's insistence on the crudity of the work and particularly of his topic is extreme. His reference here to the *sterilis materia* that is the *natura rerum* is an oblique allusion to the productive matter, *genitalis materia*, of Lucretius' version of the nature of things, *De Rerum Natura*, the fecund atoms that of their own accord produce all that exists by combining and colliding. But Lucretius' atomistic universe is unexpectedly passionate, alive with desire and fertility; Pliny, on the other hand, claims to find in his world only barrenness, dullness, crudity.

What saves his work from a corresponding dullness, according to Pliny, is the way in which it is collected from its many sources and assembled in an order – that is, it itself is a source of wonder, aside from its wonderful contents. Pliny's contribution to the nature of things is simply arrangement, but it is enough to render them palatable and, as writers like Conrad Gessner and Juan Luis Vives assure us, even engrossing. In organizing his atomistic facts, Pliny finds in them an overarching rationality that is finally, for Pliny and his followers, as wonderful as the novelty it avoids. Immediately before the passage in which he apologizes for the dullness of the *Natural History*, Pliny assures the reader that he lacks any remarkable skill (*ingenium*) even if his work had allowed for a display of such giftedness. What he can do instead is to collect and arrange, as he tabulates them, thirty-six volumes (not including a preface and a narrative index of sources, the earliest in Western literature) containing twenty thousand facts drawn from two thousand works by over a hundred selected authorities.[56] Thus textualized, quantified, and indexed, the account (in every sense) of nature acquires an interest value that is immanent in the things themselves, but invisible:

For which reason I seek to prevent those who read my works from condemning the *accounts* of them with boredom (*fastidio*), just because they dismiss many of these *things*, when in the contemplation (*contemplatione*) of nature nothing can be seen that is superfluous.[57]

Like Pliny himself, his work is marvelous in its own right. Pliny's nature itself contains many dismissable things. But the wonderful order of Pliny's text stands in for the wonderful order of nature – just as Pliny's own limitlessness can stand in for nature's. The labor of delimiting and arranging is the alchemy that changes the *sterilis materia* into an object of delight, and it is by means of his orderly text that Pliny seeks "to prevent those who read my works from condemning the *accounts* of them with boredom, just because they dismiss many of these *things*." The typical author of an encyclopedia, like Pliny, presents himself as a compiler, one who gathers together and arranges the writings of others without adding to them.[58] In a Lucretian universe, creative of its own accord, an account of the wonders of nature could be no more wonderful than the wonders themselves; there is much more danger of falling short of them. Pliny's universe, though, and even more that of Christian encyclopedists, relies on another wonder behind the wonders of the surface phenomena of the world, a logic that manifests itself in wonders even as it conceals itself behind them. This combination of dull material and fascinating collation creates a paradoxical attitude towards learning in Pliny's and similar, later works. Knowledge is carefully split up into elements, which are each carefully accounted for but also individually dismissed. The wonder of knowing is not in knowing one thing or another thing, but in knowing everything. It resides in the aggregate of parts rather than in any individual part, although the text is treated as a collection of many separate parts rather than as a unified whole. Every fact the encyclopedia contains is, numerically at least, equal to every other fact. The result is a kind of commodification of knowledge, where the tallying and dividing of elements becomes almost more important than their content or application.

Early writers minimize their own contributions and insist that their role has been limited to the manipulation of pre-existing facts that pertain to the world or textual *sententiae*, in either case atomized elements that can be shuffled, recombined, and ordered in any number of ways. Both Bartholomaeus Anglicus and Vincent of Beauvais assert that their encyclopedic works contain "little or nothing" of their own, and that they have only collected and arranged the sayings of those of greater authority in phrases close enough to suggest that even their defenses are borrowed from some third source.[59] As arrangements of pre-existing contents in an imaginary space, encyclopedic texts are simulacra of authoritative statements rather than authoritative in their own right. The same assurances that the present compiler has done little or nothing to alter what he has received from his authoritative source appear in Abraham Ortelius' *Theatrum Orbis Terrarum* (1570):

In the maps, which got their names from the authors (*Auctorum*), nothing (as we said) has been changed by us, except for two or three coasts of Belgium, which the sea altered greatly after their descriptions were published by the authors (*ab Auctoribus*) . . .[60]

Ideally, the compiler remained invisible behind the words of others and the natural order of things in the world. As these quotations suggest, however, compilers recognized that the ideal was never completely achieved. Vincent and Bartholomaeus add, they say, "*quasi* nulla," "*almost* nothing," and Ortelius must still correct his sources, even if only in a few small places. The compiler of an encyclopedia desires invisibility behind the marvelous order he proffers, but can only tend towards it asymptotically.

Although desire in Pliny originates in finite human needs, it rapidly overflows any natural limits. What begins as an attempt to master an un-nurturing world expands until what is desired is nothing less than knowledge unlimited by anything other than the world's limits. Nature's "force and majesty" are completely visible only when all of Nature is understood. It is not enough to master a single field, or even many fields; what must be mastered is the totality of things in all its marvelous complexity, the individual details and all their combinations. This, too, is a crucial element in the encyclopedic tradition – it is divorced from practical concerns not from high-mindedness, but because the *curiositas* conjured within the magic circle, the *templum*, of the knowable, exceeds all practical concerns. Hugh of St. Victor, for instance, is explicit that wonder and the desire for knowledge have no limits, and that they can only be satisfied by exhausting their objects, when he advises his reader to "Learn everything; you will see afterwards that nothing is superfluous. A skimpy [*coartata*, literally "segmented"] knowledge is not a pleasing thing."[61]

Johannes Trithemius emphasized his point with capital letters: "AND EVERYTHING THAT HAPPENS IN THE WORLD . . . YOU WILL BE ABLE TO KNOW WITH THIS ART."[62] One of Pico della Mirandola's "Conclusiones paradoxae," roughly halfway through the entire circuit of 900 theses, asserted that not only Platonists but Peripatetics had to concede that the soul could "acquire perfect knowledge of all things knowable" by being purged of its earthly dross.[63] As Pico's formulation suggests, the assumptions behind a desire for *omni scibile*, everything knowable, are vaguely Neoplatonic – man's state in the world is what ruins the wholeness of his knowing, and this original unitary wholeness is what he desires to return to. At the same time, the emphasis on a very non-ascetic engagement with the wonderful particularities of the world distances the encyclopedic project from the univocality of a simple Neoplatonism. As with the desire for wonder, Aristotle is the thinker who offers a definition that becomes part of the dogma of Renaissance encyclopedism: "We consider first, then, that the wise man knows all things, so far as it is possible, without having knowledge of every one of them individually."[64] What captured the imaginations of encyclopedists, though, was Cicero's ellipsis of Aristotle's cautious qualifications, as cited here by Pierre Gregoire: "As Cicero says, nothing is sweeter than to know everything."[65]

The difficulty raised for the encyclopedia turns out not to be generating wonder, but setting limits to the pure reverie in the marvels of nature and in moving from wonder to action. In the exemplary tale of Aristotle and Alexander, however much more ethically admirable Aristotle is to his pupil, it is Alexander who is the real master who learns the world's crucial lesson of mixing his admiration with activity – he sleeps with Homer beneath his pillow, but he is carrying him on a campaign of conquest. As Vives knew of Pliny, the author who most delighted him, "the end of one longing is the beginning of another," and so encyclopedism, seen in Pliny's sense as a sort of undirected accumulation of learning, is potentially limitless.[66] Encyclopedic desire is a kind of playing, and like play it is non-climactic and sustainable; it does not achieve a moment of satisfaction that is also its limit, but can be extended indefinitely.[67] This is why encyclopedias require the external limits of borders, rules, and goals. These limits are subsequent on the initial delimitation that calls the encyclopedia into existence – observe *here* and not there, *now* and not at another time. The marvelous threatens to be all-consuming, were it not that it always has accompanying it an outside which is given priority over it, a stable *summum bonum* that can define, in the sense of set boundaries for, the process.[68] This *summum bonum* is typically couched as a kind of practical end, an economic calculation that, like an anachronistic Pascalian wager, curtails the non-economic sense of wonder that drives the encyclopedia. Although wonder remains the encyclopedia's ground, the innate wonder that an encyclopedic text contains can be harnessed and put to work in some practical task.

What exceeds the usefulness of this task can then be labeled as excessive, parodic, or trivial (or otherwise dismissed) to that which it is subordinated, thus limiting the sustainable play of the encyclopedic text. The subsequent practical end of the encyclopedia thus seems to subordinate the encyclopedic desire that both drives and precedes it. Henningsen notes that the governing principle of seventeenth-century encyclopedias is always external to them ("'Enzyklopädie,'" 291–92). Rather, I think that encyclopedias must always be *supplied* with an external principle to harness and limit the desire that drives them. The establishment and maintenance of a distinction between theory and practice, inner and outer, text and world, is a necessary part of any encyclopedic work, just as is the establishment of a parallelism between them.

For Pliny, for instance, the human sense of wonder is balanced by the productive play of an "ingenious nature [who] makes playthings (*ludibria*) for herself, for us marvels (*miracula*)."[69] Endlessly inventive, nature produces impossibilities and then playfully matches them with still less plausible impossibilities, which the encyclopedist can then record faithfully in his own game of recording. The playthings of Pliny's nature are frequently agonistic, corresponding to the Roman tastes in games, and one animal's near-invulnerability is matched by another animal's peculiar lethalness. The basilisk, for instance, is so poisonous that it kills by sight, but it in turn can be killed by the weasel, which knows to fortify itself beforehand with rue (*Natural History* VIII, 79); giant snakes and even crocodiles are matched by the tiny mongoose, which is marvelously equipped to kill them (VIII, 87, 90). The Indian elephant and the python are also mortal enemies, astonishingly matched in their methods of attack and defense. The elephant is too large to be attacked directly by the ground-dwelling python, so the snake lies in wait for an elephant to pass and then rushes out to trip it up by knotting itself around the elephant's legs. When the elephant reaches down to untie the knots, the snake sticks its head into the elephant's trunk, preventing it from breathing. Wrapping the elephant up in its coils, the python proceeds to suck out all its blood. The elephant, though, laughs last; as it dies, it topples over, crushing the snake, now sluggish from its huge meal (VIII, 34). "What other cause of such great discord does anyone propose," asks Pliny rhetorically, "unless it is that nature thus puts on a spectacle (*spectaculum*) for herself?"[70] This natural spectacle, though, is not only to nature's benefit. Nature's *ludibria* are mankind's *miracula*, and humanity and the inhuman world prove to be strangely synchronized. The last laugh of all in the combat of the python and the elephant is the artist's, who harvests the residue formed when their blood dries together in the ground and makes a kind of artificial cinnabar from it, the only pigment that can accurately represent blood in a painting (XXXIII, 37). By rendering nature's marvels in the form of a game, Pliny does not need to adduce further reasons or causes for them.[71] As a kind of play, the wonderful becomes its own reason, explained and produced by the arbitrary rules and symmetry of Nature's game.

The games of nature, in this understanding, are finally always theatrical with respect to man, as Pliny said: *ludibria sibi, nobis miracula*, or, as Conrad Gessner phrases it, "These sorts of plays of nature (*Hi tanquam ludi quidem naturae*) are not set before us to judge, but to observe (*spectandi*)."[72]

Not all marvels in Pliny are spectacular combats, but all are spectacular in the sense that they are displayed by nature for her pleasure. Like the cinnabar maker, though, humankind in general is scarcely less ingenious than nature in turning her *ludibria* into marvels of its own. Pliny also shows a consistent interest in these reproductions and appropriations of nature, in the grafting of fruit, for instance, but especially in the myriad ways of counterfeiting natural substances, which he calls *adulterium*. The wood of the terebinth tree, for instance, can be wonderfully faked (*mire adulteratur*) by staining wild pear wood with walnut. Here the natural marvel of terebinth wood, which is the only wood that not only improves with but requires oiling (XVI, 205), is matched by the marvel of the mimetic abilities of human technology, even surpassed by them since the resulting counterfeit requires no oil.[73]

The process of *adulterium*, though, is always a slippery slope, another dangerous opening onto the limitless cycle of a negative *curiositas*. In her works Nature is essentially disinterested, but more or less well-intentioned and always even-handed, no matter how precariously, as in the combat of the python and the elephant, and the encyclopedist accurately replicates this. But the desire for knowing, cast as limitless in a figure like Pliny with his infinite willingness to expend effort in seeking knowledge, poses a potential problem when it meets with a system of values with an ordinary economic basis – one, that is, that calculates effort expended against its possible returns, that sets limits and seeks profit. This economic concern, as we shall see, continues to be a central problem for the encyclopedic tradition and its interweaving with that of the theatre – how to prevent either form from moving from *game* to *gain*. In its mimetic ingenuity, humanity always risks going too far. Human delight in nature's *ludibria* too easily becomes the pursuit of *luxuria*, the grotesque exploitation and perversion of the natural from its own playful limits. Nature's freely spectacular display is usurped by human ostentation, which instead of finding an easier or more common access to nature's marvels, perversely commodifies them by making them more difficult and rare. Like encyclopedic desire, the drive to *luxuria* knows no reasonable bounds. The practice of covering wood with tortoise-shell veneer, for example, already morally questionable, takes on a new and perverse turn when in Nero's reign artisans discover how to bleach the shell through "astonishing techniques" (*portentosis ingeniis*) and then to paint it to look like wood: "Once *luxuria* was not content with wood, but now it even makes wood from tortoise-shell."[74] The change from benign wonder at the spectacle of nature to its greedy appropriation requires no more than a change of attitude towards it, or even a change of vocabulary; moral decline is signaled by the fact that "those we call Hermaphrodites once were called androgynes and held in wonder, but now, indeed, are held in pleasure."[75] Once men stop merely observing nature from a distance and begin to investigate it for direct profit, their greed becomes a more urgent drive than even the delight that first produced it. Pliny corrects a widespread misunderstanding of the location of the Atlas mountains with the bitter observation that "I am less amazed that some things are unknown to the men of the equestrian class . . . than that they are unknown to *luxuria*, in which one senses the most effective and greatest force."[76] The object of wonder has shifted from the ingenuity of a golden nature to the brazenness of humanity. Pliny's disgust is at the lack of distance between theory and practice for the equestrians, who are not content to study a thing from a distance, but must at once put it into the economic system of exchanges.

One of the most notable skirmishes over *luxuria* and *curiositas* occurs within the Christian tradition, in which, from Augustine's fascinated appraisal of Monica's unquestioning belief or Jerome's terrified abandonment of Ciceronianism (he dreams that Peter turns him away from heaven with the words, "You're no Christian, you're a Ciceronian"[77]), desirable learning is in tension with necessary faith. Vincent of Beauvais apparently regarded *curiositas* as morally neutral, but a quote from slightly later in the same work expresses an unexplained anxiety about the desire to know. The labor of *compilatio* that the writer of an encyclopedia undertakes is not merely for convenience of reference, but for curtailment of browsing. Vincent hopes that in compiling all his readings into a single work he will not only be helping others preach and develop in charity, but

> placing a kind of limit (*modum*), as it were, on my curiosity (*curiositati*) and on that of many others who are perhaps like me, whose zeal and labor is to read many books and to excerpt passages from them, through this one great work.[78]

At the end of the preface, though, in the same vocabulary, he admits that the attempted cure has only worsened the disease, and his attempt to limit his desire for wonders has failed:

> I confess that for the most part, in my judgment, I have exceeded the limit (*modum*) of my declared purpose and intention by investigating and describing the names of those things that I did not find in the Divine Books. Thus while I wanted to assume the manner of the curious (*curiosis morem*), I fell into the vice of curiosity (*curiositatis*).[79]

In the Augustinian tradition, *curiositas* is "the lust of the eyes" (*concupiscentia oculorum*), the sin in particular associated with the watching of theatrical shows and the observation of the things of the world as if they were shows.[80] James O'Donnell observes that Augustine's anxiety about indulging in *curiositas* is based on the fear that "attending to the wonders of nature led, more often than not, to ascribing those wonders to divine powers [i.e., non-Christian ones] of various sorts."[81] For Vincent, though, curiosity and delight in knowledge are not in themselves bad, except in the risks of excess that always accompany them. In each case, a relation of incommensurability between what is necessary and what is desirable within a text is represented as one of norm and excess, with play represented as what overgoes the usefulness of the encyclopedia and corrupts it. For Pliny it is the moral gap between *ludibria* and *luxuria*; for Vincent, the Christian distinction between knowledge necessary for understanding Scripture and the frivolous learning that exceeds it, in other words between *morem curiosis* and *curiositas* proper, the mannerism of *curiositas* and the thing itself. At some point, each encyclopedia seeks to separate its use from its abuse, legitimate play from excessive play; from the outset, a limit is placed on the game in the language they use, literally, to define it. What these medieval encyclopedists require, and what is also demanded by their early modern heirs, is a way of managing *curiositas* and preventing it from overrunning the limits set for it that divide play from decadence.

The answer to this problem in both early and late encyclopedism is found, startlingly, in the idea of the theatre. The desire that overflows Varro's *templum* can be recontained by an ingenious *theatrum* that will, supposedly, neatly distinguish practical from theoretical and real from imaginary. In both Elyot's and Pliny's encyclopedias, the theatre itself offers this restricted space, providing both an opportunity for contemplation and an appropriate limit for preventing the wonder at nature's *ludibria* from turning into the greed for *luxuria*. Both theatre and encyclopedia are systems that display nature's wonders in an order and abstract them from the world, legitimating and limiting play in a single operation. Play – especially *a* play – is free and full of wonder, but as a theatre (or *templum*) it is also circumscribed by its very structure. The encyclopedia could acknowledge the power of the desire for wonder and still control it by showing itself to be properly theatrical in a positive sense, rather than the opposite of theatre as Reisch hinted at when he spoke of scholars as *histriones*. Both encyclopedias and theatres are games that authorize play and at the same time limit it to a particular space, either an imaginary one of foreplanning or an equally imaginary one of performance. By making a game of learning, setting it within definite rules and spaces, and limiting it in ways that are markedly "artificial," the desire for wonder that drives the encyclopedia can be both limited and preserved in the name of another goal – theological, philosophical, moral, but, most importantly, *purposive* – that can then be differentiated from the desire for wonder as serious from playful. Such contingent utilitarianism serves to mask what encyclopedic texts represent as essential and originary, and what will when all purposes are exhausted still remain – the desire to marvel. Under the practical claims made for the encyclopedia, the unending sense of wonder remains always half-visible, as the ground of the project that in part conceals it.[82]

Immediately after his lament about the change in attitude that has turned portentous androgynes into delectable hermaphrodites, Pliny offers a better alternative for admiration: the marvelous painted images commissioned by Pompeius Magnus for his theatre. At its dedication, Pompey the Great "placed among the ornaments of his theatre images marvelous in legend (*mirabiles fama posuit effigies*), worked out most carefully by the skill (*ingeniis*) of great craftsmen . . . ,"[83] such as an image of Eutychis, who gave birth thirty times and was carried to her grave by twenty of her children, and Alcippe, who gave birth to an elephant. The wonders of Pompey's theatre are doubly marvelous, both for what they represent and for the ingenuity (*ingeniis*) they display. This is the same term, *ingenium*, that Pliny denies to himself as the encyclopedia's compiler. What differentiates Pliny's or the theatre's kind of display-oriented ingenuity from the adulterate products of monstrous ingenuity (*portentosis ingeniis*, the same word in all three references), like the tortoise-shell painted to look like wood, is their inaccessibility to the spectator and their distance from what they represent. Their theatricality shields them from inappropriate desire, the desire, precisely, to appropriate them, commodify and exchange them as *valuable* objects rather than marvelous ones.

This abstraction, though, is not only the result of an inherent difference between what is represented in paint or sculpture and what is real. It extends to a marvelous live act that Pliny mentions, an appearance by the ancient Galeria Copiola, a retired actress who was so old that she was led out as a marvel herself (*pro miracula reducta*, *Natural History* VII, 158). Inside the theatre, Galeria Copiola's relation to the spectators is like that of the images on the walls. Like them, she is framed in such a way as to make her an object of wonder but not of use or greed. She is separated from the audience by the conventions that govern the presentation of things in a theatre. The actual conditions of performance in the Roman theatres – including the fact that what went on in theatres was not drama in our sense, but spectacle – are here less relevant than Pliny's use of the figure of the theatre to make his point about ideal spectatorship and wonder. In this theatre, the spectator remains exactly that. The images in Pompey's theatre can be viewed but not used; they cannot enter into circulation in the world of reality, unlike the *trompe-l'oeil* tortoise-shell painted to look like wood. Pompey's theatre is an idealized self-representation within Pliny's *Natural History*, a perfect encyclopedic space within a real textual encyclopedia, where objects can be removed from the circuit of exploitative, mimetic *adulterium* but preserved for admiration, paradoxically also in the form of a likeness – an *adulterium* imagined as free from economic interest, pure playful *ludibrium* with no fear of *luxuria*. Gian Biagio Conte has described Pliny's work as one in which *mirabilia* become *memorabilia*, in which marvels are recorded not as surprising but logically necessitated natural extremes, but because they are unique and unlikely to recur.[84] Such a description also fits the theatre, in which unique events become reproducible, even infinitely so – Galeria Copiola, for instance, reprises her star turn at the age of 104 (Pliny's chronology here becomes somewhat marvelous as well) – and where the real bodies of the actors are imagined as temporarily bracketed from contact with the rest of the world. The encyclopedia, in other words, is a theatre; the world is a display of the playing of nature, and both theatre and encyclopedia are devices for setting limits and rendering the desire for knowledge practical and teleological. Paradoxically, they do this by distancing it from the circuit of ordinary exchanges.

Many other early encyclopedic works also present themselves as theatrical. They stage, feign, imitate their own impossible completeness by casting themselves as dramas of knowledge, spaces for experiment in which the world can be re-presented anew, handled, examined, altered, but always through the ironizing distance of fictionality. In their self-representations they describe or enact a desire to know the source of that wonder and posit a corresponding richness of things to sustain it, an order so marvelous that it could render every part of it marvelous.[85] Like Pantagruel's amphibological praise of his teacher, the encyclopedia may be Western culture's unwitting joke on itself, as it continually reforgets what it knew about the limits of knowing and the irony of trying to master all possible knowledge and begins to take the task seriously. Naivete about the encyclopedia, in the sense of suspending its optative element and believing in its possibility outside of supernatural means, only comes after the eighteenth century, blinded by its own Enlightenment.

In premodern Europe the encyclopedic organization of knowledge had an additional feature – it demonstrated itself to be a self-defeating project. A deconstructive moment is part of early encyclopedias just as much as their idealistic pursuit of everything knowable. Having set up a tidy set of distinctions between theatre and encyclopedia, theory and practice, knowing and doing, the space of the encyclopedia, by casting itself as the equivalent of a theatre, thoroughly ironized its claims to knowledge and ultimately redefined the limits and terms within which it had taken meaning. As early as Pliny the Younger's transformation of his uncle's preternaturally large and drowsy body into a comical allegory of his encyclopedic writings, the coupling of heroism and absurdity is part of the encyclopedia, and of the encyclopedist. This reversal of values in the representation of the encyclopedia is further theorized in Martianus Capella's fifth-century CE *De Nuptiis Mercurii et Philologiae*, in which encyclopedic fantasy is belied by the actual presentation of encyclopedic information. Nominally the description of the marriage festivities of Mercury (or Eloquence) and Philology (or Knowledge), the text begins with the promise of a completely fulfilling marital union – a well-worn figure for purposefully harnessed desire – but quickly devolves into long (and to judge from the reactions of the characters in the text, harrowingly dull) speeches for the newlyweds by the seven personified Liberal Arts. Martianus ironically pits competing desires against each other – the sexual desire between Mercury and Philology, and even more the desire of the gods on their behalf, against the desirable learning the Liberal Arts offer. Instead of being observed with wonder, the actual speeches of the Liberal Arts inspire *fastidium*, "boredom," in the gods and especially in Voluptas, the goddess of pleasure; the individual speeches end with each Art being cut off in mid-stride by the complaints of the audience about how dull she is. In Martianus Capella's ironic treatment, the encyclopedia leads to knowledge, but by the same effort it also defers the ultimate union of Mercury and Philology, rhetoric and wisdom. It provokes desire by deferring its satisfaction, substituting what is only *like* knowledge – that is, the process of gaining it – from knowledge itself. The encyclopedia thus functions both as desire itself and as a limit, or at least a hedge, to its satisfaction.

Early in *De Nuptiis*, Martianus Capella describes "a sphere [which] seemed to be an image and model of the world,"[86] on which all the features of the world can be seen and in which Jupiter can intervene to raise men up or put them down. The sphere provides the watching gods with vision and access from any direction; their understanding of the sphere is completely unrestrained, in sharp contrast to the boredom and confusion they express when the actual encyclopedic contents of the Liberal Arts are revealed. *De Nuptiis* thus initially represents an ideal of encyclopedic knowledge in the sphere – total accessibility, absolute contemplation, perfect ease of action – and then deflates it by dramatizing it in the discourse of actual speakers, whose knowledge cannot be instantly or completely grasped, but must accumulate over time, in a narrative, which may not even be accurate, and which certainly lacks the fascination of the magical sphere. Perfect distance, as Martianus' double representation shows, can only be imagined schematically; merely to detail encyclopedic information begins the process of disrupting the order it was meant to represent.

But the characterization of the encyclopedia as playful or parodic, which from one perspective seems to dismiss its cognitive value, is not a dismissal of its usefulness. In their particular contexts, each encyclopedia I have cited occupies a position difficult for us to imagine, as work that is both serious intellection and frivolous pastime.[87] Each of the works I have mentioned is used until at least the seventeenth century as a storehouse of knowledge. They are not like the *Formicarium Artium* (the Anthill of the Arts) or the similar works that Pantagruel found in the library of St. Victor (once home to that earlier encyclopedist, Hugh); if they are parodies, they are the complex kind of parody that does not distinguish itself from the non-parodic. They are not games because they are empty or frivolous, but rather because they are characterized, in Borges' words, by "symmetry, arbitrary rules, tedium" – all of which serve to limit them.[88] The introduction of the idea of play or desire or game marks a passage from an epistemology in which the pleasant was supposed to be articulated with the useful to the different kind of performed knowledge. Such a shift confines the destabilizing *play* of the encyclopedia to the rules and spaces of a *game*. For the premodern encyclopedia, the theatre was the best emblem of this doubly useful delimitation.

2 The idea of a theatre

> Before the space of threescore years above-said, I neither knew, heard, nor read, of any such Theatres, set Stages, or Play-houses, as have been purposely built within man's memory. —John Stow, *Annales* (1629)[1]

It was the theatre that most completely exhibited the qualities that were associated with the encyclopedia during the Renaissance, and the spaces of contemplation imagined by Varro and Pliny during the height of the Roman Republic and the early consolidation of the Empire were regularly understood as the space of the theatre. The "theatre" of early modern Europe, however, was not equated with the various kinds of performance that had been in more or less continuous practice since antiquity. Such *playing* – the usual English word for these performance practices – had little in common with the connotations of the word *theatrum*, known to readers and speakers of Latin as a device that had been lost since the fall of Rome. John Stow's startled realization that the circular buildings that gave London a prospect unlike that of any other European city, distinctive enough in foreign travelers' eyes to characterize it,[2] were in fact the products of a single generation, suggests both the swiftness and the strangeness of this built form. In the absence of any physical objects that could be identified as theatres, the theatre in medieval and early modern Europe led a vigorous imaginary afterlife.[3] The vicious theatre of Augustine's *Confessions* and the dramatic spectacle of the damned envisioned by Tertullian, the widely circulated legend that Cicero's education in rhetoric had been completed by studying with the comedian Roscius and the great prestige of Terence and Plautus as schooltexts, combined to produce such strangely speculative, nominally "theatrical" works as Pico della Mirandola's *Oratio de Dignitate Hominum* (1486) or Juan Luis Vives' extended vision in *Fabula de Homine* (1518) of humankind as an actor on a world stage.[4] Part of the history of how the theatre became an emblem for all the qualities assigned to the encyclopedia is as old as Pliny's linking of the two. But part of it is peculiar to the idea of the theatre that developed independent of any object to define it.

Early humanist writers on theatre substituted an imaginary space for the absent social and physical one. The idea of the "theatre" during the Middle Ages and Renaissance was kept distinct from the performance practices of popular dramatic forms and even, it seems, from mental reconstructions of Roman stagings. The ruined Roman theatres that still remained throughout Italy and France are sometimes mentioned in medieval and early modern texts, although with nothing like the insistence we might expect given the importance of the theatre as a metaphor in the period. Almost without exception, though, ancient theatres are seen by their viewers not as signs of earlier theatrical practices but as opportunities for meditating on Rome's past greatness – less *theatrum mundi* than *sic transit gloria mundi*. Analogues to contemporary performance are likewise rarely drawn; in fact, theatres serve as an especially useful index of time's passage because, like obelisks, arches, and pyramids, they are impressive objects that typify ancient architecture and that moderns do not build. The ancient theatres that survived work principally as focal points for generalized melancholy at the decay of antiquity. Sebastian Münster's *Cosmographei* (first edition 1544; 1550) identifies the Colosseum in passing as "an *amphitheatrum* or playhouse" (*ein amphitheatrum oder spilhauß*, clxxix), showing that he at least understood something of its function (unlike some earlier viewers who had postulated a temple to the Sun) and is intrigued enough by the ruined theatre at Verona to supply a two-page woodcut of it (ccxxiii ff.). In general, though, he seems little interested in ancient theatres except as emblems of a rich, powerful, and absent past, "signs of a great existence that used to be."[5] The theatre at Verona, for instance, is a "wonderwork" "erected with inexpressible expense," but it, like the Colosseum, "is nonetheless half broken" (ccxxiii; clxxix). Baldessar Castiglione hones the melancholy of his reflection on Rome's "holy ruins" on the "Colossi, arches, theatres, divine works . . . turned into a little ash," (c.1515) and Joachim du Bellay asks in his *Romae descriptio* (1558): "Shall I speak of the heights of [your] pyramids, the colossal torsos, the now-empty arc of sad and silent theatres?"[6] The theatre as an emblem of the distance between ancient and modern Rome was made concrete when Sixtus IV began mining the Colosseum for stone with which to build the Ponte Sistino, as one poet complained: "In order that the foundations of a little bridge be erected,/ Must your hands bring down great amphitheatres?"[7]

To its humanist analysts, the "theatre" they read about in ancient accounts seemed to have nothing to do with contemporary popular performances they might have seen. A central element in the history of theatre practice, then, is the idea of a theatre that developed among humanists and other, mainly learned, readers. Such theatres, much like the circles of the encyclopedia, are literally ideological constructs – the basis of these stages that could only be imagined as real and figured as metaphors by their devisers is purely in the ideal realm of thought. Most humanist theatre, whether practical or imaginary, was unabashedly didactic and ideological – making Plato's connection of the visual and the visionary to the theatre as a place of seeing – but here I want to address the ideology of theatre proper: what a theatre might mean or what it could be expected to do by those who imagined it. First I will look at the connotations of the word "theatre" before the mid sixteenth century, when it became fully naturalized into the vernacular languages. The connotations attached to the word in turn led to a more thickly particularized ideology of theatre, a set of assumptions about the relations of writer and actor, audience and stage, that put pressure on theatre practices. Actual theatrical production brought with it another set of largely unarticulated pressures, and these I examine in the final section, when I look at how one humanist play, John Rastell's *Nature of the Four Elements*, thematizes the dissonance between two conceptions of theatre.

The first object since Roman antiquity to be called a *theatrum* was not a physical space for performance, but a large book that claimed to contain knowledge in a visual or visualizable form. We tend to think of the use of the word "theatre" in book titles as a metaphor drawn from the stage, but when the first circular playhouse outside London was named the Theatre, that use of the name too is a metaphor. The Theatre of 1576 was built six years after the publication of Ortelius' *Theatrum Orbis Terrarum*, a decade after the first publication of Theodor Zwinger's *Theatrum Vitae Humanae*, fifteen years after the first publication of Pierre Boaistuau's *Theatrum Mundi*, a quarter of a century after Giulio Camillo's *L'Idea del Theatro* was published, and forty years – a generation – after the Teatro described in it was designed.[8] The first realized Theatre building is thus nearly as distant in time from Camillo's ideal Teatro as Stow's well-theatred London is from the time when there were no theatres. Both the structure and the book titles are realizations of an ideal model of knowing as a species of seeing that is drawn from readings of ancient texts.[9] Although the performance space of 1567 called the Red Lion had many of the architectural features of Burbage and Brayne's later Theatre, it lacked the metaphorical gesture of completeness, abstraction, and knowledge-production that the name of the later playhouse had come to imply and that was picked up again in the universalizing name of its later incarnation, the Globe. This linking in the word *theatrum* of conceptions of a knowledge dependent upon vision, of the separation of a circular space of viewing from a real world it mirrored and a corresponding gulf between active player and receptive audience is the metaphorical basis for titles like the *Theatrum Vitae Humanae* and the Theatre in the suburbs alike. To choose the name Theatre for their second playhouse involved the two entrepreneurs in a web of assumptions and expectations about how such an object might function that had less to do with widely varied traditions of contemporary performance than with the powerful metaphorical resonance the word *theatre* had picked up in the ongoing humanist revival of antiquity.

Claims for the theatre's universal appeal and pedagogical force stem ultimately from the answer Donatus provided in his commentary on the plays of

Terence, one of the most widely read texts of early modern Europe, to the question, "What is comedy?":

Comedy according to the Greeks is the epitome (*comprehensio*) of public and private fortune without peril of life. According to Cicero it is the imitation of life, the mirror of custom, and the image of truth.[10]

In Donatus' definition, comedy served to display every aspect of existence, in terms that recall those used of encyclopedic texts – distance from risk, compression, visuality. Also frequently quoted in the context of defining theatrical performance was the tag line from Terence's *Heauton Timoroumenos*, "I am a human being; nothing human is foreign to me."[11] The quotation is more familiar as a declaration of universalism and humanism (modern and Renaissance both), but it also has a history as a comment on theatre's scope. From late antiquity onward Terence's works were regarded as exemplary in their combination of theatrical diversion, of useful knowledge of the human condition, and more narrowly of the polished Latinity that Terence above all other authors was felt to excel in. In humanist schools of the fifteenth and sixteenth centuries they were performed as well as read throughout Europe. But Terence was frequently treated as a fixed storehouse of ideas and even words – a *comprehensio*, in fact – than as a script for performance. For Erasmus and many others, Terence's works contained all the elements of both ethical behavior and copious language.[12] The tendency to credit Terence as a source of universal knowledge reached its extreme a century later, when the physician and educator Joseph Webbe made the claim that by using his properly organized edition of the text of the *Andria* (1629) and shuffling and reassembling Terentian phrases by theme, "you shall not only have power to enlarge your own conceits upon your Author's forms, and clauses, but infinitely vary words and matter, to the full extent of the whole Latin tongue, upon the style of Terence only."[13] The theatre could teach because, for the humanists, it presented a mirror of its contents, whether those were good Latin or good morality.

The word *theatre* first appears in English in a Wycliffite Bible manuscript of 1382, transliterating the Latin *theatrum* (or, less likely, the Greek *theatron*), and is glossed as a "comune biholdiyng place."[14] The use of the foreign word suggests two things about the translator of this passage. First, he could think of no English equivalent to the Latin or Greek word – "playhouse" must not have seemed adequate for whatever it connoted – and so chose to render it phonetically into English; second, that the word had not entered into ordinary usage, since he felt compelled to define it for his readers and listeners. The definition of the theatre as a "common beholding place" succinctly delineates the conceptual image of the theatre that would dominate learned European and English thought into the sixteenth century, when permanent, purpose-built theatre buildings were actually constructed in Italy, England, and Spain. Based on the

Greek root of *theaomai*, "look," the theatre was conceived of as principally an instrument of vision, a device for "beholding." *Theatre* shares its stem with the word *theory*, meaning literally "a looking," and thus also *theory*'s sense of abstraction and knowing. In some early texts the words "theatre" and "theory" are actually confused: an English text on the liberal arts from the late fifteenth century substitutes the word *theoric* for *theatric* in its discussion of the various mechanical arts.[15] Even years after the construction of the Theatre, John Rider's *Bibliotheca Scholastica* (1589), which grouped words conceptually as well as alphabetically, something like a modern thesaurus, significantly defined *theatrum* as a "looking place" and placed it under the heading "To look" rather than under "Stages to see plays."[16] The *visual* connotations of *theatre* remained dominant until public theatre became widespread in late sixteenth-century England.[17] In this idea of a theatre, the inevitable temporality of language and performance was replaced, conceptually, by a picture – a still life – in which knowledge could be seen, entire and timeless. In a variation of the Horatian dictum *ut pictura poesis*, the Spanish humanist and educational reformer Juan Luis Vives specifically linked the pictoriality of poetry to the stage: "Poetry comes onto the stage, with the people gathered to watch, and there just as the painter displays a picture to the crowd to be seen, so the poet [displays] a kind of image of life."[18] The metaphor is common: theatres are likened to pictures for their static quality, for the supposed naturalness of their signs, and overwhelmingly because of the visuality implied by the Greek meaning of the word *theatron*, which comprised both the simultaneity and the immediacy that was believed to characterize their representations.[19]

Finally, this looking was, as the Wycliffite Bible declared, "common"; it was not a private inspection, but a public display. This imaginary theatre produced, or was thought to produce, a shared experience of what was shown rather than a private one, a vision that received part of its authority from the fact that it had entered into public circulation. What allowed for this public authorization was the fact that, from its first naming and even before it was realized architecturally, the theatre was conceived of as a place differentiated in particular ways from other similar spaces around it. In his discussion of the social cohesions that made seventeenth-century science possible, Steven Shapin specifies in particular a faith in the connection of place and perception, namely the belief that the same perception of the external world is shared by those who are "attending to the same spatiotemporal region."[20] This schema is flexible enough to sustain variant reports of what occurs in the "same spatiotemporal region" through the use of such concepts as perspective, and more broadly by distinguishing between observation – which all can agree on – and interpretation – which is prone to inflection or error by any number of accidental causes. The idea of the theatre specifies these same concepts some 250 years earlier, not as a precursor to science but as a system for producing, or displaying, a shared experience of seeing. Many medieval accounts of the theatre as an imaginary object – not to be confused with the actual dramatic practices of the time – similarly suggest these emphases on commonality and vision. John Lydgate, for instance, in the *Troy Book* (II, 863 ff.), describes a theatre with an altar in its center, beside which a poet recited "the noble dedis, that wer historial [sic]." Behind the poet, mimes silently acted out the poet's words.[21] In this image of the theatre, language is connected to the fixity of a text and poetic authority, while the action of the players is subordinated to it. This relation is maintained in Tudor dumbshows such as those that introduce each act in *Gorboduc* (1559) or *Jocasta* (1566). While the silent action of the players precedes the dramatic events that it is meant to emblematize, it is limited to depictions of mood (such as mourning or threat) or at best truisms (unity is better than fragmentation, for instance) that the subsequent acts particularize.[22]

The "common beholding place" implied in these early appearances of the word *theatre* is codified in the texts of later writers. *L'Idea del Theatro* (1550), the posthumously published work of the Italian rhetorician Giulio Camillo, offers an extraordinarily clear association of theatrical display with vision, spatiality, and knowledge.[23] The work describes a device built on the model of a Vitruvian theatre that was meant to allow its user, visualizing himself standing at the center of the stage, to organize and command all humanly available knowledge by looking out into the circle of seats around him.[24] Camillo's title expresses the visual foundation of knowledge with graceful compression in the etymology of its two nouns, *idea* and *theatro*, each drawn from a different Greek word for seeing. For Camillo, though, the double sense of the title was no mere accident of definition, but one that extended to the actual nature of things. His *Theatro* was not intended merely to describe the world's structure, but actually to demonstrate it: it did not illustrate (only) that seeing is believing, in other words, but that looking is knowing. For Camillo, men in the world are like men in a wood, who cannot see the shape of what is around them unless they ascend a nearby hill: "to want to see these lower things well, it is necessary to climb to higher ones and, looking down below from above, we can have surer understanding of them."[25] The wood, or *silva*, in which earthly man is here immersed is another common image for the confused mass of disordered particulars as they appear in the fallen world of history. It is the alternative to the ordered space of the encyclopedic theatre: the *sylva* [sic] Theodore Zwinger appends to his *Theatrum Vitae Humanae* (1565), he explains, is a supplement "of certain categories and examples in the arrangement of the whole Work, whether by accident or design, either moving from their place or anyway omitted."[26] Similarly, Camillo's wanderer must rise out of the wood of particulars to a position above it. Distance rather than immersion offers the best position for understanding something, because only then does the object of scrutiny appear as a whole. Camillo's understanding of the implications of *theatrum* develops the suggestions of the word's earlier appearances. For a culture that had experience of the *theatrum* only through texts describing it, the theatre seemed to be an object that promised the abstraction necessary to combine external objectivity and absolute regularity. Its containment of the spectacles it displayed and its detachment of them from the world were ways of reducing the confusion of phenomena into an ordered whole – literally, of seeing the wood for the trees.

The imaginary theatre assumed vision as an ideal of authoritative knowing – what is definitive is not what is said, but what is seen, and hence, in this ideology that distinguishes observation from interpretation, what is "common" and can be taken for granted. Camillo's *Theatro* shows this desire to efface or neutralize the viewer in front of an absorbing and 'objective' object, mental or physical. Such an attitude separated the theatre as an idea absolutely from any empirical knowledge of playing or performance that a viewer might have acquired, where the role of the actors was typically far from objective and that of the viewers hardly passive. This idea of the theatre is also one reason why to humanist writers of the fifteenth, sixteenth, and seventeenth centuries the theatre so often looks so powerful as a learning tool. Along with the possibility of instant and complete knowledge, visual display seems to have the possibility of being self-authorizing, of speaking for itself; it seems to offer a concentrated and naturally legible form of writing, like a hieroglyph or an emblem, that could give rise to more prosaic discourse but that itself preceded it.[27] The theatre as a "place of looking" seemed to offer the possibility of a knowledge based on a shared sensual experience, prior to any reflection or interpretation. But this static kind of theatre, in which the viewer was separated from the vision before him so as to enable him to grasp it whole, was substantially different from the one suggested by the theory of public performance in the newly revitalized *Poetics* of Aristotle. For Aristotle, the key term in defining performance was *drama*, "action," with the same root as Greek *draô*, "I do (something)," a profoundly transitive verb. A *drama* was an "imitation of something being done," *mimêsis praxeos*, and there could be no action, no *drama* in Aristotle's terms, without something being affected – without change and interference in the world around the actor. The humanist idea of the theatre, then, was suspended between its conflicting concepts of *theatre* as essentially visual (and hence, in the terms of this ideology, vivid, unambiguous, mentally affecting, and completed) and *drama* as essentially imitative and active (and hence unclear, complex, unpredictable, and requiring a double awareness of the thing imitated and the thing imitating).[28]

The theatre, imagined as performed but in fact purely, even self-consciously, existing in texts, was meant to reveal a natural order of things to its observing audience, entirely apart from the drama of human intervention. But what brought forth this order was the looking that the theatre required, the proper spectatorial activity of the theatre of vision that Varro specified as *contemplatio*.[29] The circular space of the public theatre, like the imagined circle of the encyclopedia, requires the creation of a neutral space, a segment of the world set apart from the rest of the world. Independent of the world yet supposedly mirroring it exactly – comedy was "the mirror of life" – the theatre was credited with showing nature its own image undistorted for its spectators, as clear and as remote from them as the depths of a painting in perspective. Varro's understanding of *contemplatio* contains moments of both *theatre* and *drama*; there is both passive vision and active delimitation. In early modern theorists like Camillo, though, vision as a passive response serves to obscure the activity of setting aside a space within which to observe.

This tension is apparent in many of the imaginary theatres of the sixteenth century as well. In his *Universae Naturae Theatrum* (1595), the historian and political theorist Jean Bodin restages these two conflicting theorizations of the theatre, the Varronian one that acknowledges human intervention in setting aside the looking place and the Camillan one that forgets this and sees only the objects that the space holds and reveals.[30] Bodin's work takes the form of a dialogue between a master, Mystagogus, which means "Leader or Initiator into Mysteries," and a pupil, who in the heading of the first book is introduced as Theodorus, "Gift of God," but thereafter is Theorus, "Spectator." Theorus asks Mystagogus to educate him in the knowledge of the world. Hijacking Petrarch's famous metaphor of the humanist as an explorer in the ruined forum of Rome,[31] he likens his training to a group's journey through the ruins of an ancient city, where a guide

> leads them around the city, and exposes every antiquity of the place – temples, theatres, porticoes, and what he knows to be the most beautiful and most unusual, he explains in a friendly fashion. Thus I want you to educate me, a pilgrim in this city of the world (*mundana civitate*), about everything . . .[32]

In his account, Theorus imagines the truth of things to occupy a space external to him, with an objective existence of its own. As Ann Blair notes, his name is linked in alchemical and neo-Platonic literature to the human spirit, not fully at home in the world and aspiring beyond it, but unmistakably immersed in it (*Theatre of Nature*, 55–57). He also recognizes that the external objectivity of the world does not in itself make it intelligible. It is not enough to wander without guidance through the fragments and ruins of the city, which, like the melancholy cities recalled by Du Bellay and Castiglione, include both temples and theatres. Theorus here also revisits the image used by Rudolph Agricola of following in the footprints of the ancient writers, the discrete visual marks of their course through the common places, the *loci communes*, but discovers that these *vestigia* lead nowhere in particular.[33] Theorus requires the instruction of a knowledgeable guide able to point out what is most worthy of his attention. Thus directed, Theorus will be able, like Petrarch, to see the original wholeness of the city within the fragments that remain.

Mystagogus agrees to take Theorus on as a student, but he has a different idea of what is involved in such teaching. He will serve as Theorus' guide because

> we do not come into this theatre of the world (*mundi theatrum*) for any other reason than that of contemplating (*contemplando*) the spectacle (*speciem*) of the universe and all the works of the highest founder of all things, and his individual workings . . .[34]

Mystagogus' pointed change of Theorus' "city of the world" to a "theatre of the world" is critical to Bodin's understanding of the relation of man the spectator to the spectacle of things around him. For both viewers the scene before them is real; as I have been suggesting, the humanist theatre is not principally one of feigning, but a space of seeing and knowing. Theorus, though, sees humanity's work as looking at leftovers, objects that do not realize that they are being looked at and only accidentally communicate their secrets to their investigator. His teacher Mystagogus, in contrast, sees the world as a theatre, a complex and stylized play in which humanity is always participating as its spectator. As a theatre, the world is striving to show itself to us even as we strain to read what it says. The order that humans apply to the world to make it intelligible is not, as it was for Theorus, something external to it. The world is outside humanity but it contains it; as Bodin notes later, echoing Vives' *Fabula de Homine*, he was put in its center that he might see it better. One of the many parts a man in his time plays is that of the world's spectator, and, since the world is a theatre, it knows its audience and plays to him.

Mystagogus' theatre of the world is a full reversal of that proposed by Theorus, who imagines himself glimpsing his worldly city unawares, as it sleeps. This theatre has expanded from the limited *templum* of Varro (itself closer to Theorus' city, of which he is not part and to which he requires a guide) to encompass the whole natural world; there is no outside of the spectacle where things are not presented for observation. The theatricality of an object, the way it presents itself for a spectator or spectators, is also part of its truth and must be taken into account in any complete understanding of it. How it seems, in other words, is part of how it is. For Varro, *contemplatio* was an imposition of human desire onto the world for the purpose of finding out its meaning (and, I have argued, with the effect of producing further desire); for Bodin, *contemplatio* is the human realization that the world itself desires to be viewed. To look at shows in a theatre of the world in this case is vastly different from looking at the ruins of a city. In either case, man is a spectator, but in the latter he only watches, while in the former, he takes part in its playing by watching.

What Bodin identifies as nature's theatricality is also thoroughly encyclopedic. It is theatrical not through the changefulness we might associate with theatre, but by its predictability and order. Although it is the product of a God who can do as he wills, Bodin's nature is nonetheless completely subject to predictable laws that belong equally to both realms; they are "divine, that is, natural" (*divinae, id est naturae, Theatrum, Dedication,* 2v–3r). In contrast to the changeable and fickle world of human action, poignantly evoked in the concluding sentence of the work ("The end of the Theatre of Nature, which Jean Bodin compiled while all of France burned with civil war"), "in nature nothing is uncertain."[35] Unlike human action, nature follows predictable and unchanging rules. It is Bodin's understanding of the world as display or spectacle for its viewers that authorizes his representation of the world in a form that lays it out for a spectator – in short, as a theatre. When Theorus asks Mystagogus to

spread out (*explica,* lit. "unfold"), if you will, the tablet of the universe, just as in a theatre (*velut in theatro*), so that as if it were set before the eye for viewing, by the arrangement of all things the essence and faculty of each might more clearly be made out,[36]

it is because such an explicitly artificial disposition of elements most accurately reproduces their natural arrangement. We privilege the candid snapshot or the Freudian slip, the capture of an unforeseen or accidental moment, as most honest; Bodin gives this credit to carefully ordered self-display.

Theodor Zwinger's *Theatrum Vitae Humanae* seems to address this problem of contradiction between theory and practice in the realization of the *theatrum*. The text of Zwinger's book sustains on the one hand a running metaphor of being built in the form of a physical theatre: it opens with a "Proscenia," it is divided into Acts and Scenes, it describes its readers as spectators, its words as actors, *tituli* hang over its subsections like the titles that identified the *loci* in moral plays, and so on; most of all, it refers constantly to sight and vision as its modes of use.[37] In spite of this, it excludes illustration entirely. Nor is Zwinger's emphasis on the anti-naturalism of his theatre accidental; it calls attention to itself by the glaringness of its tropes. The theatre that Zwinger builds is presented to the reader as a purely verbal construction, never as a visual or spatial image that needs to be imagined. While repeatedly stressing the theatricality of his work, Zwinger explicitly rejects a visual, spatial connection for a verbal one:

Neither leisure nor life would have been sufficient for us to assemble, as many demanded and even reason bid, in imitation of geometers who wrote out the device (*machinam*) of the universe in an extraordinary globe, this great Theatre in the form of a theatre (*magnum hocce Theatrum in Theatricalii formam*), unless we were to assign more time to polishing diction than to work and study.[38]

The timeless space of print replaces the imaginary space of the world, not only ekphrastically, but by actually calling attention to the physical and spatial properties of Zwinger's book as a printed object. Instead of the literal visualization promised by the term *théatrum,* and in place of the vividly colored images provided in Abraham Ortelius' *Theatrum Orbis Terrarum* and similar textual theatres, Zwinger's work constructs its visual patterns typographically. Although Zwinger rejects spending too much time polishing his diction, his book produces its visuality solely in the medium of words, both as representations of spoken language and as physical shapes on the page. Even the title page that is so commonly rendered with an architectural motif in this period is presented entirely in type. In place of a drawn facade, the letters themselves block out a structure that distinctly alludes to an architectural space without precisely imitating one (Figure 5).[39] Zwinger delights in playing with the paradox that what defines space in his theatre are the shapes of the words on the page rather than pictures or descriptions. He explains his title on the grounds that he is presenting a specifically visual *Theatrum*, "for if you consider well the thing itself, it contains the spectacles of humanity (*tôn anthrôpinôn theamata*), and once it pleased more to say *Theatra*, from seeing (*apo tês theas*), than *Akroateria*, from hearing (*akroasei*)."[40] *Autopsis*, or direct vision, Zwinger leaves to the genre of history and its writers; with direct sight and direct hearing (*akroasis*) barred, what remains for Zwinger's visual theatre is the remaining alternative of *anagnôsis*, a simultaneously oral and visual reading, or literally "knowing again, recognizing."[41] Even the contents of Zwinger's printed theatre are to be distinguished from the language that surrounds them; the words for objects that can be sensed (*theamata*) and the actions of sensing them (*thea, akroasis*, and so on) are printed in Greek letters rather than the Latin that composes the rest of the Theatre. Zwinger insists upon the visual aspect of his theatre at the expense of conceiving of the work as a kind of aural and oral dialogue, *akroasis*, "hearing" frozen into print.

Lina Bolzoni warns against literalizing, in our terms, the theatricality of textual theatres:

this interpretation, it seems to me, threatens to overshadow the relation, although grasping an important aspect of its operation, of the one and the many, and thus the relation of the deep structure of things, which the "theatre," the ideal museum, attempts to reproduce.[42]

The literal theatricalization of elements through their actual display works against the residual neoplatonism of the idea of a *theatrum mundi*, an intuitive, extratemporal presence of the world. But this theatre in Zwinger's sense is not the *theatrum mundi* of the Platonic idea. Michel Foucault describes the space of the mirror as utopic: it represents the world in an area that lies outside the world, in a space that is not a space, which in fact succeeds in being neutral and having no positive characteristics of its own. The theatre, in contrast, is a heterotopia, "a kind of effectively enacted utopia," which juxtaposes multiple and incongruous sites ("Of Other Spaces," 24). As the encyclopedia changes from a medieval *Speculum* to an early modern *Theatrum*, and as the theatre changes from an imaginary space to a real one, each becomes more and more of a

Eheus tv, o' bone,
qui in hanc caueam non agendi, ut hiſtrio, ſed
ſpectandi cauſa deſcendiſti,

non heic Romani Curionis ligneum uerſatile, ſed
chartaceum portatile Zuingeri ſubis
Theatrvm,

opus ut quàm dicam breuiſsimè & planiſſumè
plus quàm laborioſum.

In quo ſi Tituli inſolentiam, ſi Exemplorum dele-
ctum, ſi fidem Hiſtoriæ, ſi Diſpoſitionis ordinem
reprehendes, atque adeò in publica
domo nec mutus eris, neque
ſurdus:

ecquis enim in tanta uiuendi licentia tuam
frenarit libertatem?

eſto ſanè.
De Fabula tamen ipſa non niſi lecto cognitóque
Argumento, pro tua modeſtia & æqua-
nimitate, iudicato:

cúmque tibi cum homine nec moroſo, nec ſanè
nimium loquace, res futura fiet,

Proscenia
quæ exhibemus percurrito, perluſtrato,
pellegito:

ſpectatum pòſt admiſſus, in quocunque
lubebit licebit ordine, plauſum
quem uoles edito.

Fig. 5 Title page, from Theodor Zwinger, *Theatrum Vitae Humanae*, 4 vols. (Basel: Frobenius, 1571).

heterotopia, a place in which the same space can bear radically different valences, the same structures and positions equivocally supporting and disturbing the same order.

Zwinger is able to eschew visual illusionism in his theatre because what makes his text a theatre is more real than mere appearance; it shares what for him is the deep structure of the theatre, the inner form, which ironically comes from the *dictio* that he has no wish to spend time polishing but which is what creates the theatre of his book. The inner logic that governs the theatre is that of the encyclopedia that Zwinger compiles, which lets Zwinger dismiss any visual resemblance as mere illusion and empty *forma*, while favoring a linguistic one based on *dictio*. The artificiality and foregrounding of the verbal here and elsewhere in the prefatory materials of Zwinger's work – in the almost precious divisions of the text into architectural units, in the strained comparisons the introduction makes between Zwinger's *Theatrum* and its ancestors the Roman theatres, in the rigorous exclusion of illustration from a work that nonetheless constantly refers to its own visuality both in its language and in the presentation of that language on the page – are challenges to the reader, or the *spectator*, as Zwinger frequently and pointedly reminds the user of his text, to disbelieve and reject its organization. Zwinger does not try to disguise the artificiality of his theatre (what we would now call, from a different perspective, "naturalizing"), because its artificiality, its staginess, also characterize the world it represents.

Medieval and early Renaissance dramatic performances put stress on the construction of the space of the theatre as emphatically as did contemporary theorists. The design of the Elizabethan theatre building, as the name Globe implies, had an obvious cosmological significance, and if some critics have tended to overstate this universality, it remains an important part of the ability of that theatre's plays, variously stretched by playwrights as different as Shakespeare and Jonson, to portray everything.[43] In performance, the production of space coincides with the use of the formula that begins so many early moral plays and interludes, the players' cry to the audience to "Make room!," thus allowing the space of the play to be temporarily borrowed from the space of the audience. With the construction of the Theatre and the other permanent playhouses, the function of defining the space of the play was taken over by the physical boundaries of the building's circular frame. When it was no longer necessary to renew the neutral circle of the theatre space by the effort of the actors too, it became possible to forget that the circle had ever been made, that it had not been simply found like the objects within it. The construction of the Theatre of 1576 thus had a symbolic significance out of proportion to its immediate cultural impact: by being permanent, "purposely built," as Stowe said, and by refusing the ordinary schedule of worldly events, the Theatre effectively created a time and space for representation that seemed to owe nothing to the world outside it.[44] What was set apart from the world in this way, though, was not merely the stage, which remained more or less open to the audience, but the circle of the theatre building itself. Modern discussions of theatre tend to differentiate the real world of the audience from the feigned world of the actors, but premodern writings about the theatre and performance practices tended to assimilate actors and audience to one another and to contrast them together to the world outside the theatre's circle.[45]

But such developments followed the realization that the public theatre did not fulfill the humanist ideals of separation, distance, absolute vision, and instant intelligibility. The theatre in execution was never merely a place of looking, but one of action, and this action, although marked as fictional, nonetheless participated in the world in ways both direct and oblique. The early modern theatre was in fact a place of learning, although not through the contemplation humanist scholars had imagined for it. It taught through the action of both its actors and its lookers. The public theatre's reflexive self-authorization, relying neither on some external reference nor on an externally produced authority, was perhaps its most important contribution to epistemology – that knowledge could be the creation of human action and interaction, that it was in effect performed. For those who had imagined them, though, it was as a *picture* of reality – a replica that mirrored but stood apart from its object – rather than as a *part* of it that theatres, whether buildings or books, claimed their authority.

At the same time that the theatre was becoming a physical structure – and as part of a growing association of knowledge with performance rather than revelation – the actor made an appearance as an agent in his own right. Embedded within the neutral space of the stage, the actor as an idea changed the relationship of the representations within the theatre to the world outside it. As an example of this it is helpful to look at the massive thirteenth-century compilation of sources by Vincent of Beauvais, the *Speculum Maius*, or "Great Mirror." *Speculum* is of course a common medieval title for encyclopedic works that in the sixteenth and seventeenth centuries would be called *Theatrum*.[46] Even as a Mirror, though, Vincent's work suggests a developing connection between accurate knowledge, the authority to transmit it, and the theatrical skills of the actor. The *Speculum Maius* is divided into brief chapters that address particular issues or questions of history, theology, nature, or some similar field and are composed of excerpts from one or more authorities, *auctores*, ranging in length from a single sentence to several paragraphs. Vincent is careful to label the sources of his excerpts by name and to distinguish one from another; in early printed editions, most of the names of the authorities are marked in red, even where the missing initials have not been filled in.[47] Appearing now and again in this patchwork discourse, rarely for more than a couple of lines but several times on each page, is also another rubric designated, as Vincent explains in the introductory section called *Apologia Actoris* ("The Actor's Defense"), "by my name, that is, [the name] of Actor."[48] Under this heading, Vincent fills in information that is missing from his more authoritative sources, introduces new authorities and balances them against one another, signals important or difficult points, summarizes arguments, and offers background information. The Actor is also much more personable than the Authors it supplements, sometimes addressing its readers directly. In Book 8, for instance, in a chapter that deals with different types of soil, the *Actor* announces encouragingly that the following chapter, on the colors and properties of gems, will be more interesting than the current one. At the end of a longish disquisition on dogs culled from a variety of sources, the voice of the *Actor* concludes with a mix of Scriptural allusion, folk wisdom, and ordinary observation:

Actor: Thus the dog, one reads: is born blind. Is moonstruck. Much stimulated by smell. Has sharp teeth and a wide mouth. Bites habitually, and licks; doesn't chew its cud or gnaw. Returns to its vomit; before it lies down, it circles its bed. Suffers from bolismus, that is, very rapid hunger.[49]

The result is a gallimaufry of disorganized information that, like Zwinger's *silva*, has failed to find its place elsewhere in the assembled selections.

The connection of the Latin word *actor* to the meaning that we speakers of modern English most immediately associate with it is by no means direct. Its usual meaning in both classical and post-classical Latin is "agent," less often "lawyer" or "advocate"; the modern sense of "actor" is usually expressed by *mimus*, *histrio* or *ioculator*. *Auctor* was thought to derive from *augere*, "increase," while *actor* was believed to come from *agere*, "do," and *autor* or *author* from the Greek *authentês*, "of its own kind, authentic." The *actor* thus became the writer of a work, while *auctor* and *autor* were more closely linked with ideas of originality, productiveness, and of course *auctoritas*.[50] *Actor* is a frequent variant of *auctor* in medieval Latin, but such variation takes on a particular significance in the fifteenth and sixteenth centuries. In all early manuscript copies of Vincent's *Speculum Maius*, Vincent refers to his own contributions to the text under the name *Auctor*, and the introduction, which Vincent specified was to precede each volume in its entirety, is called the *Apologia Auctoris*. The form *actor* seems to appear in Vincent's text with the advent of printing – and thus also at about the time when the works of Terence were first being revived on classical stages by humanists in Italy and Germany.[51] In these printed texts, forms like *auctor* and *auctoritas* are distinguished from *actor*, suggesting that these words were not merely seen as variant spellings of the same term, but as terms to be contrasted. Printed editions generally adopt the *lectio facilior* of *auctor* for the title to the introduction at least, but spell the section subheadings, where an author's name would have appeared, as *Actor*. This suggests that a distinction between the two forms continued to be made in the late fifteenth century.[52] When Vincent contributed the varied material that could not be assigned to a named *auctor*, he himself was labeled the *actor* of the information – a performer of words that did not originate with him and that he could neither authorize nor authenticate.

Vincent clearly defines what he includes in the category of *actor* in a passage of the *Apologia Actoris* from which I quoted earlier:

> the things which I myself learned either from my superiors [or "elders," *maioribus meis*] or from modern scholars or the notable things I found in the writings of various men, I have entitled by my name, that is, the name of Actor.[53]

Vincent's claim to transparency – to have added little or nothing – extends also to the role of the *Actor*. What he speaks in "my name," as he calls it, are still the words of others – simply others who, like him, lack *auctoritas*. As Vincent explains, he has borrowed the *auctoritas* of the work with the sentences that compose it, and so the work as a whole is not really his, either. It is "ancient certainly in its authority (*auctoritate*) and contents, new in fact in the compilation of its parts," and therefore the book belongs really to his sources "by virtue of authority (*auctoritate*)" while it is his, like Pliny's contribution to his encyclopedia, "only in its arrangement of the parts."[54] His treatments as *actor*, he explains, are thus relatively superficial, specifically not like those of an *auctor* or *autor*:

> Let him [the reader] hear again that I do not proceed everywhere in the manner of an author (*autoris*), but of an excerptor (*excerptoris*). It was not my task to have worked around the difficulties that must be handled (*enucliandas*, lit. "pitted" like a fruit or "cracked" like a nut) for any art whatsoever.[55]

In his careful distancing of his own role as *actor* from that of an *auctor* and in his insistence that he speaks only in the words of others, with their authority, Vincent is the image of the actor in a sense different from those distinguished by Chenu, and closer to our own or to that of the medieval or Renaissance theatre. "As the Parthians fight, flying away, so will we prate and talk, but stand to nothing that we say," writes Thomas Nashe about the actor's share in the prologue to *Summer's Last Will and Testament* (1592);[56] in denying his authority to verify his own text, Vincent does much the same thing. Vincent's practice in the *Speculum Maius* is a kind of performance of knowledge, a textualization of Reisch's later image of the encyclopedia as tower that shows the work of the fugitive individual behind the construction of totality. In this understanding, an actor is one who speaks on another's authority, in the words of another, one who is present in the text only in the inflections he or she gives it.

Like Zwinger's theatre, Vincent's actor is an analogy of a set of formal qualities rather than simply an imitation of some real object. Vincent's work is profoundly dramatic, not in the weak sense of being lively, but in the sense of recreating the actor's task in the mode of writing. The actor is the vehicle by which the poet communicates his thoughts, just as the Vincentian *actor* is a mouthpiece for the scattered thoughts of culture. Varro's definition of the actor specifies exactly the second-hand nature of the actor's speech that Vincent foregrounds: "it is possible to make something and not to act it, as a poet makes a play and does not act it, and on the other hand the actor acts it and does not make it."[57] Vincent's work is like a textual *disputatio*, a form Jody Enders has argued is a kind of theatre of knowledge; he imagines the actor to be invisible as he does the voices, and orders their comments, but he is no more invisible than the redactor of the *disputationes* was in fact – or than any other actor is. Vincent makes the claim of the scientist or the secretary – that he speaks in another's voice only.[58]

Robert Maniquis suggests that when encyclopedic works become "ideologically tamed" and do not strongly exhibit the particular stylistic voice and ideological vision of their writers, their readers then can no longer either identify with or reject the implied reader – in an alternative to offering a view *from* nowhere, the texts speak, as it were, *to* positional ciphers.[59] Vincent's *Actor* reveals another way for the writer to appear in his work without manifesting an individual voice or autonomous style, avoiding both the concern for *dictio* that later troubles Zwinger and the ideological decisiveness of the *Encyclopédie*. Vincent suggests instead that the encyclopedic actor appears playing many parts, including his own; as Van den Brincken has shown, much of the *Apologia Actoris* is also ventriloquized, and Vincent distances himself even from the authority of the *Actor*'s sayings: he merely enunciates them.[60] Instead of establishing a definitive position, the encyclopedic actor moves from place to place, source to source, *locus* to *locus*, always occupying the position of another who could not be given voice except through the actor. The authority and knowledge the actor assumes are not his own, but his by virtue of his action, and he dons and sheds personae as he needs to.

A series of images in illustrated editions of the works of Terence shows a similar tendency to link the actor and the author, so that the theatre is rendered as the visual equivalent of the legible, authoritative, predictable book. An eleventh-century illustrated manuscript of the works of Terence has as a frontispiece an image of Terence at one side of an *aediculum*, the frame that in medieval art signifies an interior space (Figure 6). In the center of the *aediculum* is a man labeled Calliopius, the ancient redactor of the texts of Terence's plays, gesturing towards Terence with one hand and towards two detractors at the opposite side of the building with the other. Calliopius' iconography here is that of a judge, and in the prefatory materials connected with the plays Calliopius describes himself as the defender of Terence against the sometimes pedantic objections that are brought against his stagecraft.[61] The earliest illustrated editions of Terence printed in France, Italy, and Germany, however, suggest a very different interpretation of Calliopius' role. From the first illustrated edition (Lyons, 1493), Calliopius appears not as the editor or judge of the written text, but as the actor who speaks the prologue. This shift is perhaps motivated by such glosses as that to the phrase "Calliopius recensui" ("I, Calliopius, edited [this]") at the end of *Andria*. The commentary makes it clear that Calliopius is

Fig. 6 Calliopius as judge, from Vat. Lat. 3305 (tenth century CE).

a judge only insofar as he is first an actor: "I proofread and appended my judgment, having openly recited the words."[62] In the Lyons edition, his figure changes from play to play, showing that he is not to be understood as a real person who maintains a fixed identity over the six plays any more than any of the other traditional characters; he is an actor like they are (Figures 7, 8). Actor and redactor are combined here; to reproduce another's work, even in the medium of writing as Calliopius did, is pictured as giving it a voice in the theatre, dramatic or philosophical.

Prologus.

p Oeta cum pri
    mū &c. Hic p̄/ **p** Oeta cum primū aim ad scribendū appulit: logus quē in manibus hēmus est relatiuus qm̄ in aduersariū maledicta referunt & qdē acriter ea tn̄ subtilitate ut poeta uideat oīa refellere lacessitus aduersarii male dictis. Sūt aūt q̄ttuor p̄logi sp̄es. Alius ē cōmēdatitiꝰ i quo fabula aūt poeta cōmē datur. Alius relatiuus quo aut aduersario maledicta aut gr̄æ populo referunt. Qui da est argumētatiuus fabulæ argumētū exponēs. Quida mixtus oīa hæc in se conti nēs. Hic aūt p̄logus relatiuus ē in quo defensor poetæ ītroductus on̄dere nitit poe tā modestū minimeq̨ errāte: & aduersariū in iuidiā uocare: cuius maledictis resp̄o dēdo occupatus a narrando argumēto supsedere cogit. Comici aūt solēt introdu/ cere nō seipsos in p̄logis loquētes sed aliū inducūt ex abrupto aduersariū rep̄hēde tē poetæ cōmēdatione adhibita. quod fecit Aristophanes iducēs in prima comœ/ dia sua chremetē. quod etiā satis uidere est in hoc ip̄o andriæ p̄logo in quo poetæ defensor inductus captat beniuolentiā a p̄sona poetæ eā cōmēdando & a p̄sona ad uersarii eā in crimē & in iuidiā uocādo.   Poeta cū primū. &c. Poteta a ποιε͂ω. i. fa/ cio d̄r q̄ carmia faciat. Vir. pollio & ip̄e facit noua carmia. Appello is. ex ad & pello sigificat subducē naues ad littꝰ q̄i pellere naues ad littꝰ. In appulīꝰ. i. accessꝰ & p̄pe ad

Fig. 7   Calliopius as an actor, from Terence, *Andria*, in *Comoediae*, ed. Jodocus Badius Ascensius (Lyons: [Johannes] Wechsel, 1493).

Fig. 8 Calliopius as an actor, from Terence, *Heauton Timoroumenos*, in *Comoediae*, ed. Jodocus Badius Ascensius (Lyons: [Johannes] Wechsel, 1493).

The idea that texts were performed by an *actor* who reworked the words of others rather than original works by authors or mere reflections of some real cause external to them intensified in the course of the sixteenth century. It becomes almost a commonplace to locate works of knowledge between the *poiesis* of a subject and the *mimesis* of an object. Theodor Zwinger's definition in his *Theatrum Vitae Humanae* (1565), for instance, connects the actor's practice not only with Vincent's practices, but with knowledge itself. *Histrio*, he declares, is derived either from the Etruscan word for actor, *histor*, "or because researchers (ἵστορες; it can also mean 'knowledgeable men') are those who bring forth into the scene the words and deeds of others in a kind of rebirth (*palingenesia*)."[63] Zwinger's researcher who produces (*producant*) or, in fact, *r*eproduces (palin*genesia*), the words and deeds of another, is filling the role of the actor, who likewise plays another's part by repeating his words and deeds. Stephen Batman, revising Bartholomaeus Anglicus' *De Proprietatibus Rerum* in 1582, similarly describes himself as "an imitator of the learned" in compiling their works.[64] This sense of second-hand knowledge as a kind of histrionic performance persists in Sidney's *Defence of Poesy*: "There is no Art delivered unto mankind that hath not the works of nature for his principal object, without which they could not consist, and on which they so depend, as they become Actors and Players, as it were, of what nature will have set forth" (215f.). For Sidney, of course, such histrionic knowledge is less praiseworthy than the properly poetic and creative understanding of the true author. Even the author, though, in late medieval and earlier times, could be portrayed in an actorly fashion. There was a tradition of seeing any author as a kind of fiction, literally a persona or mask of the kind associated with ancient theatre; even the trope of *prosopopoeia*, the creation of an authorial voice, could be seen as inherently theatrical.[65] The mask of the author was the vehicle for pronouncing *auctoritates* – not the people who had authority, but their authoritative sayings, which retained their authority as they passed from mouth to mouth.[66] This helps explain why sixteenth-century playwrights like George Wapull (*The Tide Taryeth No Man*, 1576) were described as the "compilers" of their plays, as virtual author-actors, and why George Gascoigne's *Glasse of Governement* (1575) provides a list of aphorisms after the prologue, noting: "This work is compiled upon these sentences." The compiler, whether of encyclopedias or plays, could thus hardly be other than an actor; he could claim nothing to rely on but the words and deeds of others, no other voice with which to speak or gesture with which to act.

Because of the conflation of actor and author, mouthpiece and source, the imaginary theatre of the humanists threatens to become a place of pure display, competent to show something exactly but not to allow it to be comfortably traced back to whatever can be said to authorize it. A variant of Varro's definition says that the actor both makes *and* acts (*agit et facit*) rather than dividing these functions between actor and poet. This is historically appropriate to the actors of early modern England, who themselves owned the scripts they played from and showed throughout the sixteenth century a tendency to play "outside the book" on their own authority.[67] In the Lyons images, the authorial function – Terence's authority in every sense – is a performance by an actor repeating another's words rather than a revelation of their origin. This is also the method for teaching Latin advanced by Joseph Webbe in his works on Terence and others – by mastering the rules with which an author used language, a student could gain that same authority in improvising new statements.[68] The Renaissance Calliopius or the student of Webbe takes the same intermediate space as does the *Actor* of Vincent of Beauvais, half dependent on another's words, half free to alter them in delivery, and as necessary to the source of the words as the words are necessary to him. The blurring of the difference between actor and author is clearest in the double image from the prefatory matter of the edition of the comedies published in Venice in 1497, an Italian response to the Northern editions of Lyons and Strassburg. Terence is pictured in the guise of an author reading, like one of the images of Calliopius; he is surrounded by listeners taking notes as he reads from his own work (Figure 9). This image draws on the medieval understanding of the theatre as a place where an author might read his work aloud, but it also echoes the lecture hall, so that Terence, corresponding to the humanist ideal, simply makes the knowledge of his text available to his eagerly annotating audience, including Donatus and some contemporary commentators. A few pages later at the start of the first play, the image of Terence lecturing is reversed by a corresponding image of an actor presenting a play in the *theatrum*. Here the illustration takes the point of view of the actor, and we look out onto the audience over the performer's shoulder. But it is as if this image simply took Terence's perspective from the first image; seen from another direction, as it were, the author of a drama becomes its actor in a theatre (Figure 10). The first view of Terence as author – as an authoritative, non-distorting medium of his fixed text – is replaced by a peculiarly directional perspective that reveals the presence of the watching audience and the necessity of the first view having been, albeit invisibly, framed. Seen from the point of view of the audience, the author's centrality is an image of the certainty of his words. From his own standpoint, or looking over his shoulder, the author is seen to be no more than a performance of authority. These illustrations from Terence outline an idea that is rarely made explicit, yet everywhere assumed in humanist writings on theatre: while the actor may know himself that he is only playing at what he does, he must not show this to the audience.

While the Lyons Terence transforms the earliest editor of Terence's comedic *comprehensio* into his actor, in the same volume the most recent editor, Guido Juvenalis, appears on the text's frontispiece in the position that earlier manuscripts and many subsequent printed editions, including the Venetian one, had reserved for Terence himself.[69] Where the Venice edition had shown Terence reading aloud to an audience that included Guido, the Lyons Terence shows Guido alone in his study, probably in the midst of editing the volume the reader holds; the books are

Fig. 9   Terence as a lecturer, from Terence, *Comoediae* (Venice: Simon Bevilacqua, 1496).

Fig. 10 Terentian actor, from Terence, *Comoediae* (Venice: Simon Bevilacqua, 1496).

Fig. 11   Guido Iuvenalis, frontispiece from Terence, *Comoediae*, ed. Jodocus Badius Ascensius (Lyons: [Johannes] Wechsel, 1493).

stacked around him in jumbled heaps to show that they are in use, and two are propped open at once, as if he were comparing two passages (Figure 11). The next page shows a structure labeled *theatrum*. Although a small figure mounts into the *theatrum* from the left of the page, the book encourages its reader to see the real actor in this theatre as neither the spectator entering it nor the piper on the stage, but the editor who compiles it; the theatre is his product. Following the image of Guido in his study with his books, the *theatrum* shows not a mimetic rendering of Terence's theatre, but, as the anachronistic costumes of the spectators suggest, an imaginary one that has been drawn together out of Guido's old books. In place of an actorly author, we are offered an authorly editor, so that the authority that is merely unsettled in the Venice edition is in the earlier Lyons edition actually shifted from Terence to his textual reconstructor. The haphazard disorder of the redactor's study is resolved into the orderly space of the actor framed by the proscenium; Guido's figurative *silva* of references is reduced to the literal *theatrum* represented on the next page, a common beholding place that displays actor, audience, and real world with equal ease (Figure 12).

Fig. 12 "Theatrum," from Terence, *Comoediae*, ed. Jodocus Badius Ascensius (Lyons: [Johannes] Wechsel, 1493).

The illustrated editions of Terence make it clear just how literal was the claim of humanists like Erasmus and Vives that a theatre presented the objects of discourse as if they were in a picture.[70] The proscenium of the stage that the reader sees only partially and from an oblique angle in the woodcut of the *theatrum* in the Lyons edition is reproduced over and over in the woodcuts to the *Andria*, the first play of the book (see Figure 7 for detail).[71] In these illustrations of the play, however, the theatre around the stage and the other spectators is invisible, and the stage itself is viewed absolutely frontally. The reader is thus to realize that she or he is an audience member looking on, as it were, from inside the theatre of the book. The tiny figure entering the theatre in the earlier image is a figure for the reader poised at the edge of the imaginary space of the theatre, representing, then, the book. The common beholding place of the theatre is not the represented stage, but the actual book, or more accurately the stage conceived on the model of its picture in a book. Once inside this printed theatre, the reader's vantage changes. The image of the *theatrum* provides a bridge between the work of the editor Guido that makes order out of disorder, but itself only performs the text of Terence, and the experience of the spectator–reader. The activity that frames each scene reverts back not to Terence, but to Guido as its source, not to the *auctor* as the authoritative origin of the text, but to the Actor as the one who reproduces those words for an audience – both the dramatic actor on stage and the bookish one in his study.

Such conflation in the illustrations to the texts of Terence was relatively unproblematic. Calliopius was in a sense the voice of Terence's own authority. But this new centrality to the actor's role could also be threatening to the imagined clarity of the theatre. Concerns over self-conscious theatricality appear, for instance, as early as Donatus' commentary on Terence, that foundation of all Renaissance commentaries. Donatus repeatedly scorns any metatheatrical moves made in the script and rejects any hints of self-reflexivity as incompatible with decorum, since how can a character acknowledge that he or she is within a play being watched by an audience without dissolving the rules of propriety? Such self-awareness would destroy the straightforwardness of character assumed by the idea of decorum, since any player would then be divided between the character he was and the character he portrayed. The relationship between actor and author, though, remains curiously balanced, for the poet falls as silent without the actor as the actor without the poet. Emphasis on the role of the actor, however figured, tended to bring out disturbing elements of self-consciousness of performance that the humanist ideology of the theatre needed to exclude. If the main force of the Renaissance idea of the theatre was to treat knowledge as objective – visual, complete, fixed, literally rooted in *objects*, in short as a version of the encyclopedic – then the self-consciousness, mobility, and changefulness that was typical of early modern performance practices found itself nearly directly opposed to the part assigned to the theatre. If the actor could be made to serve as a conceptual variant of the author rather than as an opposite to it, these competing purposes of playing could be accommodated. If, on the other hand, the actor were instead seen as a source of distortion, or even as a co-creator, the role would act as an equally strong locus of disruption, undermining the authority of the idea of the theatre. How the theatre is conceived determines which of these concepts of actor is foremost in any representation of the actor's effects on knowledge.

Humanists like Juan Luis Vives and Thomas More, while they approved of theatre as an educational tool, were as suspicious of a theatre that showed too much awareness of its own theatricality as Donatus had been. A passage from More's *The History of Richard III*, noting that political struggles are "Kings' games, as it were stage plays, and for the more part played upon scaffolds," is often quoted to show his sense of the theatricality of Renaissance statecraft,[72] but it begins with a passage less often quoted in which More insists also that the actor not show that he is acting:

And in a stage play all the people know right well, that he that playeth the sultan is percase a sowter [shoemaker]. Yet if one should ken so little good, to show out of season what acquaintance he hath with him, and call him by his own name while he standeth in his majesty, one of his tormenters might hap to break his head, and worthy, for marring of the play.[73]

The audience member who is so ignorant ("ken so little good") that he focuses on the actor instead of on what he plays is deservedly ("and worthy") beaten by the other spectators around him for drawing attention away from the portrayed role. The actor must be just as careful as the audience not to recall what is outside the role. "They act plays so as to seem to act," complained Vives of some theatrical productions, "which is an indecorum: for a play refers not to itself, but to what is done, or whatever deed is feigned, as a picture [refers] to a thing, not to itself."[74] This is an obvious rejection of contemporary performance practices, which rarely attempted to conceal the fact that what was being looked at was a performance. The anxiety over theatrical self-consciousness shown by Vives and More stems from a desire to objectify what is placed on the stage, as in the first image from the Venice Terence, to strip it of consciousness for its viewers so that it can be observed as a simple spectacle rather than the double vision of the second image. It is remedied not by a less self-aware presentation, however, but by one that consciously restricts its show of self-awareness and subjectivity. In More's example, "all the people know right well," as they should – what is culpable is the man who spoils the pretense by calling attention to it. Like Bodin's use of Mystagogus' awareness of worldly theatricality to correct the naive realism of Theorus, these theorists of theatre carefully reject not the awareness of performance as much as the willing display of that self-consciousness. In this the humanist concern for unreflexive representation resembles the later doctrine of the dramatic unities, which makes the theatre still more picture-like, comprehensive, and immediate through its highly self-conscious restriction of consciousness to the real time and real space of the imagined stage.[75] The unities are thus the logical outcome of the earlier idea of decorum. Things represented cannot differ from the things that represent them in time or space, and a stage can only "realistically" – or "decorously" – display nothing other than itself, resymbolized. The actual practices of early modern playing, which late twentieth century readers have found so compelling and which we have extended to the Renaissance as one of its principal modes of self-understanding, are regularly excluded from the imaginary theatre of the time. The theatre was of course an important metaphor for many kinds of self-definition in the Renaissance, but the theatre imagined by the humanists excludes the self-reflexivity that the image itself implies.

It was a common anxiety of the early modern English theatrical establishment that actors or spectators might learn to mimic a knowledge that they did not in fact possess – that they would gain knowledge, as Sidney feared, as its mere "Actors and Players."[76] The sixteenth-century playwright and pamphleteer Robert Greene criticized the actor's art as "a kind of mechanical labor" of reproducing empty forms of language and complained that too often the players mistook the knowledge of the writer whose words they used for their own.[77] In accounts like Zwinger's of the *histrio*-historian or in the Lyons image of Guido Juvenalis, the actor became a kind of double for the scholar. But as the ability to give voice to various positions ceased to be circumscribed by the notion of the *theatrum*, the actor became a threat to the authority that Zwinger had playfully seen it as a vehicle for.

Juan Luis Vives defined the danger to knowledge presented by the figure of the actor as *superbia*, pride, which occurs when a researcher feels all eyes turn onto him (*ubi oculos in se reflexissent*). Enjoying the sensation for its own sake, such men become completely absorbed in displaying themselves, "as if they were dancing a play before the eyes of onlookers" (*oculis intentium tanquam in scena saltarent fabulam*).[78] Vives' fear seems to mirror the dangers of *curiositas* expressed in encyclopedic writers: while *curiositas* is the threat of losing oneself in one's objects of study, *superbia* is the complementary danger of becoming fascinated with one's own self-presentation to the exclusion of anything else.[79] The actor's very awareness of his own liminal position makes that position a problem to him and his audience, whether readers or spectators, by introducing unphilosophical particularities and contingencies, of which there can be no certain knowledge, into what must be certain.[80] Human intellectual ability remedies human needs, but the investigator's sense of himself and his studies as on display threatens to make his research destructive instead of helpful, pre-empting its right usage: "A violent desire for display exciting greater admiration increased to such a degree that some persons neglected all the duties of life so as to devote and give up themselves entirely to investigation."[81] The idea of the theatre required a vision that was both distanced from action and absolutely simple – the possibility of self-reflexive feedback was not included in it, in spite of the long tradition of such self-awareness in traditional performance practices.

The attraction of the theatre for the humanists was that it promised to teach experientially rather than dogmatically. But to avoid a different kind of deviation from real life, the humanist theatre also needed to be non-reflexive. The humanist idea of the theatre thus remained a contradictory one, maintainable only so long as the theatre itself remained imaginary. When the plays of the humanists were actually performed, inevitably the seams in the imaginary theatre began to come to light. At the same time that the printed editions of Terence and the writings of Vives and More were circulating an ideology of the theatre as a neutral space of ideal representation and critiquing the grounds for seeing it as representational, humanist theatre practice was working along a similarly dialectical path. Humanists in England and elsewhere tried to put into practice their theories about the didactic potential of the theatre. Although after the building of the public theatres many opponents of the theatre, including the writers of the best-known antitheatrical tracts, based their criticism on religious principles, Henrician writers like John Bale, Nicholas Udall, and John Rastell seized on the imagined potency of the theatre as a vehicle for Protestant propaganda, believing, it seems, that its message could be controlled and put to good use.[82] The courtly audiences for these performances, set up to counter the popular mystery cycles in a variety of towns with a Protestant, nationalist alternative, were far more homogeneous and under closer supervision than the crowds in the public theatres would later be.[83] This may well have contributed to the bookish faith of such writers that they were using a lively, memorable technology to stamp an ideology of their own design (i.e., Protestant, nationalist) onto the *tabula rasa* of their audience.

The early Tudor court and the courts of its important members seem to have followed this line linking vision, learning, acting, and theatre in the vernacular interludes they commissioned. Much early Tudor theatre was explicitly didactic or propagandistic, but often of the blandest sort. Whether interlude or pageant, it tended to restate accepted *mores* rather than to question their justification.[84] With a relatively unquestioned reliance upon accepted truths – although in religious speculation "truth" was a very conflicted terrain, it tended to be clear from the context of the performance on which side truth would be found – and a general avoidance of irony except as ghettoized in Vice figures, all performed signs remained safely determinate, and the theatre could be treated as a tool for the promulgation of its sponsors' ideas, political, metaphysical, or natural-historical.

But humanist plays are distinctly different from the moral plays that they share so much with – to the point of characters and plots – in their secularity. They show a resolute interest in worldly things considered in themselves.[85] This interest was not always positive; in some texts it was closer to alarm. As M. E. Moeslein has pointed out, Henry Medwall's *Nature* excludes two of the usual evil trinity of the moral plays, the Flesh and the Devil, because "for Medwall, The World is enemy enough."[86] To counter such worldly recalcitrance, interludes like Medwall's *Nature*, John Rastell's *Nature of the Four Elements*, and John Heywood's *The Play of the Weather* combined moral and ethical instruction with straightforward natural history, geography, and cosmology, seeking to capitalize on the attributes of visibility and objectivity associated with the theatre so as to produce an educational device that could teach anyone anything quickly and without distortion. Rastell's thoughts on drama are, curiously, both pioneering and typical. He was linked to the circle of humanists around Thomas More, who married Rastell's sister, and shared with them an interest in the educational potential for drama. But his interest was also highly practical. Not only did Rastell compose several encyclopedic pageants for Henry VIII, including one in 1522 that featured "a place like heaven, curiously painted with clouds, orbs, stars and hierarchies of angels ... diverse beasts ... diverse manner of trees and flowers," he probably also printed the first play in England and constructed one of the first permanent theatre spaces in his home.[87] In *Four Elements*, Rastell shows a humanist commitment to a knowledge of things in the world and not only those in heaven:

> ... it seemeth nothing convenient
> A man to study and his time to bestow
> First for the knowledge of high things excellent
> And of light matters beneath nothing to know[.][88]

Underlying this claim is the humanist idea of the theatre as a display of information, whether of "high things excellent" or more worldly "light matters beneath," apart from action. At the same time, though, dramatic action could not in practice be avoided, and humanist productions like Medwall's or Rastell's tended to include elements of dramatic complexity that their theories could not always account for.

The title page of Rastell's *The Nature of the Four Elements*, printed between 1510 and 1520, advertises not a plot or an argument, like a Terentian drama might have, but its contents, the raw data of which it is composed. These are not its narrated events or even allegorical figures, but the elements of knowledge it contains:

Of the situation of the .4. elements, that is to say the earth, the water, the air, and fire; and of their qualities and properties; and of the generation and corruption of things made of the commixtion of them ¶Of certain conclusions proving that the earth must needs be round . . . ¶Of certain conclusions proving that the sea lieth round upon the earth . . . ¶Of certain points of cosmography . . . ¶Of the generation and cause of stone and metal and of plants and herbs . . .

as well as numerous other topics, such as tides, weather, springs, and lightning (n.p.). The interlude itself appears straightforwardly educational, taking as its topic the education of Humanity by Natura Naturata. Near the beginning of the interlude Natura Naturata reveals a visual "figure," apparently a *mappamundi* or diagram of the elemental spheres:

> Mark well now how I have shewed and told
> Of every element the very situation
> And quality, wherefore this figure behold
> For a more manifest demonstration.

In the assumptions of the play (which run counter to its narrative form), knowledge is acquired through a static and organized visual display rather than through any narrative development. The "figure" remains visible throughout the play and is repeatedly referred to by various characters, who define themselves upon entering by their relation to it.[89] In this Rastell's play can be said to be fully within the humanist idea of the theatre – its center is literally the instantaneous, complete display of knowledge in the space of the *theatrum*. The *drama* of the play, though, such as it is, does not present the learning that the play offers as its subject, but rather provides an allegory of the role of information and curiosity in an education, and thus calls into question the applicability of its own theatrical form. In a sense, then, in Rastell's play the practice of the *drama* is set self-consciously at odds with the pedagogical and epistemological theory of the *theatre*.

Natura Naturata sets up his diagram and departs, leaving Humanity with a companion, Studious Desire. What Natura Naturata merely demonstrated with a figure, Studious Desire takes more time to explain to Humanity, without, however, changing the fundamentally objective form that knowledge seems to have. The presence of Studious Desire implies that the knowledge of the world is a kind of commodity that Humanity can and should possess; as Nature Naturata reminds him, in an interesting rehabilitation of *curiositas* that overturns the examples of the previous chapter, "the more that thou desirest to know any thing/Therein thou seemest the more a man to be." Studious Desire then calls for Experience, who can give first-hand corroboration of the material that has been shown and explained, to prove to Humanity what Studious Desire can only expound. Before Experience can come in, though, Sensual Appetite enters through the crowd, asking for room. Studious Desire urges Humanity to have nothing to do with Sensual Appetite, but Sensual Appetite responds that no creature can live without him. As Humanity observes, Sensual Appetite is "for me full necessary/And right convenient," the appropriate first step towards knowledge and, as an unrelated benefit, also a source of "pleasure" and "refreshing." Studious Desire protests that Sensual Appetite alone affords "no conning," no knowledge, but Humanity insists he will only make "a pastime of recreation/ With this man for a while." He abandons Studious Desire, Experience, and Nature's figure and leaves the stage to explore the world with Sensual Appetite.

The rest of the extant playscript (the end is lost) proves Studious Desire right to be skeptical. Sensual Appetite leads Humanity to a tavern, introduces him to Ignorance, who encourages him to give up "folyshelosophy" (E. iii), and finally leads in a troupe of singers and dancers to entertain at the party. After the disguisers go out, Nature returns and explains Humanity's error to him. Although Sensual Appetite is indeed

> full necessary
> For thy comfort sometime to satisfy . . .
> . . . yet it is not convenient for thee
> To put therein thy felicity
> And all thy hole delight
> ¶For if thou wilt learn no science
> Neither by study nor experience
> I shall thee never advance.

If he refuses the knowledge displayed on the visual figure, Nature tells him, Humanity will be no better than a "beast" like Ignorance.

At first glance, the interlude presents a thoroughly normative educational system. Rastell's play in particular puts special emphasis on the importance of the visual figure in educating the audience; the *mappamundi* remains constantly on stage once Natura Naturata produces it, a kind of set for a theatre of the world that will be more subtly, but no less surely, mapped into the "heavens" and "hell" of the Elizabethan public stage. Its significance, however, lies in its visibility; in spite of the varying attitudes and interpretations the characters express, it remains unchanged, a spectacle that both requires and resists interpretation into language. Verified by Experience, it rises to the status of a *fact* – an incontrovertible presence that must be reckoned with but which, in its silent visibility, holds a true picture of the world, if it can only be understood.

Like Vives' text on the danger of performative *superbia*, or the earlier fears of unbounded *curiositas*, though, the play shows an excess beyond the norms of usefulness that can only disappoint as a source of one's "whole delight." Sensual Appetite combines features of both Experience and Studious Desire – he answers when Experience is called for and is attractive like Studious Desire – but the active and pleasurable examination of the world he promotes is not directed towards any final, fixed state of knowledge. Unlike Experience or Studious Desire, Sensual Appetite is finally no more than a "pastime." He is, in short, a version of the *curiositas* regarded warily but positively by encyclopedic writers. Except through the two authorized channels of study and experience, the play seems to conclude, there can be no learning – following Sensual Appetite, "Thou wilt learn no science." Sensual Appetite both experiences and desires, but continuously rather than towards a predetermined end-state of intellectual satiety. There is no way to subordinate his drive to a picture of reality because his relation with it is active and ongoing. Instead he is the figure of curiosity out of control, unlimited by any higher purpose or authority, which the encyclopedic texts like those of Pliny or Vincent of Beauvais defended against. Appetite is necessary to both study and experience, but in itself is too haphazard to advance the knowledge of Nature securely towards its fulfillment in the *mappamundi* figure without the structural frameworks provided by Studious Desire and Experience.

But although the play has a harder time admitting it, Studious Desire and Experience also prove not to be sufficient for learning. They remain limited in their action to explaining the figure left for them by Nature – that is, they seem to be incapable of actually advancing knowledge in any way, although they can verify and account for it. Their commitment to this pre-existing model, which they expound (as Studious Desire does) and authorize (tautologically, when Experience declares, "I know by experience"), also serves as a limit to their interpretations. Sensual Appetite, on the other hand, is wedded to mere appearance, to "pastimes" and "pleasures," that do not yield lasting knowledge. But these diversions also represent the only possibility for action in the play. Without Sensual Appetite there is literally no *drama* in the play, only *theatre* – only the contemplation of the diagram left by Nature, with no ability to act on it or use it. Sensual Appetite is, in the play's representation of knowledge and in its practical dramaturgy, the motive force of the plot. Without it, one could speculate, there would be no play at all, only the still and silent display and contemplation of Nature's figure. But *The Four Elements* does not simply reconfirm the humanist idea of the theatre as pure vision. If what Sensual Appetite produces is not truth, it is nonetheless real, and of all the characters he is the only one to be able to organize anything.[90] Because the medium of the presentation of this knowledge is neither traditional study nor actual experience, though, the relations among study, experience, and desire become still more complicated. What allows these differing positions to be represented – in the actual production of the interlude, not in its representations of pedagogy – is not the static spectacle of Studious Desire or Experience, but the dramatic activity of Sensual Appetite.

Rastell's interlude also acknowledges the double position of the audience nominally present for edification but hoping for amusement. Before Sensual Appetite brings in the disguising, Ignorance boasts that

> For they that be now in this hall
> They be the most part my servants all
> And love principally
> Disports as dancing, singing,
> Toys, tryfuls [i.e., trifles], laughing, jesting,
> For conning they set not by. (n.p.)

For better or worse, Ignorance's evaluation is probably an accurate assessment of the audience's taste and not mere sportive mockery. As if to reinforce the importance of sensual appetite to the interlude, the printed text of the play, in contrast to Nature's and Humanity's representation of these playful and theatrical displays as subordinate to real knowledge, advises potential producers that the interlude can be shortened by judicious cutting, but (in spite of what the play's argument values) not of the hijinks of Sensual Appetite's crew: "if ye list ye may leave out much of the sad matter, as the messenger's part, and some of Nature's part and some of Experience's part and yet the matter will depend conveniently."[91] The core of the play's production, in other words, is the *drama* of Sensual Appetite and Ignorance, not the imaginary humanist idea of the *theatre* that displays the knowledge of the still world promised on the title page and in the *mappamundi*. The interlude's real audience enjoys the singers and dancers and other expressly theatrical fare as much as Humanity – indeed, in exactly the same way as Humanity – and then has the added pleasure of being able to dismiss them as empty shows opposed to the authorized knowledge of Studious Desire and Experience.

In one sense, then, the experience of the audience parallels that of Humanity in the interlude, passing from learning to unchecked play to learning again, and delimiting the proper place of pleasure in learning. The interlude rehearses the action of the encyclopedia in raising the specter of boundless *curiositas* and then reassuringly confining it. More accurately, though, the pastime of the interlude presents both learning and play, containing them equally within the theatre's neutral space. Studious Desire and Experience, and Nature himself, are no different qualitatively than the disguised singers and dancers who satisfy Sensual Appetite. They are only actors differently disguised. Play and pastime are condemned, but play and pastime are also what condemn them. Taking the means of representation into account, playfulness proves not to be the excess of learning over its allotted limits, but the ground within which such limits can be established and the source of the procedures that establish them. The practice of *drama* is revealed as the precondition of the *theatre*, and the social activity that had been meant to disappear in the construction of the theatre revealed itself again within it.

Rastell's play shows how in practice the humanist idea of the theatre is necessarily in contradiction with the real theatre it can produce. The idea of the theatre requires the activity of drama, so that the idea is undercut by the very medium of its presentation. While we must look to the *ideology* of the theatre to explain its uniquely central role in sixteenth-century thought and culture, we must also acknowledge the ways in which *realizing* this idea changed it. Understanding this theatre ultimately neither depends on a sheer materialism nor accepts unexamined the declarations of early viewers of the theatre's spectacle. What Rastell's play and other humanist theatres, bookish and dramatic both, suggest is the impossibility of distinguishing in them ideal from material, *curiositas* from knowledge, Studious Desire from Sensual Appetite. The inherent tension between the two different, equally hypothetical, conceptions of theatrical performance as action and as spectation found itself played out most strikingly when humanist critics like Rastell turned their attention to actual dramatic production, when the fixity of various schemas held up for contemplation was offset by a desire to divert the audience with songs, jokes, and other action. This nuanced interlacing of the alternatively active and passive, artificial and natural, ordering and ordered roles of both viewer and vision typifies the early modern sense of the theatre. What makes the representation of the world as a theatre, or the theatre as a vehicle for displaying wordly knowledge, possible in these seemingly unrelated instances is a construction of neutral space – for Varro, the *templum*; for Bodin or Zwinger, the theatre-book within the world; for the actual stage, both the physical space of the theatre building and a social, legal one suspended in a web of regulations, prohibitions, and sanctions. When the theatres around London were at last pulled down in 1642, it was because it was recognized – rightly – that the idea of the theatre as a common beholding place of visual comprehension that safely and constructively educated its passive audience was possible only so long as it was located in the imagination alone.

3 Tricks of vision, truths of discourse: Illustration, *ars combinatoria*, and authority

> You have come in to this hollow circle not for the sake of acting, like a player, but for the sake of watching.
> —Theodor Zwinger, *Theatrum Vitae Humanae* (1565)[1]

Encyclopedias and theatres alike employ strategies that limit the threat of an endless play of knowledge, whether that play is understood as boundless *curiositas* for new objects of study or the investigator's self-absorbed *superbia*. In its place they offer a form of knowledge both complete and finite, its finitude guaranteed by the promise of faithfully mirroring the spectacle of the world within the circumscribed space allotted to it. With no visible inherent limits, though, either to *curiositas* or *superbia*, what could ensure the exhaustiveness of that mirroring or the legitimacy of its structure?

The preface to Thomas Elyot's Latin–English *Dictionary* (1538), addressed to his patron Henry VIII, reflects this difficulty. The great advantages Elyot claims for his work, the first such in English, are speed and thoroughness: by removing words from their context in discourse and framing them as alphabetically ordered objects, it enabled its readers to approach Latin directly rather than obliquely, and so to "understand better the Latin tongue in six months than they mote have done afore in three years" (*Dictionary*, Aiiiv). But Elyot's assurance that the English definitions are the same as the Latin entries they explain is both overdetermined in the preface and never quite directly faced. Elyot's preliminary text instead circles around the problem of authorizing its referentiality in a series of disconnected observations on the project's genesis, the relation of words and things, and the practices of interpretation. Elyot's indecision suggests the complexity of the issue of authority facing other compilers of encyclopedic theatres. The preface begins with a meditation on the greatness of the state of kingship, which is modeled on God's status as:

one principal ruler and moderator, by whose eternal sapience all things been governed. Unto that office of governance is (as it were by general consent of all people) one name appropried, in the which, although by diversity of languages, the letters and syllables are oftentimes changed, yet the word spoken hath one signification, which implieth as much as a KING in English, as it may appear to them, which do read holy scripture, and will mark how often God is there called king, and also the prophets do so frequently name him. (*Dictionary*, Aiir)

The discussion of rulership shifts into an explanation of how Elyot can construct a book that carries its readers from Latin to English. Like most humanist thinkers, Elyot sees language as based on popular convention rather than any natural Cratylan code. This conventionality, however, is doubly braced. On the one hand, word-by-word translation is made possible by a theory of referential signification. "Rex" and "king" mean exactly the same thing, a sense that can be extended quasi-metaphorically to pagan deities and even the Christian God: the concept of a "principal ruler and moderator" that all people share but represent differently in their variety of tongues. On the other hand, the congruence of the concept in the minds of all people is, it seems, guaranteed by the very thing this particular concept represents – by an "eternal sapience" that gives rules and order to human experience. This second anchor is never stated, merely suggested in Elyot's choice of the supposedly randomly chosen example of the word "king."[2] But Elyot goes on to recount Henry VIII's interrogation of

the most detestable heretic John Nicolson, called also Lambert, at the which time your highness, more excellently than my tongue or pen can express, declared to be in your royal person the perfect image of kingly majesty . . . extolling the just reprehensions of the perverse opinions and interpretations of the arrogant masters of the said Lambert, in whose writing, and his own proper wit, he more trusted (as your highness truly alleged against him) than in the plain context of holy scripture, and the determinate sentences of holy and great learned doctors. (*Dictionary*, Aiiv–Aiiir)

Nicolson's heresy, it seems, is a crime of interpretation: he substitutes unauthorized authorities and even his own private understanding of Scripture for official doctrine. There is, though, apparently no confuting him – Nicolson's language is unbridled by the "determinate sentences" of proper authority and thus threatens the same interminable expansiveness as the encyclopedia. Henry's majesty appears in his ability to confute Nicolson's "perverse opinions and interpretations," which is to say, in his ability to pronounce them perverse. As represented by Elyot, Henry's authority brooks no disagreement. Henry's power over interpretation is so naturalized as to all but conceal its own glory; it emerges at the end of a chain of being, at once rigidly hierarchical and exactingly mimetic, that extends from the divine truth of God realized in the words of the Bible and the divine image of the "KING." The act of Henry speaking is a double sign of both these images, simultaneously the visual "perfect image of kingly majesty" that verbally "declare[s]" itself. The very naturalness and obviousness of the "plain context of holy scripture" in

Henry's presence, or, better, the revelation of the context's plainness, rather than Henry's brilliance or extravagance or the context's difficulty, pronounce Henry's majesty. To argue against him, as Elyot says, is simply *perverse*; it is an action not against a kingly power that might be resisted or challenged, but against the "plain context" of the words, the true allegations of perversity and "just reprehensions" which the king merely observes. The gesture of royal power with which Elyot introduces his analogously structured dictionary is both performative and referential, both theatrical and encyclopedic. It rests on yet another unresolved tension, this time between words and things, or rather, between discourse and vision: Henry's discursive refutation of the perverse interpretations of Nicolson reveals him to be "the perfect image of kingly majesty." Control over words is effected by the true authorizing vision which anchors their meanings; the vision comes into focus because discourse is seen to be mastered.

Elyot's episodes are an extension of the older fantasy of a purely intuitive and instantaneous knowledge that does not enter time at all, conceived on the model of vision. Bartholomaeus Anglicus holds up such infinite, timeless knowledge as an ideal for which he strives in his work even as he regards it as a limit on human understanding. The angel, midway between God and man, is an example of this human ideal:

An angel has an intellect of the same form as God's. It is above time and understands everything simply (*simpliciter*) and not one thing after another or one thing from another, as a conclusion from its premises, like a human intellect, which puts together one thing from another (*qui est unius ex alio collativus*). As a comparison of a simple thing to a compound thing or a point to a line, so is the comparison of the angelic intellect to the human in understanding and judging.[3]

Men are condemned to knowledge of things from other things, in a collative process that is necessarily linear like the setting together of elements as in a syllogism. For Bartholomaeus this knowledge by collation is simply the best that humankind can do; angelic knowledge serves as a limit that the human mind cannot reach.

In his 1397 translation of Bartholomaeus' *De Proprietatibus Rerum*, John of Trevisa suggests an alternative to the opposition of human narrative understanding or angelic intuition. In a rare addition to Bartholomaeus' work, Trevisa inserts an example of how he understands gathering to work:

As if a child knoweth that if the nominatif case and the verbe discordith in persone and in noumbre, thanne the resoun is incongrue, as in this manere: *puer sumus bonus*. Thanne take [for] on premis: no reason is conger in the which the nominatif case and the verbe discordith in noumbre and in persone. And take for the othir premis: in this resoun, *puer sumus bonus*, the nominatif case and the verbe discordith in noumbre and in persone. And make thi conclusioun in this maner: ergo this resoun is not conger, *puer sumus bonus*. Thanne if he knowith the forsaid tweye premisses he knowith the conclusioun by the premisses, for he concludeth that on of that othir.[4]

None of this passage appears in Bartholomaeus' Latin, and, as with Elyot's example of the king, John's choice of grammar seems far from unmotivated. Grammar can be expanded, as John does here, into the discursive form of a syllogism, but it is not primarily a temporal phenomenon; although any given sentence unfolds according to grammar in time, the logic of grammar is synchronic. The phenomenology of discourse is temporal, but that of grammar is not; more precisely, it may be inaccurate to speak of a phenomenology of grammar at all, since any empirical experience of it is only ever of its particular instantiations within time. Even if the nature of human understanding is necessarily a collation, it still tends towards instantaneity, and the encyclopedia, the collation of all possible elements, is the materialization of the tendency towards that ideal. As the reduction of discourse to its synchronic elements and to rules for combining them, grammar as an ideal seemed to mediate between discourse and the instantaneity of vision. Most significantly, it seemed to precede all forms of rhetoric, considered in the largest sense as moving or contextualized discourse.

With the European invention of printing, the desire for instant and total comprehension that had been answered by an eternal grammar of elements and rules for combining them gained a powerful new metaphor. The earlier metaphor deepened radically as the elements that composed words and sentences no longer seemed tied to human production. Instead of requiring the temporal motion of the hand across the page every time a document is to be reproduced, printing offered an image of knowledge that was both textual and instantaneous. With every impression of the press, printing gave its Renaissance readers a utopian – or uchronic? – knowledge that lay outside of time and discourse, visual and reproducible in a single stroke. Printing begins with the literal manual traversal of a space in composing the types, but then leaves it behind, presenting itself as a window onto the eternity of things – as a narrative device providing the escape velocity necessary to free itself from narrative. Where Bartholomaeus used an angel to visualize the difference between divine and human intellect, Pierre Gregoire saw in printing an analogy for the revealed wisdom received directly from God and knowledge gathered by human means:

revealed knowledge (*infusa*), like the art of the printer, with a press instantly (*simul*) fills the pages with sentences and clauses; but acquired knowledge (*acquisita*) imitates the arrangement of writing, in which one then another and a third letter are depicted, and then syllables joined, words and lines minutely finished. (Gregoire, *Syntaxes* I, 112)

Not only the printed page but the practice of printing itself could be understood as an eruption out of time into a timeless eternity. Unlike other arts, asserts

Pierre Boaistuau in his *Theatrum Mundi* (1561), printing was born fully formed and already perfected:

> And although one can adjust something in all other arts and human discoveries, this one alone has made its entrance in this world with such impact and perfection that one cannot adjust or criticize anything that makes it defective or deformed.[5]

In the same way that Gregoire in his metaphor conveniently forgets the labor of the hand placing the type in a manner that mimes that of writing, Boaistuau imagines the art of printing as a fixed state that has been achieved through time but now somehow lies beyond it. Spatialization in these printed works gives the illusion of eternity. The printing press, at least in the imagination of those who read its products, erased the labor that went into the making of texts that had been so much a part of scribal copying.[6] Knowledge was no longer taken to be part of an ongoing process of accumulation and assimilation, but idealized as instantaneous. Hence it could also be ever more commodified into an "account," as Pliny had predicted – discrete quanta of information arranged according to synchronic rules.

Even the ideal forms of grammar and print could not wholly eliminate the agent whose presence was always implied in the construction of sentences from words. The corresponding means that later encyclopedists turned to were twofold, each one possessing the advantage of restricting the freedom to stray that seemed inherent in the concepts of encyclopedia and theatre and each corresponding to the rough demands of those concepts. The first was like grammar, a combinatory – a system of a finite number of elements and a set of rules for combining them in regular ways; the second was a reliance on vision as a dependable, shared common sense basis for knowing. While both methods could delimit the improvisation of the actor/author, the former is, roughly speaking, a subjective limit, answering to *superbia* – it limits the possible actions that can be undertaken – while the second is objective – it puts limits on the objects of knowledge. As before, these encyclopedic techniques were interpreted as overlapping and as typical of the theatre as a comprehensive spectacle of the world. In this chapter I will trace how two writers in particular, Giulio Camillo and Conrad Gessner, attempted to authorize their discourses on the two parts of the combinatory system, Camillo on the rules for combination and Gessner on the elements to be combined. But these two different ways of focusing attention on the problem of authorizing the performance of knowledge brought into conflict an open system of visual representation and a closed one of algebraic combinations.

The desirability of a combinatory system for recording the nature of the world was grasped as early as the thirteenth century in the works of Ramon Llull, who sought to eliminate the religious conflicts between Christians, Jews, and Muslims in the Spanish peninsula. Llull realized that there could be no final appeal to an authoritative text when each faith recognized a different one. By reducing the teachings of the three religions to axioms of divinity, ethical behavior, and the nature of the world on which he believed all human beings could agree, and then creating a mechanical, automatic system of combining the axioms to produce universally recognizable truths, Llull attempted to prove that only Christianity was logically tenable. Llull's influence, though attenuated and often unacknowledged, was immense in the intellectual circles of the later Middle Ages and the Renaissance, as Frances Yates and subsequent scholars have shown.[7] The idea of a combinatory method can be naturalized to elucidate the workings of an unexpected combinatory or made strange with equal ease. The alphabet is a recurrent trope of the way in which a finite number of elements of knowledge can combine to form an apparently inexhaustible set of things and a correspondingly unbounded capacity for knowing. Lucretius makes the letters of the alphabet a metaphor for the way the finite kinds of atoms can come together in infinitely many ways (*De Rerum Natura* II, 682ff.). Francis Bacon's idea of experimentally derived Forms of things also makes explicit use of this metaphor.[8] Pierre Gregoire describes the same process of combining elements, but makes it into a kind of marvel. Letters are the elements (*elementa*) of reason, its hidden sinews and its force (*implicitis nervis et viribus*); whoever speaks must do so by combining the limited number of letters and the sounds of the five vowels, but the infinite is produced by the finite, since with the letters a speaker can pronounce any possible sentence and refer to any existing thing.[9] But the idea that the combination of letters into words might be a model for the organization of the world finds its most striking, because most extreme, expression in the writings of Peter Ramus, who based his logic upon a combinative method:

> Let us suppose that all the rules, definitions, and divisions of grammar have been ascertained, that all the examples used in grammar have been found, and that all these things have been truly and correctly "judged." Let us suppose that all these prescriptions are written out, each on a separate little ticket, and all of these thoroughly mixed in an urn, as for a game of *blanque*. Now I ask what part of dialectic would teach me how to put together all these mixed-up precepts and to reduce them to order.

Since the elements of grammar are all accounted for, there is no need for a method of dialectical invention; since they are all true, there is no need for syllogistic. All that is required is a method of arrangement, to ensure that the elements are put in proper order:

> Let our dialectician, then, by the light of the method first pick out from the urn the definition of grammar . . . Next let him look for the parts of grammar in the same urn . . . Then let him separate out the definition of these parts . . .[10]

One of the most famous of those who adopted Llull's methods to produce an art of arrangement was Giulio Camillo, whom I discussed briefly in the second chapter. In the wooden circle of his Teatro, Camillo sought to organize and make accessible all knowledge, human and suprahuman.

Camillo's theatre has been given a degree of notoriety by Frances Yates' valuable account of it in *The Art of Memory*. The Teatro, mentioned in several contemporary accounts in addition to Camillo's own lengthy but vague description in his book *L'Idea del Theatro* (1550), seems to have been a physical structure that took the form of an amphitheatre, large enough for one or two users to enter and stand on the stage.[11] Arrayed in a semicircle around them, in the place of the audience, and recalling the decorations of Pliny's theatre of Pompey, were images, probably statues or paintings, of mythical and quasi-historical figures. These images were arranged – cross-referenced, as it were – in twelve vertical columns, one for each sign of the zodiac, of seven ranks each, one for each of the astrological planets. Scholarly consensus has long followed Yates in seeing the Teatro as a magical structure for calling down astral influences, and there has been a tendency to leave it at that, with scholars standing on the shores of reason watching Camillo float off toward the horizon of madness. In recent scholarship, though, Camillo has been looked at less from the point of view of how wildly wrong (but nonetheless valuable for theorists of the theatre) he was, and with greater sympathy for why he might have thought what he did – and even what he might have thought he was doing.[12] While Camillo may very well have hoped to harness astral forces to help him accomplish his tasks, it now looks much more as if his Teatro was a method of arranging and storing passages from Cicero by topic, with the idea of being able to locate them quickly and recombine them into new speeches that could express any idea in a style that was genuinely Ciceronian.[13] Such a design fundamentally reconceives the problem of *collatio*. *Collatio* remains the locus of the individual and the contingent, since the language of Cicero and any other Latin writer is identical. But Camillo's goal was to determine Cicero's own rules of collation and to use them to make an encyclopedic theatre that was not merely demonstrative like the Llullist tracts but productive – a finite collection of elements and rules for combining them that would yield Cicero's style.

L'Idea del Theatro is a guide to the system by which Camillo organized the Teatro but does not include a discussion of how the Teatro worked.[14] Based on the descriptions of contemporaries who saw it as well as on Camillo's own sketchy account, the Teatro seems to have been a literal storehouse of examples of text.[15] This is borne out by Camillo's description of his new system of writing poetry in *Trattato delle Materie* (cited hereafter as *Delle Materie*) and its demonstration in *Trattato della Imitazione* (cited hereafter as *Della Imitazione*).[16] The confusion about how exactly Camillo's wooden structure was supposed to work seems to have come from the critics' concentration on the weirder and more seductive *L'Idea*, at the expense of drier works like *Della Imitazione* and *Delle Materie del Teatro*. In this scholars have responded exactly as Camillo predicted his peers would to his Teatro, becoming absorbed by the gaudy and fascinating images and neglecting the more prosaic reams of paper beneath them that in fact supply the material upon which the theatre relies. Camillo's emphasis was not on the visual images he presented, but on what was beneath them – texts, carefully collated and indexed for recombination. In this deflection from visuality his theatre resembles that of Zwinger. What both writers reveal is the structure underlying vision that secures it from the endless seeking of *curiositas*, the lust of the eye.

Camillo's project in constructing his Teatro is the same one undertaken by Llull of uniting philosophy and rhetoric – that is, of devising a linguistic system that would adequately represent the true state of the world. The real problem with this union, as Camillo saw it, was the nature of invention, or the finding of material, peculiar to each field.[17] In rhetoric, invention is carried out by the writer (*Scrittore*) according to his own particular qualities and abilities; in philosophy, on the other hand, invention takes place through things themselves. Rhetoric then serves to adorn the things discovered by philosophy: "Every subject (as I have said in one of my Latin orations) in the hands of an Orator or Poet is of necessity modified by some of the passions (*passioni*), as Aristotle so learnedly teaches us . . ."[18] For Camillo, passions are not merely the emotions that an orator might display or arouse, but more technically the categories or "sufferings" that any idea or concept must undergo to enter into language – the changes to which the particularity and materiality of language subject the pure idea. In a commonplace of this problem, one cannot imagine *man* generally without imagining *a* man in particular, of a unique age, condition, and so on.[19] Without rhetoric, thought is like a skeleton – stripped to its essentials, but also dead – as Camillo implies recalling an exemplary moment in the development of his theory:

> I remember once in Bologna that an excellent anatomist enclosed a human body in a casket pierced all over, and then set it in the current of a river, which within a few days consumed and carried away the flesh of that body through the holes, so that afterwards it revealed its marvelous secrets of nature in its bare bones and remaining sinews. A body thus stripped down to the bones I compare to the model of eloquence stripped down to its material and to its bare design.[20]

For Camillo, there is no question of gaining any direct access to philosophical truths in an actual, living speech. As a body is adorned with accidental qualities like beauty, age, and gender, rhetoric particularizes the universality of the things treated of by philosophy – and just as any body necessarily has such accidental qualities, so must the universal truths of philosophy subject themselves to the particularities, or *passioni*, of speech and concrete thought. There is no alternative to the use of rhetoric, since we understand and reason from particulars, and contingencies color all ideas, covering them as flesh covers a body and like the flesh responsible for outward signs like beauty or age. What Camillo poses, then, are not really the alternatives of philosophy and rhetoric as if they were distinct, but rather the combination of philosophy and rhetoric, and rhetoric without philosophy. Whether adorning the things provided for it by philosophy or making them up out of nothing, rhetoric is the collative process of setting things into words and so is part of every use of language. At the level of the skeleton, all human bodies are alike; so too are all similar discourses, for instance speeches of praise, at the level of structure. But the underlying structure is not a speech any more than a skeleton is a person; the rhetorical ornament cannot be discarded without changing the totality of what is displayed, as from a living body to a dead one.

In order to ensure that rhetoric only *adorns* philosophy and does not set out on its own errant way, the orator, according to Camillo, needs a consistent method of standardizing the effects of these passions and accidents so that they can be trimmed from or added to their base topic in predictable ways. Returning to the image of man, for example, if I conceive of man as being middle-aged, dark-haired, and horse-loving, and you conceive of him as being youthful, uxorious, and noble, we need to devise something to ensure that neither of us becomes distracted by what are really only ornaments, albeit ones necessary to imagine *man* with. Our idiosyncratic imaginings need to be re-universalized so that they can be compensated for by abstracting them from each of our images of man. For this Camillo created a device (*artificio*) that, given an idea and a variety of passions that could affect its representation, would standardize their relations:

When the thing is not adorned, or indeed is deficient, if the writer places it within the center of this our artificial circle (*artificiosa rota*) . . . , drawing and taking on from the circumference to the center all these things [the variable passions] which are able to amplify (*aggrandire*) it, he will be able without doubt to make it accept such things as are great.[21]

Camillo called his device a *Gorgo*, because it consisted of a central circle with lines radiating from it, apparently suggesting to him the snaky head of a Gorgon (Figure 13). In the circle was located the central idea; the radiating lines were various modifications that the essential idea could undergo. In a sense the *Gorgo* was a visualization of the late medieval and Renaissance use of the Aristotelian categories in rhetoric, which were seen as providing additional detail to a concept rather than logical or systematic description. By beginning in the central idea and moving out along the radiating lines of the *Gorgo*, one could vary the passions in predictable fashion, intensifying or decreasing a passion by fixed increments or moving at a given radial distance to another passion of equal intensity.

In addition to moving around the circumference of the circle to discover the particular passions and locutions appropriate to any circumstance, Camillo

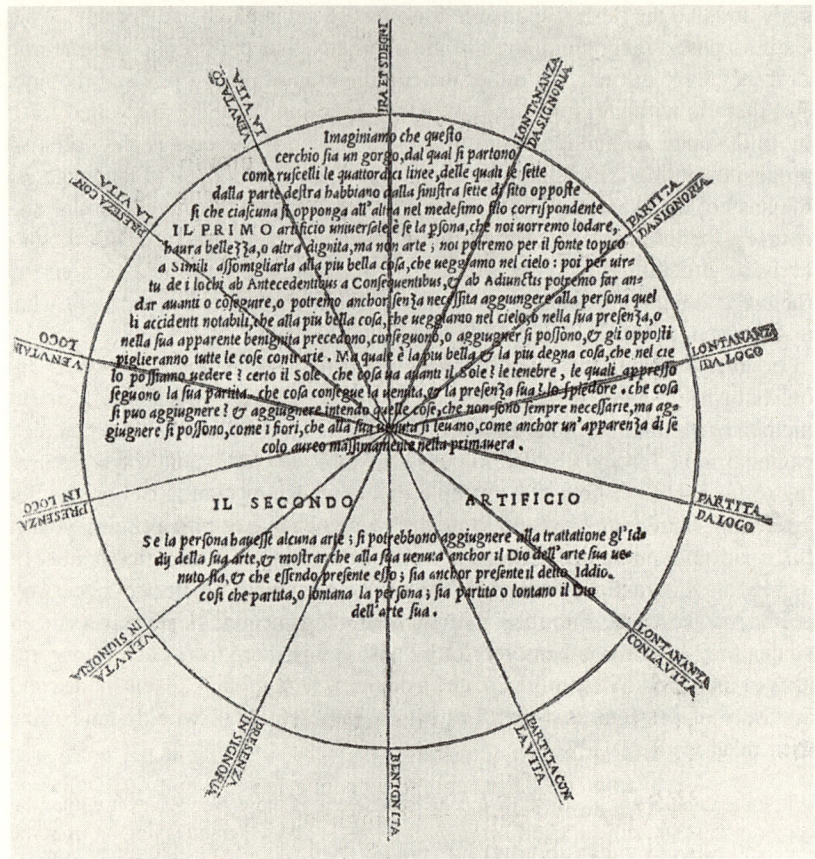

Fig. 13 *Gorgo*, from Giulio Camillo, *L'Idea del Theatro dell'Eccelente M. Giulio Camillo* (Florence: Lorenzo Torrentino, 1550).

distinguishes degrees of closeness or distance from the central idea. Camillo distinguishes *proper* (*proprio*) terms, which stand for an idea or thing transparently; *translated* or *metaphorical* ones (*traslatione*), which involve a slight embellishment (in his example they are simply the proper word with another word or words added); and *topical* (*topica*) ones, which express the same idea without repeating any of the words, but move from one expression on the circumference to the logical center of the *artificio* and back out to another point on the circumference:

We will offer the example concerning *sigh*. When I say "to sigh," I pick the proper word; and these accompanying words say the same, and they provide a nearly pure translation: "to give a sigh," "to heave a sigh." But if I would say "to crack the air with the weight of sighs," that would be a topical figure, drawn from a necessary place, that is from the consequences of sighing.[22]

The place from which the figure is drawn is necessary because air is necessarily moved in the act of sighing; Camillo refers to the sigh as cause indirectly by bringing in one of its effects, the movement of air. Camillo also shows how a weaker figure can be generated from non-necessary consequences, for instance, "to move small objects with sighs" – weaker, Camillo notes, because small objects do not always move under these circumstances.[23] Presumably there are a number of relations that one could draw on – to take "sigh" as an effect, for example, to move to its cause, or to make a more properly metaphorical transference. Mario Carpo distinguishes Camillo's method as an "encyclopedia" from a scholastic "system" or a humanist "example." A system, Carpo explains, organizes rules and prohibitions in relation to each other and uses them to locate individual events; an example provides an instantiation of a particular quality, but without explaining how it is to be replicated. Camillo's encyclopedic system, though, guarantees that the same results can be obtained by any practitioner, even the most mechanical – and perhaps *especially* the most mechanical.[24]

Camillo gives as an example of the use of his *artificio* his handling of the charge to write a poem in praise of Ercole D'Este's first entry into Ferrara as Duke. Since Camillo is writing a poem of praise, he first selects a related concept (that is, a praiseworthy one) that will serve to magnify Ercole's importance. He chooses the sun as the image to place at the center of the *Gorgo* which he will use to metastasize Ercole into poetry, referring to him in terms properly associated with the sun, but applicable to Ercole – his brilliance, his hoped-for appearance, his power to make those around him flourish, and so on. Then Camillo cites passage after passage describing the sun in various ways from various writers, principally Petrarch and Vergil, but also Seneca, Cicero, Lucretius, Tibullus, and the Psalms (*Delle Materie*, 170–91). Only with these all in place is Camillo able to set what he calls the *materie* of his work into what he calls the *lingua*. He does this by varying the particular qualities that can be expressed around the general ideas of the sun and sunniness.[25] The sun provides the motive force for the image, but is itself invisible or at least unviewable, while making the vision of everything else possible. What remains unrepresentable is what is allowed to structure the troping of the system, the mechanization of the *Gorgo* itself. Camillo's *materie* here are themselves *lingua*, words collated and arranged in order, and not the things he had claimed they would be. Rhetoric is supposed to be a way of adorning and particularizing the idea at the center of Camillo's device. But Camillo does not present the idea as divisible from the ornamentation of rhetoric; it cannot appear as itself, but only as dressed in words, as the example of the sun makes clear – it stands at the center of the *Gorgo*, but it remains inexpressible except in *passiones*. What can appear is not the sun itself, but only a name, like Ercole – and neither name in itself is particularly impressive nor has any inherent meaning. Both are empty placeholders, which is why Camillo can readily switch them. What makes Ercole meaningful (explicitly) and also the sun (tacitly) is their insertion into a set of discursive elements. Crudely put, the static idea *the sun* becomes meaningful only in a sentence, for example: *the sun also rises*. But this sentence can also contain *Ercole* in the same position, because as names they are interchangeable: *Ercole also rises*. The sun, like the skeleton discovered by the anatomist, does not simply appear in a poem; both are revealed by a device, whether a perforated box or Camillo's *artificiosa rota*.

The *artificio* of Camillo works as a kind of panegyric template for perfectly exchanging words, so that the same idea can be said in a variety of different ways, each appropriate to a different audience or set of circumstances – for instance, the absolute idea of emerging brightness expressed in the particular contexts of Duke Ercole's emergence or the sun's emergence. But instead of moving from circumference to center and back, as he claims, from absolute idea to various manifestations, as Elyot's contemporaneous *Dictionary* can do, Camillo's *artificio* only lets him move from one point on the edge of his imaginary circle to another one, from one set of words to another set. This artificiality, although not the result sought by Camillo, is what guarantees the accuracy, or at least the reproducibility, of the imitation, whether it is of things or of particular authors. Its device is a book of references to words, to language conceived along the model of a lexicon or grammar, and not to ideas conceived as images. As Camillo observes, "There is no idea visible apart from the passions of language" (*L'Idea*, 12r).

Another version of Camillo's *Gorgo* could be made to function with much greater rigor and inflexibility, literally reweaving the words of other authors to match a new context. In the *Discorso in Materia del suo Theatro* (1544, hereafter cited as *Discorso*), Camillo shows more clearly how his system works by rewriting a line of Petrarch, to use his term, topically. The length of the line is fixed by the form of the poem at eleven syllables, providing one fixed formal condition. If one is trying to write a line of only three words, one each of five, four, and two syllables in any order, there are a smaller number of possibilities, smaller still if one limits oneself to words and phrases used by Petrarch. If one has a particular subject to write on, for example the entrance of Ercole into Ferrara, the possibilities become still more limited. Camillo gives examples of some possible lines with the words of different lengths in a variety of orders, but for the order of 2–4–5 he says that

> at present an example does not occur to me. But if I had my book with me, where my labors are already ordered, . . . I could show your Lordship not only how many times Petrarch sang in a given measure, but how he, or rather his good ear, sang . . . [26]

Camillo's claim is thus not only to be able to reproduce *what* is distinctively Petrarchan, but to have discovered at an archeological (or anatomical) level the underlying mechanism of production of Petrarchan writing. The book that Camillo does not have with him must be something like a concordance listing all of Petrarch's vocabulary in its contexts, or at least most of it, and in fact such a book was published posthumously under Camillo's name, the *Annotationi Supra le Rime del Petrarca* (1557). Camillo's actual notes to the poems are of relatively slight interest, but the attached tables, credited to Lodovico Dolce, list, he claims, all the varied figures of speech and thought occurring in the *Rime sparse* by type – metaphors, contraries, antonomasia, and so on. Most like what Camillo describes broadly in *Delle Materie* are tables of nouns in various cases with all the possible adjectives Petrarch uses to modify them, which Dolce calls "epithets"; a list of Petrarchan vocabulary; and a Petrarchan rhyming dictionary.

The rules for combining the elements of the concordance, whether the imaginary ones of Erasmus' *Ciceronianus* or Camillo's (apparently) real ones, detail exactly what elements of composition must be placed where, and in a way that is no longer subject to non-quantifiable, subjective vagaries – Camillo understands not the vagueness of Petrarch's spirit but rather the concreteness of "his good ear." He dismisses as silly the objection "that I do not believe that [the *artificio*] can ever be the nature of the author (*la natura dall'autore*), but only those principles (*consigli*) that proceed from him."[27] The mechanism of Camillo's method of course does not reproduce what is literally native to the author; it does, however, accurately reproduce the results that proceed from that authorial nature, although by a different means. The attempt to find some indefinable authorial nature to imitate – espoused by humanist theorists from Petrarch onwards – was thus a dead end, and what had been mistakenly credited to genius was in fact the product of invariable rules of practice.[28] There is no *natura* recoverable apart from the *consigli* and the "good ear" of the author. An author's *auctoritas* is reinterpreted as a set of distinctive stylistic and lexical features rather than any personal quality. "My whole art," Camillo boasts in conclusion, "is governed by necessity and sufficiency."[29] When one has such an art, one has made authority itself standardizable.

Camillo mentions that he wishes to construct similar books for the *corpus* of both Vergil and Dante (*Discorso*, 31) and in *Della Imitazione* he is still more ambitious. "It is my intention," he declares, looking ahead to his memories of the body in the perforated box, "to make of the most excellent (*perfettissimi*) authors a minute Anatomy," so that of their scattered parts he will be able to reassemble whatever speech he desires.[30] Here Camillo's project becomes different from what he attempted to show with Petrarch, Vergil, or Dante. There the aim was the perfect imitation of a single authorial style. Here, though, the goal becomes good style in general, on the assumption that the *perfettissimi* that Camillo collects are not merely individual instances of various good styles, but that there must be a single kind of good style that underlies all of them – something like the idea of "Latinity." What Camillo assembles here are not like his evidences of Petrarch's "good ear," but of good Latin. Like the elements of metaphor or the individualities of Petrarch's or Dante's styles, the working knowledge of the language could be reduced to a relatively simple mechanism. With it, Camillo boasted that he could teach, depending on which contemporary account one consults, either Francis I of France or a complete illiterate to speak and write Latin within a few months.[31]

It is significant that Camillo undertakes this project with Latin rather than with a vernacular language. A dissection of the structure of Latin is necessary because moderns are not born into the Latin rhetoric that Camillo is trying to teach, but only learn it later (*Della Imitazione*, 207). Thus they cannot easily distinguish the various levels of meaning of expressions that compose the *Gorgo*, whether proper, metaphorical, or topical, as they can in Italian or the other vernaculars. Latin is a dead language, shut up in books, and it is only from those books that correct Latin can be learned.[32] Some moderns, Camillo explains, persist in misrecognizing the subject of Camillo's anatomy and their own skeletal grammars as still living: "There are some, although they were not born into the Latin tongue, who burn to introduce – I do not say topical figures, I do not say praiseworthy metaphors, but a new proper use of words."[33] From Camillo's standpoint this is plainly ridiculous, but since the system is based on a proper locution which can be philosophically analyzed for rhetorical adornment, there must be a recognized set of terms which are proper not only in the sense of belonging to a thing itself but also in the sense of being correct Latin. What must be done is to collect and sort a body of Latin from which one can systematically and mechanically deduce the proper Latin ways of connecting words, so that one's book knows as certainly and automatically as oneself that, in Italian, *gettare sospiri* is the same as *sospirare*. In fact, as Camillo suggested earlier, this requires a return to the books in which the dead language remains sealed.

But while Latin's deadness requires a project like Camillo's, Camillo's project of building rules of composition likewise requires a dead language, in which there is no authority left in any living speakers, but only in written texts. If one "born into" a language is given authority to produce that language spontaneously, Camillo's system becomes not only unnecessary, but impossible, because its rules of "necessity" and "sufficiency" can be challenged by any native speaker. One can construct an *artificio* for an *auctor* like Petrarch, since Petrarch can no longer introduce new praiseworthy metaphors or authentically Petrarchan topical figures, but not for Italian generally, where any speaker can potentially add to the linguistic *silva*. One of the things that Camillo's project relies on is the possibility of establishing a restricted set of texts with which to stock the categories of the *artificio*.[34] If, as is the case with Petrarch, the goal is really to discover every possible word or phrase exhaustively, and not in the more haphazard way of a writer thinking through at random what he can remember of what he has read, the number of texts to be consulted must be restricted and finite – in a word, dead. This set of texts is quite literally a corpus. The anatomy described earlier by Camillo becomes the figure not only for detailed analysis, but also literal dismemberment; Camillo's operation relies on the deadness of the language he performs it on. The authors Camillo designates as *perfettissimi* are not only "most perfect" but (punning on the Latin) "most thoroughly finished," as dead as the anatomist's skeleton which, like the *perfetto*, yields up its form to the knowing eye of the scholarly graverobber (*Della Imitazione*, 227–28). The closure of the authoritative corpus is what ensures the iterability of its style through Camillo's device, and what enables him to see the common framework supporting the works is its dismemberment.

Camillo's slightly ghoulish image of the anatomist resonates with the name he gives his *artificio*, the *Gorgo*. Like the Gorgon, Camillo's device petrifies the language it operates on, reducing its flux to a set of predictable and fixed exchanges. When Alciati mentions Camillo's claims to make people as eloquent as Cicero or Demosthenes, he means it to the letter: he makes them not eloquent to the extent that Cicero was, but eloquent precisely in the way Cicero was eloquent, using only his words and phrases.[35] Camillo's effort is to standardize and regulate the *Actor* to return to him the authority of the *Auctor*. By working from the corpus of one such *perfetto*, one need not take a haphazard or idiosyncratic approach to copying, taking one part from one text and another from another, like Zeuxis had to in painting Helen; the *perfetto* has done it for you already:

Thus one who imitates a *perfetto* imitates the perfections of a thousand joined in one, and so much the better, insofar as in that One appears a uniform (*continuata*) perfection, not one composed only in one part of the composition . . . In the opinion of Zeuxis, we ought to be bold to take from many the most beautiful elements (*le parti piu belle*), as Cicero does, or any other *perfetto*.[36]

According to Cicero, though, what Camillo proposes is exactly the opposite of what Zeuxis did; not finding any single model for his Helen, Zeuxis had to assemble his beautiful parts from life, and not from the imitation of another artist who had already done so. Camillo's system, however, in striving for accurate imitation, must bypass the vagaries of haphazard copying which made *perfetti* of the native speakers of Latin or the artists of the ancient world. By limiting the elements to be imitated to the few that were already chosen for imitation by earlier artists, Camillo secures a kind of representation that does not depend for its success on the individual talent of its maker, but on the iteration of the collective genius of tradition:

And if these same Sculptors and Painters, when they want to make a figure, in general they prefer (*si contentano*) to make an imitation of an ancient statue made by some great artist who, from many individuals made by nature, in which the beauties (*le bellezza*) are not united – and it is not unusual when one cannot find even one – nevertheless in an ancient figure by a skilled artist one sees already all the beautiful things (*tutte le belle cose*) united . . .[37]

Camillo's image makes it clear that whatever his claims to approach the underlying order of the world are, in practice he works from artifice to artifice. The most beautiful and lifelike statue is the one copied from another statue, an object already distilled from life into art. A user of Camillo's method, then, is not like Vincent of Beauvais' actor. The actor browses idiosyncratically in the treasure house of the dead *perfetti*, the collection of their imitable excellences. Camillo's system takes the works of these *perfetti*, divides them into elements, and supplies rules for their reassembly. In so doing he eliminates the arbitrariness of the actor browsing the authoritative texts and selecting from them at random. In Camillo's devices, the necessary elements are reduced to a manageably finite number, and all are immediately present to the user. The user may still determine what thought he wishes to express, but for a line of a certain length expressing a certain thought, there is *one* excellent line; for a hand in a particular gesture, *one* superlative hand. "Necessity and sufficiency": Camillo's system projects exactly enough elements to answer every need, so that there is neither excess to cull nor shortfall to make up. When this kind of system is imagined to be capable of producing every piece of information it becomes a metaphysical version of the compiler's work; as Hugh of St. Victor observes, God creates forms in his mind and realizes them in the world, and all that is left to the human *artifex* is "to conjoin the scattered and separate the conjoined."[38] It is the same as the combinatory technique used by other compilers, but extended to its logical limit.

Based on the very fragmentary descriptions that remain, Camillo's finished Teatro seems to have been another of his *artifici* designed to carry out the process of arrangement, but vastly more inclusive and powerful than his others; based on the works of Cicero, it would describe not just Cicero's style but the real shape of the way things were.[39] As Camillo explains, the works of Cicero provide sufficient material for expressing any idea, once they are properly distributed by subject in the structure of the Teatro. Camillo's Teatro thus conflates the two concepts of the *artificio* that I have discussed. It is both an imitation of an individual style – Cicero's – *and* of the best Latin, here assumed to be the most accurate and expressive way of describing reality. The Teatro collapses the distinction between word and thing, object and representation. It relies on the grammatical substitutions that Camillo used in his other *artifici*, but takes them as genuinely productive of meaning – more, they are capable of completely expressing *all* meaning. It is for this reason that Camillo's work takes the form of an encyclopedic theatre, in which representing and represented are folded into a single machine of vision.

Camillo does not intend for his *artificio* to limit its user to pagan topics, or to stifle his ability to speak of what he chooses. Even things that Cicero himself did not speak of, because they were not part of Roman culture, can be adapted to fit Camillo's culture by judicious use of Ciceronian vocabulary, as Camillo explains:

> And here I will say a few words about the utility of my labor, that, proposing to myself the state of this age, and of our religion, I have sought to accommodate many things to our custom, as for example: while Cicero never spoke of Christ or of the Holy Spirit, I have prepared, considering our need of speaking and writing of the Divine Persons under the breadth of the images of beings, a great wood (*gran selva*) drawn from the writings of Cicero, with which one can clothe the name of the Son and the Holy Spirit Ciceroniously (*Ciceroniamente*).[40]

In a passage I cited earlier, Camillo compared the user of his Teatro to a man who is lost in a wood (*selva*) who climbs a tree to see his way out. This wood is the same as the wood (*selva*) of Cicero's writings which serves as a matrix for the construction of speeches. The *selva* requires an ordering structure that will allow all possible ways of expressing a topic to be grouped and compared:

> In the great construction of my Theatre are arranged, by means of places and images, all those places that are capable of being sufficient to hold in order and manage all human concepts, all the things that are in all the world, not excluding those that pertain to all the sciences, and all the arts, liberal and mechanical.[41]

The Teatro was not merely rhetorical, as perhaps some of his smaller *artifici* for writing poems may have been, but philosophical in the fullest sense that it could have for Camillo, which is to say rhetorical and philosophical simultaneously. It was a device for finding the words that could describe all things. The structure of the theatre is so complete that it even enables one to see flaws in a language, such as concepts mandated by the logical order of things for which there are no words.[42] Rhetoric dealt with ephemeral things, and so could use ephemeral and idiosyncratic mental places or categories for its invention of phrases and ideas, but Camillo's system is tied to the eternal order of the world.[43] The orator finds his subjects in the places in which, following the mnemonic tradition, he has put them, but Camillo finds them in their own eternal places (*loro luoghi eterni*). Like Zwinger, for whom *epistêmê* was simply a sufficient accumulation of the *stasis tôn horômenôn*, the state of things seen, Camillo's project grows out of the faith that a sufficient accumulation of terms into a *selva*, no matter how obscure, will eventually develop into an order. Camillo ensures the ability of his device to represent all of nature by insisting on its absolute artifice. The idiosyncrasy threatened by the part of the Actor is brought back under control. In place of the *artifex* or actor there is now an *artificio*.

Camillo's *artifici* that sought to reproduce the style of a particular master were devices to tap the irreducible authority of their originals – to speak as

Petrarch or Cicero would have spoken. But they also point to a problem that beset other writers of multi-voiced texts. From its beginnings, encyclopedism had differentiated itself from other forms of writing on the basis of its disinterest in style; its marvelousness lay elsewhere, in the things it represented. Pliny, for instance, saw his own absence of style as a kind of crudity, which nonetheless emphasized the wondrousness of his subjects. Theodor Zwinger follows Pliny as a model (as he announces in the "Proscenia" to his Theatre, *Theatrum* (1571), I, 5) and tries to arrange his *Theatrum Vitae Humanae* according to the internal qualities (*internas habitus*) of the things themselves. He rejects the extremes of aestheticism and expressionism, the excess over things themselves of either verbal ingenuity or personal charisma, which he associates respectively with the genres of rhapsody and history.[44] In other words Zwinger wants to concentrate on the "bare facts" (*nudas res*, 27), rejecting all superfluous material (*parerga omnia respuimus*, 27). In the end, however, he admits that within the stable structure of his Theatre, there is an element that cannot be reduced to the orderly stillness and objective logic of the rest of the work: "there remains Style (Λέξις) or type of diction, which enters (*inseruit*) in place of actors for us, and is constructed (*fingitur*) for the office of an intermediary."[45] Conrad Gessner's *Historiae Animalium* (1551) also relies heavily on the writings of other authors, preferring, like Zwinger, to subordinate verbal style to the things themselves. But Gessner's polyglot, cut-and-paste process of composition means that he finds his text to be constantly disagreeing with itself – not in content, which as he says is fairly stable, but in stylistics and grammar. "Quotations (*parentheses*) especially, as grammarians call them, pertain to style (*stilum*)," he admits, "and there are very many of them throughout the whole Work."[46] Zwinger has the same problem: "Now in fact the very style of this Theatre is various, even as the writers whose authority we have followed make use of a diverse character."[47] Gessner finds that setting a variety of texts into a conceptual order produces exactly the stylistic variations that Pliny found himself denied. This stylistic variation extends even to the level of spelling, since Gessner, as he says, follows the usage of individual authors.[48] The material is just as sterile as Pliny's but the language he assembles is surprisingly fertile; it produces at best a thematic whole that remains a *cento* of others' voices and styles. Style appears as the irreducible residue of the disappearing compiler. Either a compiler simply quotes his sources, in which case the work of assembling appears in the juxtaposition of the different styles and formats of the *auctores*, or the compiler consolidates and rewrites, in which case he produces a visible style of his own.[49] In the absence of highly artificial and self-referential controls like those of Camillo, the contingencies of writing tend to break down the link between representation and world in the same way that Vincent's *actor* does. Style, like the actor, creates a variability that does not exhaust itself in the service of some higher goal.

The combinatory method that Camillo outlines is a model for the ordered mastery of an artificial discipline. In principal at least, Gessner's *Historiae Animalium* (1551) heartily endorses it:

Of those who want to advance rapidly in the art of grammar, and to make ready for themselves the use of some language, the ones who seek knowledge of the art from the best grammarians, who pass on the art by the compositive method (*methodo compositivo*), as they call it, progress from letters and syllables to words and the eight parts of a speech [or "of speech," *sermonis*], and later to speeches themselves and syntax; but meanwhile he [sic] nevertheless does not neglect the usefulness of Lexicons, in which individual words and expressions are listed very differently than in the precepts of the art, where they are reviewed neither singly nor in the same order, not so that he would read them through from beginning to end, which would be of more work than use, but that he might consult them at intervals. Thus whoever wants to know the subject of animals, and wants to read through it in a continuous narrative (*serie*), let him find it in Aristotle, and anyone else who has written it similarly. Our Volume, in truth, is to be used like an Onomasticon or Lexicon.[50]

Despite Gessner's enthusiasm for the form, though, the *Historiae Animalium* is not a compositive guide at all, but rather its complement. Gessner recognized that the supposition that "all the rules, definitions, and divisions . . . have been ascertained" that Ramus, Llull, and similar practitioners granted themselves was not at all the case. Camillo in a sense avoided this problem by concentrating on the *corpora* of his *perfetti*, but with animals Gessner was working in a less fixed field. An encyclopedic system that devised the rules of combination had at least as much need to establish the parts that could be combined. This is what Gessner's onomastic text is for; like a lexicon, it provides only the elements that must be combined in a grammar of animals, as Gessner's other works did in their fields of bibliography, herbology, and proverbial lore. As in a dictionary, all the elements necessary for expressing a universe are present, but dissociated and insulated from each other. Bernardino de Sahagun, a Spanish Franciscan who in the mid sixteenth century compiled an encyclopedic account in Spanish and Nahuatl of the culture of the Aztecs of Mexico, expresses this function of the encyclopedia more clearly. When contemporaries asked Sahagun if he were compiling a *calepino* (that is, a dictionary, named after the compiler of the first Latin-vernacular dictionary), he responded that a *calepino* required a written language; what he was doing was writing the book that had to precede the *calepino* of Nahuatl by providing the elements that such a lexical work would be made of. Instead, "if it were finished, it would be a treasury (*tesoro*) for the knowledge of many things worthy of being known, and for the easy knowledge of this language with all its secrets."[51] Gessner's *Historiae Animalium* similarly contains the units that the compositive method requires to work with, the givens without which, like the letters in grammar or the axioms in Aristotelian logic, it cannot function. Since Gessner's encyclopedia is meant to be a description of the world and not of language, however, unlike in Camillo's *Teatro*, the units are animals and not terms, actual things and not the signs that combine to represent them.

Unlike Vincent in the *Speculum Maius*, for whom the elements of learning have already been combined to handle a variety of topics, Gessner provides the elements that one could use to complete a specular project of one's own. It is a complete archive of information through which each reader must find his own way rather than an organic totality, or even an artificially organized one, less a tool kit than a stack of lumber and a box of nails. Camillo tried to eliminate the need for an actor in favor of a mechanism; in contrast, in Gessner's *Historiae Animalium*, there is no organizing system but the reader. When Hugh of St. Victor said that the proper use of a text involved imitation, and Vincent gave admiration and imitation as the defining responses to a mirror, both referred to the contents they represented. Gessner's readers, though, imitate not the contents the author has represented but the authorial (or perhaps actorly) work of selection and organization that produces such representations. In leafing through Gessner's *Historiae Animalium*, pulling out what he needs and applying it to the situation he is in, Gessner's reader is doing what Hugh and Vincent would both have recognized as imitation – imitating Gessner's research and so providing the link between the static space of the encyclopedia and the particular context in which the reader uses it to intervene. Gessner's explicit request that the use of his work be, in contrast to the work itself, performative and not constative, effective and not merely descriptive, shows the encyclopedia as a collection of detached units ready for rhetorical reapplication to particular circumstances. What differentiates Gessner from Hugh or Vincent is his revelation of a relation of likeness between his own actions and those of the reader. Author and reader are bound together as two common *actores* of the text, each imitating the other.

Within their shared admiration for the compositive method, Camillo stresses the *teatro* and the rules of combination, Gessner the *selva* and the elements that are combined. This difference in turn is reflected in the relation established in each of these works most clearly between words and things. The governing metaphor in Camillo's Teatro (and Zwinger's *Theatrum* as well) is, in spite of its resolutely discursive composition, a visual one; and in spite of the metaphor through which Gessner's *Historiae* is a "Lexicon, or Onomasticon," it is organized primarily around its illustrations. In spite of its practical claim to be lexical, Gessner's encyclopedia seems to strive towards the theatrical ideal of vision as authoritative knowledge. Each author, then, names his work for a prioritization of word and thing that the work reverses.

Camillo's use of visual images in relation to words treats them as very different from one another, although they mirror one another. His system relies on an ability to distinguish with absolute certainty between words and things, whatever names the two sides of that relation are given. As his practice suggests, though, since the split is absolute, the things and ideas can never appear except in the changeable ground of rhetoric; the closest he can get to them are his "proper terms," which quickly enter into his linguistic equations and alterations with a status no different from that of his other terms. His project thus becomes how to divide up and recombine the verbal elements he has accumulated. In his smaller *artifici*, this would create a system which in effect had no originals or axioms, no final resting place to which all rhetoric could eventually be reduced. In the Teatro, though, Camillo provides himself with an irreducible sign of an order that cannot enter his system of linguistic exchanges in the form of the images that adorn the rows and orders of the theatre. The statues or images he describes as being on his Teatro are explicitly allegorical and so no less artificial than the words he draws from his *selva* to recombine. In particular, they are fixed by Camillo's intention; he admits that the meanings he has assigned them are not the ones necessarily given them by others. But by contrasting with the stacks of texts beneath them, the images provide an indexing system not composed of the elements manipulated by the *artificio* of the Teatro. They offer a relative still point to which interpretation can return for reference, as artificial and as necessary as putting north at the top of a map.

Camillo's emphatic artificiality and his mechanization of the beholder's share was one response to the dangers of a public audience newly released from external authorities. In the *Historiae Animalium*, Gessner set out not to overthrow error, but to provide his readers with a new common ground based, in a familiar gesture, on the things themselves. Like Camillo in his Teatro or Elyot in his *Dictionary*, Gessner is eager to stress both the contingency and the comprehensiveness of language. Gessner's reputation in the sixteenth century was based on his facility in ancient and modern languages and in particular on his massive *Bibliotheca Universalis*, an annotated bibliography of all works ever written in Greek, Latin, or Hebrew, rather than on his natural science.[52] After completing his *Bibliotheca*, an encyclopedic account of everything ever written, Gessner began a corresponding record of everything that ever existed with the *Historiae Animalium*, the first in a projected series of works that would include accounts of plants and of fossils.

In its emphasis on the exchangeability of the words he uses, Gessner's project is similar to Camillo's. At the front of each volume, Gessner's *Historiae Animalium* includes a set of tables giving the names of the animals arranged alphabetically in a variety of languages with the numbers of the pages they appear on and a Latin synonym. In case the order that he has established as singular and eternal is not actually the one instituted by God for the universe, Gessner explains, he has also included alphabetical indexes to the work in the three sacred languages of Greek, Latin, and Hebrew, as well as several vernaculars – English, French, German, Italian, Spanish, and Arabic (I, B1v). Gessner makes no attempt – surprisingly, in this period which felt so strongly the need for a hierarchy of tongues – to justify Latin or any other language as superior to the others; he draws evidence in the text, when he finds it, as readily from German as from Greek.[53] The easy shifting between languages in the tables suggests that every language, Latin included, is equally contingent – equally useful as well, since there seem to be few if any marked deficiencies in any of the tongues, although some tables are much shorter than others. Because of its very arbitrariness, emphasized still more by the several languages and alphabetical orders it includes, the alphabetical index has a consistency and permanence that the world may lack, or rather, may conceal too well. Gessner's tables promise that, given an adequate level of linguistic competence in the reader, the exchange rate of words, so to speak, will simply present itself. This is a contrast to Camillo, who had to rely on the difficult and laborious use of an *artificio* to find the equivalence between words in the absence of any non-verbal medium. On the one hand, then, what is hard for Camillo is easy for Gessner. What at first seems to be an authorization of language prior to any earthly power, though, is simultaneously a de-authorization of it. For Gessner, words can be exchanged, but they never touch the truth of what they are meant to name. The straightforward operation of matching words, though it can be undertaken readily, is ultimately a dead end on the way to organizing the lexicon of worldly things.

In *Historiae Animalium*, Gessner claimed that he had put the concern for words behind him. He discovers that, like Pliny, he is constitutionally suited to his task of tabulating data by brute force rather than cultivating niceties of expression:

It happens, too, that by nature excessive cultivation of style and every affectation are foreign to me, and so this concern is left to those who take words more than things (*verba magis quàm res*) to heart.[54]

In this he takes up Camillo's encyclopedic project from the side of what exists rather than of the means of representing it. But a few lines after declaring himself uninterested in words and style, Gessner finds *himself* in the degraded category of those who take words more to heart than things when he admits that too much space in his work is spent on philology, which, Gessner notes, repeating the phrase he had just used, certainly "pertains to words more than to things" (*ad verba magis quàm res pertinet*, "Ad lectorem", I, B1r). Indeed, the longest part of the entry for most animals is what Gessner calls "Philologia." Coming after the zoological information and culled from the *silva* of written accounts in all languages, this section can contain things like other names for the animal, what it is called in other languages, its epithets, and poetic and historical references to it.[55]

Gessner's awareness of style as a material presence in his text forces him to speak, like Camillo, of rearranging the *dicta* of others; conceived of as discrete passages, knowledge of discourse can be culled from *auctores*, compared, rearranged, localized, and manipulated in ways that are not possible with phenomena. While Gessner's claim is always to work from phenomena, his actual methodology relies much more heavily on the mediation of a variety of representations, linguistic and pictorial, and it is these that he means when he refers to actual observations of things.[56] In this Gessner's work goes further than that of his contemporaries in representing the nature of language as wholly conventional. But this insistence in Gessner's work leads to a complication that did not trouble Camillo, who authorizes one artificial system with another. In his work Gessner is looking to find something that exists outside the conventions of language, whether that is to be called experience, reality, or, in Gessner's own favorite term, "life." Like Camillo, Gessner arrives at the image as a guarantee of the possibility of accurate representation, but by moving in the opposite direction. He relies on the image as a natural sign with which to unify the dozen tongues that make up the rest of the work. The image is not merely another legible, conventional sign, as it is in Camillo's *Theatro*. For Gessner, the image has its own authority; it speaks, as it were, for itself. The five volumes of the *Historiae Animalium* are copiously illustrated with plates, both those cut especially for Gessner's work and others either copied or cannibalized from other sources. The entry on each animal is built around a woodcut image; it is surrounded by a commentary on the animal's size, habits, and so on. A note from the printer promising to publish the illustrations in a separate edition with a minimum of Gessner's extensive commentary suggests that they were considered to be one of the work's main selling points.[57] Vision, Gessner imagined, had the advantage over discourse that it was not treated as having the same problem with authorization that language did.

Gessner intends his engravings to look like the thing itself. With their help, the text can be transcended because it is only accidental, as for Camillo a kind of ornament abstracted from reality. Its very insubstantiality gives language a kind of transparency. In his partially autobiographical "Epistola Nuncupatoria," Gessner records how he first began to study natural history. He had always desired to be a physician, but knew that

> there was never an excellent or even a learned physician who had not drawn deeply from the rudiments of the first method of healing from the books of nature, as from the source; I therefore began myself, to learn the writings of those philosophers who are commentators on the things of nature . . .[58]

Trying to go to the source of the book of nature, Gessner quite naturally turns to the books of the philosophers. Like Camillo explaining the necessity of choosing a *perfetto* to imitate so that all the particular beauties of a variety of individuals can be smoothly incorporated into one, Gessner depends on a mediated relation to his source. Camillo relied on an absolute break between the beauties of Crotona and the painting made from them, carried out through the agency of the irreproducible *natura* of Zeuxis that luckily left behind its material *consigli*. Gessner, on the other hand, admits no such break or mediation – like a stream from a spring, in spite of the usual use of the metaphor, which counsels drinking from the source, for Gessner the water is the same all the way down. In Gessner's own work, which lacks the *auctoritas* of the philosophers, the vehicle for this continuity is the image constructed as natural. A gaudy porcupine, for instance, appears with the caption, "We arranged to have this picture made to life (*ad vivum*) at Zurich, when some beggars were leading around the porcupine for a spectacle (*spectaculi gratia*)."[59] The beggars' spectacle transforms seamlessly into the book's spectacle, and Gessner's only effort, unlike Zeuxis' or Camillo's, is to arrange for the image to be "ad vivum" and so to render the small spectacle of the porcupine over into the eternal medium of the printed image.

Here and elsewhere, Gessner connects the use of pictures in his work to theatrical spectacle and, like Pliny before him, he discovers that in some ways the theatre has advantages over reality. In a short introductory section, Gessner recounts how the Roman emperors "used to offer animals to the people to be looked at." This reliance on living beasts, though, had disadvantages:

But who could inspect and consider in that hardly other than brief period, namely, for which spectacles endure? Our images, all of which have been made to life (*ad vivum*), which I either took care of myself or accepted, completed as they are, from friends worthy of trust (unless I note otherwise, which is seldom), offer themselves to be viewed by those who wish for any length of time, even perpetually, and apart from labor and danger.[60]

The animal spectacles were offered by the emperors, but the images obligingly offer *themselves* to the spectator. Gessner mentions other practical considerations, too; large sea animals cannot be brought out alive as part of a spectacle, and dangerous or poisonous animals are threats to their viewers. The admonition that a theatrical display is safer than the actual experience it represents is familiar from Donatus' commentary on Terence, where he notes that comedy is an imitation of life – without the attendant risks.[61] Gessner also knows that representations let us take pleasure from looking at what would in reality be unpleasant to see: "But we see these same things depicted not only without terror of the things, but even with pleasure."[62] In a sense in both Gessner and Camillo the encyclopedic impulse overtakes the dramatic one – the controlled, limited display of symbolic equivalents is preferred over the chancier, less clearly separable mimetic one.

Gessner's pictures, though, have a very different function from Camillo's. Like contemporary theories of the theatre advanced by humanist thinkers, they are meant to be mimetic, not allegorical.[63] This is a relatively recent development in book design. Mary Carruthers discusses the meditative element in the diagrams found in medieval manuscripts, which were not meant to be photographically accurate, but allusive "invitation[s] to elaborate and recompose."[64]

They were intended to stimulate reflection on things rather than to represent them with exactness. The difference between such a diagram and Gessner's images lies in the expectation of the audience's role, between an audience imagined as unconstrained, which is free to understand according to its particular abilities and memories, and one which *must* understand the image properly or risk exclusion from a group which recognizes such images as correct.[65] Comparing one of Gessner's images to a similar one from De Worde's edition of Bartholomaeus Anglicus makes this clearer (Figures 14, 15). Gessner's

Fig. 14 Animals, from Bartholomaeus Anglicus, *De Proprietatibus Rerum*, ed. Wynkyn de Worde (London: Wynkyn de Worde, 1495).

Fig. 15   Dogs, from Conrad Gessner, *Historiae Animalium*, vol. I (Frankfurt: Bibliopolium Camberiano, 1603).

group of dogs is at least an imaginable juxtaposition of animals; they are particularized and interacting in contrast to the emblematic rendering of the animal kingdom of De Worde, in which the animals are not only stylized – that would be true of Gessner's dogs as well – but, more importantly, symbolic of nature's variety. De Worde's creatures are distinguished by emphasizing their *differentia*, for instance, the elephant's corkscrewed trunk or the lion's dagger-like claws. Gessner offers an image one might see, with all the assumptions of naturalized vision that such a statement makes; De Worde's image must instead be read both as individual creatures displaying their most remarkable qualities, and, in their unlikely grouping, as the introduction to a section in the encyclopedia on animals.[66]

Because for Gessner the image has such a strong and natural connection to its model, once a visual representation has been authorized, it quickly becomes a kind of evidence in its own right. As Hans Fischer has noted, Gessner's research for the *Historiae Animalium* was largely a careful study of prior written sources and authorities, with the additional support of substantial correspondence with his peers in other geographical areas and with different expertises, and even with members of artisanal classes, including especially the exchange of drawings and other images.[67]

Because [of my poverty], it was not practical [to travel, so], I did what I could – I enlisted some friends in various regions of Europe, who helpfully, openly, freely communicated to me many images (*effigies*) of animals of every kind represented from life (*ad vivum repraesentatas*), and even their names in diverse tongues (*etiam nomina in diversis linguis*), and their histories (*historias*).[68]

What validates this process, overcoming the two problems of Gessner's own distance from the animals he is describing and the confusion of terms for them, is in fact that the images provide an immediacy capable of nullifying both difficulties. The "names in diverse tongues" are superadded, introduced with an *etiam* that suggests their superfluity, although a generous and not threatening one. The names here are oddly unnecessary so long as they are present. The images, on the other hand, all speak the same language, the language of life, from which and to which they are drawn; the linguistic representations of the animals' histories, connected by their position in the sentence with the names but not explicitly modified by the phrase "in a variety of tongues," hover between the two primary representations, neither quite as lifelike as the images nor quite as contingent as the names. Gessner's introduction is not meant to be misleading in its reliance on the image as natural; for him, an *icon ad vivum* was, unlike a representation in language, simply an equivalent to an actual *animal vivens* in terms of its fidelity. The univocality and accuracy of the images are secured by the linguistic multiplicity to which they are compared.

Gessner's elevation of the mimetic image at the expense of non-mimetic language makes it very hard for him to reject any image as completely fanciful. For instance, he offers two conflicting images of the pelican, the first a stylized cut representing the Christian allegory of the pelican and labeled, "Pelican as it is commonly feigned by painters," and the second, larger and more modern in style, "Figure of a pelican, or, as we say, a spoonbill."[69] Gessner explains that the pelican has mistakenly been thought by many to be some exotic bird because of the way in which it is drawn, solely according to the whims of the artist (*pro arbitrio pictores hactenus finxerunt*), wounding itself to feed its young, "when there is no such bird, I think, in the nature of things."[70] The truth of the pelican, as the second image both shows and tells, is (apparently) the more prosaic European spoonbill. Gessner here looks momentarily like a defender of empirical observation ahead of his time, but then his analysis continues: "unless one thinks the Egyptians speak truly about the vulture what Horus insisted in his writings, that, lest its chicks should die of hunger, it wounds itself in the thigh, and the blood coming out is lapped up by them."[71] In spite of his commitment to writing a faithful and accurately updated natural history, it is finally too hard for Gessner to discard any pictorial evidence completely. The evidence of the image is too pressing to be totally ignored. A picture may be more or less accurate, but not simply false; Gessner will label the second of two woodcuts of a giraffe as a "more accurate image (than the one shown above)," but he still includes both.[72] Images that differ from each other or seem improbable need to be explained back to an originary difference in the real world, since they cannot be entirely discredited.

Gessner is thus every bit as reliant on the material ground of his representations as Camillo, although Camillo bases his encyclopedic representations on artificial and automatic technique and Gessner bases his own on the mimesis of nature. Because for Gessner there is no clearly defined break between image and reality (as there is between reality and language), his interest in the faithful reproduction of the animal's appearance leads to what can only be called a literalism in his rendering of the animal's appearance in the medium of print. On the one hand, the experience of an animal can be transferred by the image; on the other hand, however, Gessner makes this lack of experience into a *kind* of experience in its own right. He acknowledges the distance of the printed image from the living animal and is fascinated by the possibilities the medium of print presents with the image *ad vivum*, but is unwilling to accept the need for the materiality of the paper image to differ from the phenomenality of the perception of the real animal. Gessner had originally wanted to have color plates in the books, but it proved too expensive. He did get most booksellers to agree to make colored copies available to interested buyers, who could then color in their own woodcuts according to the models at the bookshops. When the size of the page allowed, images were made life-sized (*qua vivunt magnitudine*).[73] But his interest in mimetic likeness extended beyond color, size, and appearance even to number. His entry on the weasel includes two identical figures of the animal on facing pages, the second one accompanied by the note that "This figure was inserted twice because the white weasel differs from the other only in color" – but two colors require two images in order to be numerically accurate to life.[74]

This emphasis on the materiality of the images themselves instead of only the materiality of the things they represent can also backfire. The pictorial does not supplant the real world in Gessner, but it threatens to supplant *interest* in the world by becoming an object of scrutiny in its own right. It supplements the real world with its appearance instead of simply gesturing to the world and fading from view, the way Gessner expects language to do. What looks mimetic may instead be a kind of inverted ekphrasis; that is to say, it may be the drawing of a verbal description rather than of an object. Although they are not drawn from words directly, three images of lynxes show such a dependence on words to order and correct them (Figures 16 and 17, *Historiae Animalium*, I, 677, 678).[75] The first confesses its inaccuracy: "This is the figure of a lynx . . . such as we were able to get," but Gessner hears (*audio*; significantly, the source

Tricks of vision, truths of discourse

Fig. 16 Lynx, from Conrad Gessner, *Historiae Animalium*, vol. I (Frankfurt: Bibliopolium Camberiano, 1603).

of information is aural, not visual) that it is fairly good, "except for the head and nose, in which it ought to remind more of a cat."[76] The second, he has been told, is better.[77] The third is clearly medieval in style, and Gessner makes no attempt to judge its accuracy, simply citing its subject, a lynx chasing a wild cat, and its source, the *Tabula Regionum Septentrionalium* of Olaus Magnus, a near-contemporary.[78] This last lynx stands out most clearly by its style. The image is indeed from Olaus Magnus, but has been intentionally hyperstylized. This lynx is cut to look more imagistic than the original image. In recutting the block for the *Historiae Animalium*, Gessner's copyist has emphasized its medieval character, at once refining the execution and stressing its stylization. It is there to represent not the lynx, but an opinion (*ideology* would sound both too strong and wrongly systematic) about the lynx. Like the allegorical image of the pelican or the mass of data on each animal included by Gessner under the heading of philology, it pertains to the animal in its *doxa*, its reception into common knowledge, which constitutes a necessary part of knowledge about the animal. The multiple styles of the images mark their heterogeneity – and their distance from their purported object – as much as the linguistic styles in Gessner's text had called attention to themselves. The third lynx also serves another purpose: its marked artificiality produces an effect of reality in the other images. Its foregrounding of style and its obvious lack of transparency to the represented object conceal the fact that the other drawings of the lynx are also expressions of *doxa* – as Gessner says, his corrections of them are not based on his experience, but on what he has read or heard translated.

Fig. 17 Lynxes, from Conrad Gessner, *Historiae Animalium*, vol. I (Frankfurt: Bibliopolium Camberiano, 1603).

It is still not so simple, though, as saying that Gessner's artists naively drew what they believed, just as he corrected their drawings according to his own more educated but not otherwise different set of standards. The last volume of the work contains images of sea creatures, including both shellfish of great fidelity and huge cartoonish whales and sea monsters with stylized spouts, showing by their style that they are what is commonly believed to be out there in the deep, but not by the artists or Gessner (Figure 18). They are drawn as fictions. Near the end of the book is an astonishing head of a hammerhead shark (Figure 19, *Historiae Animalium* V, 1254–56). A hammerhead shark must be one of the more improbable-looking things in existence, but the artist has rendered it with almost photographic accuracy in a style that is startlingly like that of a nineteenth-century engraving, with thin, even lines and meticulous attention to the delicate contrasts of its shading. It is, in fact, remarkably close to what later periods will judge to be "scientific." Its recognizability now as almost transparent and indeed as *stylized* for transparency argues that the accurate drawings are

Tricks of vision, truths of discourse

Fig. 18 Fictional sea monsters, from Conrad Gessner, *Historiae Animalium*, vol. IV (Zurich: Christophoros Froscherus, 1558).

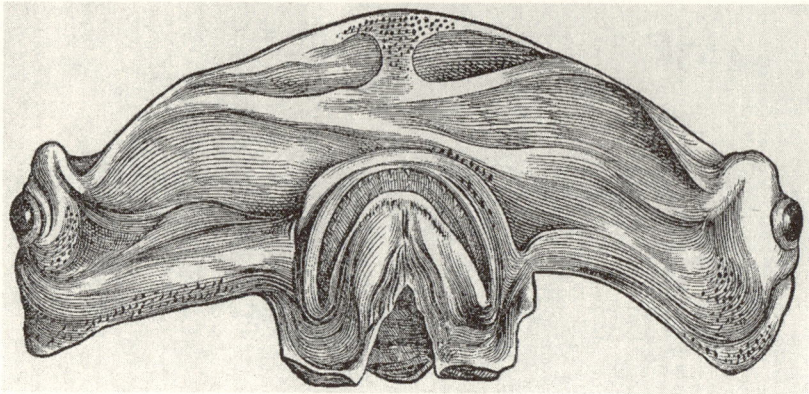

Fig. 19 Hammerhead shark, from Conrad Gessner, *Historiae Animalium*, vol. IV (Zurich: Christophoros Froscherus, 1558).

themselves reflections of a *doxa* of what it means to be accurate and objective, drawn into the works as surely and materially as outmodishness and superstition are drawn into the representations of the sea monsters.

Camillo and Gessner both try to limit the heteroglossia produced by compiling excerpts from all sorts of authors, and both rely on the materiality of their works to do it. Camillo chooses a highly artificial method of exchanging words for words that, he suggests, is capable of expressing any thing, or all things, in a single voice; Gessner tries to replace the contingent signs of language with natural ones. It is Gessner, though, who finds his natural sign representing subjective whimsy, while Camillo's expresses only an objective material reality, not of things but of language. Ironically, Camillo's highly artificial system is the self-consistent one, because it remains closed. Opening his work to things, Gessner finds that he can never reach them in themselves. Closed systems can raise and dismiss subversion, and this perhaps begins to explain both the success of encyclopedic works in introducing elements that seem antithetical to their project of edification, and the consistent anxiety – in both the sixteenth century and the twentieth – about the subversive potential of the theatre, which shows people the things they look for.[79] Open systems have no such mechanism; when the border that separates the representation from the world begins to weaken, the transfer between representation and reality – the way that the representation is recognized as, or becomes, part of reality, but always as a representation – rapidly levels the distinction altogether. It is for this reason, though, that Gessner's text, in its attempt to do no more and no less than to document the possibilities of experience in the animal world, ends up producing new experiences. By acknowledging the materiality of his medium, the result of Gessner's *Historiae*, unlike that of Camillo's *Theatro*, is not merely combinatory, but inventive. It produces new possibilities of experience. The realization of the imagined theatre, in short, even as a book, led to new complications in recording and transmitting knowledge.

4 Holding the mirror up to nature?: The humanist theatre beside itself

> CLAUDIUS: "I have nothing with this answer, Hamlet. These words are not mine."
>
> HAMLET: "No, nor mine now." —Shakespeare, *Hamlet*, 3. 2. 87–89

The physical theatre, in its humanist conception at least, was imagined in terms very similar to those set out in the textual theatres of Conrad Gessner and Giulio Camillo. The subversion/containment model that has been so influential in New Historicist readings of the early modern theatre in fact draws on this early modern conception, however unwittingly or unwillingly. This model, in which the threat of subversion ends up contained by the ideological and material conditions that instantiate it, mirrors the success with which early encyclopedic and theatrical texts could set their right hands against the left without completely destabilizing their purposes. A description of "An Excellent Actor," published in a collection of Theophrastan characters in 1615 and perhaps written by John Webster, suggests a formation as closed and schematic as that of Camillo's *Gorgo*: "Sit in a full Theatre, and you will think you see so many lines drawn from the circumference of so many ears, while the *Actor* is the *Center* . . . what we see him personate, we think truly done before us . . ."[1] The difficulties in errant agency foreseen and ostensibly forestalled by the *artificio* in the texts of Camillo and by lifelike illustration in the work of Gessner are completely overlooked in "An Excellent Actor." Rather, the actor himself becomes the organizing center around which the audience forms. The actor is here credited with an almost marvelous agency to assemble a space for representation around himself. An early emblem of the power of rhetoric pictured it as a man with a golden chain emerging from his mouth and fastened to the ears of his listeners to signify the political speaker's ability, literally, to lead his audience by the ears.[2] Whereas the usual image stresses the speaker's power over each individual in the audience, though, Webster's image stresses the distributive force of the actor's golden chain, the "lines drawn from the circumference" that cut out, or produce from within, an almost magically defined circle of neutral space – the complete and encyclopedic circle of learning envisioned as folded onto the physical space of the public theatre. But Webster's image is also in a sense curiously at odds with itself here – the actor is the charismatic focal point of the staging, but in such a way that he disappears and the audience sees not him, but whom he "personates," or represents.

In Webster's account, the actor's ability to organize space around himself is as mysterious as that of a conjurer, and like the necromancer, the actor calls upon a spirit greater than himself to do it – the person he represents. This fading of the actor into the more forceful character he portrays explains why the utopian limit of representation in Shakespeare's *Henry V* is to present, tautologically, "the warlike Harry, like himself" (prol. 5); in the impossible perfection of Harry representing Harry, there is no room for a distracting actor. But the prologue seems to connect this perfect representation and the power of the actor to generate it to the pre-existent and strictly delimited physical space that surrounds both:

> But pardon, gentles all,
> The flat unraisèd spirits that hath dared
> On this unworthy scaffold to bring forth
> So great an object. Can this cock-pit hold
> The vasty fields of France? Or may we cram
> Within this wooden O the very casques
> That did affright the air at Agincourt?
> O pardon; since a crookèd figure may
> Attest in little place a million,
> And let us, ciphers to this great account,
> On your imaginary forces work.   (*Henry V*, prol. 8–18)

Shakespeare's famous apology for acting, performed at least fifteen years before the publication of Webster's character sketch, serves as both a prior inscription of Webster's image of the actor at the circle's center and as a demystification of it. The insistence with which the prologue returns to the *shape* of the public theatre building – the wooden O, the cock-pit, the crooked figure of the cipher – with all its paradoxes of emptiness and infinity, shows that while the actor makes the stage space, the shape of the theatre gives him permission to do it.

Space remained as important as vision in imagining the theatre, as it had been to the encyclopedia. Tom Conley notes that works like Pierre Boaistuau's encyclopedic *Theatrum Mundi* (1561) and Abraham Ortelius' atlas, *Theatrum Orbis Terrarum* (1570), both participate in the shift away from a vertical hierarchization of the world to a horizontal expansion of it that recast high and low as near and far.[3] Conley's analysis recognizes that a planar graphing of elements allows for a very different set of manipulations than a linear chain of being, where elements are linked in a fixed and unalterable order. Elements imagined in a neutral plane are all equally accessible – and inaccessible – to one another; they have become, as in Foucault's analysis of the Enlightenment *tabula*, a different sort of image, disengaged from one another.[4] The *theatrum* of the humanists, book or building, was similarly imagined on the model of instant access and visual display, combining to create a pedagogical tool of unrivalled potential.

During the course of the sixteenth century, as *theatre* became linked more and more frequently with the actual space of performance, the idea of the theatre changed significantly from the encyclopedic ideal that earlier writers with less concrete ideas in mind, like Elyot or Camillo, had defined for it. Unlike the text of the encyclopedia, which denies history both in its own longevity as a text that continues in use for generations and its description of a world that is apparently static – as late as 1535, editions of Gregor Reisch's *Margarita Philosophica* still do not mention the New World in the section on geography[5] – theatrical presentations take place at a particular moment before a particular audience. Late medieval and early modern theatrical works, in spite of humanist theories of a neutral space and a controllable audience, are flexibly but firmly tied – one might embrace the pun and say "with play" – to a set of present circumstances on which they frequently comment and, minimally, insert themselves into. The cry "Make room!" with which so many fifteenth- and sixteenth-century plays open is a physical, actual displacement of ordinary activity by the efforts of a group of players.[6] Further, the intervention is literally from *within* the crowd, not from one side of it – playtexts direct actors to call out from within the crowd, to shoulder anonymously through the onlookers before making themselves part of the spectacle, or to push back bystanders to give themselves space to act. Even the term "interlude" was often understood as "enterlude" – a drama in which the actors came to the audience and appeared among them.[7] These plays present themselves not as descriptions drawn from a distance, but as events, as interventions into the larger world around them.[8] The effect of this strong occasionality is debatable: in some cases it certainly served to limit possible meanings, or to produce very context-specific ones, but it may also have provided an impetus to design plays that could be shifted from one pronounced context to another.[9] There was nothing new in this occasionality of performance, of course. For hundreds of years drama had almost always been associated with particular events, the stable and recurrent festivals of the church year or the body politic, or the less predictable arrivals of groups of players from outside the community. But the Elizabethan theatres simultaneously abstracted themselves from the other, more traditional rhythms and spaces of their society and established their own place and time, acquiring in the process a partial autonomy. As Steven Mullaney has argued, part of the shock of the early modern theatre for its contemporary critics was its apparent ability to disregard the rhythms and space of the world outside it, setting, for instance, its own regular time and place for performances rather than subsuming them to the larger temporal and spatial patterns of the city at large. This new place of the stage, in other words, was seen as threatening to displace older ones like the place of the church and the position of the aristocrat.[10] Theatre-going involved both a particular experience and the bracketing of that experience from the rest of life; it was thus both, in the literal senses of each word, im-mediate and abs-tract.

As theatres became a part of the physical landscape of London, the question facing those who supported them was this: if one believed that theatres were justified by their ability to represent and transmit the universal knowledge of everything, what steps needed to be taken to ensure their continued usefulness? If the distortions and misprisions that attended them could not be separated from the theatre, what claims could continue to be made for it? There is a change in attitudes towards the possibility of controlling misprision and authorizing correct understanding in the plays of the sixteenth century, roughly paralleling the interest shown by Camillo and Gessner in controlling right understanding. Although John Rastell's *Four Elements*, I argued, shows in its directions for shortening the performance an awareness that what would most appeal to its viewers was not necessarily what was most in accord with its declared purpose of playing, there is no sign that Rastell was concerned with the audience failing to understand the proper choice for Humanity to make. Nicholas Udall's *Respublica* (1553), on the other hand, begins with the warning:

> Indeed, no man speaketh words so well fore pondered,
> But the same by some means may be misconstrued.[11]

In this passage, Udall raises the possibility of misunderstanding his interlude but goes on to treat it as a preventable accident. He seeks to avoid the possibility of misunderstanding by alerting the audience to the danger of misconstrual and by laying out his intentions in advance. The play begins by trying to safeguard against misunderstanding; after this initial warning, the prologue goes on to explain that the play is an allegory, and so there is a deeper meaning behind the words and actions of the characters, whose identities are conveniently indicated by their names. In the course of the play, it is precisely "words" that prove to be deceptive. As in many interludes in which the Vices take on new and more palatable identities to fool the hero, the Vices of *Respublica* do not disguise themselves physically; they take false names, but because they declare their intentions to do so in front of the audience, the false identities of the Vices are an open secret. In the first scene, Avarice, Insolence, Oppression, and Adulation explain to the audience that they will fool the heroine, Respublica, by assuming the false names of Policy, Authority, Reformation, and Honesty. There is never any doubt for the onlookers, then, that what is passing for Reformation is nothing other than Oppression. The tricks of speech are quite literally *seen through* by the knowing audience; it is only the characters within the play who are taken in by the deceptive names. The certainty of visual appearance, as in Gessner or Camillo's encyclopedic works, is contrasted to shifting and shifty language.

A similar confusion of the identities of allegorical characters occurs half a century later in Jonson's masque *Hymenaei* (1606) for the marriage of Frances Howard and Robert Devereux, the third Earl of Essex. On the second night of the ceremonies, there was a trumpet fanfare and out of a perfumed cloud

did seem to break forth two *ladies*, the one representing *Truth*, the other *Opinion*; but both so alike attired, as they could by no note be distinguish'd.[12]

As Jonson explains in his tendentious preface to the published version of the masque, it is not outward appearance that is significant, even in the spectacle of a play, but its inner meaning: "Though *bodies* oft-times have the ill-luck to be sensually preferr'd, they find afterwards, the good fortune (when *soules* live) to be utterly forgotten." But the compensation for the eventual oblivion of the physical forms of the masque is to be "preferr'd" in two senses. The obvious one is that the body of the performance is liked better than its inner soul, or meaning; here, though, Jonson's second (more bodily) meaning is that the body is *held out in front of* the soul, preceding it or even, in the case of *Hymenaei*, screening it from clear sight. In the masque, both of Jonson's figures claim to be Truth, and "as they could by no note be distinguish'd," the viewers of the masque (although not the readers of the printed text) have no means of telling one from the other. Between Udall's court-sanctioned performance and Jonson's, vision ceases to be reliable, and Udall's disguising has become actual instead of merely symbolic. In Jonson's masque, Truth and Opinion argue about what state is best for women to maintain, with Truth arguing for the primacy of marriage and Opinion taking the side of virginity, and although the occasion is a wedding, the recent history of Elizabeth makes Opinion's case harder to dismiss. The debate between the two proves inconclusive, as does a series of combats at barriers which are meant to resolve the impasse; Truth is only at the end distinguished from Opinion by a literal *deus ex machina*, an Angel who appears at the last minute and correctly identifies them (*Hymenaei*, 239). Jonson holds his audience in suspense before revealing to it the real identities of his disguised figures, unlike Udall who tells the audience from the beginning of the identities of the villains that are hidden from the characters of the play. Both playwrights share, however, the opposition of a single right reading against all wrong ones, however deceptive or seductive, a clear vision (whether actual or metaphorical) that strips the shades of gray from wordplay and leaves the Manichean alternatives of true and false. The signs of the theatre may be difficult to read, but as the *mappamundi* figure in Rastell's play suggests, they can be read in a single correct way. Misprision is thus represented as a correctable accident.

This belief in the controllability of an audience's interpretation was shared by representations as varied as Tudor moralities and Jonsonian masques. The assumption in each of these cases was that, in the theatre as in the encyclopedia, experience – physical perception, contact – was a mere supplement to a more purely intellectual and disembodied understanding. Authority could control vision, or, more accurately, vision and authority coincided so that what was seen was wholly contained and reproduced in what was said. In the humanist interpretation that saw the encyclopedia and the theatre as extensions of one another, understandings that did not conform to the correct norm, whether stated or implied, were rejected as errant. This is the process exemplified in Elyot's preface to his *Dictionary*, where Henry's roles as the "perfect image of kingly majesty" and the "author" of the definitive text on the meaning of words come together in the act of pronouncing Nicolson's opinions "perverse" and against "plain context . . . and determinate sense" (A. iii. r). Even the visual displays that were intended to represent a sensual experience that could be shared were left to particular authorized viewers to interpret and make meaningful, and even to decide if there had been a shared experience at all. When vision or experience becomes public, even though it remains figurative, it becomes necessary to authorize some guide for its management. Such a guide also serves as a marker or a guarantee of the accuracy of the original knowledge. As I have argued, the information embodied in the figure of Rastell's *Nature of the Four Elements* is doubly affirmed by the authority of Studious Desire and the experience of Experience, and Jonson and Udall use the same model of double articulation. A doubtful display is definitively interpreted by some agent who nominally stands outside, but is able to draw out its hidden meaning. In a not unrelated field, Steven Shapin has detailed the ways in which the discourse of seventeenth-century science distinguished between the *knowledge* of the gentlemen experimenters, who had the ability to produce truth by observing and reporting experimental phenomena, and the mere *skill* of their "laborants," the servants and technical workers who prepared and enacted the experiments, often made the physical observations and recorded them, and even designed both the experiments and the equipment, worked out the implications, and wrote the final drafts of reports.[13] In the earlier practice of the sixteenth-century anatomy theatres, the common sense spectacle of the dissection, physically performed by unlearned assistants, was supplemented by the voice of the doctor, standing back from the actual work of cutting, verifying what the audience saw by comparing it to a written text.[14] It was in the power of the authorized observers to uphold or reject the work of the laborant; conversely, when an experiment failed to perform as expected, the operant was a figure upon whom blame could be placed "costlessly and consequently" (Shapin, *Social History of Truth*, 392; cf. 389–92). Early performances similarly divided authority and spectacle for the purpose of reuniting them in figures like Rastell's or like Justification in Lewis Wager's *The Life and Repentance of Marie Magdalene* (c.1550), whose appearance as a character at the end of the play is used by the character speaking the epilogue, Love, to authorize the accuracy of his explanation of salvation by faith:

> Such persons we introduce into presence,
> To declare the conversion of her offense.[15]

The evidence of Justification's body and the concurrence of Love's voice work together as if they were independent proofs.

For the most famous Elizabethan defender of poetry, Philip Sidney, theatre challenged even the system of meaningfulness that allowed for the recovery of poetry as useful. The indefinability of theatre is not tied simply to the correctable abuse of mingling kings and clowns in "mongrel tragicomedy"; for Sidney, theatre itself has an irrecoverably mongrel quality:

I do it [that is, mention plays] as they are excelling parts of poesy, so there is none so much used in England, and none can be more pitifully abused; which like an unmannerly daughter showing a bad education, causeth her mother poesy's honesty to be called in question. (*Defence of Poesy*, 246)

Even though it finds a place in Sidney's *Defence of Poesy*, theatre remains awkwardly indefinable. Theatre is poetry's daughter, although a bad one, and Sidney does not make it clear, or rather makes it clear that it is not clear, whether this is an accidental fault of theatre's "bad education" – in which case, presumably reformable – or some innate and irremediable defect resulting from the question of her mother's "honesty," that is, from theatre's possible bastardy. Whether Sidney uses "honesty" here as a synonym for "chastity," and thus suggests that poesy's carelessness has produced in theatre a bad and hybrid offspring, or whether it is theatre's badness that forces us to question poesy's commitment to theatre's upbringing, theatre is both exemplarily bad and exemplarily good, a border case uncomfortably on both ends of poetry. It threatens to discredit *all* poetry because of its possible bastard origins, but it also excels as poetry. In the paragraph that immediately follows this, in fact, plays are tacitly absorbed into poetry proper when Sidney begins, "Other sorts of poetry almost have we none, but that lyrical kind of songs and sonnets . . ." But the truth of drama's unstable relation with its more codified parent remains lost in the gap between Sidney's paragraphs. For Thomas Nashe, writing the introduction to Sidney's *Astrophil and Stella* (1591), the assimilation of playing to poetry can be reversed as well: after the "Scene of Idiots" and "puppet play" of other writers, Sidney's sonnets are a "tragicomedy of love" set out in a "Theatre of pleasure" (Nashe, *Works*, III, 329).

The practical experience of the performed drama, and what set it apart from the imagined theatre of the humanists, was precisely that factor that made "experience" possible at all – an audience which responded to, changed with, and in its own turn shaped the presentation of the written script. The imaginary theatre of the humanists had presupposed an audience as well, of course, but with its emphasis on decorum – on consistency, uniformity, and the coordination of characters with "appropriate" and therefore expected roles – and its circumvention of self-consciousness, it envisioned an audience that responded predictably and homogeneously. That the audiences of the public theatres of the sixteenth century did not so respond is amply documented; from demanding the performance of an entirely different play to fighting with the actors, theatregoing crowds could approach the worst predictions of unruliness made by their antitheatrical critics, shouting, clapping, hissing, fighting.[16] These empirical challenges to the didactic theory of theatre led some antitheatrical writers to reject the ordinary audiences of public performance as the real problem with drama, while allowing the benefits of school drama, with its rigidly defined purpose and tightly controlled audience. In practice, the school dramas were often as licentious as other forms, both in execution and in conception.[17] They permitted critics, though, the illusion of a predictable and uniform audience.

Yet the encyclopedic ideal persisted among learned writers for and about the theatre. In fact, whatever the actual conditions of performance, most of the writers who took up the topic of the theatre, whether in prose works or in plays, seem to connect any value that the theatre has to its pedagogical potential. Based on readings of the few extant eyewitness accounts of individual performances, Richard Levin has suggested that Elizabethan playgoers were interested almost exclusively in the plot and in the depiction of naturalistic emotions.[18] Simon Forman, a fortune-teller who saw four plays in April 1611, recorded the details in a book that he designated as being "for common policy," that is, for general practical knowledge. *The Winter's Tale* provokes him, for instance, to observe "Beware of trusting feigned beggars or fawning fellows," a conclusion so simplistic and incongruous that it suggests the strength of Forman's commitment to seeing plays as a mere vehicle for (in this case, rather banal) lessons.[19]

Following the humanist emphasis on pedagogical theatre, protheatrical writers tended to stress the socially constructive *content* of plays rather than questioning the effects of their dramatic *mise-en-scène*, performance, and context. Thomas Nashe does little more than update and particularize the positive assessments of Cicero and Donatus of theatre as the mirror of life when he notes ironically in *Pierce Pennilesse* that

in plays, all cozenages, all cunning drifts over-gilded with outward holiness, all stratagems of war, all the cankerworms that breed on the rust of peace, are most lively anatomized; they show the ill success of treason, the fall of hasty climbers, the wretched end of usurpers, the misery of civil dissension, and how just God is evermore in punishing of murther. (*Works*, I, 213)

Nashe's defense has an additional area of interest, though, and that is his linkage of the social event of theatregoing to the development of a particularly English sense of history and identity. What is seen on stage is morally and ethically improving not just in general, but in particular for an English audience that can identify itself with the actors of the deeds performed before it:

The subject of [plays], for the most part it is borrowed out of our English Chronicles, wherein our forefathers' valiant acts (that have lain long buried in rusty brass and worm-eaten books) are revived, and they themselves raised from the grave of oblivion, and brought to plead their aged honors in open presence; than which, what can be a sharper reproof to these degenerate effeminate days of ours? (*Works*, I, 213)

Here Nashe, while making a claim for theatre following the long-standing rhetoric of educability, also clearly distinguishes it from the remoteness of books. There is something unusually striking in the raising of "brave *Talbot* (the terror of the French) . . . after he had lain two hundred years in his Tomb . . . to have his bones new embalmed with the tears of ten thousand spectators, who, in the Tragedian that represents his person, imagine they behold him fresh bleeding" (212), not only because of the vividness of the display, but because of its Englishness. Thomas Heywood, following Nashe in seeing theatre as a site for the formation of national identity, asks rhetorically,

what English blood seeing the person of any bold English man presented and doth not hug his fame, and honey at his valor, . . . as if the Personater were the man Personated? . . . What coward to see his countryman valiant would not be ashamed of his own cowardice? (*An Apology*, [B4r])

Both Nashe and Heywood in these passages emphasize the morally upright matter that is portrayed onstage and the "as if" quality of the tragedian within his character. Dramatic form is relegated to a secondary position, responsible for its vividness and appeal. Theatre, in other words, does exactly what "worm-eaten" encyclopedic texts do, but better than they do it.

It was the antitheatrical writers who most quickly recognized that the theatre would be hard to critique on the basis of its content alone and that, surprisingly, "for some subjects, playgoing itself could be as disruptive of established social relations as watching the most iconoclastic drama."[20] Rather than concentrating on the "man Personated," in other words, who might well be virtuous, they called attention to the much more questionable "Personator." The very distance between the two served Stephen Gosson in 1582 as evidence against the possibility of a truly didactic theatre: "If any goodness were to be learned at Plays, it is likely that the Players themselves, which commit every syllable to memory, should profit most . . . but the daily experience of their behavior showeth that they reap no profit by the discipline themselves."[21] Even the best-behaved audience threatened numerous social conventions merely by attending plays, mingling classes and genders in a single, minimally hierarchized space of the theatre, a fact reflected in the concentration of the antitheatrical writers from Gosson onwards mainly on the theatre's form and practices in the broadest sense – cross-dressing, dissembling, unbridled speaking, and even the idleness or rowdiness of its audiences. Philip Stubbes turns the humanist defenses of a didactic theatre on their head in *The Anatomy of Abuses* (1583):

> whereas you say there are good Examples to be learned in ["Plays or Enterludes"], truly so there are: if you will learn falsehood; if you will learn cozenage; if you will learn to deceive; if you will learn to play the Hypocrite, to cog, lie, and falsify; if you will learn to jest, laugh, and fleer, to grin, to nod, and mow; if you will learn to play the vice, to swear, tear, and blaspheme both heaven and earth; if you will learn to become a bawd, unclean, and to devirginate maids, to deflower honest wives; if you will learn to murther, slay, kill, pick, steal, rob and rove; if you will learn to rebel against Princes, to commit treasons, to consume treasures, to practice idleness, to sing and talk of bawdy love and venery . . .[22]

The education that Stubbes foresees is a kind of schooling in the worst sorts of behavior, but significantly it comes as much from watching the audience as from watching the actors. "Falsehood" may be the province of the actors, but "cozenage" sounds like it could take place on either side of the stage. The blaspheming, lying, and sexual misconduct that Stubbes warns against are frequently mentioned as threats to playgoers, since the gathered crowds concealed pickpockets and ruffians, and the enclosed spaces in the galleries or the inns where performances were sometimes held presented opportunities for trysts or rapes – or so at least it was claimed. For Stubbes, then, the actual practices of staging plays added to their threat; these could not be forestalled simply by presenting a moralizing story. Like Stubbes, other antitheatrical writers, with their interest in the bad behavior of spectators, also tend to present a more vivid view of early modern theatre practices than their idealizing, protheatrical counterparts, who are often content to assert the vague moral uplift that viewers got from the plays they saw.

Protheatrical writers too, though, express considerable, and understandable, interest in the problems posed to interpretation by an audience and an actor. John Marston took a positive view of this difference, or at least could see how to exploit it; in the introduction printed with *The Fawn* (1606), he admonishes his readers that "Comedies are writ to be spoken, not read: remember the life of these things consists in action," and to excuse any thinness of plot or character their reading reveals as the fault of their choice of medium.[23] The first edition of John Webster's *The White Devil* (1612) opens with a note "To The Reader" that explains that one reason for publication in print was an incompetent audience for the first performances:

> it was acted, in so dull a time of winter, presented in so open and black a theatre, that it wanted (that which is the only grace and setting out of a tragedy) a full and understanding

auditory: and that since that time I have noted, most of the people that come to that playhouse, resemble those ignorant asses (who visiting stationers' shops, their use is not to inquire for good books, but new books) I present it to the general view with this confidence . . .[24]

When Webster blames the setting together with the audience for his play's poor reception, he is close to acknowledging that the theatre is not simply a text but a web of experiences which generate a new kind of cognition. Webster focuses, though, on the limitations of his audience and finally likens the bad playgoers to bad readers, remaining within an essentially humanist view of the theatre – the printed text is presented as the ideal form of the play. Except for the unusual vividness that it was given credit for having, the theatre functions, apparently, in the same way as a written text, Nashe's "worm-eaten books."

The dedicatory epistle prefaced to Francis Beaumont's *The Knight of the Burning Pestle* (1613; performed 1607?) similarly confesses the play's bad reception, and credits it to an inability of the audience, "who, for want of judgment, or not understanding the privy mark of irony about it (which showed it was no offspring of any vulgar brain) utterly rejected it." The edition, the epistle tells us, is published in the hopes of remedying their mistaking, and the publisher adds, "if it be slighted or traduced, it hopes his father will beget a younger brother, who shall revenge his quarrel and challenge the world either of fond and merely literal interpretation or illiterate misprision."[25] Something outside the simple opposition of "literal interpretation" and "illiterate misprision" is required to understand the play properly, something that stands between them – something literate but not literal. But the concern for misprision is not confined to such late and self-reflexive works as *Troilus and Cressida* or *The Knight of the Burning Pestle*; misprision and misinterpretation are connected with the theatre very early. The ongoing connection of the theatre with such misprision, willful or otherwise, is almost ludicrously overdetermined. The diction used by early playwrights and playgoers insistently suggest the theatre's indeterminacy, where, as John Lyly observes in the prologue to *Midas* (1590), "Time hath confounded our minds, our minds the matter," and what was formerly neatly compartmentalized has become what he calls a "gallimaufrey" of social classes, prejudices, ages, and genders poured together to behold the performance of a "mingle-mangle" that, in its confusion, mirrors the "hodgepodge" world.[26] It was this that most clearly distinguished the performed play from a written text, which was assumed among more educated readers to follow the pattern of writing and remain in some sense the author's property, and under his control. From early on it was clear that the theatre would need to rely on other than purely discursive tools to ensure clear and proper communication.

This uncertainty built in to performance, echoing the anxiety of More and Vives about a self-conscious theatre, stands as a counter-position to the dominant humanist assurance of the controllability of the theatre, represented by, for instance, Elyot, Camillo, or Bodin. But in accord with this dominant strain of understanding theatre, writers who observe the uncertainty tied up in the production of plays link it to a specific failure to mirror reality on the part of the actor or the audience. These two co-participants – the two that most decisively separate a performed play from a read playtext – are treated in these discussions as *external* to the truth of the play proper, which is the printed text and ultimately the product of the writer's "brain" (Beaumont, Epistle, *Knight of the Burning Pestle*). In spite of the actual conditions of production, the truth of the play in this way of thinking is its concept, prior to being translated into the accidents of time, place, action, and experience. In this light, actor and audience are seen as contingent elements that foil both the attempt of a writer to reflect things as they really are, and the assumption that with proper discipline to actors and watchers, such errors can be eliminated. This is the same project as that of Camillo or Gessner, but now carried out in a literal space of performance.

Certainly the most famous statement of this assumption that error can be tied to the misprision of the producers is Hamlet's advice to the players who visit Elsinore:

Suit the action to the word, the word to the action, with this special observance, that you o'erstep not the modesty of nature. For anything so o'erdone is from the purpose of playing, whose end, both at first and now, was and is to hold as 'twere the mirror up to nature; to show virtue her feature, scorn her own image, and the very age and body of the time his form and pressure. (*Hamlet*, 3. 2. 17–24)

So familiar is this description of what happens in a theatre, often even treated as Shakespeare's own theatrical manifesto, that it requires careful glossing. The most salient feature of Hamlet's "purpose of playing" is a kind of mimetic realism, the long-standing likening of the theatre to a mirror, but this realism is itself subordinated to a conception of humanist decorum – even the famous metaphor of the theatre as a mirror is carefully qualified with a coy "as 'twere." What makes Hamlet's idea of the theatre mirror-like is his insistence on the elision of all incongruous elements, whether those are pitifully ambitious clowns who speak outside their parts, actors who roar like the products of nature's journeymen, or simply a lack of dovetailing between word and gesture. Such insistence on the uniformity of the stage is supported by and simultaneously ensures a single and eternal "purpose of playing," holding good at all times and in all situations – "the purpose," rather than merely *a* purpose, "both at first and now." This double interest in decorum and the exact duplication of reality comes together in the charge to "o'erstep not the modesty of nature," where an inherent natural appropriateness ensures that any exact copy will at the same time be a suitably decorous one. Hamlet's "purpose," unsurprisingly, is the humanist idea of a theatre we saw in More and Vives, which portrayed the theatre as an exact representation of the world, and therefore as educational and non-self-reflexive. The concept of decorum itself is a kind of inscription of the expected (the literally normal) as the inevitable, so that any particular slave or old man must act like all other slaves or old men. What Hamlet primarily wishes the players to understand is the point made also by Udall and Jonson, that there is a single meaning that they as its actors are responsible not for producing or embodying, but rather for not contaminating.

At the same time, though, Hamlet expresses another, seemingly unrelated component to his single "purpose," a desire to produce discernible effects in the world that will become more central as he devises his trap to catch the conscience of the king. What is not clear is how Hamlet imagines his decorous, specular theatre will be able to produce these real effects, since it is itself bound to duplication – Hamlet has already dismissed from his theatre whatever deviates from an original. By the time he speaks these words, Hamlet has already significantly distinguished his own theatrical interests from the wild and uncontrollable Termagants and Herods of earlier performance, with its traditions of actorial innovation. The players are explicitly enjoined from such improvised and changeable action; instead, they must "speak not more than is set down for them . . . ," for Hamlet "would have such a fellow whipped for o'erdoing Termagant. It out-Herods Herod. Pray you avoid it" (3. 2. 13–14). Even Hamlet's professed concern with an apparently single and timeless "purpose of playing" suggests a shift away from the irreducibly plural occasionality and situatedness, the affiliation to context, of earlier drama.

In another oft-cited comment on playing, Theseus in *A Midsummer Night's Dream* observes of players that "the best in this kind are but shadows, and the worst are no worse if imagination amend them" (5. 1. 210–11). In comparison with Theseus' lofty dismissal of drama as mere entertainment, Hamlet's reference to the players as "the chronicles and brief abstracts of the time" and his physical language of molding with "form and pressure" the "very age and body of the time" puts him firmly in the humanist camp of More, which took theatre seriously enough to worry about it. It is clear from Hamlet's advice to the players, as well as from his attempt to rewrite his own history with "The Mousetrap," that he imagines the theatre to have an educational effect through its mirroring of nature. But in spite of the pointedly topical discussions of what is occurring in the world of the theatre that surround Hamlet's advice – the rise of the children's acting companies, or (perhaps) the departure of the irrepressible clown Will Kemp from Shakespeare's company, for instance – Hamlet also speaks of theatre as a timeless phenomenon, a mirror that reflects but does not distort or even interrupt. Moreover, Hamlet does not seem to be aware that in the few lines in which he insists on *one* purpose of playing, he describes two that are not only distinct, but incompatible. The relation of theatres to the world is complicated by the ways they simultaneously connect to what surrounds them and deny any direct connection to their circumstances. The "purpose of playing" is, according to Hamlet, itself uniform and unvarying in its conveyance of a single determinable message, and it relies on the players subordinating their own understandings and "ambition," everything that might individuate or contextualize their performance, to its single purpose, which Hamlet presents as an overdetermined synthesis of naturalness, decorum, and textual fidelity. But there is a remarkable degree of incoherence here, as Hamlet insists on a theatre that is both reflective and active – is theatre, or should it be, a copy of reality or an intervention in it?

This contradiction in the very terms with which theatre could be handled forced a kind of conceptual fuzziness on those, like Hamlet, who tried to describe theatre from a humanist standpoint. In spite of Hamlet's insistence on a single coherent "purpose of playing," and much closer to the double business that he actually demands of it, Hamlet expects the theatre to represent the present and at the same time to intervene in it. Thus the solution, so to speak, embraced by Hamlet is to see the perfect representation of an event as having an effect not just similar to, but in fact indistinguishable from, the event itself. Neither fully reflection nor interference, the copy's fidelity to the original must be such that its viewers respond to its re-production as true, indeed that they confirm its truth by the expression of their own secret truths:

> I have heard
> That guilty creatures sitting at a play
> Have by the very cunning of the scene
> Been struck so to the soul that presently
> They have proclaimed their malefactions. (*Hamlet*, 2. 2. 584–87)

Hamlet's assumptions are again less obvious than the familiarity of this passage suggests. His "Mousetrap" for Claudius is consistent with the humanist mirror-theory of the stage of his advice to the players. It is clear that he is drawing on the same paradigm for a good theatre as Nashe and Heywood earlier, where a staged action, seen necessarily as the repetition of some prior, original, and inherently meaningful event, elicits a response similar to the response elicited by the event itself. Nashe's and Heywood's English heroes prompt imitation in the English audience, "as if the Personator were the man Personated," and so, ideally, will Hamlet's play.

Hamlet, in short, wants to do what he can to recreate his own vision of the ghost for his uncle, using what he identifies as the mirror-like quality of the stage to force in Claudius a purely reflective – and, equally important, an unself-reflexive – response. Abandoning the ability to dissemble the real past that he shows in his first speech to the court, Claudius will respond to the enacted event as if it were real. The force of the play depends on its exact duplication of the original murder scene in its essence (leaving curiously open what it might mean to capture an event's essence – the mode of death is apparently part of it, but not the relation of the murderer to the victim), while leaving its contingent details open to change. Interestingly, Hamlet's plan here reverses the order of the stage and the audience, suggesting further the exactness of the mirroring implied. The reflection is so close that actor and audience may almost change sides. Where More and Vives – and Hamlet's earlier advice to the players – insisted on actors who responded without self-consciousness, Hamlet here imagines an absolutely un-self-conscious Claudius, one who cannot or will not think, but only react, one who will unthinkingly betray himself at the sight of his misdeed. Theatre is the medium by which Hamlet's knowledge about his father's death will be put into effect – in this case, an anticipated reaction by Claudius. What in other works for the stage was cast as purely verbal assurance becomes itself a kind of experience with its own authority, like that of Gessner's images, by reproducing the original event of the father's murder. Hamlet's play tests the truth of the ghost's claim by displaying it. As in Udall's interlude or Jonson's later masque, Hamlet expects the authority of telling to be subordinated to the experience of seeing – and as in these other works, Hamlet believes that showing something is akin to the truth devoid of tricks of speech like particular names, relations, and so on. In the act, though, what happens is that talking and seeing do not combine into a single truth, but open up a refractory matrix of possible meanings. Like the characters in earlier plays and interludes, the play imagined by Hamlet is intended to provide proof of its own accuracy, but now as something known because it is (again) experienced.

It is easy to imagine what Hamlet is hoping for. It is again the ideal of the controllable, educational theatre, the theatre that is bookish because it is also wholly defensible against misprision. Thomas Heywood reports a similar situation in his *Apology for Actors* (1612) as evidence that the theatre teaches by repeating and displaying prior experiences. I quote it in its entirety because of its curious fullness of detail and the density of its allusions to contemporary drama:

What can sooner print modesty in the souls of the wanton, than by discovering unto them the monstrousness of their sin? It follows that we prove these exercises to have been the discoverers of many notorious murders, long concealed from the eyes of the world. To omit all far-fetched instances, we will prove it by a domestic, and home-born truth, which within these few years happened. At Lynn in Norfolk, the then Earl of Sussex' players acting the old History of Friar Francis, and presenting a woman, who insatiately doting on a young gentleman, had (the more securely to enjoy his affection) mischievously and secretly murdered her husband, whose ghost haunted her, and at divers times in her most solitary and private contemplations, in most horrid and fearful shapes, appeared and stood before her. As this was acted, a townswoman (till then of good estimation and report) finding her conscience (at this presentment) extremely troubled, suddenly screeched and cried out Oh my husband, my husband! I see the ghost of my husband fiercely threatening and menacing me. At which shrill and unexpected outcry, the people about her, moved to a strange amazement, inquired the reason of her clamor, when presently un-urged, she told them, that seven years ago, she, to be possessed of such a Gentleman (meaning him) had poisoned her husband, whose fearful image personated itself in the shape of that ghost: whereupon the murderess was apprehended, before the Justices further examined, and by voluntary confession after condemned. (*An Apology*, Gv–G2v)

Heywood's account is grounded rhetorically as a real history of nearby and familiar places – a "home-born truth" set in "Lynn in Norfolk" "within these few years" – with an exactness of detail that suggests reference or remembrance rather than retelling. Not surprisingly, though, local records reveal no such confessions were ever made or murderers ever tried.[27] Like Hamlet's play within a play, Heywood's account is an explanatory fiction rather than a sociological record of actual audience responses; it deals with ideas of the theatre rather than theatre's practices and what the theatre *means* rather than what it *does*. Heywood's example, half the ghost from *Hamlet* and half the ghost from *Macbeth*, reveals a belief in a kind of automatic reaction to what is represented on stage that is ultimately not far removed from humanist didacticism. The play's effects on the viewer are in each case calculated as if they were directly referential to and purely reflective of the real world they press against but are absolutely distinct from; whether good precepts or bad practices are staged, they have predictable effects on the crowd.

In "The Mousetrap," Hamlet is counting on Claudius to have a similarly automatic response to seeing the murder re-enacted before him. The metatheatrical elements that twentieth-century critics have found so attractive in this and other Elizabethan plays within plays are in fact minimalized in this particular play. Rather than disturbing the relation between theatre and reality, Hamlet's play, in both his theory and the actual practice of it, serves to reinforce them. The play recreates an event that is past, but leaves that event untouched – unresolved, unrevised, merely mirrored back in such a way that the play cannot be confused with the murder, but can only confirm it. Hamlet wishes to occupy the middle ground between mirror and intervention, to create an intervention-as-mirror, or a mirror-as-confirmation-of-a-story, but his attempt produces (for Claudius, at least) an entirely new experience, an event that grows out of the past but does not reproduce it. For Hamlet, too, the play is a turning point (it leads directly to his interview with Gertrude, Polonius' murder, and Hamlet's exile) but not because it reflects the past. Instead, it recreates something related but altogether new in the present. It is the continuation of history as the sequence of events following one another, not an imaginary recursion to some prior point and recovery of some certainty of what is now lost with time.

Hamlet seems convinced after seeing the play, confident enough in his dramaturgy to link himself imaginatively to those who make the stage their profession: "Would not this, sir . . . get me a fellowship in a cry of players? . . .

O good Horatio, I'll take the ghost's word for a thousand pound!" (3. 2. 269–81). But to Horatio, the play within a play yields much less solid proof than Hamlet seems to believe; the performance is worth only "half a share" of a theatre company. What Hamlet has based his optimism on is apparently his dumbshow of a man pouring poison into a king's ear and taking his crown. It is the only event in the play that particularizes the otherwise nameless crime, but it leaves Claudius completely unmoved. He storms out only after the murder is repeated with words in the play proper. Hamlet's rational meaning- and knowledge-producing mimesis escapes his control and begins to produce the knowledge in the wrong places. It bothers Claudius not at all to see an anonymous king poisoned by an anonymous man; he stands up when he discovers that the murderer is "one Lucianus, nephew to the king" (3. 2. 248) – Hamlet's relation to Claudius.[28]

Claudius pays attention not to the supposed truth of what he is shown, but to the trick that language plays on Hamlet – linking him as another "nephew to the king" to the character of the murderer and thus also, indirectly, to Claudius.[29] The truth of the scene, this suggests, lies not in the supposedly unambiguous showing of the things themselves, but in the doubleness of language that Udall and Jonson had worked to expose as deceitful and, more importantly, clarifiable. Claudius reads the play not, as Hamlet had hoped, as a passive spectator, but as another actively interpreting participant, like Hamlet himself. While the play within a play produces knowledge in Claudius, the play *Hamlet* as a whole also shows Hamlet falling prey to the confusion that he sought to stand outside and in control of; he gets caught, in a sense, in his own "Mousetrap." During the play, Hamlet responds only to information that he himself has inserted into it; twice he responds to lines in which the Player Queen vows never to remarry, once with an aside about its bitterness ("wormwood") and once by asking Gertrude rather pointedly how she is enjoying the show (3. 2. 184, 232). His conviction that he is learning something from the play by analyzing the reactions of the viewers appears to be mistaken. Rather, he is reacting to the vivid objectification of his own confused desires on the stage.

If Hamlet sees the play as producing knowledge of the real world, though, none of the other onlookers seem to think of it as more than an entertainment. It is in fact because he is *not* looking for truths in the play that Claudius can recognize Hamlet's desire in it instead of his own. The exchange between Hamlet and Claudius before the start of the play within a play that I have chosen as this chapter's epigraph is emblematic, a mad bit of banter that captures this play's concern with reliable witnessing, reporting, and performing. In these lines, Hamlet believes that, like the humanist author of an encyclopedic theatre, he can control his words. What he says here, but will not know until later, is that words cannot be controlled – they belong to no one. Likewise, as I have been arguing, Hamlet's theatre shows that vision is deceptive as well, since the scene amply demonstrates that each of the viewers – skeptical Gertrude, baffled Ophelia, dismissive Polonius, Claudius, Horatio, Hamlet himself – responds very differently to what they see. A play within a play may confuse the distinction between theatre and reality, but if this confusion is represented as purposeful and under the control of a character who stages it then it is contained and framed – re-staged, in fact. The moment of reflexive self-consciousness may in fact be only partial and thus scarcely a confusion or disturbance at all, but a gesture of stability. This assumption of authorial control over the play event is, of course, a highly contestable one, as I have tried to suggest, and the ascription of blame to ignorant audiences or errant actors was one way to secure it in the face of evidence. One may also think of how Hamlet's play fails to tell him what he wants, but says something completely different, or of the painfully inept play in *A Midsummer Night's Dream*, which comments on and criticizes Theseus' own pursuit of love as well as his critical abilities. For both these theatrical producers, the idea of directorial control is not realized in the event of the play, but only reveals their desires for particular kinds of control over meaning. As readers or audience of Hamlet's play, we are put into the same unsettled situation as Hamlet – our supposedly privileged and distanced viewpoint on the action before us does not secure our understanding of it.

In performance, of course, the univocality of the theatre imagined by Nicholas Udall, Ben Jonson, or Hamlet proved harder to secure. Nearly as much effort was spent by playwrights protesting that they could not be responsible for the misinterpretations of their plays by ignorant or captious audiences as by antitheatricalists insisting that the theatre had direct and harmful effects and rendered the innocent viewer liable to vicious interpretations. Most often, though, the scapegoat for these errant interpretations was the actor. Hamlet's proposal that the players "Suit the action to the word, the word to the action" and that the clowns "speak not more than is set down for them" is, as Robert Weimann has argued, a historically particular one – to reduce the whole panoply of the actor to the supposedly univocal control of the text. Traditions from the earlier years of the professional theatre like jigging after the play, scripts calling for improvised scenes, jest-books claiming to preserve Richard Tarlton's repartee, and even the weeping of the leading actor for Hecuba all suggest something of the richness of the actors' resources that Hamlet forestalls. But not only Hamlet was concerned about clowns speaking outside their parts. In 1537 the Duke of Suffolk complained to Thomas Cromwell that the player playing Husbandry in "A play, which play was of a king, how he should rule his Realm" wandered from "the book of the play" in order to abuse some of the gentlemen watching.[30] A certain level of audience abuse was to be expected in moralities; what made this play objectionable to Suffolk was its unscriptedness, and presumably the fact that because unscripted, it seemed to touch its hearers much more directly than a line that needed to be spoken because it was in the book. Robert Weimann also recovers substantial evidence in early English theatre for a mode of self-expression among players, in which the part was temporarily set aside while the actor spoke in his own voice as an actor; this is the self-consciousness that Vives and More found so worrying. Actual performance thus followed the imaginary theatre and the encyclopedia in attempting to regulate the actor: the more visible the actor, the more threatening, because in every case his visibility distorts the material by drawing attention from it to himself.[31]

The relation of the actor to the textual play – of *drama* to *theatre* in my earlier formulation – is the relation of self-expression to representation. To enforce particular meanings, as Hamlet attempts, meant to reduce the actor's part to a purely reflective one where he could only repeat some authorized text, and further to ensure that what was represented was morally and legally acceptable. To ban or limit certain statements through censorship, whether through the Office of the Revels prior to production or through penalties after it, was of course the easiest kind of control available to the legal authorities, though even this was by no means certain, since an actor might always "speak outside" the censored book. But this kind of censorship of text also suggests, along with Jonson's and Udall's dramatic scripts, More's and Vives' critical evaluations, and Camillo's and Gessner's "theatres," that interpretation was ultimately controllable by controlling what was written – as if books alone were the nerve center and source of meaning for a performance, with actor and audience as mere accidents. Weimann's argument about the inherent doubleness of the actor's voice and gesture is more radical: that the very means of representation in the theatre, divided among text or plot, actorial innovation, and audience reception, ensure that no single meaning can ever be securely delimited. To control a script or even a gesture was one thing, but to control the audience's understandings of the actor's self-expressive parts, and more broadly its interpretation of even validated representations, was another thing entirely. Lest the narrative of a play become confused in production, medieval dramas had often fenced it in by licensed interpreters – doctors, prophets, and the like (to whom, one could add, Vincent of Beauvais' *Actor* is roughly homologous) – who would explain to the audience what they should be seeing. There is in the plays, of course, a great deal else to see, which is precisely why these glosses are necessary. Their presence does not prevent an audience from forming other interpretations, but it does demand that an audience forming them recognize them as errant and unauthorized. What effect this recognition has remains open to question.

Just as the humanist conception of the theatre carried with it a disregard for actorly intervention, and in fact included a built-in scapegoating mechanism (the errant clowns in *Hamlet* and the errant audience of *The White Devil* are equally cast as ignorant, and straying from written authority is increasingly guarded against during this period) to explain the occurrence of misprision, it also made use of a limit case that defined the other extreme to which it could be carried. This was imitation so perfect that it confused itself with reality – another form of error, in which the represented became the real. As he did with its good double of confession-inducing mimesis, Thomas Heywood again provides an apt example of this anxiety:

> Julius Caesar himself for his pleasure became an Actor, being in shape, state, voice, judgment, and all other occurents excellent. Amongst many other parts acted by him in person, it is recorded of him that with general applause in his own Theatre he played *Hercules Furens*, and amongst many other arguments of his compleatness, excellence, and extraordinary care in his action, it is thus reported of him: being in the depth of a passion, one of his servants (as his part then fell out) presenting Lychas, who before had from Deianeira brought him the poisoned shirt, dipped in the blood of the Centaur Nessus: he in the midst of his torture and fury, finding this Lychas hid in some remote corner (appointed him to creep into of purpose) although he was, as our Tragedians use, but seemingly to kill him by some false imagined wound, yet was Caesar so extremely carried away with the violence of his practiced fury, and by the perfect shape of the madness of Hercules, to which he had fashioned all his active spirits, that he slew him dead at his foot, and after swung him *terque quaterque* (as the Poet says) about his head. (*An Apology*, E3v)

Here Heywood's play out of history provides a contrast to the more wholesome English versions that he and Nashe discuss, the bloody forays against the French of Talbot and Henry V which, reproduced on stage, inspire imitation from good Englishmen. As Katherine Eisaman Maus has observed, such imitation is imagined to depend on some real similarity between represented action and audience that allows for an identification to take place.[32] Julius Caesar is still admirable – he is no deranged Nero, another famous imperial performer with a much less positive reputation. Heywood makes it clear that he understands this transgression as an unfortunately lethal instance of "compleatness" and "excellence." But Caesar is also threatening; in his response to Heywood, John Greene observes that "it's not unlikely but a player might do the like now, as often they have done" (*A Refutation*, 28). The force of his performance is not just an example to his modern audience of readers, but an intervention into reality in his own time.

The paradigmatic instance of this confusion of staged and real action is Thomas Kyd's *The Spanish Tragedy* (c.1586), one of the earliest revenge tragedies. Kyd's play possessed admirable staying power, remaining a standard in the repertoire for almost fifty years, and is often regarded as the first play in the family line of Marlowe and Shakespeare. Like *Hamlet*, *The Spanish Tragedy* features a character who turns to a play to satisfy his desire for revenge. Hieronimo, the protagonist, is a Spanish courtier and apparently a regular maker of masques for the court (he is asked twice during the play to produce a masque for a festivity, and seems to have a script ready for the second one). Hieronimo's son, Horatio, is murdered by two other courtiers – Lorenzo, the king's nephew and the brother of Horatio's lover, Bel-Imperia, and Balthazar, who loves Bel-Imperia as well. Hieronimo goes intermittently mad with grief and frustration because he cannot get justice at court; when he is finally approached by Lorenzo and Balthazar to write a masque to celebrate Balthazar's engagement to Bel-Imperia, he agrees provided that the four of them will be the actors. The masque – which takes its title from an earlier play, probably also Kyd's, *Solimon and Perseda* – has as its plot the story of a king who murders a lower-ranking rival in order to win the woman they both love. As with Hamlet and *The Murder of Gonzago*, Hieronimo selects a play that comes suspiciously close to the recent events of his own life, in which a member of the ruling family murders a man of lower rank in order to seize the subordinate's beloved. Hieronimo takes his play in a different direction from Hamlet, though: rather than tampering with the plot to make it closer to the event of his son's murder, Hieronimo leaves the connection between play and reality tantalizingly oblique. In fact, he further distances the action of the play from the events of his life by translating the tragedy into foreign languages, so that every character speaks his or her part in a different tongue:

> Each one of us must act his part
> In unknown languages,
> That it may breed the more variety:
> As you, my lord, in Latin, I in Greek,
> You in Italian; and, for because I know
> That Bel-Imperia hath practiced the French,
> In courtly French shall all her phrases be.[33]

I will discuss the more particular effects of Hieronimo's babel of tongues later. Here I want to examine the startling directness of the mimesis of reality that Hieronimo hits upon.

In terms of the mirroring of reality in drama, Hieronimo substitutes a much more direct similarity for the mimesis of Hamlet or even of that suggested by Nashe and Heywood. In the tragedy, he casts Lorenzo and Balthazar as actors in the play, rivals for the part played by Bel-Imperia, and then murders the two men who murdered his son while their fathers watch on, unaware of Hieronimo's murderous designs. In his tragedy, Hieronimo secretly replaces the props with real daggers. Thus when the script requires that he and Bel-Imperia, whom he has informed of the plan, kill the characters played by Lorenzo and Balthazar, their characters die in the play in fiction, but the actors Lorenzo and Balthazar die as well in actuality. Standing over their (in fact) dead bodies,

Hieronimo proclaims his dramatic production's difference from what is expected and required from the didactic theatre:

> Haply you think, but bootless are your thoughts,
> That this is fabulously counterfeit,
> And that we do as all tragedians do:
> To die today, for fashioning our scene
> The death of Ajax, or some Roman peer,
> And in a minute starting up again,
> Revive to please to-morrow's audience.
> No, princes . . . (4. 4. 76–83)

In Hieronimo's unexpected finale, there is no distance between representation and presentation, the copying of an original event and the display of one that can replace it. The distance between actors and audience assumed by Hamlet is collapsed.

The shocking violence of Hieronimo's tragedy seems to possess the bracing freakishness of a snuff film. In fact, though, the eruption of the play-world into the real world in the form of murder is a recurrent cultural fantasy, or nightmare, and a regular part of the furniture of Elizabethan and Jacobean drama virtually from the opening of the theatres to their closure during the reign of Charles I. In the latest of these deadly plays, *The Roman Actor*, Philip Massinger draws, like Heywood, on the tradition that Roman emperors at times really murdered their fellow actors.[34] This fantasy of playing murder and death in the theatre is not, in other words, an aberration, but a linchpin in the collective thinking of the early modern theatre. Humanist ideas of mimesis as a mirror and as a preparation for real action required this apparent perversion of performance as a necessary obverse of the good, controlled mimesis they imagined. In Kyd's play, educational drama opens to reveal mimesis to infinity, collapsing or swelling into the reality – the final real, where Personator and Personated are no different – of death.

Hieronimo's insistence on the difference between the plot of his play of feigned death and that of his "latest tale" of real murder conceals a much more pronounced similarity. Both his theatre and Hamlet's are predicated on the idea of an exact copy of reality; in Hieronimo's case, that copy has come so close to the original as to be able to serve as its substitute. The reception of an earlier masque that Hieronimo writes for the King of Spain and the Portuguese ambassador after the Spanish have just defeated the Portuguese provides a kind of model for a successful didactic production. It is a simple dumbshow: three knights with shields walk across the stage and hang them up. The king's response shows him to be an ideal audience for this kind of educational presentation, delighted and eager to learn:

> Hieronimo, this masque contents mine eye,
> Although I sound not well the mystery. (1. 4. 138–39)

It is also a straightforward demonstration to Kyd's audience of the naive playwriting that Kyd is pointedly leaving behind, in which characters cheerfully announce their psychological and emotional states for the edification of the audience. Hieronimo explains that each of the knights represents a semi-legendary English king, two of whom conquered Portugal and the last, Spain. The king and the ambassador then draw the appropriate ethical conclusions – the Portuguese should not feel shame because they have been defeated in war before; the Spanish should not grow too proud because so have they.[35] The theatre, this masque and its reception suggest, is dark, but interpretable with the proper key; its purpose is explicitly and directly didactic, aimed toward a specific audience. Appropriately for such decorous metatheatre, the levels of reality here remain neatly in place – the function of the play (here the play within the play) is to instruct the viewers outside it (here the King of Spain and the Portuguese ambassador).

This is the viewers' relation to *The Spanish Tragedy* as well – its meaning is presented initially as being dark, but ultimately discoverable. The play begins with the entrance of the ghost of Andrea, a friend of Hieronimo's son, and Revenge personified, who both sit on the stage during the play and watch the performance. Andrea has been dishonorably slain in battle and has been brought back to view the aftermath of his death in the community of the Spanish court, which includes his friends and rivals, his fiancée, and his killer, who was captured after the battle. At the end of every act, Andrea demands to know why his requested revenge is not working the way he has imagined. He is repeatedly assured by Revenge that everything will come to a satisfactory conclusion. Andrea serves as a model for the actual theatre audience. He is invited to sit on the stage by Revenge as part of an explicitly theatrical experience:

> Here sit we down to see the mystery,
> And serve as Chorus in this tragedy . . . (1. 1. 90f.)

The last lines of the performance, spoken by Revenge over the bodies of the dead as he descends into Hell, return to the same apparently metatheatrical theme:

> . . . though death hath end[ed] their misery,
> I'll there begin their endless tragedy. (4. 5. 47f.)

From the first, the actions of the play thus present it as already staged, already a play. In a sense, the perversion of theatre represented by Hieronimo is only a logical corollary to the humanist idea of theatre as reflection. A perfect copy cannot be distinguished from its original; a perfect play, then, becomes, at its limit, indistinguishable from reality and identical to experience itself. Significantly, not just any experience is chosen as the exemplar of this crossing over from stage to reality. In the deadly masque that Hieronimo stages, meaning is replaced by violence, as the representation of murder is replaced by its reality. Violence and death are treated as irreducibly unequivocal events; they are themselves impossible to interpret or make sense of, but at the same time they do not require any interpretation and so provide a contrast to the confusion of tongues, or the inexplicable performance, of the masque. Death itself becomes a kind of semiotic, and although the foreign languages of the tragedy may never be comprehensible to the onlookers, death communicates its hard message universally.[36] At the same time, at least for Hieronimo, death escapes complete translation into any other form. His son's death drives him outside of rational speech into madness; his revenge remains equally inexplicable. When at the tragedy's end Hieronimo announces, "Here break we off our sundry languages/And thus conclude I in our vulgar tongue" (4. 5. 74–75), he reveals that there is another vernacular in addition to the spoken one – the vernacular of violence. The multiple languages, which can be (and in the printed edition are) translated into a more readily understandable form, serve as a pale shadowing of the final incomprehensibility of the onstage murders, which find no equivalent in our speech. Death serves as the real not only for Hieronimo, who is baffled when the king of Spain and newly arrived king of Portugal fail to comprehend what they have just seen, but for Kyd himself as the designer of the largest frame in the play. More exactly, the dead body stands in, in the cultural context of the Elizabethan theatre, for the one thing that, although it is repeatedly invoked, cannot be completely feigned; an actor playing dead still breathes and stirs.[37]

While the characters Hamlet and Hieronimo are each responding, in different ways, to a humanist ideal of educational and encyclopedic drama, the plays within which they appear provide a critical stance that mediates between the equivalent extremes of Hamlet's mirror view of theatre and Hieronimo's frightening and absurd double. *The Spanish Tragedy* in particular uses Hieronimo's two masques to develop an alternative, if not fully enunciated, theory of how the theatre can take effect. The tragedy that Hieronimo stages later at the request of Balthazar and Lorenzo, as well as the larger framing device of Andrea and Revenge, gets much of its significance from the way it deviates from the ideal model of the first masque. Paralleling the didactic structure of the first masque, the deadly second masque contains a hidden meaning, but one whose obscurity is produced in an extraordinarily perverse way. The first masque is obscure because wordless and emblematic – much like the humanist interludes it imitates, it presents obscurity as a problem inherent to the dramatic form, but is easily overcome by the intervention of an authorized interpreter, in this case its deviser Hieronimo. In the second masque, though, silence is replaced by a superabundance of words and languages that still fail to make sense to the viewer, and the obscurity is the result of this excess of words. Instead of stemming either from an attempt to delight and exercise the mind or from the difficulty of the material, the play's obscurity is pointedly artificial, even meaningless on the level of content. The babel of languages is there, as Hieronimo says, simply "That it may breed the more variety," and the languages are chosen in part apparently just because different actors know various tongues.

On the level of their form, however – that is, simply as foreign and incomprehensible – the obscure languages are not just an expendable absurdity, although they seem so to Balthazar, who protests, "But this will be a mere confusion,/And hardly shall we all be understood" (4. 1. 180–81). They do not conceal meaning, since what is said in the foreign languages is irrelevant to Hieronimo's revenge plot. There are none of the parallels between real and represented that typically occur in double plots or in Hamlet's play, or else they are so attenuated as to disappear. Instead, the masque's action misdirects interpretation by calling attention to itself rather than to its content. What they hide is not the sense of the words that they speak, but the fact that the deaths in the tragedy are real events. When, as after the first masque, Hieronimo is called upon to give the interpretation, he does not bother with the plot, which was a mere lure, but announces that the deaths were real; his "tongue is tuned to tell his latest tale," – which is not, notably, the tale the audience has just seen – "Not to excuse gross errors in the play" (4. 4. 85–86). In place of the plot in the tragedy, he tells of the plots around the tragedy: how his son was killed by Lorenzo and Balthazar and how he and Bel-Imperia decided to take revenge. Although Hieronimo has explained his whole revenge plot, the king continues to demand that he reveal who helped him, and Hieronimo refuses to speak. In fact Hieronimo has already told the king everything; it simply remains incomprehensible to his audience within the play.[38] With the mirror of mimetic drama cracked, it is as if the possibility of meaningful transaction has leaked away altogether. In a move more unsettling of the difference between the play and real life than the rather more predictable murders on stage, Hieronimo borrows a device from his own tragedy and pretends to conceal a meaning that does not exist:

> What lesser liberty can kings afford
> Than harmless silence? Then afford it me.
> Sufficeth, I may not, nor I will not tell thee.   (4. 4. 179–81)

When the king presses him harder, Hieronimo bites off his tongue rather than reveal that he has no secrets. Somebody suggests that he be made to write the names of his accomplices, and when he is given pen and paper, Hieronimo gestures to say that his pen is dull. He is given a penknife, with which he kills Lorenzo's father, then himself.

What Hieronimo's tragedy suggests about theatrical illusion, then, is the opposite of what his first masque does. In the second play, the performance does not conceal a hidden meaning, it hides nothing at all.[39] Mimesis, mimed in the form of the play within a play, reveals only its ability to misdirect the audience from the real events that are placed in front of them, but behind, as it were, the screen of performance. In the tragedy, the glorious indeterminacy of the confusion of tongues lures the audience to take it as an object for interpretation ("*King*: Here comes Lorenzo: look upon the plot,/And tell me brother, what part plays he?", 4. 4. 33–34) while in fact their own sons are being killed on stage. Even with real corpses, Hieronimo's drama fulfills its entertaining and its didactic functions. The real deaths of Lorenzo and Balthazar are in fact set seamlessly into the tragedy's plot, and it is almost a hundred lines after they are killed that anyone recognizes it. Hieronimo writes a theatrical piece in which reality and theatre overlap, and in which he exploits the audience's willingness – like that of Theseus in *A Midsummer Night's Dream* – to see the theatre as mere entertainment, wholly fictional: he casts the killers of his son in a tragedy and then uses the play's fiction to screen his real revenge by really killing them according to the plot. Conforming to the humanist ideal that erased the actor's share in the role as conceived by the author, Hieronimo's tragedy hides the real actions of which Hieronimo is both author and agent behind the empty role he fills as actor. The "real" actions that take place during the theatrical illusion are heterogeneous to it on the level of reality, but identical to it in terms of how they are carried out. In other words, the theatrical illusion is shown to be not a sign, as it is in the first masque, but something else – a misdirection. The pose of enlightenment and mastery staged by the play within a play is here merely a theatrical one, whether its author recognizes it or not. Hieronimo's enlightenment proves illusory when he cannot in the end explain the justice of his actions to those around him; it is only the audience in the real world that can see the sense of his actions (Altman, *Tudor Play of Mind*, 281–82). But Hieronimo achieves at least part of what he wants. The plays within plays in *Hamlet* or *A Midsummer Night's Dream* debunk the illusion of authorial control while insisting, like *The Spanish Tragedy*, on the theatre's real effects. They maintain at all times a distinction of levels within them, and the players, while acting, are never more than life-*like*.

In the interrogation scene of *The Spanish Tragedy*, though, interpretation itself becomes not merely complicit with violence, as when it is misdirected by the confusion of tongues, but in fact what incites it and makes it possible. Interpretation is here misguided; the desire to uncover all the meaning of something is shown to exceed the amount of meaning that there is. The tragedy continues after the deaths of the children because Hieronimo and the king continue to raise the stakes of understanding. In the interrogation, the king's desire to get behind the surface of the play to find its meaning is what makes Hieronimo's final acts of violence possible. The king's mistake is to see one set of theatrical signs concealing a different truth. But Hieronimo's tragedy is not a sign with a meaning figuratively *beneath* it, which explains or justifies it; it is an action with another action *beside* it, so that acting the play and acting the murder are not reducible to a single meaning. What in Shakespeare's *Hamlet* is apparently metatheatrical – the theatre's comment on itself in the mode of representing something else – is flattened out in Kyd's *Spanish Tragedy*, in which there is no clear way to separate different levels of representation. This is not metatheatre, in the usual hierarchical sense of the word, where one level frames and comments on another. This is a theatre beside itself, theatre attaching to theatre accretively, altering both levels, multiple heterogeneous strands interacting without conclusiveness.

Hieronimo's tragedy relies on a confusion, a mistaking of the boundary between play and reality as the same as that between a signifier and a signified. In leveling this difference, it enacts an idea that is the dream (or perhaps the nightmare) of the humanist ideology of the theatre – that the sign could perhaps be what it represents. It is thus motivated by the same desire that drove both hermetic magic and the Jacobean masque. It is important to recognize both the reality of this desire and that it was, precisely, a desire rather than a description of an event – despite the device of the play within a play, the recurrent trope of the murderous masque, the stories of Julius Caesar (when positively valorized) or Nero (when negative) actually killing fellow actors during performances, and even the staging of executions within theatres, people were not killed intentionally during performances in Elizabethan playhouses and everybody knew it[40] – that is, on the few instances when people were killed or injured, it was treated as an accident. The collapse of the Paris Garden during a performance in 1583 continues to appear in city documents limiting the theatre for the next two years, but always as an example of actual physical danger posed by playgoing rather than as an emblem of divine wrath.[41] In spite of its frequent appearance, the play that turns murderous is consistently represented in the sixteenth- and seventeenth-century theatre as a monstrosity, an anomaly of extreme literalism and a gross misunderstanding or abuse of the theatrical form. This error can be comic as well as tragic: the rude mechanicals in *A Midsummer Night's Dream* show their rudeness in part by worrying whether the ladies in their audience will mistake the costumed Snug for a real lion. Here, too, though, the confusion of play and reality is literally mad. *The Spanish Tragedy* is typical in the way that it presents the murderous masque as a possibility, but also distinguishes it from the theatre that the audience is watching. To confuse theatre and reality, comically or tragically, is for early modern writers always symptomatic of a disordered consciousness, whether that of a clown like Bottom, who wants to reassure the ladies that the lion's part is played by an actor, or the merchant of *The Knight of the Burning Pestle*, or of a grief-maddened avenger like Hieronimo.

In plays about deadly plays, the action is also distanced from the present of the audience by space, time, or both – crossover violence is a *Spanish* tragedy, or the concern of *Roman* actors, or in the remote and alien past of English *history* (in the anonymous *Woodstock*), but not in the present of Elizabeth's England. Further distancing the danger of the theatre that it has exposed, these plays, once they broach the possibility of violence crossing over into the audience, readily shoot over the top into the realm of campiness. The violence that is pointed out as real is simultaneously exaggerated into hyperreality, at once expanded and reduced into something emblematic. *The Spanish Tragedy* concludes with Hieronimo biting his tongue off and spitting it onto the floor, then gesturing first for a quill with which to write his confession and, then for a penknife to sharpen it, and finally, when he is given the knife, using it to stab the king's brother and himself. *The Revenger's Tragedy* (1606) includes two groups of murderous masquers simultaneously roaming the halls of the palace looking to kill the duke. The murderous play thus serves the early modern theatre as a limit case of its own power, insistently threatening but never achieved in reality. It expresses a cultural anxiety about the disturbing proximity of theatre and reality and the threat of their permeability while at the same time distancing it. Such theatre is presented as just possible – but not now, not here, not like this.[42] The problem posed by Hamlet's mirror of nature, consciously or unconsciously, remains: a play can either reflect reality or intervene in it – but the latter possibility is presented as impossible, at best a fantasy, at worst a nightmare. *The Spanish Tragedy* concisely spells out the anxiety or the desire for this kind of collapse of theatre and world, and in so doing accurately represents one aspect of this relation.

Thomas Heywood's *Apology for Actors* provides a corrective view to both Hamlet and Hieronimo's theatres. As I have indicated, Heywood raises the theatrical possibilities both of Hamlet's oblique pressure and of Hieronimo's more direct intervention. The overt argument of Heywood's *Apology* is the usual didactic defense of the theatre (e.g. "What can sooner print modesty in the souls of the wanton, than by discovering unto them the monstrousness of their sin?", Gv). Jonas Barish observes that Heywood shares the belief in the affective power of playgoing with his antitheatrical opponents, but does no more than invert their arguments that the theatre corrupts its viewers (*Antitheatrical Prejudice*, 117–21). In support of this Hamlet-like faith in the power of reflection, though, Heywood adds a strangely aberrant example. A group of players were putting on a show late at night in a town in Cornwall. Unbeknownst to them, a group of Spaniards had made a landing nearby to capture the town,

> when suddenly, even upon their entrance, the players (ignorant as the townsmen of such attempt) presenting a battle on the stage with their drum and trumpets struck up a loud alarm: which the enemy hearing, and fearing they were discovered, amazedly retired, made some few idle shot in a bravado, and so in a hurly-burly fled disordered to their boats. (*An Apology*, G2r)

Alerted by the noise, "the townsmen were immediately armed, and pursued them to the sea, praising God for their happy deliverance from so great a danger." Barish finds the example of the thwarted invasion particularly inept because the event that Heywood seizes upon is a mere coincidence and has nothing to do with any improving qualities of the performance itself;[43] it is, as Heywood calls it in a marginal note, "A strange accident" rather than a defense of anything essential to the theatre. But if this anecdote fails as a defense of what Heywood seems to want to defend, it does suggest the doubly blind way in which the theatre takes effect in the real world. The Spanish mistake the theatrical alarms for real ones, and are chased off, but as important is the way in which the actors and the audience mistake their real alarms for theatrical ones; they think they are acting, but in fact they are not. Had the townspeople set off charges of gunpowder, for instance, to make the Spanish believe that they were under attack, this would be an example of how a theatrical display can be controlled to offer an audience – the Spanish – a fixed meaning. As Heywood narrates it, there is truth and misapprehension on both sides. More significantly, the Spanish clearly experience the performance as a real event. Their experience simply is not the event that the actors perform.

In fact, each of Heywood's examples, unlike the models offered by Hieronimo and Hamlet, is predicated on the ignorance of the performers as well as of the audience. The acting company that successfully unveils the secret murder succeeds, if it can be called that, without any intention to do so, and when Julius Caesar kills his fellow actor, it is because he has lost control of himself in the excitement of the performance. Rather than – as Barish sees it – unreflectively repeating classical and humanist defenses of the theatre, what Heywood points out is in each case a double mistaking, and so one that resists the directorial control that Hieronimo and Hamlet both count on and that both find finally to be insufficient to achieve what they want completely: Hamlet at the end of his play, as Horatio's skepticism suggests, cannot be sure that it has revealed what he wants it to, and Hieronimo cannot get the full measure of his revenge because what he has accomplished is at first unrecognized by those who have wronged him. In his anecdote, regardless of what he may have wanted it to say, Heywood does not distinguish the theatrical world from a prior real world with absolute clarity; one notices, for instance, that the Spanish, like actors on a stage, "enter" and "retire." But neither are the realms of theatre and reality indistinguishable; the townspeople, warned in their turn by the theatrical "bravado" of the Spanish return of fire, take steps of actual defense by chasing the Spanish down to the shore. The two realms overlap and infuse, not in a way controlled by the authority of truth – such as one would posit for a didactic play, for instance, or the illustrated figure of Rastell's play – but outside it, contingently. What is involved is also different from a simple switching of real and theatrical, through which the priority of truth and fiction, staging and reality, is temporarily reversed. The theatre is neither the *theatrum mundi*, showing an action that seems meaningful from one perspective but empty from another, nor an ordinary sign referring to an absent reality. Most significantly, Heywood's theatre is not even clearly delimited from the reality he describes; like Hieronimo's theatre, it is set firmly and inextricably within its context. It partakes of both, inside and outside, presentation and representation, and in such a way that it mystifies its participants. But that confusion is what ultimately frustrates the perfection of Hieronimo's staged revenge; for Heywood, that confusion – the fact that its effects are finally as real as any real event, but are equally unpredictable – is the source of his theatre's power. What Heywood sees, but Hamlet does not, is that the power of the theatre to have real effects in the real world cannot be isolated from the possibility of mistaking. The confusion it engenders is not a side effect, but the source of its powers. Heywood's theatre, in which we must include the whole landscape of his example, is revealed as a space of radical misprision.

The misprision that characterizes the theatre, not only the ways in which its plays presented misunderstanding but in its own status in society as an object that could, and maybe could only, be misunderstood, is not simply a correctable one that can be stabilized by reference to something outside it, like the watchman in the Induction to *Bartholomew Fair*, whose "mistaking words" are meant to be understood as misunderstanding and so are comical. Characters like Dogberry or the rude mechanicals are funny in contrast to a standard of language usage which they cannot meet but which their audience can. This certain error, as one may call it, is one end of the indecidability of theatre – a hierarchy where the theatrical representation represents another representation as inadequate. At its most complex, the indeterminacy that the early modern stage demonstrates is far more, and more threatening, than a simple indeterminacy or vagueness, which closer scrutiny or divine revelation might make clear. Theatre produces a confusion that does not allow itself to be fully localized and managed; it sets itself on both sides of the question. Rather than a metatheatre that centers one vision of mimesis squarely within another, it is a cluster of representational means that mutually support and undermine one another.

The theatre is an object that is divided between itself and its audience. Many discussions of the uniqueness of Elizabethan stage space have proposed some form of split within it, and I have made free use of several of them: Steven Mullaney's acute discussion of the liminal space of the liberties in which the theatre buildings were first constructed; the horizontal/vertical division variously proposed by Frances Yates and Alvin Kernan, in which the theatre building itself was a map of the universe with its own Heaven and Hell and middle ground of human action; Robert Weimann's division of the playing space into the two stylistic zones of *locus* and *platea* with different representational and performative traditions; Kent van den Berg's distinction between the visual and aural aspects of the drama; even, in fact Harry Berger's post-performance attempt to reconcile reading and viewing in "imaginary audition."[44] The range of these theories and their pervasiveness suggest that rather than determining which, or how many, of these apply to Elizabethan theatre, we should perhaps concentrate on the recurrence of this cleft form as an incommensurable and irreducible difference internal to the theatre.

No less important, though, is the unlocatability of this difference, which resists definition as it demands it. To fix the split between different registers of performance or different modes of characterization is not in essence different from the now-discredited attempts in the early part of the century to determine which parts of which plays were for the groundlings and which for the more learned nobles, or the similar seventeenth-century figurations of Webster, Middleton, Jonson, and others, to locate error in their audience or their actors. If the division between what is accurate and what is distorted, or what is full and what superficial, or any other hierarchizable pairing, can be completely and predictably understood, the theatre – its practices and physical spaces – no longer threatens meaning the same way. But as Heywood, the practicing actor among the theorists, spells out, the space of the theatre is not so much split as folded and doubled over, so that the same word or gesture simultaneously means more than one thing and produces unpredictable results. It objectifies the things it represents in a subjective mode – that is, it shows how one action can mean severally from several positions of understanding it, in a way that is not reducible to eliciting a single correct or authorized meaning for it. Most of all, though, it negotiates the likeness of its signs to things and cannot disguise the conflicting legibility of these elements. Not only can what is represented never fully mask what Robert Weimann calls the "neutral materiality" of the actor and the stage,[45] but that materiality also calls attention to itself with theatrical metaphors and self-reflexive gestures. Further, the split in the theatre can never be absolutely defined; it is heterogeneous, but not separate, and each form of acting or map of topography appears through the lens of the other. To return to my earlier metaphor, this is not metatheatre as it is usually defined, but theatre beside itself – one might almost say at its wit's end, or at the limit of its inventiveness.

While such a split is unavoidable in any theatrical performance, the uses to which it is put, and even the extent to which it is recognized are of course historically determined.[46] The same sort of idea is seen in Hamlet's advice to the players to suit the action to the word and the word to the action, and his prohibition on clowns ad-libbing. In action, though, as the use of the play within *Hamlet* suggests, the plays of the Elizabethan and Jacobean public theatres tended to flaunt rather than suppress the partial discontinuities between elements and so their lack of naturalism. In its joining of visual and verbal elements, the Elizabethan stage constructed not a *Gesamtkunstwerk* but one that was disassembled and disassembling, one that requires the audience to accept its conventions in order to repeatedly break them down and expose their limits.[47] In the performance – that space of misprision – meaning cannot be secured finally because the authority that should support it has splintered, not dissipated, but divided and spread. This diffusion forces the theatre into a realm that is neither fact fully nor fiction, neither poesy nor something else, but which levels all distinctions through second-guessing and always demands at least a second corrective reading to rework a first reading that is recognized as insufficient.[48]

What I suggest is neither that the theatre offered a real threat of spilling over into reality nor that it failed to offer one, but that in fact even to pose this question is to make the error of Hieronimo and Hamlet. Plays do not project themselves outside of the stage and into the real as what they represent, nor are they somehow contained and prevented from doing so; they are always outside of themselves and active in reality, but in the strangely contradictory muddle of empowerment and impediment that characterizes them. They are active as representations are active. This is a fairly obvious point, but easily elided in seeking to understand what a play does. Because mimesis demands of its audience that they suspend their disbelief in it and that they accept its rules, it must begin to screen out its existence as an actual practice, however patchedly. This indeterminacy is also the death blow to the humanist idea of the encyclopedic theatre, since it effectively excludes the possibility of an un-self-conscious representation. In being set apart from the real world, the theatrical fiction paradoxically becomes an indissociable part of the real world, yielding meaning only when seen precisely as an event on the same interpretive plane as all other events. The relation of the play to the world is not conceived of as a merely didactic or representational one, nor is it portrayed as a confusion of illusion and reality. For Hamlet, Hieronimo, and Heywood alike, the play within a play does not simply confuse life and theatre only to settle finally on a particular interpretation of the relation between the two – not even on the interpretation of life as performance. Instead these plays use this device to suggest an understanding of the theatre as a way of producing knowledge while deferring any definitive interpretation by turning it into the performance of an experience. In their own ways, each of these works critiques the possibility of circumscribing the encyclopedic knowledge produced by the staging of theatrical performance.

5 The show of learning and the performance of knowledge: Humors, *Epigrams*, and "an universal store"

> In being able to counsel others, a man must be furnished with an universal store in himself, to the knowledge of all nature: that is the matter, and seed plot; there are the seeds of all argument, and invention. But especially, you must be cunning in the nature of man: there is the variety of things, which are as the elements and letters, which his art and wisdom must rank and order to the present occasion. For we see not all letters in single words; nor all places in particular discourses. That cause seldom happens, wherein a man will use all his arguments.
> — Ben Jonson, *Timber*[1]

The early modern theatre in action did not look very much like the mirroring encyclopedia it was meant to be. While deceitful or errant mimesis was obviously possible, that possibility was much less disturbing to the unified vision of theatre and encyclopedia than the possibility that the poles of deceit and verity did not operate in the encyclopedic theatre as they ought to do in the world – the possibility that even at its best theatre refused that distinction altogether. Rather than offering a distanced but exact reflection of reality – the ideal of theatre as a metalanguage – theatre proved instead to be an intervention into reality on its own terms. The frame the theatre of performance provided, unlike the one the encyclopedic theatre had promised, was not timeless and eternal, but itself mobile, and it seemed to draw its motion from the mobility and changefulness of the world it represented. The realization of encyclopedic ideals in the public theatres ultimately opened a new realm of existence – human experience – to intelligibility. But this potential was initially overshadowed by its difference from the things it was meant to represent. The *mappamundi* of the world displayed in Rastell's *The Four Elements* had tried to mirror the world itself exactly; the practice of drama, though, showed that it was not as reflection but as involvement that theatre represented its objects.

In the final two chapters I want to examine how theatre and encyclopedia continued to exert pressures on each other after the experiment of the publicly performed drama in purpose-built theatres in England seemed to deny the possibility that these forms were the same. If the ideal of an encyclopedic theatre could not survive unchanged, that did not, however, mean it could not survive. In early seventeenth-century England, two writers in particular, the scholar–playwright Ben Jonson and the scientist–politician Francis Bacon, undertook the reform of the theatre and the encyclopedia, finding in their apparent failure to coincide the outline of a project for improving each of them. Jonson and Bacon were each deeply moved by the double spur of *superbia* and *curiositas* to shape their outputs in encyclopedic terms. Each man insisted, improbably, that the entire body of his broad, varied, and never completed work of writing and describing was part of a single, unified life-project. In Jonson and Bacon, the resistance to fragmentation and the desire to totalize are explicitly cast as contests between the theatre and the encyclopedia, in which one form becomes the model for the reformation of the other.

Ben Jonson was a capacious writer in every way, and contemporary portraits of him as well as later ones remain partial; there are few categories large enough to contain him, in part because he worked so hard himself to establish the categories, in part because he crossed them so recklessly. Jonson throve on contradiction. Opposing the restraint of his *Epigrams* to the excess of his plays, the tight dramatic plots of his theatre of humors to the loose collections of lyric, or the antimasque to the masque, his career shows a commitment to *discordia* and an ongoing struggle to make it *concors*.[2] Jonson adopted the encyclopedic strategy of reframing his contradictions within a larger whole capable of containing and unifying them, units vast enough for anything – authorial genius, the folio *Works*, the masque.[3] At various stages in his career, Jonson revisited the close relation between real knowledge and its bogus imitations in a number of guises: in his disputes with Inigo Jones about their masques; in the hierarchy of noble spectator over understanding-man in the theatre, and of the reader over both; and in the minute nuances of meaning he would establish between two closely related terms in his poetry. To Jonson, the subtlety of these differences, indeed their apparent insignificance, reflected the difficulty of distinguishing the truth from the falsity that so closely imitated it. Not only did they make the minute but crucial distinctions in what they described, they also revealed the intellectual and moral acuity of the describer who judged them properly.

For Jonson, the root of his contradictions lay in the double problem that poetic work, as both particular and universal, necessarily confronted. As he explained it in the printed introduction to his wedding masque *Hymenaei* (1606),

It is a noble and just advantage, that the things subjected to *understanding* have of those which are objected to *sense*, that the one sort are but momentary, and merely taking; the other impressing, and lasting . . . So short-lived are the *bodies* of all things in comparison of the *souls*. And though *bodies* oft-times have the ill-luck to be sensually preferred, they find afterwards the good fortune, when *souls* live, to be utterly forgotten.[4]

As a result, concludes Jonson, the "greatest *persons*" are "not only studious of riches, and magnificence in the outward celebration, or shew; (which rightly becomes them) but curious after the most high and hearty *inventions* to furnish the inward parts." Jonson justifies the masque because its outer glitter is anticipated by its inner richness; its gaudy and evanescent exterior gestures in its fading at an enduring inner "soul." Depth and surface are distinguished, but the surface is the screen across which the truths of depth are manifested. Bodies and souls, surface and depth, though, are Jonson's redescriptions of yet a different distinction between temporality and timelessness. Although here he treats specifically the masque, the ability to offer timely counsel from one's "universal store" – the encyclopedic *silva* – is the task of poetry and of learning generally, and in Jonson's terms, it is simultaneously a theatrical concern for showing and an encyclopedic one for retaining. As he described it in *Hymenaei*, poetry "must be taught to sound upon present occasions," that is, to intervene in the present, but poetry can only justify itself on an inner meaning which no present occasion can exhaust, one that "should always lay hold on more removed *mysteries*." The particular realization of truth and the unchanging truth that underlies it exist in constant tension with each other, not simply as veil and reality or essence and ornament.[5]

The complicated circularity of the masque is one of Jonson's reinventions of the theatre along the lines of the encyclopedia in the wake of the actual public theatres. His attempts, though, not only encompass his varied dramatic writings – his humors plays as critiques of theatre, his popularly and critically successful middle comedies, his masques, and his late attempts at rewriting older genres like the Robin Hood play, the moral play, or his own humors plays[6] – but his corpus as whole. All of Jonson's texts – drama, verse, and prose – show a split between the atemporal store of universal knowledge and the present occasions of the historical moment to which consciously or unconsciously it must sound. What characterizes Jonson in all his works, and what has been variously identified as a mechanistic aesthetics, a manifestation of anal eroticism, empirical materialism, and above all antitheatricalism,[7] can instead be explained as encyclopedism, a desire to find a means to present his own "universal store in himself, to the knowledge of all nature" without sliding into the error Jonson warns against in *Timber* of mechanically putting "all letters in single words" and "all places in particular discourses."

In *Poetaster* (1601), a late salvo in the so-called Poets' War, Jonson represents the falsely encyclopedic setting of "all letters in single words" and the failure of poetry to distinguish souls and bodies, the present occasion and the lasting, as a particularly theatrical problem.[8] John Marston, one of Jonson's opponents, in the guise of the hack playwright Crispinus, is given a purge by a suspiciously Jonsonian Horace, and vomits out his ersatz learning word by word:

> CRISPINUS: Oh, I am sick –
>
> HORACE: A basin, a basin, quickly; our physic works. Faint not, man.
>
> CRISPINUS: Oh – *retrograde* – *reciprocal* – *incubus* . . . Oh *glibbery* – *lubrical* – *defunct* – oh –
>
> HORACE: Well said: here's some store.
>
> VIRGIL: What are they?
>
> HORACE: *Glibbery, lubrical,* and *defunct.*
>
> GALLUS: O, they came up easy. (5. 3. 457–69)

In this passage Jonson grotesquely literalizes the idea of the encyclopedia as a space containing knowledge in the form of discrete units. Crispinus' body holds an actual "store" of knotty words, which, as Virgil's curiosity reveals, remain physically in the basin that Horace holds for him after he coughs them up. In *Satiromastix* (1602), Thomas Dekker struck back, portraying a Jonsonian Horace as poetically bankrupt as Crispinus, and in similar terms. Dekker presents the poet laboring at his desk to come up with a poem, scanning through his own mental store of words to find a rhyme:

> O me thy Priest inspire.
> For I to thee and thine immortal name,
> In – in – in golden tunes,
> For I to thee and thine immortal name –
> In – sacred raptures flowing, flowing, swimming, swimming:
> In sacred raptures swimming,
> Immortal name, game, dame, tame, lame, lame, lame.[9]

While Crispinus suffered from a kind of verbal bloat of "terrible, windy words" (*Poetaster*, 5. 3. 397), Horace's store is meager and thin, full of possibilities of only the most mechanical and unproductive kind.

Translating Vives in *Timber*, Jonson divides "speech" into the two categories of words and sense: "In all speech, words and sense are as the body and the soul" (2333–35). "Words" are the material elements out of which speech is made, a self-contained system with its own rules. "Sense" makes up the content of speech, and ultimately the encyclopedia itself, and is finally, if mysteriously, linked to the things of the world: "Sense is wrought out of experience, the knowledge of human life, and actions, or the liberal arts, which the Greeks called 'Ἐγκυκλοπαιδειαν'" (*Timber*, 2336–39). In both Jonson's and Dekker's representations of bad composition the elements of dramatic poetry are words as most fully opposed to sense – words-as-things that are stored, combined, hunted for, but that take on sense almost as a side effect. Both writers also rely on the encyclopedic idea of a totality of knowledge stored in the mind of the dramatic poet. The poet has ready access to a store of all human knowledge; the bad poet can be distinguished from the good one by his inability to reproduce it except as idiotic repetition, whether in the inkhorn terms of Crispinus or the pedestrian flaccidity of Horace. The process of combinatory that looked so promising to the Llullists and to Camillo, in which meaning depends on the recombination of the words that serve as mechanical chits to be shuffled and rearranged, is shown by both Jonson and Dekker to yield undigested and meaningless sentences.[10] The good and the bad poet are distinguished not by a difference in their relations to knowledge, which for both is a "store" of discrete bits of information, but in their ability to apply those elements selectively to the world rather than merely to repeat them. For Jonson, the real test of knowledge is in the way it leaves the atemporal circle of its own structure and is set to work in the world of time and history, and the only way to ensure that the right information is available at the right time is to have all of it to hand. In Jonson's version, encyclopedism is necessary for discussion or thought, but also necessarily hidden from view; too obvious a reliance on it produces intellectual nausea like that of Crispinus or reveals an automatic and idiotic repetition like the sterile rotation through the alphabet a letter at a time of Dekker's Horace, musing "name, game, dame, tame, lame, lame, lame." Lame indeed.

Jonson's early plays *Every Man In His Humor* (1598) and *Every Man Out of His Humor* (1599) directly address the problem of mechanical repetition and the gap between words and sense.[11] The humors plays are novel in form, drawing on the contemporary fad for "humorousness" but shaping it differently from any other writer. T. S. Eliot observed that while Shakespeare's characters interact organically, Jonson's fit together mechanically, like the pieces of a machine, and this feature is especially pronounced in the humors plays.[12] Eliot's phrasing recalls the combinatory works in the tradition of Camillo's theatre, the same ones which had emerged as critiques of bad writing in the Poets' War. What Jonson does in his humors play is examine the application of various forms of combinatory to the performed theatre. Jonson's humors characters piece together speeches from predigested elements like a user of Camillo's Teatro or Webbe's Terence; Jonson's plays piece together the characters. Early printed editions of Terence sometimes adopt a similar technique in their illustrations for purely practical purposes – different scenes are illustrated by combining individual blocks representing characters and landscapes into a single image. As in Jonson, the results are sometimes comically incongruous (Figures 20, 21, 22). Using *Every Man Out of His Humor* as an example, I want to suggest that Jonson's early playwriting is a theatricalization of the encyclopedic combinatory method, in which individual elements are manipulated and arranged to produce every possible combination while they remain unchanged.

Fig. 20   Illustration from Terence, *Andria*, in [*Comoediae*], ed. Sebastian Brant (Strassburg: J. Grüninger, 1496).

The plot of *Every Man Out of His Humor* is simple. Characters afflicted by what the play calls humors, so that they can only respond to their world in the most mechanical of ways, are forced to encounter one another until their limitations become unsupportable, at which point they are jarred into a more normal state of flexibility and reactivity. The main catalyst in the process of undoing the humors is Macilente, but even he is very often a kind of bystander to a play that seems to run itself far more than to be run by any of its characters. He is portrayed by the play's supposed author, Asper, and is more akin to an onstage chorus than to the other characters. Early in the play Macilente remains on stage, while other characters stumble upon him, as his lines at the end of several scenes show: "Soft, who be these?/ I'll lay me down a while till they be past" (1. 1. 37–38); "Stay, who's this?/ Now for my soul, another minion/ Of old lady Chance's: I'll observe him" (1. 2. 236–238); "Here comes another" (2. 5. 51). His role is that of a fixed element past which variables are rotated in a combinatory – Macilente and Fastidious Brisk, Macilente and Deliro, Macilente and Sordido. The play can only present in sequence a variety of meetings between characters.

Fig. 21 Illustration from Terence, *Andria*, in [*Comoediae*], ed. Sebastian Brant (Strassburg: J. Grüninger, 1496).

After a scene which combines Puntarvolo's wooing of his own wife with the meeting of the fashionable Fastidious Brisk and the fashion-mad Fungoso (2. 3), one of the play's two interior commentators, Mitis, complains that although the humors of the characters have been made clear, the author "might have altered the shape of his argument, and explicated 'em better in single Scenes." Cordatus, the other critic, objects that "That had been single indeed: why? Be they not the same persons in this, as they would have been in those?" It gives more variety, he continues, to fill a stage with characters than if "the actors come in (one by one) as if they were dropped down with a feather into the eye of the spectators" (2. 3. 288–301). In fact, though, this is how they have been presented until this scene, and even here the actions of Puntarvolo and Fastidious Brisk are kept as distinct as the events in the different mansions of a play like *The Castle of Perseveraunce*. But Cordatus is right that combination does not alter these characters. The conventional television situation comedy, in which the humor is generated not by the impact of characters upon one another and their world, but where typed characters are thrown into discordant juxtaposition, is an exact tactical equivalent to Jonson's plot, which makes a rustic into a rich man and then introduces him to a court lady, or puts a dog-loving knight with ethical values derived from romances in contact with a foppish, would-be Machiavellian, would-be Petrarchan courtier.

Fig. 22 Illustration from Terence, *Andria*, in [*Comoediae*], ed. Sebastian Brant (Strassburg: J. Grüninger, 1496).

As the play's detractors have noted, nothing in *Every Man Out of His Humor* really develops, but really nothing can. The characters of the play are triply fixed in their ways: by their descriptions at the front of the text; by the script that Asper supposedly has written and which they as actors follow (of course the real actors are similarly bound by Jonson's script); and finally, within the fiction of Asper's play, by the humors which govern their actions. With such a structure and such characters, no real change is possible except for the binary one of being in or out of a particular humor. Characters do not develop, they persist in their humors or they cease them altogether; Fungoso or Fallace out of love with fashion and the court are not so much reformed as extinct – they have almost no content aside from their obsessive behavior. Sordido, the first to be put out of his humor, must literally die and come back as somebody else to be free of the humor of avarice; he hangs himself in despair only to be cut down and literally revived as a kinder, gentler landlord. Contrary to our expectation of a play showing some change from beginning to end, this one simply lays out a set of positions that it then mechanically undoes. The rising and falling of the play's action are nearly perfectly symmetrical. The first half of the play is dedicated to "mak[ing] the humors perspicuous enough" (2. 3. 291), with Cordatus and Mitis dutifully recording each one as it comes on stage: "Do you observe that, Signor? There's another humor has new cracked the shell" (2. 3. 125–26). The play's second half, beginning with Sordido's attempted suicide (3. 7) and rebirth into charity (3. 8) is given over to reversing them. Anne Barton sees in the suddenness of the characters' reforms a parody of such unrealistic psychology, but these characters are in some ways so far from having a psychology as to make its parody impossible. Their mechanical reversals, like that of Sordido from stereotypical miser to equally stereotypical saint, worthy of inclusion, as his surprised neighbors say, in the next edition of Foxe's *Actes and Monuments*, are simply a continuation of their equally mechanical humors.

Immediately before Sordido's conversion, when the characters are all introduced and the machinery of the play's analysis is in place, Mitis offers another objection:

the argument of his Comedy might have been of some other nature, as of a duke to be in love with a countess, and that countess to be in love with the duke's son, and the son to love the lady's waiting maid: some such cross-wooing, with a clown to their servingman, better then to be thus near, and familiarly allied to the time. (3. 6. 195–201)

Mitis' complaint now is that the play lacks a real plot. Plot in the sense of *muthos* is not in general Jonson's strong point, in spite of Coleridge's judgment that *The Alchemist*, along with *Tom Jones* and *Oedipus the King*, was one of the three greatest plots in literature.[13] Rather than plot in the sense of action, Jonson's work here is *plotting* in the sense of ballistics, the art of the air traffic controller rather than the more conventionally cited one of the weaver. *Every Man Out of His Humor* is Jonson's clearest substitution of arrangement for action, a tendency that continues in the sharply restricted spaces and the proliferating activity of *Volpone* (1606), *Epicoene* (1609), and *The Alchemist* (1610), and reaches its extreme form in plays like *Bartholomew Fair* (1614) and *The New Inn* (1629), which are held together not by any unity of plot, but strictly by a unity of place. Their restriction to one location is a conscious spatialization of Aristotle's dictum about a play concerning a single action. Jonson's characters are spectacular trajectories across the stage, and even in recognized masterpieces like *The Alchemist* or *Bartholomew Fair*, the lack of individual roundness that many of them show, also noted by Coleridge,[14] makes them flirt conspicuously with grotesqueness. They gain vitality from their startling juxtaposition and the neatness with which their predictable tracks are executed across one another. In *Every Man Out of His Humor*, the combinatory structure is more rigorously preserved than it is in Jonson's later plays, so that rather than coming to a climax and resolution, the play seems almost to die of exhaustion.

The text of *Every Man Out of His Humor* begins not with action, but with a list of the *dramatis personae*; after the names of the characters are given, brief prose "characters" in the style of Theophrastus follow, a satirical genre describing various undesirable character types which was becoming popular in the early seventeenth century. The first figures on stage are Asper, the playwright; Cordatus, an astute critic who has read the play; and Mitis, essentially a straight man for the cleverer Cordatus. Asper retires to play the part of Macilente in the play; Cordatus and Mitis remain on stage as a *Grex* – Terence's word – or Chorus, commenting on the action from a single-mindedly literary-critical point of view. From the start the humors are explicitly central to Asper's project, which is the reform of the popular conception of the humors. Asper's plan for social reform is directed at those who superficially mimic what they cannot actually be:

> O, how I hate the monstrousness of time,
> Where every servile imitating spirit,
> Plagued with an itching leprosy of wit,
> In a mere halting fury strives to fling
> His ulcerous body in the *Thespian* spring
> And straight leaps out a Poet!   ("Second Sounding," 66–71)

The poet, according to Jonson, combines the roles of "philosopher," "divine," and "politic," and must have "exact knowledge of all virtues, and their contraries" (*Timber*, 1276–83); the poetry he practices is "the queen of arts, which had her original from heaven" (*Timber*, 2952–53), and so the poet must master all the other liberal and ethical arts as well (*Timber*, 2981–85). The "servile imitating spirit" merely copies this truly encyclopedic learning. Such self-professed poets address themselves to the correction of the humors that plague society, but without the true poet's mastery of virtues they cannot act correctly. Nor do they even understand what "humor" means; one of Asper's particular goals is to define this complex word rightly and

> To give these ignorant well-spoken days
> Some taste of their abuse of this word Humor.   ("Second Sounding," 79–80)

Although "well-spoken," the servile imitators do not understand their own language when they speak of humors. Asper insists that the primary definition of the humors is medical, based on the ratios of "choler, melancholy, phlegm, and blood" in the body, but adds that the term "humor" may also be used metaphorically:

> ... when some one particular quality
> Doth so possess a man, that it doth draw
> All his affects, his spirits, and his powers
> In their confluction, all to run one way ...   ("Second Sounding," 105–08)

Humor as physiological quality already begins to flow towards ways of defining it and its metaphors in Asper's discussion. But Asper absolutely draws the line at the "ridiculous" misuse of the word by the ignorant, well-spoken age in servile imitation of those who know its true sense, to associate humors not with an internal quality of disposition, but with some external, material display, whether it reflects an internal state or not:

> But that a rook, in wearing a pied feather,
> The cable hat-band, or the three-piled ruff,
> A yard of shoe-tie, or the Switzer's knot
> On his French garters, should affect a Humor!
> Oh, 'tis more than most ridiculous. ("Second Sounding," 110–14)

Although Asper is clear that such external posturing is also ridiculous, his central complaint is with those who call such odd choices of clothing a humor. Ridiculous as French garters or Swiss knots are, to attribute them to a physical humor is still more absurd. For Asper, then, "humors" are actually physiological or metaphorically psychological, but never merely superficial behaviors or appearances. Contrary to normal usage, insists Asper, not every whim or quirk can be called a humor.[15] To do so is to reduce all such absurdly humorous behavior to the level of physical reflex.

This physiological or psychological understanding is supported by Asper's definition of humors at the beginning of *Every Man Out of His Humor*, but it disregards the way the humor characters actually act, as opposed to how Asper describes them as acting. In spite of Asper's certainty, the humors that Asper's/Jonson's play diagnoses seem socially rather than physiologically dictated. Possibly in *Every Man In His Humor* the characters' humors are physiological, like Kitely's obsessive jealousy, for instance, or Clement's whimsy. But the colorful oaths and gestures of Bobadil and their pallid re-renderings by Stephen glance ahead to a tendency in *Every Man Out of His Humor* and later plays by Jonson and others for humors to be exactly what Asper rejects – highly visible and repetitive mannerisms and ticks that do not have a clear origin in any underlying physiological disturbance. While it is possible to associate some of the characters in *Every Man Out of His Humor* with a particular psychological humor, such as Maciente with envy or Sordido with avarice, the humors of characters like Fungoso, who mimics Fastidious Brisk's fashions, or Deliro, who fawns on his wife, are more immediately identifiable as a set of external behaviors than as physiological humors.[16] What seems to distinguish a humors character is not, as Asper would argue, an *internal* disposition but rather a drastically reduced range of *external* reactions, often centered on some physical object or even a phrase.[17] Such characters tend to respond automatically in the same way regardless of their situation, so that any given input produces identical output. Characters like Captain Otter or Sordido, rather than being receptive to external circumstance, mechanistically project their behaviors indifferently onto any and every scene. Outwardly colorful and expansive, their display of character points to a poverty of inner resources.

Jonson's humors plays thus emphasize not the underlying psychological structures that produce a particular humorous behavior, but the empty repetition of external behaviors themselves. Clove and Orange in *Every Man Out of His Humor* offer the most distilled portraits of humors characters. They are wholly disconnected from what little plot there is, "mere strangers," as Cordatus notes, "to the whole scope of our play; only come to walk a turn or two, in this Scene of Paul's, by chance" (3. 1. 17–19). Their place in the play is to instantiate just this alienness from everything else in it; they are so completely caught up in their own closed circles of empty and mechanically repetitive behavior that real interaction with any other character is effectively impossible.[18] They can be completely characterized by external elements like their names, clothes, and styles of speech. These they merely repeat, regardless of the appropriateness of their responses to the circumstances. Orange, as Cordatus observes, "is as dry an orange as ever grew: nothing but *Salutation*; and, *O god, sir*; and, *It pleases you to say so, Sir*;" (3. 1. 23–25) – and indeed Orange's lines in the play are limited to salutations, "O lord, sir," "O god, sir," and "It pleases you to say so, sir." Because in any interaction Orange will perform predictably, producing one of his three phrases, his words only mimic meaningfulness. It may take a while before this is noticed – and thus Cordatus' warning is useful – but Orange's words can no more take part in a conversation than the language on a street sign. Clove's scholarly discourse, while generated by repetition of a broader set of samples, is in the end no more meaningful:

Monsieur Orange, yond' gallants observe us; pr'y thee let's talk fustian a little, and gull 'em: make 'em believe we are great scholars ... Now sir, whereas the *Ingenuity* of the time, and the soul's *Synderisis* are but *Embrions* in nature, added to the paunch of the *Esquiline*, and the *Intervallum* of the *Zodiac*, besides the *Ecliptic line* being *optic*, and not *mental*, but by the *contemplative* & *theoric* part thereof, doth demonstrate to us the *vegetable circumference*, and the *ventosity* of the *Tropics*, and whereas our *intellectual*, or *mincing capreal* (according to the *Metaphysica*) as you may read in Plato's *Histriomastix* – You conceive me, sir? (3. 4. 6–30)

Like Orange, Clove can only repeat things he has heard or read, and parrot them back automatically and uncomprehendingly. His language is also a parody of the encyclopedia. It falls neatly into the category of speech that J. L. Austin calls theatrical – their words may appear to have illocutionary force, but in fact they only make use of empty forms.[19] They might be imagined as the combinatory project of a Camillo or a Llull gone horribly awry, so that they produce seemingly sensible, or self-consistent, statements that nevertheless have only the slightest relation to reality, external or internal. Contrary to Jonson's warning in the epigraph to this chapter, Clove and Orange *do* use all their arguments in a single discourse.[20]

For Jonson, humors is a disease of the theatre, marked by theatre's excessive display and repetition. The public theatre uses such repetition as its medium, putting writer's lines in the mouths of characters and resurrecting long-outdated plays, *Hieronimos* and *Andronicuses*, to entertain its masses. This is what makes it such a good vehicle for exposing humors. Unmonitored, though, the public theatre can become a place for endless and empty repetition without critical edge. This is why the playwright Asper rails so harshly against the otherwise innocuous "servile imitating spirit" of the poet and scorns the "apes" of his society, not those who suffer physiologically from a humoral imbalance, but those who "affect" to.[21] Jonson parodies a similar absurdity when Wasp and some other fair-folk in *Bartholomew Fair* play a game called vapors, "which is nonsense, every man to oppose the last man that spoke, whether it concerned him or no" (4. 4. 28s.d.) To play at vapors is to refashion oneself into the flatness of a humors character; it is also, of course, exactly what an actor does, responding at his cue with anger, or love, or anything else, regardless of his actual internal state. The irony of the theatrical repetition that Jonson pillories is that it never succeeds in actually repeating what it seems to want to, precisely because of its mechanical exactitude. Something repeated is always marked as a repetition by something extra that distances it from the original, a jarring lack of fit with circumstance. In the representation of Clove's learned discourse, it is his inability to combine the individual words he accurately produces with a discernible meaning; for Orange, what marks his speech as repeated is its incongruity with the context. To repeat something accurately, one must change its external form; only then can its inner essence remain stable. Theatrical repetition, then, is in a sense a problem of scale; the person who repeats fails to take into account the proper scope of what is to be repeated, taking too small a unit, as Clove does and Jonson accuses Marston of doing, or failing to see his words in a larger context, like Orange or Marston's Jonson.

To circumvent this problem, Jonson manipulates the scale of his encyclopedia. Instead of being contained in a single text, Jonson's ideal encyclopedia is a particular kind of knowledge embodied in a person. This person serves others not only as an epitome of ethical excellences, but also as a means of putting the total knowledge of the encyclopedia into practice. With a larger repertoire than that of one of the humors characters, this encyclopedic self avoids the danger of senseless repetition; it has, apparently, nearly inexhaustible resources to draw on in responding to the world. This shift from book to person is part of a larger development within Renaissance humanism that linked the encyclopedia to a knowledge that was global, and because of that was in particular ethical. It was still possible to see the encyclopedic text as simply the necessary concatenation of the standard school subjects, or any of the other organizing systems that delimited a finite body of things it was needful to know. But rather than Elyot's or Reisch's image of the encyclopedia as the articulation of the different fields of knowledge, writers like Angelo Poliziano, Guillaume Budé and Juan Luis Vives also viewed the encyclopedia as a whole greater than the sum of its parts, a quintessence of knowledge that exceeded the individual disciplines from which it was composed and that was translated in the mind of its possessor/beholder into the prudential, humane skills concerning the life well-lived as a whole rather than in its specialized sub-disciplines:

The practice of life, the examples of our ancestors, the knowledge of contexts makes one who is called in Greek *polyhistor*, as if it were "knower of many things" (*multiscius*): to us, let him be called by a truer title, simply *prudent*, and his studies *prudence* (*prudentia*).[22]

Polyhistory, or Prudence, as Vives prefers to call it here, is a kind of master art (Budé and Volaterranus both called it *philologia*, the love of words and other material traces as opposed to the love of abstracted ideas[23]). Nonetheless, it cannot be gained by the programmatic study of texts; it requires a very different approach to knowledge than the traditional arts that it was meant to cap. But even innovative forms that relied on a method, such as Camillo's theatre or Ramus' universal system, could produce mechanical and senseless results like those dramatized in Jonson's Crispinus and Dekker's Horace. Polyhistory itself was all-encompassing but unsystematic, exhaustive but not exhausting; prudence in particular was the knowledge of the right thing at the right time, the proper application of one's knowledge to the contingent flow of the world. In this sense, knowledge was not possessed so much as deployed, or enacted.

Vives offers a sample of the kinds of knowledge that contribute to prudence, but these parts are never the whole, and laid out all together the effect is slightly silly. Truly encyclopedic, prudential knowledge includes topics like eating habits and the names of different types of transportation:

All of which subjects are [part] of the encyclopedia, on which Pliny, Athenaeus, Aelianus, Macrobius have all touched piecemeal, but old men in their groups (*circulis*) and clubs (*exhedris*) discuss these topics better, just as Cicero says, than the most learned men in their academies (*gymnasiis*), which Pliny bemoans in his preface.[24]

Here Vives is in particular working in a critique of the scholastic university and praise of the new learning of the humanists. Encyclopedic knowledge is strangely resistant to formalized genres of exposition, like the disputation or the essay, and instead comes from a different kind of less formal social interaction – old men in clubs rather than scholars in academies. To realize Vives' ideal one must undoubtedly read widely in all sorts of texts, because only through texts can one hope to get a sufficient breadth of experience, or any experience at all of the ancient world or far-off places.[25] But such book-learning is necessarily partial because it is only made up of fragments and never completely digested. Some other form than a purely textual one must be called on for understanding the world itself.

In contrast to the fragmented treatment the encyclopedia receives in the texts of even its most distinguished practitioners, Vives holds up the example of a schoolteacher, Carolus Virulus of Louvain, "a man not so much well-read as good, though neither natural gifts (*ingenium*) nor diligence were lacking to him, but time and place."[26] He had pupils from every walk of life, and in order to maximize his opportunities for learning new things, he would invite the relatives and friends of his pupils with skill in various trades and disciplines to dinner parties. Before the dinner, Virulus would select a topic of conversation upon which his guest was expert, and learn just enough about it to be able to ask some elementary questions. During dinner, then, after prompting his guest, Virulus "would hear in a very short period what he could scarcely have learned through practice in many years; and so he used to learn from the conversation, and the dinner became more cheerful and the diner more prudent and more accomplished."[27] Vives is careful to point out that Virulus is not particularly well-read (*literatus*), although he could have been in better circumstances. What Virulus learns is not knowledge that is already safely gathered in books, but a more haphazard, more comprehensive one that comes from what Ben Jonson would call "language such as men do use" (*Every Man In His Humor*, Prologue, 22) as they talk about their work around the dinner table. If he had merely read an encyclopedic text to gain his learning, Virulus' knowledge would be contained in that text, and he would only serve as its reflection; even if he had been a scholar, his learning would still exist materially in a library. As it stands, though, this encyclopedic knowledge is collected only in Virulus. But Virulus does not merely record and store the knowledge of any of the individuals he invites to dinner. The conversion of the experiences of the individuals whom Virulus invites into language enables him to distill their years of practice into a few hours at the dinner table, and so to master in an evening the knowledge it would otherwise take a lifetime to acquire. This change in the manner of knowing also converts the particular knowledge of one field by a kind of epistemological alchemy into *prudentia*, which is not the knowledge of particular things but of all things pertaining to human activity taken together.[28] Virulus becomes the sole *locus* in which his guests' particular knowledges are combined, providing a unique place for a comprehensive knowledge where before there was none. The result is a differently conceived encyclopedia, one that is a characteristic of a person rather than a book, and which we can perhaps label as a *prudential* or *ethical* encyclopedia, in distinction to the encyclopedic text. In essence, this polyhistory or prudence is not a quality of a book that contains all knowledge, but of a person who can master and order it within him or herself. This location within an individual resulted in somebody who was skillful at voicing the knowledge of others in such a way that it was useful or entertaining. It is, in other words, the incarnation of the encyclopedic actor of Vincent of Beauvais, or Zwinger's all-knowing *polyhistor* who is also an all-becoming *histrio*. The hallmark of prudence is sound judgment, but judgment is an intervention in the world, a comparison of its contingency with the still accumulation of knowledge.[29] In a reversal of earlier encyclopedic concerns, interest shifts to the application of static encyclopedic knowledge to history, rather than on the problem of achieving complete knowledge from particulars.

Virulus is part of a long line of knowledgeable diners who use their suppertimes to uncover, variously and sometimes indiscriminately, central and trivial truths about the world. Plato's *Symposium* comes unavoidably to mind, as does perhaps the encyclopedic *Convivio* that Dante abandoned to pursue his less culinary universal project, the *Commedia*. Vives mentions in particular Athenaeus and Macrobius, two compilers of late antiquity whose works were prized by humanist readers for their wealth of wildly various information on all subject matters, both couched in the form of vivid dinner conversations. Francis Bacon's biographer and chaplain, William Rawley, alluded to these authors' works when he described Bacon's own table as "like the *Noctes Atticae*, or *Conviviae Deipnosophistarum*."[30] The opinions of scholars in various fields were often circulated in quasi-fictional accounts of their mealtime conversations. For instance, John Selden's views on a variety of subjects were gathered and published posthumously as *Table-Talk* (1689), which the editor proudly claimed to have methodized and arranged properly – that is, given an encyclopedic order to the shapeless mass of Selden's wisdom; Luther's *Tisch-Reden* were similarly recorded. For Jonson, as for Vives, the feast is an occasion upon which knowledge is shared and verified in conversation, providing a sense of community that is often lacking elsewhere, as in his poem "Inviting a Friend to Supper" (where the friend may be the learned John Selden[31]), in the unseen feasts that end *The Alchemist* and *Bartholomew Fair*, or in the half-joking rituals for admitting a new member to the Tribe of Ben (*Underwoods* 47) and recorded in the *Leges Conviviales*, the drinking rules that Jonson established for the Apollo Room.[32] These feasts of learning, so different from Dante's incomplete, encyclopedic *Convivio*, are an emblem of the peculiarly humanist hybrid of theatre and encyclopedia – complete understanding in a convivial, informal setting, a natural interaction selectively displayed by sincere actor/authors who understand their world well enough to show and conceal their understanding depending on circumstance.

The learning these learned early modern suppers promise surprisingly never finds its way fully into their texts – it is promised, referred to, anticipated or remembered, but not shown. The encyclopedic knowledge that Virulus gathers does not appear in Vives' account of it; the conversation at Bacon's dinners is praised by Rawley but its exact content remains a mystery. To display the encyclopedic goods is ultimately less impressive than keeping them hidden and talking around them. This resembles the strategy of the wedding feast described in Martianus Capella's *De Nuptiis*, which promises universal knowledge of the liberal arts and casts the desire to know as an analogue for the erotic desire ratified by a wedding. In practice, though, while the stores of knowledge seem limitless – no allegorical Liberal Art is ever at a loss for what to say – the lectures quickly spiral down into such depths of uninteresting trivia and inspire such boredom (*fastidium*) that the wedding guests invariably cut the speakers off. The dinners of Virulus do not decay into the pedantry of those described by Athenaeus or the other ancient sources, partly because we never actually see their contents, but only hear of them at second hand. When Vives does describe the information contained in the encyclopedia, it sounds as trivial as anything in Martianus Capella or Macrobius. From a recapitulation of Vitruvius's discussion of the architect as encyclopedist, Vives and his imagined encyclopedist proceed to acquire a thorough knowledge of

conveyance, in which category is the horse, the mule, the ox, and every sort of vehicle, within which definition is navigation and even hauling; let him investigate for what reason and in what way all these were discovered, sought, improved, preserved, applied to our use and benefit. Now the things kept in store for the entertainment of all the senses, what is society in a private house, of a husband, of a wife, of children, of relatives, of neighbors, of contemporaries, of servants; what it is in the public state; what has been thought out and discovered about it by human ingenuity, [and] what made up through stupidity in name and opinion but without any basis at all in fact. These are all [part] of the encyclopedia...[33]

This passage is curiously double-edged. It is perhaps a legitimate review of necessary fields of knowledge, but can equally well be read as a parody of those who turned from the great texts of antiquity to study its material minutiae. It is finally something of both, a serious program that one could not undertake without laughing, ridiculous in exactly the same way as Budé's massive and revered work *De Asse*, a universal cultural history of ancient Rome and modern France through the study of a Roman unit of measure.

The encyclopedia must answer to two requirements – it must be comprehensive and it must be useful. At least it must be *usable*. But encyclopedic texts from Martianus Capella's through the early modern period habitually pit these qualities against each other. As the encyclopedia progressively reveals its impossibility as a text, its performance and execution in "language such as men do use," as opposed to fantastic and bookish talk, acquires a new importance. The idea of the encyclopedia shrinks from a text to a person and the place of information moves to the dinner table. Vives was at the forefront of humanist thought that emphasized the historical embeddedness of language. Language, he believed, gained its meaning from its employment in human activity.[34] The critical relation to be investigated by language was thus not an unchanging one between words and things, but the relation of language to prior acts of language. The table talk staged by Virulus was not, then, mere talk; it was an *investigation* carried out into the way particular individuals, representing different discursive communities concerned with a variety of skills, assigned meanings to things and came to consensus on terms and actions. In the anecdote, neither Vives nor Virulus show much interest in gaining the technical skills of their conversation partners, but only in acquiring their professional idiolect. What makes Virulus' knowledge unique and valuable is its residence wholly in discourse. His ability to consolidate the many partial and particular languages of his dinner partners is what constitutes his *prudentia*. Whereas encyclopedias like Camillo's Teatro (if not the texts about the Teatro) or Gessner's *Historiae* were meant to *display* recondite knowledge, and hence a kind of spectacular theatre of ideas, the ethical encyclopedia necessarily conceals knowledge, or at least always holds some in reserve. As Jonson notes in this chapter's epigraph, "we see not all letters in single words; nor all places in particular discourses. That cause seldom happens, wherein a man will use all his arguments." The ethical encyclopedia of the centered self holds knowledge whole, but produces it in fragments suited to the immediate context – *performs* it, in fact, as an actor plays a part in a drama rather than as he might in a fixed tableau. The *locus* of knowledge shifts from the library, where knowledge is stored, to the dinner table, where it is taken from its place of storage in memory and deployed in learned conversation.

Jonson's model for the useful application of knowledge is someone like John Selden, who combines centeredness and capacity in a single contradictory image of experience and retirement:

> Stand forth my object, then, you that have been
> Ever at home: yet have all countries seen:
> And like a compass keeping one foot still
> Upon your center, do your circle fill
> Of general knowledge; . . .   (*Underwoods* 14, 29–33)

In their careful translation of *enkuklios paideia*, the last two lines make clear that at least part of Selden's greatness is a literal encyclopedism; "knowledge" is, conventionally, *paideia*, while "circle" and "general" translate *enkuklios* in both its senses. Like an encyclopedic text that exists as the terrain between a single, centered meaning for all phenomena and the dazzling manifold of worldly details, Selden encompasses both a breadth of contingent particulars and stability: he has "all countries seen" while, like Virulus, remaining "ever at home." The characters whom Jonson singles out in his collection of praise poetry are those who, like Selden or William Camden (*Epigrams* 14), keep themselves centered on a single truth that directs their actions and gives them a wholeness that other figures lack, or those who contain within them a host of disparate qualities. Jonson's *Epigrams* in particular single out for praise certain individuals who contain within themselves all the resources they need to negotiate the vicissitudes of historical existence. In a world where most individuals are marked by their want of wholeness, these "centered selves" provide models of integrity in every sense.[35] This ability to maintain a still center in the midst of the changing world is characteristically the highest praise that Jonson can offer.[36] Their prudence – the practical ability to negotiate worldly events – relies on vast resources of learning, which let them elect from among a range of options the most appropriate response to any situation in which they find themselves.

As a genre, the epigram's slight outward form is only an index of the fullness of its sense, just as the epigram is only an index and not a description of its subject. This ability to turn *words* into *sense*, *theory* into *practice*, is what the Jonsonian epigram as a form both embodies and praises. Dense yet plain and ordinary-seeming, it seeks to present an individual in his or her timeless essence. Jonson's epigrams and other poems rarely offer descriptions of the precise qualities of their praiseworthy subjects. The brevity of the epigram as a genre perhaps requires this, but not all of Jonson's poems of praise are brief, and some of his disparaging poems in particular do describe their subjects.[37] In place of description, as Edward Partridge has noted, Jonson often uses a name. In a poem to Lucy Harington, Countess of Bedford, for instance, Jonson imagines describing a lady in conventional Petrarchan hyperboles, but concludes the poem with the recognition that his eighteen lines of fantastic description can be removed from the fiction of Petrarchan love and made real, by reducing them to one proper term:

> Such when I meant to feign, and wished to see,
> My muse bad, *Bedford* write, and that was she.   (*Epigrams* 76, 17–18)[38]

Other figures are similarly praised because they contain in précis every human quality, and preserve them untroubled against the decay of the world in the flux of time. These denials of metaphor – for Jonson's burden in these poems is to replace the figurative, suggestive language of the poet with the pure referential force of the name – are examples of a faith in words-as-things quite different from Crispinus'. In these poems names alone retain accurate meaning, while description fails, falls short, or is false. Jonson ends an epigram to Mary Wroth:

> So you are Nature's index, and restore,
> In yourself, all treasure lost of th'age before.   (*Epigrams* 105, 19–20)

The word "index" suggests comprehensiveness, compression, and order, and Wroth's uniformity and self-sameness lets her be expressed completely with great brevity. She resembles Thomas Elyot's Henry VIII in his *Dictionary*, at once the representation and the embodiment of virtue. Her wholeness makes her relation to nature reversible – she is an index to nature's wholeness herself, and such is her uniformity that all her excellences can themselves be indexed with a single name. In another epigram, Jonson begs Wroth to

> Forgive me, then, if mine [i.e., my poems] but say you are
> A Sidney: but in that extend as far
> As loudest praisers, who perhaps would find
> For every part a character assigned. (*Epigrams* 103, 9–12)

Wroth collects all the virtues in herself and becomes a kind of synonym or abbreviation for them, like Bedford both exhaustively compendious in her worth and neatly contained in her (family's) proper name. In Wroth's case, her status as a Sidney is also like the reticent virtues of the epigram in that it is neither visible nor audible in her given name and title. With the inexorable logic of a romance plot, being a Sidney is a hidden truth that Mary Wroth, *née* Sidney's, virtue reveals to have always been the case. The first epigram to William, Earl of Pembroke, the dedicatee of the *Epigrams*, begins, appropriately, by recognizing Pembroke's likeness to what Jonson offers him:

> I do but name thee Pembroke, and I find
> It is an epigram, on all mankind. (*Epigrams* 102, 1–2)

Pembroke himself, or at least his name, is a model for all good behavior and a warning against all bad. Standing as he does as an example and corrective to *all* mankind, Pembroke's epigram is also a kind of encyclopedic rendering of human virtue in fine, infinite riches in the little room of one individual, a quality Pembroke shares with other epigram dedicatees like Bedford and Sidney.

In all these poems a proper name is substituted for an enumeration of a set of qualities or a description, becoming a kind of shorthand and substitute for all imaginable virtues – naming a Pembroke or a Sidney evokes all one could say and more. The "Epistle to Selden" and the epigram upon Lucy Harington both offer a hypothetical listing of the qualities they can imagine enumerating, but in each case the list is shown to be supplanted by the individual or by her name. The name is represented as a full word in contrast to the empty words of the theatre; it guarantees the content of anything associated with it as an index of the actual *locus* of virtue rather than any falsifiable claim in discourse. In order to show encyclopedic content, Jonson must paradoxically avoid displaying it. In all its detail, as Vives' explanation of its content quoted above shows, the encyclopedia tends towards the ridiculous. But the name can hint at hidden depths without needing fully to sound them. "Bedford" contains more than the sum of its parts, just as *prudentia* in Virulus is more than the absorption of the dinner conversations he arranges, or the encyclopedia he names is more interesting than the vehicles he lists as examples of it.

This hinting at an offstage fullness which cannot appear, and then hinting at the representation's insufficiency, is also the strategy Jonson's *Epigrams* use to evoke the centered wholeness of their praiseworthy subjects. The form of the epigram mediates, like the encyclopedic selves it praises, early modern ideas of encyclopedia and theatre. Other genres are limited by decorum to what they can express and in what context, but not epigrams; in his *Poetices*, Julius Caesar Scaliger notes that "there are as many kinds of epigrams as there are of things."[39] Scaliger's parallelism between poem and object inflects the variety of topics available to the epigrammatist towards an idea of complete coverage of experience, and links the genre of epigram to the encyclopedic ideals of a Selden or a Camden, both of whom are praised for their "faith in things,"[40] their mastery of the kaleidoscopic variety of wordly *data* and human history as distinct from potentially deceptive or empty language. The epigram, with its tradition of being able to address every human topic, its brevity, and its obscurity, is a perfect demonstration of this forever only partially visible totality. As it is discussed in Renaissance treatments of genre, it distills an observation to its maximum density for its greatest possible force – that is, it simultaneously reflects and displays, like the encyclopedic theatre. The breadth of subject matter makes a collection of epigrams, like the names Bedford, Pembroke, or Sidney, or the person of Mary Wroth herself, a container capable of holding and unifying everything. Jonson's choice of titles for parts of his collections – *Underwoods* and *The Forest* – additionally allude to the disorganized *silva* of materials from which the *theatrum* is assembled.[41]

Because of their great variety, epigrams could also serve as a skeleton for a more literally encyclopedic collection. One of the earliest humanist texts to serve as something like a dictionary, the *Cornucopiae* of Nicolaus Perotti, was organized as an exhaustive lexical commentary upon the first two books of Martial's *Epigrammata*. Perotti's massive commentary, written in the mid 1480s and printed about a decade later, discusses words in the order they appear in Martial's text, delineating fantastically nuanced shades of connotation, adducing near-synonyms, near-antonyms, and near-homonyms to thicken its definitions, so that Elyot declared it "too compendious" and offered his own *Dictionary* as an alternative (Aiiir). Martial's spare Latin proved to be capable of supporting a vast edifice of philological scholarship; the first poem alone, eight lines of forty-three words (the same number as this sentence), demands one hundred and sixty-eight folio pages of Perotti's dense experimentation to gloss. He describes it as "an interpretation of the first book, that is of the whole work, and thus practically of a half of the entire Latin tongue."[42] With each modification, Perotti broadens his claims for the material that the work covers, until it extends to embrace a complete knowledge of Latin. Perotti's introduction reveals him to be something like a Selden or a Virulus captured in book form; his ability to extract meaning, or more aptly to draw discourse, out of Martial's poems seems to be limited only by the time and energy of the reader and the practical limits of the size of a codex. He concludes with a gesture that makes his text truly encyclopedic and all-encompassing. He passes the task of completion on to the reader: "It will be the duty of the reader to compare others' writings diligently with our own."[43]

The epigrammatic encyclopedia, or the encyclopedic potential of the epigram, is also curiously but consistently theatrical. The two books of Martial selected by Perotti for his lexical commentary are both connected to the theatre by Martial. The first, often called *On the Spectacles* (*De Spectaculis*), was written to celebrate the inauguration of the Colosseum in 80 CE. It consists of poems on some of the individual events that were part of the first games held in it and thus revises the ideal of a theatrical encyclopedia realized in Pliny's description of the encyclopedic theatre of Pompey. Pliny's theatre had presented natural marvels in a way that protected them from greedy but ingenious replication in money- and *curiositas*-driven *adulterium*, but Martial's *De Spectaculis* traces the use of a similar display to show the wealth and might of the emperor. In the introductory epistle to his second book of epigrams (usually numbered independently of *De Spectaculis* as *Epigrams* book I) Martial refers to the volume as "my theatre" (*theatrum meum*) and compares its contents to those of the theatre that Cato was said to have ostentatiously walked out of to protest its lewdness. Martial's recommendation that Cato either stay wholly in or wholly out of his epigrammatic theatre ("non intret Cato theatrum meum, aut si intraverit, spectet" ["Let not Cato enter my theatre, or if he has entered, let him watch"]) is explained by a concluding poem that suggests that Cato's gesture was intended solely to make a spectacle of himself:

> Why did you come into the theatre, stern Cato?
> Or did you come in only so that you could go out?[44]

A less calculating Cato appears in the epistle to Pembroke that prefaces Jonson's collection of chaster epigrams, "my theatre," (as he too calls it) "where Cato, if he lived, might enter without scandal."[45] Mary Thomas Crane has uncovered other connections between the Renaissance idea of the epigram and the ideas of the theatre that had currency in humanist circles.

One of the collections that served as a model in sixteenth-century England was the *Actors* (*Mimi*) of Publius Syrus; another was the *Disticha Catonis*, attributed incorrectly to the same Cato the Censor whom Martial found so irritatingly peripatetic and whom Jonson invited to stay.[46] The genre of the epigram thus offered in the Renaissance an unparalleled opportunity for exploring the relations of performance, didacticism, and encyclopedic knowledge, however confusedly knotted together.

But the epigram did not offer its knowledge as a kind of static clarity. It required a certain kind of understanding to discover in a name the index of all the virtues that it contained. The "Epistle to Selden," for instance, begins with the poet's assurance that "I know to whom I write." His evidence, though, is that he has been mistaken before in distributing his praise to the seeming wholeness in another person. In contrast to the certainty of the name, the words of the poet can miss the truth:

> I confess (as every muse hath erred
> And mine not least) I have too oft preferred
> Men past their terms . . .   (*Underwoods* 14, 19–21)

Now Jonson is much more careful when he writes poetry:

> Since being deceived, I turn a sharper eye
> Upon myself, and ask to whom, and why,
> And what I write? And vex it many days
> Before men get a verse: much less praise;
> So that my reader is assured, I now
> Mean what I speak: . . .   (23–28)

Jonson makes the issue not the general knowledge possessed by Selden, but Jonson's particular knowledge of himself – he must only praise when he is sufficiently sure of his own accuracy. Praise is not a test of the recipient as much as it is of the praiser. His belated recognition is that what he praised in error before was only his desire for encyclopedic completeness ("with purpose to have made [the recipients] such") instead of an accurate description. Jonson must examine *himself*, not even so as to know the accuracy of his praise, but only to ensure that he praises honestly, that he *means* what he speaks.

For the demonstration of completeness of knowledge present to the viewer, in other words, Jonson substitutes the desire for wholeness elsewhere. Selden, though, remains just as much a projection of Jonson's desires as those others Jonson wrongly praised as centered selves, distanced not temporally now but spatially, set in the body of another, finally inscrutable individual. Accurate judgment depends on abstraction and distance, and Jonson's argument is just as likely to cast doubts on his current praise of Selden as it is to assure the reader that Jonson has learned from his mistakes. Jonson first asks where he will begin to praise Selden, and then asserts that he has been swept away by an irresistible flood of Selden's greatness, but the paucity of information about Selden followed by the retroactive insistence on its arrival suggest that Selden's sudden manifestation here is a wish-fulfillment, as Jonson turns inexpressible absence into equally inexpressible overflow.[47] The poem displays his struggle to control his praise of Selden, and the final proof of Selden's worth is that in the end, cautious though he is, Jonson cannot:

> I yield, I yield, the matter of your praise
> Flows in upon me, and I cannot raise
> A bank against it. Nothing but the round
> Large clasp of nature, such a wit can bound. (*Underwoods* 14, 61–64)

The result of this abundance, though, is a net loss. Jonson has erred again, in his enthusiasm, by overreaching his ability; Selden's "circle . . ./Of general knowledge" exceeds Jonson's capacity to list it, and his poem cannot contain Selden's wit any more than it can keep it out. Selden's prudential circle cannot be held in language, but only in the circular world itself, the "round/Large clasp of nature." Small wonder that Selden and similarly centered selves have "faith in things," since things alone – sense, not words, and their performance in the world – seem to be able to express them fully. The ethical encyclopedism of such selves remains absent, another's share and not part of the author or reader except in those fragments that appear across the table or in the text, hints at a wholeness of learning that will never be fully manifested.[48]

What Jonson demonstrates in his epigrams is how desperately we *want* there to be an encyclopedia, a *locus* of true and whole knowledge, even if it remains inaccessible to us. This representation of completeness as always another's and as a kind of subjective loss suggests one interpretation of Jonson's *impresa*: "a compass with one foot in the center, the other broken, the word, *Deest quod duceret orbem*"[49] – "That which draws the circle (or 'leads the world') is missing." But Jonson could almost have said "Quod deest ducit orbem" – "that which is missing leads the world." In a congratulatory poem printed with Jonson's *Sejanus* (1603), George Chapman notices this drive to fill in the whole from the part in Jonson's work. Jonson, he says, drew "the Semicircle of *Sejanus*' life" to show "the whole Sphere and Law/ To all State Lives" (Jonson, *Hrs*, XI, 309, lines 30–32). When something is missing, it provides an impetus to fill out the world through desire, as a fragment implies its completion; yearning posits the missing leg of the compass as Jonson posits Selden's knowledge. A broken compass, then, is the only kind that works. This working is necessarily limited, of course. In a reading of Jonson's comedies, Edward Partridge defended their frequent portrayal of cruelty and exploitation by arguing that

The show of learning and the performance of knowledge 167

aesthetics are the other of history, so that what is portrayed is not necessarily done. Because of this inversion, all aesthetic objects – and Jonson would certainly have seen his works in such a light, however many questions Partridge's interpretation may raise – whether ethically good or bad, are always positive in both senses of the word: they are ethically improving and they set up things. But Jonson's compass is also broken because the comic writer cannot perfect the world except fictionally. Towards wholly formed characters and better things in reality, he can only make the gestures and inexplicable dumb shows of discourse without being able to complete his image of things in reality.

Although the good theatre of conversation opposes its empty double of repetition, it is not always easy to distinguish the humors characters of the theatre of repetition from the centered selves of the *Epigrams*. The clearest distinction – and the most apparent association – between the totalizing ethical encyclopedia and the exhausting theatre of repetition is Jonson's ode "To the Immortal Memory and Friendship of Sir Lucius Cary and Sir H. Morison" (*Underwoods* 70). In this poem, Jonson attempts to reform the theatre and to present a perfected version of it as an ethical encyclopedia. The question that Jonson, prompted by the early death of Henry Morison and the patronage of Lucius Cary, seeks to answer is one that seems to be rhetorical: "what is life, if measured by the space,/ Not by the act?" (21–22). To prepare his response, Jonson calls on two other characters, the infant of Saguntum and the stirrer, before turning to Morison. The poem opens with Jonson addressing the infant, being born into a town under siege, who

> looking then about,
> Ere thou wert half got out,
> Wise child, didst hastily return
> And mad'st thy mother's womb thine urn.   (5–8)

This is a life at its logical and practical minimum, but it is critical for Jonson that the child make its tiny odyssey out and back rather than merely being stillborn. Like William Roe's, whose journeys "perfect in a circle always meet" (*Epigrams* 128, 8), the infant's brief career describes a perfect circle, and one which, Jonson imagines, contains all the knowledge that we need for this life:

> How summed a circle didst thou leave mankind
> Of deepest lore, could we the center find![50]

Jonson's experimental use of the three-part structure of the Pindaric ode (the first such in English), which he translated Turn (strophe), Counter-Turn (antistrophe), and Stand (epistrophe), is a formal attempt to find the center of that circle. The poem thus embodies the same process of going out and returning to stop where it began, while at the same time moving forward with its language.

Jonson's attempt to sound the circle in the Counter-Turn following the introduction of the brave infant of Saguntum is inconclusive,[51] and he turns to the counter-example of the "stirrer." The stirrer's title implies the same circular motion that characterized the infant, but not the infant's decisive circuit; instead the turn and return of the infant is changed to a vague and undifferentiated mixing. In fact, as Jonson relates, there is nothing wrong with the course that the stirrer initially follows, and he might well have been another infant of Saguntum writ large: "He entered well, by virtuous parts,/ Got up and thrived with honest arts" (33–34). What ruins his beginning is his inability to move beyond it. The stirrer begins promisingly, but never advances and never concludes; his circling defines not a single, decisive act of completion like the infant's, but its empty repetition or imitation.[52] Ironically, the stirrer could have had the same success as the infant or as Morison had he only died sooner; as it is, his unseemly dilation subtracts from his early achievement:

> What did this stirrer but die late?
> How well at twenty had he fallen, or stood!
> For three of his four score, he did no good. (30–32)

William Kerrigan reads this poem as Jonson's recognition that the stirrer has lived too long and that only a short life like Morison's or the infant's can have real nobility. *Pace* Kerrigan, the stirrer could have done well had he *either* fallen or stood; the trouble is that he did neither. It is not death but decisiveness that Jonson looks for in perfection. Morison is the third character to appear, and he combines the perfection and fullness of the infant of Saguntum with the first twenty years of the worldly activity of the stirrer, these not marred by the stirrer's repetition of his good entrance until it becomes a kind of histrionic idling in one place. Like Selden or Roe, Morison is an encyclopedic character, a living demonstration of completeness of human knowledge and action:

> All offices were done
> By him, so ample, full, and round,
> In weight, in measure, number, sound,
> As though his age imperfect might appear
> His life was of humanity the sphere. (48–52)

Like the infant, Morison's figure is the perfection of the encyclopedic "sphere."

The circling of the stirrer, on the other hand, is presented as theatrical. He is said to "enter" well, and he benefits by "virtuous parts," not only his natural gifts but the roles he is given to play. The Stand that follows the introduction of

Morison makes the theatricality of the stirrer's life still clearer:

> Go now, and tell out days summed up with fears,
> And make them years;
> Produce thy mass of miseries on the stage,
> To swell thine age:
> Repeat of things a throng,
> To show thou hast been long,
> Not lived; for life doth her great actions spell,
> By what was done and wrought
> In season and so brought
> To light: her measures are, how well
> Each syllabe answered, and was formed, how fair;
> These make the lines of life, and that's her air. (53–64)

This language, appropriately, echoes that used to describe the infant; here, though, it is not a circle that is "summed" with lore, but days "summed up" with fears. The miseries of life that the infant avoids with his circle become the means by which the stirrer extends his life. The difference is that between an infinitely rich encyclopedic *summa* and an infinitely extensible sum of numbers to be totted up. A circle like Morison's closes a path off by completing it, but the transgression of this boundary opens up a potentially endless series of stale recapitulations, a theatrical pattern unlike the perfect actions of the infant of Saguntum or of Morison or even the young stirrer. "Years" grow from the repetition of identical "days," themselves compounded of undifferentiated "fears"; "things" are repeated rather than completed. This repetition of the "mass of miseries on the stage" is what the stirrers of the world mistake for life, when in fact life lies in the proportion all its elements bear to one another. Merely to "repeat of things a throng" endlessly is theatrical inanity instead of life, the existence of a Clove or an Orange and not a Morison.

But the relation between ethical encyclopedism and personal theatricality is not entirely so simple. Without the benefit of dramatization, the encyclopedic secrets of such centered characters remain lost to us; as Stanley Fish has observed, the circle within which such characters contain themselves can easily become an impermeable barrier against the outside world.[53] "Could we the center find", the lore of the infant of Saguntum would be ours, but it is lost to us, except in our uncomfortable awareness of its absence; Selden's would be lost, too, did he not know how to speak with "Newness of sense, antiquity of voice" (*Underwoods* 14, 60), fitting his meaning to his audience. The encyclopedic selves must also be players. Mary Wroth's greatness, for instance, is her ability to manifest in a single name, Sidney, what otherwise would need to be praised as a whole cast of types, "For every part a character assigned" (*Epigrams* 103, 12). The encyclopedic figures participate in a theatre differently conceived from that of the humors characters, deploying their knowledge not mechanically and reductively but carefully tempering it to the situation. The Cary – Morison ode is this alternative kind of theatre; encyclopedic selves still recite lines, but they are "the lines of life," united by the melody of "her air," and not the stirrer's empty and shapeless repetitions. Jonson composed the Cary – Morison ode after the dismal failure of *The New Inn* and his renunciation of the public stage in "Ode to Himself," with its bitter opening lines, "Come leave the loathéd stage,/ And the more loathsome age."[54] With its three voices and Pindaric reference to choral performance, the Cary – Morison ode intimates what a perfected theatre would look like – balanced, predictable, orderly, composed, none of its three parts suggesting any disruptive identity. Each is subordinated to the whole, and there is no single dominant role for any of them. It is a theatre for the display of an encyclopedic self. But Jonson can achieve this good theatre only between the covers of a book.

While difficult, the judgment between good and bad theatre is as necessary as any of the other fine *differentia* that Jonson requires of his readers. The centered self may be *like* the humors character, and the encyclopedia may *seem* to be reliant upon theatrical repetition, but ultimately each particular instance is to be distinguished. The necessity of this distinction is what divides the role of Asper, in *Every Man Out of His Humor*, into two characters – the theatrical persona of the envious Macilente, who is as much a victim of humors as any of the other characters in the play, and the impetuous but reasoned Asper, who is Macilente's more centered near-double. But clarity of vision is not entirely on the side of Asper, who misinterprets the nature of the humors he critiques. It is because he is *outside* the empty repetition of the humors characters that he must look for an explanation of the humors in the hidden parts of their psyche. Because he has some interiority – a hidden source of rage and the ability to distance himself from his own reactions enough to take on the character of Macilente, a persona both like and unlike himself – he assumes that the other characters must as well. The final difference between ethical encyclopedia and humors character, then, may rest in the *spectator's* position, and whether he views the character from within, in which case its behavior seems mechanically repetitive, or from without, in which case the viewer can project his own encyclopedic desires into the object, imagining it into fullness.

Inverting the imaginary theatre of the Cary – Morison ode, *Every Man Out of His Humor* is an example of actual theatre reformed along the lines of the encyclopedia. The second part of Mitis' complaint, it will be remembered, was that the play was too closely allied to the time. As Cordatus asserts, comedy is indeed the *imago veritatis* and the *speculum consuetudinis*, although this one has less a plot than a schema. It is not an Aristotelian mimesis of an action, nor does it pretend to be. When Mitis asks if the play will observe the unities and the traditions of "the Terentian manner," Cordatus responds that comedy's form has changed continually to fit its context, and that "we should enjoy the same license, or free power, to illustrate and heighten our invention as they did; and not be tied to those strict and regular forms, which the sickness of a few (who are nothing but form) would thrust upon us."[55] Like Selden, the encyclopedic theatre of *Every Man Out of His Humor* must have "Newness of sense, antiquity of voice!" – stored truths must be duplicated, but not theatrically or mechanically in their original form, which would necessarily empty them out. To give a plot of actions such as the "cross-wooing" Mitis requests is to offer one kind of merely theatrical repetition – not only because Mitis proposes what sounds like a well-worn romance plot, but because the emphasis is then on the passive reception by the audience of a series of old lines recited by actors. One danger of the theatre was that there was no place in it for encyclopedic richness of the encyclopedic self, discoursing freely on any topic at the dinner table. Actors and even playwrights were like Sidney's artisanal "Actors and Players ... of what nature will have set forth," bound to their words and bodies, hinting at a poverty of sense and soul. But the theatre was also a device like the broken compass for eking an acceptable representation out of an inadequate one by supplying ciphers to a great account. Furthermore, in the absence of an encyclopedic dinner companion, theatre could be a source of information about what can be said or imagined – not the theatre of effects that Jonson differentiates his own from in *Every Man In His Humor*,

> Where neither *Chorus* wafts you o'er the seas;
> Nor creaking throne comes down, the boys to please;
> Nor nimble squib is seen, to make afeared
> The gentlewomen; nor rolled bullet heard
> To say, it thunders; nor tempestuous drum
> Rumbles, to say a storm doth come;　　　　(Prologue, 16–21)

but one that presents, necessarily in bits and pieces because that is how it occurs, "language such as men do use," or the variety of languages that make up a society.

The obviously mechanical structure of *Every Man Out of His Humor* distances and alienates its watchers, refusing to present them with easily digestible plots of cross-wooing or distract them with spectacular, if empty, effects. As with an encyclopedia, the viewer of *Every Man Out of His Humour* must find his or her own way through the work, with Cordatus and Mitis as "Guides, not Commanders" – Jonson's description of the help the classics can provide us (*Timber*, 171f.). In contrast to the passive-aggressive Macilente, who simply sees what comes his way and then rails at it (although as Asper he is also the play's author), the audience must actively organize and interpret the elements that make up the combinatory of the play, "For to all the observations of the ancients, we have our own experience: which, if we will use and apply, we have better means to pronounce" (*Timber*, 166–69). We must render its universal store into some flexible form, not merely repeating it senselessly, but finding new applications for its universal store of knowledge. As Jonson warns in the first line of the first poem of his *Epigrams,* it is not enough for a play's viewer merely to "take [it] up" passively; the spectator, like the reader, must try "to understand." Ultimately the ideal spectator, as so often for Jonson, *is* a reader; even the most spectacular of theatrical genres, the masque, was ideally legible rather than fascinating:

> Then, as all actions of mankind
> are but a Laborinth, or maze,
> so let your Dances be entwined,
> yet not perplex men, unto *gaze*.
> But measured, and so numerous too,
> as men may *read* each act you do.
> (*Pleasure Reconciled to Virtue,* 261–66; my italics)

Jonson reverses the usual encyclopedic claim that privileges vision; what links the epigram and the encyclopedic self is their reserve – their ability to retain information in their depths until it is cozened out of them by a careful reader. *Reading* is active, solicitous, whether at the dinner table or in the library. *Gaze,* its theatrical counterpart, is not; it is dull, passive, mystified. The difference between gaze and reading, fascination and analysis, figuratively, is distance.[56] Jonson's books and his plays require *readers*, while his usual image of the actor is of a bad reader of another's text, not as the text for a spectator.

Jonson's poem to Edward Alleyn, the leading actor of the King's Men, recapitulates this movement from author to text by way of the stage. Jonson compares Alleyn to his classical predecessors Roscius and Aesop, who were said to have taught Cicero his skill in oratory. Like Horace in *Poetaster*, Cicero in *Catiline* (1611) is a quasi-Jonsonian figure. Since "Cicero, whose every breath was fame" (6) had praised his actor–teachers, Jonson can do no less for Alleyn, who outstrips them both:

> How can so great example die in me,
> That, Alleyn, I should pause to publish thee? (*Epigrams* 89, 7–8)

Of course, Alleyn had published Jonson on the stage long before, but as Jonson explains in the last two lines of the poem, publication as text is better than embodiment in the theatre:

> Wear this renown. 'Tis just, that who did give
> So many poets life, by one should live. (13–14)

The life Alleyn can give is as different from that which Jonson offers as the skillful but necessarily mimic actors Roscius and Aesop are from their greater pupil Cicero, who (as Jonson demonstrates in *Catiline*) both writes and performs his own part on the stage of the world. Alleyn realizes the writings of the poets and brings them to life in the moment, and it is only through him that their words can take on the physical form and pressure of the time. Jonson's publication of Alleyn as an epigram, however, can take Alleyn out of history again and make him eternal; once the words have been embodied in an actor, they can be embodied again in a text that will last beyond the realm of merely human action as they were in the Cary–Morison ode.[57] Epigram again appears as purified theatre, preserving and recreating Alleyn anew from his place "in" Jonson with every reading.

The quarto edition of *Every Man Out of His Humor* flaunts this new kind of newness that the good theatre can offer, the newness of something freshly repeated. The motto on the title page of the quarto *Every Man Out of His Humor* boasts that "I have not set my foot in another's [tracks]; if you stand closer, they will please you more, and ten times repeated (*repetita*; lit. 'sought again') they will please" ("Non aliena meo pressi pede *si propius stes/ Te capient magis *& decies repetita placebunt"). Jonson's epigraph is, predictably, not original, but neither is it simply a repetition; he compiles it from three separate sections of Horace's *Epistles* (*Ars Poetica*, 361–62 and 367; and I, 19. 22), demonstrating the kind of circular reading he demands of his reader/spectators, moving within the text and recombining its elements selectively and with judgment.[58] True to his preference for encyclopedic circling over mere repetition, Jonson's cento of Horace does not simply restate Horace's claim in the *Ars Poetica* that some works repay study more than others. Plays were not staged ten times in succession in early modern England. Jonson's motto is a reminder to the reader of the play to distinguish the printed text he or she holds, and which can be read at his or her pleasure, from the play that was performed at the Globe.[59] The motto's use of the first-person perfect *pressi*, from the verb *primo*, suggests both the Latin word for print, *imprimo*, and its English derivative, "press"; not only is Jonson breaking new ground, he is doing so by printing a book. Printed plays almost always presented themselves as deriving originally from a theatrical performance; in fact, early quartos especially may have had a cultural status closer to baseball programs than to texts, souvenirs of having been there rather than works to be read again.[60] Jonson reverses this. The epigraph is only the first part of the play that is "more than hath been publicly spoken or acted," as the title page boasts; it is one of many elements in the printed text that will let the reader get closer to the work, "As it was first composed by the Author B. I.," than its spectators did in the theatre.[61] The work's new medium literally requires that its reader "stand closer" to it than he would have in the theatre; the payoff is that in its new form it can be "sought out ten times" and enjoyed anew every time.

This ideal audience of readers is explicitly a theatre in its own right. The folio *Works' Poetaster* concludes with an epilogue that was performed only once to answer what Jonson felt were the libelous and ignorant reactions to it.

In it, he declares his intention to move on to the genre of tragedy,

> Where, if I prove the pleasure but of one,
> So he judicious be; He shall b' alone
> A Theatre unto me: (226–28)

Here Jonson draws on the Senecan conceit of the philosophical theatre of two like minds absorbed in mutual contemplation.[62] But *Sejanus*, the tragedy in question, was hardly more successful than *Poetaster* at securing for itself a learned and critically aware audience, in part perhaps because Jonson seems to have been writing for readers rather than spectators. The margins of the published versions of *Sejanus* (1603) and the contemporary *Masque of Blackness* (1605) and *Masque of Beauty* (1608) bristle with learned commentary invisible, one assumes, to their viewers.[63] Jonson's demonstration in the epigraph to *Every Man Out of His Humor* that words set into a new context thereby assumed renewed meaning – quite literally Selden's "newness of sense, antiquity of voice" – grew bolder in works like *Poetaster* and *Catiline*, which both include long passages from the works of Ovid, Horace, Vergil, and Cicero rearranged and translated into English. Set within Jonson's new, theatrical context, these become not the mere theatrical repetitions he dismissed but challenges to read encyclopedically, recognizing the work and seeing how it has changed in moving from an ancient text to a public stage, and finally, with the publication of Jonson's works, back into a book. In a revisionary return to the earlier humanist idea of the theatre, the single ideal reader is alone a theatre, because such a theatre could force each of its spectators to apply his or her timeless encyclopedic knowledge to his or her particular historical circumstances. Although in the Poets' War Jonson had been figured both by himself and by others as Horace the satirist, in *Poetaster* the encyclopedic poet who understands most clearly how to distinguish times is Vergil:

> That which he hath writ
> Is with such judgment, labored, and distilled
> Through all the needful uses of our lives,
> That could a man remember but his lines,
> He should not touch at any serious point,
> But he might breathe his spirit out of him.
>   . . . . he might repeat part of his works,
> As fit for any conference he can use? (5. 1. 118–25)

A burden of judgment remains on the reader, but, read correctly, Vergil's work offers guidance in any circumstance, a perfect ethical encyclopedia in the form of a poem and not a centered self. The motto on the title page of John Selden's *Table-Talk* was "Distingue tempora!" – "Distinguish times!" or perhaps,

"Always historicize!" – and employed properly, Jonson's encyclopedic theatre could do just that.

In his humors plays Jonson had offered a critique of an encyclopedic theatre; in his epigrams he had outlined an encyclopedic ideal, and in Vergil's poetry in *Poetaster* and the ideal theatre of the Cary–Morison ode, he offered a solution to the problem as one of distinguishing times – that the theatre was encyclopedic insofar as it dramatized the apt and skillful deployment of a "universal store"of learning. Any other theatre threatened to be a mere display. But Jonson and his contemporaries attempted to present an encyclopedic theatre onstage as well. In his great middle comedies, Jonson also revised his understanding of what the theatre was capable of and what real knowledge might consist in. One example of how an audience might "distinguish times" by applying the authorized knowledge of the encyclopedia in the mobile context of the theatre comes from John Webster's *The White Devil* (1612), when Flamineo addresses his seemingly ungrateful patron, Brachiano, who has taken Flamineo's sister as his mistress:

FLAMINEO: Lo, you, sister.
Stay, my lord; I'll tell you a tale. The crocodile, which lives in the river Nilus, hath a worm breeds i' th' teeth of't, which puts it to extreme anguish: a little bird, no bigger than a wren, is barber-surgeon to this crocodile; flies into the jaws of't; picks out the worm; and brings present remedy. The fish, glad of ease but ingrateful to her that did it, that the bird may not talk largely of her abroad for non-payment, closeth her chaps intending to swallow her, and so put her to perpetual silence. But nature loathing such ingratitude, hath armed this bird with a quill or prick on the head, top o' th' which wounds the crocodile i'th' mouth; forceth her open her bloody prison; and away flies the pretty tooth-picker from her cruel patient.
BRACHIANO: Your application is, I have not rewarded
The service you have done to me.
FLAMINEO: No my lord;
You, sister, are the crocodile: you are blemished in your fame, my lord cures it. And though the comparison hold not in every particle; yet observe, remember, what good the bird with the prick in the head hath done you; and scorn ingratitude. (*Works*, I, 159; 4. 2. 221–40)

Flamineo's tale is literally encyclopedic theatre. It comes to Webster from Pliny and Herodotus by way of Bartholomaeus Anglicus, perhaps through Stephen Batman's edition of 1582.[64] But it is not a simple statement about the nature of the world; it is a contest in which the nature of the world, in particular the human world of obligation and gratitude, is variously defined. In the space of twenty lines, it has three separate meanings applied to it: Brachiano's interpretation, Flamineo's correction, and Flamineo's sexual joke to his sister about the bird with the prick in its head.

It is hopeless to try to determine what Flamineo "means" here: the most likely candidate, and the least interesting, is the dirty joke he explicitly denies. He simply means, in all the banality of this analysis, what he says – that is, each of these meanings, and any others that could be spun from his curious anecdote. Flamineo tries to explain his multivalent tale in an aside: "But this allows my varying of shapes,/ *Knaves do grow great by being great men's apes*" (4. 2. 244–45). Flaminio's *sententia*, like the story that it further glosses but does not interpret, is here shown to be an element of discourse that is only distinguishable as true or false, or even apt or clumsy, in a particular context. Flamineo is in fact theatrically aping a great book, an encyclopedia, pulling it into history by citing it in a particular context. Context alone, though, is also insufficient to give the story a fixed meaning; context, too, is determined through discourse. This structure is analogous to that of the theatre beside itself; Webster uses drama to show how knowledge is something that must be constructed rhetorically rather than accepted as given. At least one further application of Flamineo's universal store passes unremarked. If Flamineo is the bird, Flamineo presents himself as a well-intentioned victim of Brachiano's ruthless crocodile. If Brachiano is the bird, then it is an off-color joke. But Bartholomaeus' story is different. Bartholomaeus' bird waits until the crocodile is asleep and then flies down its throat into its belly, where it uses its "prick" to rip the crocodile open from the inside (XVIII, 33). This application is perhaps Flamineo's "meaning," but it is certainly also (one of) Webster's; it reveals the opportunistic, amoral Flamineo for the Machiavel he is, not the wronged servitor but a predatory opportunist. This interpretation, though, is no more fixed than the others. The story's meaning varies with its audience.

What Flamineo and Brachiano – and no less Webster – are fighting for is the conviction of their audience, and they each rely on a surprise discovery for that conviction. The truth must catch them off guard, as it were, in order to secure the belief of their reader. In a reversal of the reliance on the *auctores* that continued to be so important, these authors try to show that the truth is *not* their possession. Instead it is a discovery; alienated knowledge appears to them unexpectedly, as something opportune rather than as something they have structured for themselves. Like the characters of Jonson's epigrams, they seem to find knowledge in a store of learning. But the store is not theirs to master – the elements that emerge fortuitously from it can, indeed must, be interpreted or applied to the immediate situation to become meaningful. Their skill, then, is not founded on endless reserves of closely-held knowledge, like those Jonson attributes to Selden or Camden, but on a sense of readiness and mutability that allows them to assign meanings to the information that flashes up before them. The theatre was a form of mechanical reproduction, preserving and repeating things from one context in an infinity of possible others, each of them particular. The emphasis on the application of things to the moment was what distinguished the theatre of practice from the encyclopedic theatre of the imagination. Such application begins as an interruption of ordinary discourse, such as Flamineo's triple interjection, "Lo, you, sister!" However calculated, application relies on a rhetoric of accidence rather than on a shared reliance on an inevitability. In doing so, it puts its authority up for grabs. Speaker and listener, rather than sharing an experience of reality, come to some tacit agreement of what their words mean by proposing interpretations, judging them, agreeing on them, marshalling fellow debaters, compelling assent. Knowledge cannot merely be shown, it must be performed.

A generation before Webster, Marlowe's *Doctor Faustus* relates a kind of humanist catastrophe of the centered self as born in performance. Contemporary reception and later criticism of this play have focused, rightly, on the issue of Faustus' sinfulness, but the play is also concerned with Faustus' knowledge and in particular, its failure to protect him. Not for nothing is Faustus represented as a scholar, first revealed in his library searching for a way to extend his knowledge and thus his power. Marlowe's play dramatizes the shortcomings of the encyclopedic conception of knowledge as a possession without being able to specify a workable alternative. The first scene demonstrates that the knowledge that Faustus seeks is already his, at least in the sense that he possesses – owns, in fact – its contents; not only is his library complete in "Aristotle's works,/Sweet *Analytics*," the logical and rhetorical texts of the *trivium* (1. 1. 5–6), but in medicine ("Galen"), law ("Justinian"), and divinity ("Jerome's Bible"), the advanced university faculties open to those trained in the *trivium*.[65] Although Faustus' repeated admonition to himself to "read no more, thou hast attained the end" (1. 1. 10) is premature, the accounts he offers of his successes ("Is not thy common talk sound aphorisms?/ Are not thy bills hung up as monuments,/ Whereby whole cities have escaped the plague/ And thousand desp'rate maladies been eased?" 1. 1. 19–21) suggest that he is not simply ignorant of the substance of the fields he professes, however selective his quotation from his source texts.[66]

Faustus' anticipatory sureness of the finality of his intellectual achievement and his disturbing ability to misread texts that he clearly knows and even has nearby in his library have a common root in his encyclopedic conception of knowledge. As Paul Budra has pointed out, Faustus is far more concerned with *having* books than with understanding them, as if they somehow contained knowledge physically and possession itself provided for a kind of mastery. What fascinates Faustus is not the application of knowledge that Flamineo excels at. It is precisely his real achievements that Faustus dismisses, and his inability to connect what he reads and hears with his own life is precisely opposite to Flamineo's serpentine ability to interpret. Faustus is instead dazzled by the idea of the power of the word itself, a power seemingly contained materially in the magical "Lines, circle, scenes, letters and characters" of the "necromantic books,"[67] which he cannot read but which he believes to have an inherent power that has nothing to do with human comprehension. In this he is the forerunner of Jonson's more comically costive Crispinus, full of incomprehensible words. Faustus' vocabulary invokes combinatory, theatre, and circle, the tropes of the encyclopedic theatre, but his relation to it is what Jonson terms *gaze* – Faustus is dazzled by the visual display of the magical symbols just as he is by the empty figures of the Seven Deadly Sins in Lucifer's feigning theatre when the Good Angel appears to tempt him back to God (2. 3. 108ff.).

Faustus sees words-as-things – books, spells, contracts – as possessing power not in their application to situations but inherently, and as sufficient to interpret and enforce themselves, although the play will continually point out their failure to do so. The disconcerting action of the play's clowns, whose scenes follow and parody those of Faustus and Mephistopheles, underlines the protagonist's great shortcoming – his strange faith in the power of the material book as a physical token of knowledge in place of its internalization in a reader. When the clowns half-accidentally summon Mephistopheles by reading aloud from Faustus' book (3. 2), they suggest to what extent Faustus, too, is relying on the power of the book's words without having any sense of what he is doing or how to control it. When Mephistopheles appears in a rage to "*set squibs at their backs*: [so that] *they run about*," the clowns' slapstick is not fundamentally different in its uncontrolled technique from their master's conjuring.[68] Faustus' actions are regularly echoed and undermined by corresponding scenes with Wagner and the clowns, who show the buffoonishness of Faustus' actions underneath the loftiness of his idealizing claims. Faustus' first summoning of Mephistopheles (1. 3) is followed by Wagner signing the clown into servitude (1. 4); Faustus' disruption of the Pope's banquet (3. 1) is followed by a tussle between Robin, Rafe, and the Vintner (3. 2). Nonetheless, the "tragic" scenes with Faustus are kept separate from the "comic" ones with Wagner and the clowns until the conceptual climax of the play. Immediately after the apparent triumph of Faustus' magical power in conjuring Alexander is the Horse-Courser scene (4. 1), in which Faustus passes over entirely into the world of Wagner, clowning away his immortal jewel with a false leg.

This plunge into tragicomic bathos reflects Faustus' crucial epistemological, rather than exclusively spiritual, problem. In spite of the knowledge that he possesses, both internally and materially in the form of books, Faustus is never able to move from knowing the world to acting intelligently in it. He repeatedly confounds things of slightest importance with things of great weight, preferring to watch a masque of sins rather than to save his soul, being distracted from the ominous clotting of his blood before he signs Mephistopheles' bill, vaulting across Europe only to slap the Pope or fetch grapes for the pregnant Duchess. He has technical mastery from the first lines of the play, but conspicuously lacks, and fails ever to develop, humanist *prudentia*, the practical knowledge of using one's learning to one's profit that Jonson celebrated in the centered selves of his *Epigrams*. What Faustus cannot do is *apply* his knowledge to his particular circumstances and needs in the way that Vives, More, or Jonson demanded. When Faustus fantasizes about diabolical knowledge that can "Resolve me of all ambiguities," he seems to be speaking less about knowing the world's secrets than of finding a single immutable meaning lodged in things themselves, the encyclopedic goal of a knowledge outside of time or perspective. Faustus possesses this complete knowledge already; he simply wishes to hold it beyond the accidents of interpretation and circumstance. As a result, Faustus repeatedly fails to give the encyclopedic learning he possesses a local habitation and a name; he cannot make his encyclopedic understanding work theatrically in Jonson's revised sense.

After his humors plays, Jonson's own sense of instruction becomes more indirect. The audience is much more closely associated with the characters of Jonson's plays than with their writer – they become Jonson's "Theatre" in the sense of being additional performers in it. The result is that they must increasingly understand the plays, as it were, from inside out. The search for understanding explicitly becomes a theme, as characters and spectators alike seek to decipher the play's world. When Jonson's texts take encyclopedism and the uses of knowledge as a theme rather than merely as an opportunity and a technique for praise, they suggest very different things about the acquisition and possession of a "universal store." In the Folio, this thematization of the encyclopedia is most obvious in Jonson's play of knowledge, *The Alchemist*. Vives' description of encyclopedism ends with the complaint that because men neglect encyclopedic studies, they know Cicero's or Pliny's times better than their own, preferring to master the trivia of an earlier time than to do the work of applying knowledge in the practice of the present.[69] Within this same half-serious, half-mocking mode, the prologue of *The Alchemist* sets out specifically to remedy this:

> Our *Scene* is *London,* 'cause we would make known,
> No country's mirth is better than our own . . .   (Prologue, 5–6)

Jonson's claim to knowledge in the play is founded in the humanist idea of *prudentia*, the practical, experiential, worldly knowledge lying worlds away from Faustus' fugitive and cloistered book-learning. Unlike *Every Man Out of His Humor*, though, which depended on the *reader* (whether of performance or text) to supply it with an order, *The Alchemist* shows its *characters* putting a kind of knowledge to work in the world.

The Alchemist is a play full of things – hardware like alembics, retorts, and pelicans, hard abstractions like cibation and mortification, even (and maybe especially) things that do not exist, like *sanguis agni*, the "white shirt" that matter puts on as it becomes the philosophers' stone. For the most part, these things never appear on stage; in fact, the role of the most important thing in the play, the philosophers' stone, is precisely *not* to appear while remaining always on the verge of arrival. What defers its materialization while at the same time making it imminent is the skillful use of language by the "venture tripartite" of Subtle, Face, and Dol Common. What marks all three of them as exceptional, in distinction not only to the collection of gulls in the play but to the ungulled and in the end apparently triumphant Lovewit, is their protean ability to reproduce a variety of discourses particular to a wide range of disciplines. In fact, it would be better to say that the play is full of hard words than full of hardware:

> SUBTLE: Your *lapis philosophicus*?
> FACE: 'Tis a stone, and not
> A stone; a spirit, a soul, and a body:
> Which, if you doe *dissolve,* it is *dissolved,*
> If you *coagulate,* it is *coagulated,*
> If you make it to fly, it flyeth. (2.5. 40–44)

> SUBTLE: O, this's no true *Grammar,*
> And as ill *Logic*! You must render causes, child,
> Your first, and second *Intentions,* know your *canons,*
> And your divisions, moods, degrees, and differences,
> Your predicaments, *substance,* and *accident,*
> *Series extern,* and *intern,* with their *causes*
> *Efficient, material, formal, final,*
> And ha' your *elements* perfect — (4.2. 21–28)

> DOL: And so we may arrive by Talmud skill,
> And profane Greek, to raise the building up
> Of Helen's house, against the Ismaelite,
> King of Thogarma, and his habergeons
> Brimstony, blue, and fiery; and the force
> Of King Abaddon, and the Beast of Cittim;
> Which Rabbi David Kimchi, Onkelos,
> And Aben-Ezra do interpret Rome. (4. 5. 25–32)

These speeches, dazzling though they are, are emphatically not outpourings of knowledge as conventionally understood, but mechanical repetitions of other discourses: Face ventriloquizes the jargon of alchemy, Subtle's science of quarreling is a hash of bogus Aristotelianism, and Dol's rabbinical history is lifted from a book by the Hebraicist Hugh Broughton.[70]

In their regurgitation of specialized discourses, Dol, Subtle, and Face are like the humors characters of Jonson's early plays, or Crispinus and Horace with their bloated or meager stores of words to use.[71] What distinguishes the three con-artists from their humors character counterparts in *Every Man Out of His Humor*, who also have taken over, or been taken over by, specialized discourses, or even from the learned but ineffectual Faustus, is their ability to put their knowledge to effect. Dol behaves like the humors characters Orange and Clove when, acting as the scholarly lady, she begins to rave about the mystical history of Israel to Sir Epicure Mammon. But Dol knows she is only acting and her words, although having no real meaning, nevertheless have at least an unmystified function; her mechanical (and theatrical) repetitions are expressly meant to cozen Mammon. The knowledge she and the others have is not empty. It has no referent on the level of alchemy or history, but it still has rhetorical force; it is in fact very successful at conning the gulls out of their money, a different kind of production of gold than that promised by alchemy, and one that is purely social. This language produces palpable effects without having any degree of adequate reference to any palpable thing. *The Alchemist* demonstrates that there is always something other than truth, in the sense of adequate representation of the thing, going on in issues of belief. When there is no thing present in reality, what counts as its truth can become a question of dazzling with words.

In *The Alchemist*, Jonson proposes a counter-argument to the Platonic epistemology of works like *Every Man Out of His Humor*, where knowledge is a kind of enlightenment and ignorance is its absence. In *Every Man Out of His Humor*, characters can be made to see, though sometimes with difficulty, the emptiness of their humors by confronting them with a strong enough refutation. When their eyes are opened to the idleness of their humors, they abandon them. I use the language of vision here intentionally, for in *Every Man Out of His Humor*, the "de-humoring" is often a literal demonstration of some destructive fact that cannot be reconciled with a particular humorous view of the world. At the end of the play, as Macilente shows the citizen Deliro his wife kissing the noble fop Fastidious Brisk, he taunts him to explain away what he sees: "Nay, why do you not dote now, Signor? Methinks you should say it were some enchantment, *deceptio visus*, or so, ha?" (5. 11. 9–12). Deliro cannot, as Macilente knows; in *Every Man Out of His Humor*, such ocular proof is definitive, and corrects the intellectual blindness from which Deliro and the humors characters have been suffering. When one is misled, it is the result of *deceptio visus*, or a trick of vision. To see things rightly, in this scheme, is to know the truth. *Doctor Faustus*, too, relies on the principle of the *deceptio visus* in a different sense. From the scene of his library full of books to the spectacular ekphrasis of the duel between Christ and Lucifer for Faustus' soul, it is always the appearance or the surface of knowledge that fascinates Faustus rather than its practice or application – with its spectacular pageants of the Sins, its mirages of wives, and its vain conjurings of dead phantoms. But not all visions are equally persuasive. Faustus' almost literally blind faith in the power of words as univocal things causes him again and again to overlook the hollowness of the particular images of power he fixes on. When, as he signs his pact with Mephistopheles, he sees the blood clot on his arm to form the words *Homo fuge*, Faustus can literally overlook that visible omen by simultaneously dismissing the sign as uncertain and at the same time believing that the contract he has agreed to has already bound him to Mephistopheles through its wordy force. Most important, the sights seen by Faustus that dazzle and confuse him in the play are *seen through* by the audience, just as they can see through the deceitful appearances of the disguised Vices in an early morality like Nicholas Udall's *Respublica*. The *deceptiones visus* of the play are, to the watching crowd, clearly that; there is no real deception about the kind of deception that they are watching.

The deceptions of *The Alchemist* are not mere *deceptiones visus*, although Jeremy desperately claims at the end of the play that "'Tis all *deceptio visus*" (5. 3. 62) as Lovewit stands outside the locked house hearing about the goings-on from the neighbors. Alchemy and the cozenage of the "venture tripartite" are not simply misapprehensions that can be corrected by better or even different viewpoints. Knowledge is more than enlightenment. When Surly, taking on the aspect of an Asper, reveals the scheme of Face and Subtle to Dame Pliant, he expects her to join him immediately on the side of what he takes to be a self-evident truth. He cannot imagine that she or anyone would persist in their error once the truth stood revealed. But it is as if Surly were transplanted from the simpler world of *Every Man Out of His Humor*. Like Dol, Face, and Subtle, Surly is a professional cozener, but the importance of this detail lies less in how it puts his project of revelation on the same shaky ethical footing as theirs than in the distance it sets up between their two approaches to deception. Surly's tricks rely on mechanical deceptions like marked cards and loaded dice that must be concealed, because if he reveals them, they lose their effectiveness; they must give the appearance of being ordinary. He mistakenly believes that the cheating he is trying to uncover is something similar:

> Alchemy is a pretty kind of game
> Somewhat like tricks o' the cards, to cheat a man,
> With charming. (2. 3. 180–82)

What makes the "venture tripartite" different from a cheat like Surly is their ability to weave together languages. The impenetrable jargons of Face, Subtle, and Dol instead fascinate without ever being deciphered or even decipherable. In *The Alchemist*, the languages of alchemy, kabbala, and other occult practices dazzle their hearers rather than escaping their notice; they are, to use the distinction Jonson makes of masques, gazed at rather than read. Subtle's alchemical discourse, unlike Surly's card tricks that only work until uncovered, must be disseminated; the exposure that serves in other contexts to bridle cheating here fosters it. Each time a new gull is brought in to Subtle, Subtle displays a mastery of language and thus implies a related power over the mysteries he deals in. Drugger is shown – in language, for the power of Subtle's words lies in *not* seeing their referents – the wonders of metoscopy, chiromancy, and kabbalistic angelology (1. 3. 43–49, 52–57, 63–68); Ananias sees Subtle run Face through an alchemical catechism (2. 5. 7–45); and Kastril is promised a tabular exposition of the art of quarreling (3. 4. 25–37). Only Dapper, who spends most of the play locked in the privy with a piece of gingerbread in his mouth and a dead mouse in his hand, waiting to be visited by the Queen of Faery, is simple enough to be taken in without a display of extraordinary language.

In *Doctor Faustus*, Faustus fantasizes that all his desires can be made real through the accumulation of sufficient knowledge, and the course of the play is about that failure of knowledge to equal ability. In *The Alchemist*, on the other hand, the poles of knowledge and power collapse into each other, so that the knowledge of Dol, Face, and Subtle produces its own power to validate itself.[72] Surly finds that his plain-dealing enlightenment of Dame Pliant is much less seductive than Subtle's jargon, and Ananias is quickly confuted – to his own satisfaction, significantly – by Subtle and Face. Subtle does not attempt to show Ananias referents in the world for "*sapor pontic? sapor stiptic?* . . . *Ars sacra,/ Or Chrysopoeia*, or *Spagirica,/ Or the pamphysic*, or *panarchic* knowledge . . ." (2. 5. 10–15), the encyclopedic (*pamphysic* means "all of nature") comprehension of all things that he claims to have and that Ananias challenges as "heathen Greek." Instead he proves that his speech is meaningful by asking Face questions about it:

> Sirrah, my varlet, stand you forth, and speak to him,
> Like a *Philosopher*: Answer, i'the language.
> Name the vexations, and the martyrizations
> Of metals, in the work.
> FACE: Sir, *Putrefaction*,
> *Solution, Ablution, Sublimation,*
> *Cohobation, Calcination, Ceration*, and
> *Fixation*.
> SUBTLE: This is heathen Greek to you, now?   (2. 5. 18–24)

What convinces Ananias that Subtle's alchemical catechism is not meaningless is the ability of Face to respond to it. In other words, the evidence of a social context for the language of alchemy serves as a guarantee of its truth. Ananias' only error is mistaking the meaning socially established by the speech, which is not about alchemy at all, but about ensuring that Ananias and the Holy Brethren continue to believe in it and give their money to Subtle.

Subtle and Face are aware that they are cozening Ananias, and so their cant could be seen as an aural version of *deceptio visus* – there remains an undeceived point of view from which all comes into clear focus. But the discourse of alchemy can operate even without an enlightened user. Mammon is the character who most perfectly rehearses the alchemical jargon of Face and Subtle, the character who has been most thoroughly absorbed in it and who is least able to resist it. When Surly remains skeptical and demands ocular proof, Mammon's astonishing language dazzles Surly in describing the effects of the stone, not only on Mammon's credit, but that of the past:

> Pertinax, my Surly,
> Will you believe antiquity? Records?
> I'll show you a book, where Moses, and his sister,
> And Salomon have written, of the art;
> Aye, and a treatise penned by Adam[.] (2. 1. 79–83)

Mammon overrides Surly's objections by establishing a socially ratified history of "antiquity" and "records" which renders Surly's objections senseless. While the catechism required a difference between Subtle and Face, who know the "truth" of their speech, and Ananias, who is taken in by it, there is no such difference here; Mammon believes what he is saying. The discourse of Subtle and Face is contagious: Mammon does not realize that his language is fulfilling its purpose precisely because he does not know what he is talking about. The power of language, as opposed to Surly's card tricks, is that it does not require an enlightened cozener and a hoodwinked cony. It is not simply a tool to be used, although of course it is also that; it is the ground of the social knowledge that circulates around the tables of the great and the ordinaries of the lowly alike. The language of alchemy literally speaks itself through Mammon, a mechanical repetition that does not rely on a knowing subject for its appearance. The deceptions of Face, Subtle, and Dol require exposure and dissemination rather than concealment. They grow more rapidly the more widespread and visible they are, and spread by advertising rather than hiding their impossibility. They are a set of seductive discourses that the gulls inhabit and from which they cannot exit; the more the gulls talk – skeptically or not – the more their language makes what they talk about convincing.

Jeremy's plea that Lovewit understand all as *deceptio visus* is his attempt to simplify and domesticate the true complexity of these overlapping languages. In Jeremy's version, there is the good servant Jeremy and the bad Captain Face, and they are distinct. Whether Lovewit believes that they are different individuals, as Jeremy implies, or whether he sees with the audience that they are both roles played by a single actor, makes little difference to the stability this explanation offers. In either case Jeremy and Face can be kept separate, and where one is, the other is not. The truth is instead that Jeremy and Face, and for that matter the other characters he plays, Ulenspiegel and Lungs, are all the same, and that what lets one appear in place of the others, in Jeremy's explanation to Lovewit no less than any of his other explanations during the play, is an effect of language. Who appears is literally a function of what is said. Truth then resides in the ability to structure discourses that are logically seamless in their own terms, regardless of their aptness to the world around them. More accurately, the interest in "truth" is suspended in favor of effectiveness, the ability of speech to shape reality.

In their interactions, the characters of *The Alchemist* develop the distinction between performative and constative forms of knowledge. Jonson's criticism, and the source of the three plotters' power to deceive, is that we ignore the performative elements in knowledge and mistake them for constative knowledge. Mammon's misunderstanding of the status of his descriptions thus in no way hinders their suasiveness. Different viewers weave different discourses around the things they find in the world, and what makes them right or wrong is not the things themselves; the things change depending on the languages, which must in turn be authorized or dismissed within other discourses. But we reduce the qualities assigned to objects within various discourses to the objects' essential *properties* and treat them as kinds of possessions, acting much as Faustus does in Marlowe's play. The power of language to shape things is revealed when Subtle and Face suggest an alchemical laboratory full of equipment in a conversation they have for Mammon's benefit:

> SUBTLE: Are you sure you loosed 'em
> I' their own *menstrue*?
> FACE: Yes, sir, and then married 'em,
> And put 'em in a *Bolt's-head,* nipped to *digestion,*
> According as you bad me; when I set
> The liquor of Mars to *circulation,*
> In the same heat.
> SUBTLE: The process, then, was right.
> FACE: Yes, by the token, sir, the *Retort* brake,
> And what was saved, was put into the *Pelican,*
> And signed with Hermes' seal.
> SUBTLE: I think 'twas so.
> We should have a new *amalgama*. (2. 3. 71–80)

Later, in the same room, Lovewit discovers only

> The empty walls, worse then I left 'em, smoked,
> A few cracked pots, and glasses, and a furnace,
> The ceiling filled with poesies of the candle:
> And Madame with a dildo writ o' the walls. (5. 5. 39–42)

Lovewit's rhetoric of deflation does not expose the alchemical laboratory as a wholecloth fabrication. There really was some sort of activity there – there are broken pots and candle burns to prove it. Instead, Lovewit sets the same furnaces and equipment into a different discursive context, one that strips them of their power by reducing their power to that of words, imagination, and desire – suggestively a desire that is doubly substitutive, no more satisfying than the writing of a dildo – as opposed to hard facts and real objects.

The display of learning and tongues put on by Subtle, Dol, and Face for their victims seems to have no boundaries – it is, in other words, a caricature of encyclopedic learning, not the minute reproduction of the world in thought, but the ability to shape the world in speech. According to Robert Greene, even primitive cony-catching depended upon a kind of perversely encyclopedic knowledge:

> The taker-up [a kind of cozener] seemeth a skillful man in all things, who hath by long travail learned without book a thousand policies to insinuate himself into a man's acquaintance. Talk of matters in law, he hath plenty of cases at his fingers' ends, and he hath seen, and tried, and ruled in the King's courts. Speak of grazing and husbandry, no man knoweth more shires than he, nor better which way to raise a gainful commodity, and how the abuses and overtures of prices might be redressed. Finally, enter into what discourse they list, were it into a broom-man's faculty, he knoweth what gains they have for old boots and shoes ...[73]

Subtle, Face, and Dol, like Greene's taker-up, speak with ease on any subject, including those of which they have no practical experience – and those like alchemy and kabbalistic history, of which nobody has any experience. But this limitless learning is proper not only to the con-artist, the abuser of knowledge. It is rightly the province of the poet as master of language, possessing "exact knowledge of all virtues, and their contraries" (*Timber*, 1283). This knowledge of all the arts necessarily includes the immoral alternative to real encyclopedic knowledge: "It is an art to have so much judgment, as to apparel a lie well, to give it a good dressing" (*Timber*, 386–87). Prudence, gained through encyclopedic learning and the ground for good judgment, is equally apt for crafting a convincing lie. Judged in practical terms of its effectiveness, the knowledge to cozen is as much a part of the circle of knowledge as any other discipline. The ideal of learned conversation treats language as a kind of currency rather than as a passive reflection of reality, and makes of it an activity rather than an object.[74] The elite intellectualism of the humanists and the gritty world of the cony-catchers come together in the house where the alchemy is staged.

What Subtle, Face, and Dol show in *The Alchemist* is a kind of negative knowledge that takes effect through mystification and not through enlightenment, a way of knowing that, contrary to Jonson's earlier Platonic doctrine, is both positive *and* immoral, prudent in its structure but reckless in its practice, a discourse with all the characteristics of knowledge including, significantly, prudential "judgment," except for the ethically uplifting ones. The goals of the "venture tripartite" are more limited, of course, than those of Faustus – they seek to master ideology rather than physics and metaphysics – and they succeed, unlike Faustus, because they do not confuse the power of their language with power over the extrahuman world. Human speech is powerful enough to achieve almost anything within the realm of belief or hope, but, as in *Doctor*

Faustus, not within the world of things. The learning displayed by the taker-up or by Dol, Face, or Subtle has no outside, or rather there is *only* an outside, and it provides no way to tell a well-appareled lie from the naked truth. It is true that Subtle's alchemy and Dol's Hebrew learning have no referent in the world of objects, as Lovewit's deflating description of the laboratory reveals. But they are not for that reason without effect. They have functions without having meanings; rather than reflecting or representing a world, they go to work within a world, and they work by exploiting the belief of the gulls that they make a reference to something that is outside the social world of discourse. This is also what gulls Faustus – he believes in the limitless power of Mephistopheles, although he is repeatedly shown that it consists of empty shows and illusions, and in the end these cloudy fictions result in the loss of his soul, which in the terms of the play is the truly real thing about him.

In *The Alchemist*, language, like alchemy, works by projection. It intimates things to come by emphasizing their current absence; it presents parts, and lets the desire of the gulls fill them in as wholes. The represented space and time of the play commingle with the actual space and time of its first production: Lovewit's house, like the theatre building, is in the Blackfriars district; like the theatre building, it has recently been abandoned due to the threat of plague.[75] The first line of the prologue sets the limit of the play at "two short hours." Almost Face's first words to Mammon are the command to "three hours hence, prepare you/ To see projection" (2. 2. 4–5), informing the audience that the promised transformation of base metals into gold will fall outside the time limits of the play. This double vision of the play – both the play *in* the theatre and the *dis*play *of* the theatre – lets *The Alchemist* take the form of an unfulfilled promise or, more accurately, a promise to remain unfulfilled. But the play is also honest about its limits. The "venture tripartite" of Face, Subtle, and Dol never claims that its words are magical, that the language that the gulls hear can in any way be exchanged for gold or power. Unlike Surly's material tricks, there is no bogus evidence other than language in their deceptions – even the Spanish costume procured by Face is never used except by Surly and Lovewit. The world of things does not deceive on its own, but only by means of the languages in which it is made meaningful, and then only because, encyclopedically, those languages are confused with things. What convinces is in every case the foolish desire of the gulls, and the commitment of each victim to his or her desire is why, contrary to what Surly expects, ending the deceptive play is not as easy as exposing it.[76]

My analysis of *The Alchemist* to this point, it will be noticed, only shifts the distinguishing quality between good knowledge and bad knowledge from content to effect. It acknowledges that at one level the social knowledge of Face, Subtle, and Dol is like every other kind of legitimate knowledge. In this play, in contrast to his centered selves of the *Epigrams* and the tragicomically decentered ones of the humors plays, Jonson looks at the productivity of knowledge not as a physical capacity – to reflect the world or materially reshape it, for instance – and certainly not as a material entity that can be "possessed," but as social transformation through the capture of human belief. Whereas Marlowe presents Faustus conjuring the fictive Alexander at the emperor's court as a critique of such merely apparent knowledge, Jonson fully gives words the partial credit they deserve. Not what truly is, but what truly *seems*, and thus can dazzle or fascinate, has real power in *The Alchemist*. But the play also rediscovers a way of distinguishing one kind of knowledge from the other in a metadiscourse of cozening, in which some characters, like Face and Subtle, are able to manipulate the discourse of alchemy to defraud other characters like Ananias, while still others, like Mammon or Drugger, unwittingly continue to dupe themselves and even project the deception onto others without recognizing their own ensnarement. The language of alchemy is split by the knowledge of it that its users bring to it, and the binaries of true/false or meaningful/meaningless are replaced by an analogous one of socially beneficial (or at worst neutral) and socially predatory. In other words, we are apparently left with the same kind of distinction as that between true knowledge and seeming knowledge, re-emerging under ethical terms – helpful knowledge and empty knowledge.

In fact, though, the knowledge of Subtle and Face is not so neatly contained. The wildest claims for the material power of the stone are Mammon's; Subtle and Face rely on a language about the stone's production, but their discussion of its magical properties after it is made is kept to a minimum. Instead they present the stone principally in terms of social interactions. When he urges the Puritans Tribulation Wholesome and Ananias to continue to invest in the making of the stone, Subtle rushes past the mere material wealth it will bring them and emphasizes instead its power to make a place for them in a culture that currently rejects them:

> As, put the case,
> That some great man in state, he have the gout,
> Why, you but send three drops of your *Elixir*,
> You help him straight: there you have made a friend.
> Another has the palsy, or the dropsy,
> He takes of your incombustible stuff,
> He's young again: there you have made a friend.
>
> A lord, that is a *Leper*,
> A knight, that has the bone-ache, or a squire
> That hath both these, you make 'em smooth and sound,
> With a bare fricace of your med'cine: still
> You increase your friends. (3. 2. 26–32, 37–41)

Real alchemy, this hints, is skill in manipulating social connections, the production of friends through the manufacture of belief. Subtle's advice shows the real knowledge of human affairs that Jonson specified as encyclopedic: "Sense is wrought out of experience, the knowledge of human life, and actions, or the liberal arts, which the Greeks called 'Εγκυκλοπαιδειαν" (*Timber*, 2336–39). There is nothing to distinguish this advice from what Tribulation Wholesome might hear from one of the centered selves of the *Epigrams*. Two scenes later, an even more remarkable education takes place as Face describes to Kastril Subtle's ability to train a man in quarreling and the other fine points of being a gentleman.

>   The whole town
>   Study his theorems, and dispute them, ordinarily,
>   At the eating Academies.
> KASTRIL: But, does he teach
>   Living, by the wits, too?
> FACE: Any thing whatever.
>   You cannot think that subtlety, but he reads it.
>   He made me a captain. I was a stark pimp,
>   Just o' your standing, 'fore I met with him:
>   It i' not two months since.   (3. 4. 39–46)

Face, while deceiving Kastril, is also being absolutely forthright with him. Subtle really has, by Face's own admission, made him a Captain, if not out of a stark pimp at least of a "good,/ Honest, plain, livery, three-pound thrum" (1. 1. 15–16). Subtle's real alchemy is just what Face offers Kastril, the knowledge of the social conventions that allows him to pass from one form of existence to another. There is no reason to distinguish the gentlemanly education Face promises Kastril from his own, in which Subtle (as he says to Face)

> *Sublimed* thee, and *exalted* thee, and *fixed* thee
> I' the *third region*, called our *state of grace*?
> Wrought thee to spirit, to *quintessence*, with pains
> Would twice have won me the *philosophers' work*?
> Put thee in words, and fashion? Made thee fit
> For more than ordinary fellowships?
> Giv'n thee thy oaths, thy quarreling dimensions?   (1. 1. 68–74)

The social transformation "in words, and fashion" of Face into a Captain is Subtle's real alchemical achievement. In this light, the remaining line between conies and cony-catchers disappears; they are not irreconcilable opposites, like rabbits and foxes, but a continuum like graduate students and professors, simply at different stages in a process.

Doctor Faustus is a tragedy because in the end, the protagonist's ambitions are unmet, and it turns out that in spite of his – and his play's – hopes, there is no real difference between the educated doctor's conjuring and the student Wagner's much more obviously inept dabbling. In *Faustus*, the clowns serve as foils to Faustus' pretensions and to their ultimate failure. In *The Alchemist*, in contrast, Face is not Subtle's foil but his counterpart and ally; the absolute distinctions that *Faustus* imagines, tries and ultimately fails to maintain, are never present except as delusions. Mammon's belief that he will exceed all human wealth, for instance, is instantly recognizable as folly. It is learning that these differences do not exist that ensures that *The Alchemist* is a comedy, and this knowledge – of the alchemy of social relations – is what the gulls get for their money. Jonson's play revises the tragic deflation of Faustus as comic bathos. When Faustus quotes Ramus as Aristotle, *Bene disserere est finis logicis*, "to speak well is the goal of logic," that apparently limited goal is for Faustus reason enough to abandon logic. But for Jonson, in *The Alchemist*, speaking well is sufficient power to do almost anything, so long as it relies on human weakness and not material change. Kastril thinks he is paying for an education, but paying and being deluded is itself the education. The education of the spectator in *Every Man Out of His Humor* involves the same delusion. Mitis wanted a plot he could view passively, a content to be taken in, but it is Mitis who is taken in; what he pays for is the opportunity to interpret, arrange, and work on the play he is shown. He learns by being disappointed, and by paying for it.

This payment is the sole difference between the gulls and the cozeners. The gulls in *The Alchemist* all in one way or another believe that they can get something for nothing, while the cozeners know better than to believe in that or in any other kind of alchemy. Being deprived of their money, the gulls of *The Alchemist* will eventually learn, as Face does, this lesson of the constructive powers of discourse. The burden of the play is precisely that the traffic in language carried on by Subtle, Face, and Dol is not nothing. It is an activity that produces effects of its own rather than a mirror that reflects whatever is set before it without distortion. Language is not alienated – or alienable – from its users, as knowledge is in *Doctor Faustus*, as when the books are treated by both Faustus and the clowns as containing knowledge like an object. The true poem makes a demand on its consumer like the one made on its maker: "Indeed, things, wrote with labor deserve so to be read and will last their age" (*Timber*, 3055–56). In *The Alchemist*, Dol, Face, and Subtle are intellectual laborers who exchange words for goods. They can gull the other characters because the others believe that it is possible to get gold for nothing; in the process of learning that there is no increase without work, they surrender their wealth.

In this, too, alchemy is like a theatre. As Jonson observes in the Induction to *Bartholomew Fair*, in entering the theatre, we pay our money "preposterously"; we buy a product that we have not seen and cannot know what it is, whether we believe it to be entertainment or, with Jonson, education in the ways of the world.[77] In the Induction of *Bartholomew Fair*, Jonson offers his audience a contract in which they are given certain rights of interpretation and in return forfeit certain lines of understanding. As in an antimasque, a limited amount of disorder is allowed – in this case, by admitting that interpretive authority has been given to the audience – in order for it to finally be recuperated by Jonson as the author in strict economic terms:

> It is further agreed that every person here have his or their free-will of censure, to like or dislike at their own charge, the author having now departed with his right: it shall be lawful for any man to judge his six pen'orth, his twelve pen'orth, so to his eighteen-pence, two shillings, half a crown to the value of his place, provided always his place get not above his wit. And if he pay for half a dozen, he may censure for all them too, . . .[78]

According to Jonson's terms, the audience has already entered into the contract, "as you have preposterously put to your seals already (which is your money)." This intrusion of the real activities of the audience into the play world of the theatre makes the contract other than the usual joking induction directed to the audience.[79] Once the spectators have bought into it, however, their judgment is of limited interest to the theatre company, which has made its money whether the audience likes or understands the play or not. Their seals are literally pre-posterous, putting first what should come later.[80] These judging spectators, moreover, are by the same contract enjoined against "censure by contagion, or upon trust, from another's voice, or face" and required to maintain consistency: "what he approves, or not approves to day, he will do the same tomorrow, and if tomorrow, the next day and so the next week (if need be)." In short, the theatrical contract creates an audience of centered, stable selves, capable of (and constrained to be) remaining critically ever at home, like the consistently decorous and predictable actors that Hamlet praises who never stray beyond the bounds of the norm.

Within a single theatrical setting, *The Alchemist* shows both the power of theatrical illusion and its emptiness, and it is through this play of presence and absence that the theatre has the effect of producing knowledge. Like the prologue to *Bartholomew Fair*, in which the cash is determined to be both the ultimate basis of the real and, simultaneously, revealed to be a social construction, *The Alchemist* comes as close as possible to showing off the theatre itself in all its duplicity. The theatre, too, both the one staged by the "venture tripartite" and the one in which they are staged, falls into this structure of a single object that shifts with its different interpreters from within and without the discourse it establishes. From one point of view, *The Alchemist*, like alchemy, is only theatre. From another perspective, the theatre, for the same reasons that the first dismisses it, is full of all the disciplines needed for human life – in fact, truly encyclopedic in the way first imagined by the humanist critics of the theatre. The final *differentia* between legitimate and illegitimate knowledge, the play shows, is not in the knowledge at all, but in how it is framed by the spectator. The difference between a Selden and a Subtle is one that finally we cannot make, as long as we insist on making one between text and theatre, good repetition and bad, reading and gazing – but only these latter distinctions give the first one any meaning.

The performative knowledge disseminated in *The Alchemist* is Jonson's response to the community of the *Epigrams*. The *themes* of *The Alchemist*, *Bartholomew Fair*, and *The Staple of News* reveal that individuals are not in themselves centered or humorous, but that a social network produces both sorts of individual through the exchange of money and the investment of desire. The encyclopedic knowledge of the social whole is held before us like the promise of the philosophers' stone, but like Mammon, we always await projection in three hours' time, although we will be at the theatre for only two hours. The perfect understanding and unity promised by characters like Mammon or Faustus is imaginary, projected, cast ahead of itself into the discourse that gives it meaning. The idea of the encyclopedia is an object of intense desire in all of Jonson's works, but it is always cut with nostalgia, melancholy, anticipation, or the other feelings one may experience in relation to an absent object. From within a discourse, such total knowledge is always impending and awaited with anticipation; from outside it, it is already lost or impossible, viewed with disappointment or ridicule. In the present, it is never more, but also never less, than a theatrical show – a knowledge that exists not as a reference to the way things are or even to the way they are said by authorities to be, but one that is enacted and renewed in each moment by chains of desires, beliefs, promises, hopes.

6 Francis Bacon's theatre of Orpheus: "Literate experience" and experimental science

> Dramatic Poesy, which has the theatre for its world, would be of excellent use if well directed. For the stage is capable of no small influence both of discipline and of corruption. Now of corruptions in this kind we have enough; but the discipline has in our times been plainly neglected. And though in modern states play-acting is esteemed but as a toy . . . among the ancients it was used as a means of educating men's minds to virtue. Nay, it has been regarded by learned men and great philosophers as a kind of musician's bow by which men's minds may be played upon. And certainly it is most true, and one of the great secrets of nature, that the minds of men are more open to impressions and affections when many are gathered together than when they are alone.
> —Francis Bacon, *De Augmentis* 2. 13

Works like Ben Jonson's demonstrate the limits of the encyclopedic theatre as well as its promise. In them, a vision of the world is shared, but for all that not secured; interpretation is not separated from observation, and the surface of things itself does not speak univocally. Jonson's works propose two alternatives to the empty show of learning that the theatre can be: the ideal audience reading a poem as the exemplary case of perfect theatre, or the performance of knowledge rooted in human activity but without a foundation in things or authorities, as in *The Alchemist*. He grounds both alternatives in a grasp of the real practices and forms of human interaction, whether as an ideal in the centered selves (and a corresponding negative of that ideal in the humors characters) or as a real sort of knowledge of behavior in plays. Ultimately, though, what both encyclopedia and theatre must focus on to be true is *us* – human beings in a world defined by their behaviors and labelings.

Francis Bacon offers another perspective on the relation of theatre and encyclopedia that in a sense is a culmination of the encyclopedic theory of the past thousand years and the theatrical thought of the previous hundred. Bacon's most well-known reference to theatre is of course his dismissal of what he calls the Idols of the Theatre as one of humanity's self-imposed obstacles to knowledge of the world. But as the epigraph suggests, Bacon's attitude towards theatre is not simply to reject it, as is sometimes suggested. Bacon's long intellectual engagement with theatre – his own writings for it, his ongoing interest in it as a symbol, his payment of £2,000 to sponsor a masque for the wedding of Robert Devereux and Frances Howard – demonstrates a relation more complex than simple dismissal.[1] Like Jonson's, Bacon's project is a reformist one of bringing theatre and encyclopedia profitably together. It is not, however, Jonson's theatre as an encyclopedia of social knowledge, but an encyclopedia that would truly theatricalize knowledge by performing it and experiencing it. Bacon's experimental science as described (we know less of his practices) relegates the idea of the theatre to the background so that the voice of real objects can be heard, what Bacon calls the "discourse of things" (*sermo rerum*). But this verbalization is simultaneously a visual receptivity: "all depends on keeping the eye steadily fixed upon the facts of nature and so receiving the images simply as they are" (*Instauratio Magna*, *Works*, I: 145, IV: 32). In this view, the transition from theatre to science demands invoking things themselves to speak their truth along the model of writing – to use Jonson's distinction once more, to subject them to reading rather than gazing; to return to mine, to make them drama rather than theatre, and to tie the knower's productive activity into the performance of knowledge. Bacon's explicit linking of the encyclopedia to power relies on his sense of knowledge as something produced, performed, pursued, rather than as something that confronts the viewer in stupefying completeness.

In 1591, at the age of thirty-one, advancing rapidly at Gray's Inn but unable to secure a significant government appointment, Francis Bacon wrote a letter to his uncle William Cecil, the Lord Chancellor, protesting his lack of political ambition:

Lastly I confess that I have vast contemplative ends, as I have moderate civil ends: for I have taken all knowledge to be my province; and if I could purge it of two sorts of rovers, whereof the one with frivolous disputations, confrontations and verbosities, the other with blind experiments and auricular traditional impostures, both committed to so many spoils, I hope I should bring in industrious observations, grounded conclusions and profitable inventions and discoveries . . .[2]

Bacon's careerism here, like the Aristotelian science he will critique later, "carr[ies] a show of perfection in the whole, but in the parts ill filled up" (*Instauratio Magna*, Preface, *Works*, IV: 16); it is a master plan without clear contents.[3] The letter shows an oblique and doubled commitment to both knowledge (but why then write to Cecil?) and civil service (but why then protest one's unfitness for it?). In fact, Bacon's self-description seems at first glance simply confused – he prefers, he says, contemplation to engagement, but his ultimate goals are active ones, *industry* and *profit*.

But Bacon protests that a similar confusion governs most fields of human learning. In his letter to Cecil, Bacon views "all knowledge" spatially, as a colony; it is his "province," a territory of the mind to be conquered and governed in lieu of an actual one. It will only be recovered by replacing the "rovers" who terrorize it now, impractical theorizing and untheorized practice, the piratical methods through which its dominion is pursued.[4] Elsewhere Bacon offers another image that contrasts his new method with the two older ones:

> Those who have handled sciences have been either men of experiment or men of dogmas. The men of experiment are like the ant; they only collect and use; the reasoners resemble spiders, who make cobwebs out of their own substance. But the bee takes a middle course, it gathers its material from the flowers of the garden and of the field, but transforms and digests it by a power of its own. (*Novum Organum* 1. 95, *Works*, I: 201, IV: 92–93)

With his province of all knowledge cleansed, Bacon will join these two methods together again to produce theoretical "conclusions" from empirical "observations," rather than to spin the one from thin air or to gather the other at random as it comes. Like the work of the empiricists, Bacon's work begins in the external world and in its close observation. Like the theoreticians and dogmatists, Bacon processes this information through the use of memory and reason. Unlike the mechanical arts, which laudably combine thinking and doing, "philosophy and the sciences of the intellect, on the contrary, are like statues, worshipped and celebrated, but not moved or advanced."[5] Bacon here refers to the moving statues of Hermes Trismegistus' *Poemander*, marvelously animated by the astral influences to which they had been meticulously attuned; Bacon too seeks that union of artifice and animation as an alternative to either heaps of antlike experience or veils of spidery theorizing. Only by joining theory and practice, system and experience – and the flowers of both garden and field, that is, of both experimentalism and empiricism – can Bacon open the way again to progress and advancement instead of the empty repetition of received knowledge that has characterized learning in philosophy up to Bacon's time.

Bacon periodically became re-enchanted with his epistemological project, usually when his political career was faltering, and threatened to dedicate the rest of his life to it – when he failed to obtain the posts of either Solicitor General or Attorney General in 1594, for instance, and again in 1621 after being stripped of the Chancellorship for accepting bribes.[6] But Bacon did not simply use the pursuit of knowledge as a substitute for political power, a kind of consolation prize or even a lure which he could repeatedly hold out for himself as his always-anticipated true calling;[7] for him knowledge and power maintained an inverse but deeply implicated relationship. Revising the earlier example of Alexander's sponsorship of Aristotle's encyclopedic research, Bacon concluded that ultimately "human knowledge and human power do really meet in one," but also that their meeting is only their eventual end-point, to be reached after a number of intermediate steps in which they do not reflect and sometimes even seem to oppose one another.[8] Ultimately, Bacon's conception of a unified field of knowledge, marked into divisions that were in the end transcended, blended action and contemplation, and simultaneously put science in the service of practice and human activity in the realm of the scientifically knowable.[9]

Bacon is not usually given much credit for having succeeded in his task. Certainly his experimental science remained largely imaginary, and his entire encyclopedic project, the reform of all the arts and sciences according to the reality of the world rather than to the desires of humanity, is explicitly no more than a gesture showing the direction in which Bacon believed that others must advance without him.[10] Bacon's project is significant for another reason – not because of his scientific achievement as usually defined, but because of his achievement of establishing and simultaneously exposing an ideology of science. His apparent inconsistencies are rather signs of his double motion of developing a series of conditions for a knowledge that is absolute, visual, timeless, objective, and of revealing the necessary forces of desire and illusion behind such a conception of knowledge, desires and illusions which, paradoxically, make it function. Later interpreters of Baconian science, like the Royal Society and D'Alembert in his introduction to the *Encyclopédie*, would forget the second half of Bacon's task – of revealing the technologies through which his science hid its human origins and made itself into pure fact. This doubleness of representation, which shows simultaneously its object and its process, also characterizes the spectacles of the public theatre of Bacon's time, and for Bacon, as for so many previous encyclopedists, the theatre becomes a governing metaphor for his vision. Bacon's emphasis on what he calls "the vicissitude of things" in the last of his essays, "On Truth," points towards a tentative transcendence of the difference between theatre and encyclopedia, one that replaces the earlier humanist dream of theatre as a device for encyclopedic education and instead suggests that means and end, knowledge and power, really do finally coincide – that the theatre is an encyclopedia because the world is a theatre.

Bacon's epistemological project of looking into the vicissitude of things themselves meant turning away from the different, but equally domesticated, versions of the philosopher and the common man: "For I am building in the human understanding a true model of the world, as one finds it, not as one's own reason would have it to be; a thing which cannot be done without a very diligent dissection and anatomy of the world."[11] Although they offer very different views of the world, philosopher and commoner alike unwittingly put their own desires in place of true descriptions, "For what a man had rather were true he more readily believes" (*Novum Organum* 1. 49, *Works*, I: 168, IV: 57), substituting a "philosophical theatre" for less pleasing realities (*Novum Organum* 1. 62, *Works*, I: 173, IV: 63). Even when he is not explicit about the theatricality of these other versions of reality, Bacon emphasizes their circularity, both figural (they are tautologies) and actual. Early attempts to understand the world were, according to Bacon, only "a whirling round about and perpetual agitation, ending where it began" (*vertigo quaedam et agitatio perpetua et circulus, Instauratio Magna*, Proemium, *Works*, I: 121, IV: 8).[12] In a dramatized set of speeches written for the Earl of Essex to perform at the tilt on Ascension Day, 1595, Bacon gave a vivid image of the sort of circling sterility he was trying to avoid: "Shall he [anyone] exchange the sweet travelling through the universal variety, for one wearisome and endless round or labyrinth?"[13] But sweet travelling and universal variety are features of an endless labyrinth as well; earlier philosophers and encyclopedists in fact claimed that the works that Bacon now finds to be labyrinths contained the universal variety he attributes to a less-centered world.

The true variety of Bacon's model of the world as it is rather than as we wish it to be is another circle, but a different kind: "it is a matter of common discourse of the chain of sciences how they are linked together, insomuch as the Grecians, who had terms at will, have fitted it of a name of Circle Learning" – or encyclopedia (*Valerius Terminus*, *Works*, III: 228). The evidence Bacon cites here, though, is itself bound to language; the chain of sciences is a circle "in common discourse," named by Greeks who "had terms at will" in an apparently lost linguistic freedom and perhaps another exercise of desire. In a strange way, what best reflects this labyrinthine world are precisely the tensions between disordered antlike empiricism and the twisted webs of reason that characterize Bacon's representation of knowledge as province. This distinction between what something seems to be and what it is, and the complications of representing this distinction, are at the center of Bacon's project of science. They are also, we recognize, central to Jonson's multiple re-centerings of the theatre. In his work, Bacon takes up the problem of the encyclopedic theatre, as it were, from the other side. The theatre offers Bacon a solution to the difficulties of the overly theoretical, and thus distorted, or overly empirical, and thus unusable, encyclopedia.

For Bacon, the image of the theatre also suggests the danger not only of playful and endless experiencing, but of distancing oneself too far from the phenomena that one studies and getting lost in a view of a single reality. This spectator-like investigation trails off into error if it fails to recognize when the time has come to act on its knowledge instead of simply waiting and having things shown to it, for "men must know, that in this theatre of man's life (*humanae vitae theatro*) it is reserved only for God and angels to be lookers on" (*De Augmentis* 7. 1, *Works*, V: 8, VII: 718). It is to ward off the endless circular error of the labyrinth that Bacon must root up all existing knowledge: "But the instauration must be made from the lowest foundations unless it is to be whirled around in a circle with slender and almost contemnable progress."[14] The Latin word *instauratio*, which Bacon took as the title for his entire encyclopedic undertaking, originally meant the re-beginning of a ceremony that at some point had gone awry; rather than correcting the error or continuing from where the mistake had occurred, the performer of the ritual was obliged to begin all over. Instauration is thus an exact repetition of another, perfected instance of the ceremony – albeit an imaginary one – and both the correction and the cancellation of another repetition of that imaginary performance that had diverged from their shared original.[15] It is a renewal by repetition, corresponding to the resurrection of a playscript by its actors on the stage, but an improved one – not the theatre of things as we wish, but the theatre of things as they are.

The way Bacon proposes to get outside of misleading theories and into the changeless facts of worldly philosophy sounds relatively simple: "Let us observe the discourse of the things themselves" (*sermo rerum ipsarum*, *Historia Ventorum* [1622], *Works*, II: 46, V: 167). This language is not to be found in the restatements that have already been made in the form of traditional encyclopedic texts, which Bacon called, "the corruptions and moths of histories . . . things that have fretted and corroded the bodies of many most excellent histories, and wrought them into base and unprofitable dregs" (*De Augmentis* 2. 6, *Works*, I: 506, IV: 304). Bacon intends instead to produce what he calls a science

simple, and without any infusion of dogmas; all theoretical doctrine being as it were suspended: a history embracing only the phenomena themselves (now almost incorporated with the dogmas) pure and separate; a history in short, setting forth a simple narrative of the facts . . . the experiments detached from the art . . .[16]

By collecting data and resisting the temptation to shape or epitomize it, he will listen neither to men's words about things or systems arranging them into orders, but merely list, without commenting or arranging, their facts and qualities. Bacon's explicit model is Pliny ("Something of this kind indeed Pliny has touched on cursorily and loosely," *Descriptio Globi Intellectualis* [c.1612], *Works*, III: 734,V: 511); the goal sounds as if it will be something like Gessner's *Historiae Animalium*, but pointedly lacking the section on each animal's philology. Certainly Bacon's description touches on a number of familiar encyclopedic tropes, beginning with the invocation of Pliny as progenitor. But Bacon's rehearsal of terms is a kind of instauration on a small scale, repeating and renewing a form already commenced in error, here in the epitomes. Unlike the Grecians, who "had terms at will" and invented the name Circle Learning, Bacon here and repeatedly insisted on using the terms that he was given by the past, but he worked to develop a language that doubled back on itself, saying two things at the same time, alluding to earlier thought and replacing it with his own.

The new Baconian Circle Learning differs from that of other encyclopedias precisely in its doubly articulated purpose. Its characteristics are suggested in two tales in *De Sapientia Veterum* (1609), a collection of allegorized myths which Bacon refuses to treat either as wholly his own interpretations of old tales or as evidence of lost ancient wisdom. By itself, then, this is an example of Bacon's linguistic coyness – rather than starting from nothing, he insinuates his own understandings into the received fabric of myth, freely inventing meaning and event. The first figure Bacon presents as a model for the new philosopher is Echo. In Ovid's *Metamorphoses*, which Bacon essentially follows, Echo's story has two main parts. First she is punished for revealing Jupiter's secret amours by being deprived of the ability to initiate conversation; she can only repeat what is said to her. Later she wastes away for love of Narcissus, desperately pleading with him, in his own repeated words, to love her in return. In *De Sapientia Veterum*, contrary to usual mythography, Bacon makes her the only wife and true love of Pan, his figure for the whole of nature. Working from the pun on the Greek τὸ πᾶν, "everything" or "the all," Bacon declares that "the world therefore can have no loves, nor any want (being content with itself) unless it be of discourse (*sermones*)," (*Works*, VI: 640, VI: 713f.). Without a hint of paradox, Bacon declares that only what can contain also itself can be said to contain everything:

For that is the true philosophy, which echoes most faithfully the voice of the world itself, and is written as it were from the world's own dictation; being indeed nothing else than the simulacrum and reflexion (*simulacrum et reflexio*) of it, which it only repeats and echoes, but adds nothing of its own. (*De Sapientia Veterum*, s.v. "Pan", *Works*, VI: 640, VI: 714)

Echo is the faithful "simulacrum and reflection" of the world into discourse. As Bacon says elsewhere, the philosopher gains his power over nature by first becoming her servant (e.g., *Novum Organum* 1. 3, *Works*, I: 157, IV: 47 and 1. 129, *Works*, I: 222, IV: 114). Bacon suggests that the philosopher can proceed to the works of nature that his project anticipates only once he learns to reflect accurately all the varied phenomena of the world in their own language, without addition or variation.

But Bacon's insistence on the unoriginality of his science, which will translate the world's events into language without affecting them in any way, is apparently reversed in the second of the philosopher-heroes of *De Sapientia Veterum*, the much more conventional figure of Orpheus.[17] Although regularly a symbol for human knowledge and power, Orpheus seems to fit awkwardly with Echo. Where Echo can merely repeat, Orpheus is a poet in the fullest sense of maker – he creates his verse, and creates the effects of life through his verse. In Bacon's account, Orpheus first tries to use his poetic powers to bring Eurydice up from the dead. He would have succeeded, but so great was his love and impatience that he looked back to see if she was following him before he had reached the surface and so lost her forever. With his first desire forever out of reach, Orpheus consoled himself by singing alone in the wilderness. Apparently without any intention on his part to do so, through his playing

he drew to him all kinds of wild beasts, in such manner that putting off their several natures, forgetting all their quarrels and ferocity, no longer driven by the stings and furies of lust, no longer caring to satisfy their hunger or to hunt their prey, they all stood about him gently and sociably, as in a theatre (*in morem theatri, illum circumstarent*), listening only to the concords of his lyre. (*Works*, VI: 647, VI: 721)

Orpheus' power, as Bacon sees it, is the power of the theatre. He creates a still space around him as he plays that transfixes and controls his spectators, as the humanist theatre had hoped to do. But the fascination that he eventually achieves is not Orpheus' goal at the outset, but a by-product of his initial failure. As Bacon makes explicit, his story of Orpheus is twofold, just as Orpheus' own achievement is double (*Duplex est Orphei cantio*, Works, VI: 647). Orpheus' first song, sung to free Eurydice from death and to please the infernal gods, represents natural philosophy, while his second, which calms the beasts and makes stones and trees move of their own accord, is moral and civil philosophy. Orpheus' first song fulfills its aim of recovering Eurydice; Orpheus' failure to keep her is not one of knowledge or technique, but of self-control – that is, of a field covered by the second song. In other words, Orpheus possesses Echo's knowledge, but is unable to use it successfully for power over the world – life and death – because he does not have control over his own desires and cannot resist looking back for her. In less allegorical terms, a concern for government, persuasion, laws, and virtue – here, the theatrical mastery of the animals – only arises "after the experiment (*experimentum*) of restoring the mortal body has been diligently attempted, and finally in vain" (*post experimentum corporis mortalis restituendi sedulo tentatum, et ad extremum frustratum*; Works, VI: 648).

According to Bacon, this power over life and death, which Orpheus both has and does not have, is the ultimate goal of natural philosophy, to which Bacon himself returned over a decade later in his *Historia Vitae et Mortis* (1622). The desire for that power serves to produce other discoveries, apparently less significant and so less attractive, but in the end more productive. Unlike the first song, which Orpheus sings with a clear intention, the power of the second song seems to be fortuitous; there is no hint that Orpheus means to charm the animals. His real, effective power to control desire, his own and others', appears only when he has abandoned the hope that his singing can fulfill his desire, or, more accurately, that his technical ability to fulfill his desire will be matched by an ethical ability to control those desires.[18] The unexpected power to control the wills of the animals is gained from the lesson of his earlier failure to control his own, but not as conscious knowledge. Rather, his failure drives him to another sort of practice, which has unexpectedly powerful effects. It is for this reason that Bacon recalls the unmanaged, errant power of the theatre to describe Orpheus' knowledge. For Echo's simulacral philosophy fails Orpheus; it allows him the ability to recover Eurydice, but not to control himself and put his power into effect. Real learning must include the management of desire, and this, in a sense, is Orpheus' first hard lesson: self-knowledge of the ways in which one's immediate desires distort and hamper one's real desires. In Bacon's allegory, the philosopher turns to moral and civil philosophy, represented by the second song, only when he fails at natural philosophy because of his inability to control and defer his desire. Like the power of the theatre, Orpheus' power is limited to shaping desire and susceptible to reinterpretation and mistaking. For all that, it has an efficacy in the world of human action that is hard to rival.

For Bacon, the story of Orpheus depicts two different kinds of Circle Learning: the full circle of learning of natural philosophy, which takes Orpheus on a circuit through the world and into the land of the dead,[19] and the learning that produces the circle of the theatre in which Orpheus charms the animals. Bacon's theatre of Orpheus is a disappointed encyclopedia, knowledge of what men desire substituting for a potentially superior knowledge of nature that nonetheless forgets to consider human desire and so falls short of the success of which it is technically capable.[20] While not capable of the miracles of Orpheus' first song, the performer in the theatre of Orpheus can realize his full potential by recognizing and leading the desires of others rather than by indulging his own. Using the same image of the theatre of Orpheus in the earlier *Advancement of Learning* (1605), Bacon had emphasized the theatrical elements of moral and civil philosophy, and its effectiveness, still more strongly:

Neither is certainly that other merit of learning, in repressing the inconveniencies which grow from man to man, much inferior to the former, of relieving the necessities which arise from nature; which merit was lively set forth by the ancients in that feigned relation of Orpheus' theatre . . . (*Works*, III: 302)

The circle of the theatre, in potential at least, encloses the knowledge of governing and persuading people – not because of what it represents, in an important difference from humanist theories of theatre, but because of its mode of representation: the doubleness of intention and accident, knowledge and desire, and the subconscious indirection of how it answers the needs of its audience, of which neither they nor it are fully aware.

Bacon finds the theatre not only to be a useful metaphor for the Orphic structure of knowledge, where desire is both denied and exploited in the service of unanticipated productivity. As he notes in this chapter's epigraph, Bacon found the theatre of his time inadequate, but somewhat mystifyingly so, as it reveals great and untapped potential even in the physical layout of grouping men together. The practice of drama is the actualization of the lesson of Orpheus' double story:

. . . even mean faculties, when they fall into great men or great matters, sometimes work great and important effects. Of this I will adduce a memorable example, the rather, because the Jesuits appear not to despise this kind of discipline, therein judging (as I think) well. It is a thing indeed if practiced professionally of low repute; but if it be made part of a discipline, it is of excellent use. I mean stage-playing . . .[21]

What is needed, and what the encyclopedic, theatrical system envisaged by Bacon was intended to provide, was a knowledge that combined the two kinds of Circle Learning, natural and moral, as they had not been since the time of the pre-Sokratic philosophers, before Sokrates first separated rhetoric and philosophy (*De Augmentis* 4. 1, *Works*, I: 580, IV: 373). In Bacon's synthesis, mortal knowledge and power over nature – the mastery of life and death – serve as lures to ensure that the less fabulous social disciplines are instituted, while the social and moral disciplines organize the human effort to strive after knowledge of the natural world. Like knowledge itself, the resulting structure is, or is meant to be, or (perhaps most accurately) is because of the power of the belief in it, self-sustaining.

The two kinds of Circle Learning that Bacon outlines in his tales of Orpheus and Echo are explained further in his theories of pedagogy. Bacon distinguishes two methods of instruction, Magistral and Initiative. The first, Magistral, involves handing knowledge over to the learner in its complete form. Because it accidentally makes use of the desires of both the teacher and the pupil, it

is a kind of contract of error between the deliverer and the receiver; for he who delivers knowledge desires to deliver it in such form as may best be believed, and not as may be most conveniently examined; and he who receives knowledge desires present satisfaction, without waiting for due inquiry; and so rather not to doubt than not to err; glory making the deliverer careful not to lay open his weakness, and sloth making the receiver unwilling to try his strength. (*De Augmentis* 6. 2, *Works*, I: 663, IV: 449)

This is the method of Bacon's own theatrical works – a simple presentation of data that lulls presenter and audience alike into passivity, stasis, and therefore inaccuracy. Theatre as it is usually conceived by humanist writers – indeed, as Bacon himself seems to conceive it in his occasional dramatic works – is Magistral; it attempts to impress the writer's ideas as completely and accurately on the viewer as possible, and takes advantage of the vividness of theatrical presentation to do so. Such staging as is currently used, argues Bacon, is a kind of theatre of memory, recalling what is already known and transmitting it rather than producing new knowledge: "Again, men help the memory by putting images of persons in places; could the same thing be done without the places by connecting actions or habits with persons? So much for the Production of Experiment" (*De Augmentis* 5. 2, *Works*, I: 627, IV: 416). The actual theatre of the Jesuits or even the professional players is an improvement over the memory theatre for Bacon because it retemporalizes the static memorial figures, and sets them into contexts of experience, or experiment. It replaces architecture, dismissed along with the rest of Ramism (*De Augmentis* 6. 2), with action; instead of a semiotically coded figure frozen in the mind's eye, there will be one that acts as it crosses the real eyes' field of vision. But while this is a potential improvement, there is yet a better kind of staging, the shift from Magistral theatre to Initiative experience that the mobility of the figures allows for.

Returning to his Orphic imagery, Bacon takes the word *Initiative* "from the sacred ceremonies, which discloses and lays bare the very mysteries of the sciences" (*De Augmentis* 6. 2, *Works*, I: 663, IV: 449); it is a form of education that initiates one as an adept who must repeat the originary Orphic journey himself rather than as a student who pores over the accounts of a traveler on a passage he himself never makes. To do this, the Initiative method does not offer a thinker's conclusions, but the route he took to reach them, including his missteps and uncertainties. It requires the learner to re-experience the process by which the knowledge he seeks was attained or produced by personating its other knowers. The Initiative method presents knowledge in fragments rather than already digested into a philosophy, and in so doing demands active interpretation. Since the first thing the Initiative learner must understand and master is his own encyclopedic desire to know at once and completely, he must first encounter the elements of human activity, recorded in history and relived in experience: "For knowledges are as pyramids, whereof history and experience are the basis. And so of Natural Philosophy the basis is Natural History."[22] Natural history almost automatically recalls one *Natural History* in particular, that of Pliny, "the only person who ever undertook a Natural History according to the dignity of it; though he was far from carrying out his undertaking in a manner worthy of the conception" (*De Augmentis* 2. 2, *Works*, I: 497, IV: 295). History – that is, the accumulation of particulars – and experience are the same thing, as are philosophy and the sciences (*De Augmentis* 2. 1, *Works*, I: 495, IV: 293), but whereas philosophies contain the possibility for error as they systematize and organize their material into generalizations, history and experience, lacking explanation, hold the seeds to true understanding. The Baconian experiment serves as theatricalized experience – spatially delimited, it provides the distance of the theatre of Pompey without the danger of the commodification of wonder in Pliny's theatre. Making use of the opportunities of planned experience, the Initiative learner heaps up material until he achieves his own understanding.

The theatre appears far more strikingly in Bacon's philosophical works as a metaphor than in his dramatic scripts as a practice. While Bacon's limited theatrical production was closely wedded to ideas of theatre as an educational tool – like many other talented courtiers during Elizabeth's reign, Bacon had a hand in writing entertainments, including the 1594 Christmas revel at Gray's Inn and some devices for his patron Essex – his use of theatre as an idea shows all the complexity that critics have found in actual Renaissance theatrical practices. The single most sustained use of the metaphor of theatre is in Bacon's discussions of his doctrine of the Idols of the Mind. Bacon's intent in defining the Idols is to eliminate the fallible human elements from his system and so gain a true knowledge of the nature of things. In contrast to the errors in the human understanding of the world that have arisen from carelessness, lack of interest, or some other accidents of knowledge, the Idols are various potentials for error inherent in the nature of the mind and the ways it organizes and communicates its experiences:

> Idols are the deepest fallacies of the human mind. For they do not deceive in particulars, as others do, by clouding and snaring the judgment; but by a corrupt and ill-ordered predisposition of the mind, which as it were perverts and infects all the anticipations of the intellect.[23]

Like the deceptions of *The Alchemist*, Bacon's Idols of the Mind represent a tendency to error that cannot be corrected by any clarity of vision. Neither simple – and thus simply correctable – misinformation nor false consciousness, the Idols that Bacon distinguishes are tendencies towards specific types of misprision that one must be aware of and compensate for, but cannot eliminate.

Bacon first mentions the Idols in *Valerius Terminus* (1603), and they receive their fullest explanation in the *Novum Organum* (1620).[24] Here Bacon lists the complete set as the Idols of the Tribe, the Idols of the Cave, the Idols of the Market-place, and finally the Idols of the Theatre. According to Bacon, the first three each have a certain inevitability.[25] The Idols of the Tribe are patterns of thinking that human beings as a group are always prone to – in particular, a belief that the universe is more ordered than it is, that it is made to the measure of man's senses, and that these senses are therefore adequate to investigate and understand it. The Idols of the Cave are the prejudices and predispositions of the individual, whether by education or temperament. The Idols of the Market-place are the ambiguities, confusions, and dissimulations that arise from the ways men communicate, most importantly from the instabilities and vagaries of language, corrected in part by the use of Initiative learning. The Idols of the Theatre, though, unlike the other sorts, "are not innate, nor do they steal into the understanding secretly, but are plainly impressed and received into the mind from the play-books of philosophical systems and the perverted rules of demonstration" (*Novum Organum* 1. 61, *Works*, I: 172, IV: 62). They are not misperceptions but systematic misrepresentations of worldly information that exaggerate its order, symmetry, and similar anthropocentric features.

Here and elsewhere Bacon associates theatricality not with the naive assumptions of the unlearned masses, but with the carefully plotted and seductively organized structures of previous thinkers. In the introduction to his *Historia Naturalis et Experimentalis* (1622), his collection of individual natural histories into several phenomena, Bacon dismisses the ancient philosophers who "invented systems of the universe, each according to his own fancy, like so many arguments of plays (*fabularum*); and these their inventions they recited and published, whereof some were more elegant and probable, others harsh and unlikely." Moderns, too, "have come upon the stage (*scenam tentarunt*) with fresh stories, neither honoured by approbation nor elegant in argument" (*Works*, V: 131). Elsewhere as well Bacon uses theatrical vocabulary to describe the work of scholars: philosophers participate in a *ludum*, or take the part of a *pantomimus*.[26] The Idols of the Theatre are representations of the world constructed according to human desire and not the truth of nature, the theoretical counterpart of the Magistral systems constructed to pass learning comfortably on to their passive recipients:

And in the plays of this philosophical theatre you may observe the same thing which is found in the theatre of the poets, that stories invented for the stage are more compact and more elegant, and more as one would wish them to be, than true stories out of history. (*Novum Organum* 1. 62, *Works*, I: 173, IV: 63)

Here Bacon seems simply to pick up the obverse of the humanist praise of theatre: while the idealized humanist theatre is truthfully representational, Bacon's theatrical Idols are entirely deceitful, even if their content is true – they fool the student by allowing him to rest secure in another's store of knowledge rather than forcing him to acquire his own.[27] The philosophical theatre is where old knowledge is performed over and over again in a circular repetition, while books of aphorisms, which require the reader's active engagement, and the scientific experiment are where the drama of discovery really takes place.

What makes the Idols of the Theatre different from the other sorts of Idols is that they are not unconscious, but chosen and developed by men in full consciousness of their constructed and appealing qualities. Like Orpheus on his descent, they incorporate affect – delight in order, the decorous sense of rightness, antipathy for complexity – without acknowledging its presence or knowing how to govern it. They can be seen as the manifestation in practice of the tendencies named by the first three types of Idols. The other three kinds are as objectively present as the objects they distort, but the Idols of the Theatre are the deflection of the empirical world by the force of desire – the same desire that Orpheus failed to take into account and through which he lost Eurydice, the same desire he accidentally tapped in the animals who stood around him "in the manner of a theatre" when he sang his grief, and the same deflection that transforms the discrete aphorisms of the Initiative method into the smoothed and soothing narratives of the Magistral. For Bacon, the consciousness with which the Idols of the Theatre have entered human thought makes them uniquely susceptible to deconstruction; while they are "adventitious" and "hard to eradicate," the "innate" Idols "cannot be eradicated at all" (*Instauratio Magna*, *Works*, I: 139, IV: 27). This, curiously, lets Bacon claim that an acquaintance with the Idols of the Theatre is superfluous in understanding possible errors – because, unlike the other Idols, they are accidental to learning, they can also be omitted from his propaedeutic works. In fact, in *De Augmentis Scientiarum* (1623), published three years after the *Novum Organum* and the *Instauratio Magna*, Bacon lists only the first three kinds of

Idols in the heading of the chapter in which he discusses them. The Idols of the Theatre creep in unannounced only in the body of the chapter, and then only to be dismissed without engagement: "There is also a fourth kind which I call the Idols of the *Theatre*, superinduced by corrupt theories of systems of philosophy, and false laws of demonstration. But this kind may be rejected and got rid of: so I will leave it for the present" (*Works*, I: 643, IV: 431). It is as if in the development of his thought, Bacon cultivated an intentional blindness to the Idols of his fellow thinkers. Like the desire that they delineate in shadowy outline, the Idols of the Theatre are only ever half-visible and half-serious – but like Orpheus' desire, they remain at the center of Bacon's project in spite of his attempts to dismiss and ignore them.

Bacon's certainty that the Idols of the Theatre can be entirely rooted out informs his decision to leave these Idols out of the chapter heading, but the theatre is not so easily removed from Bacon's own systematization of knowledge. Bacon's encyclopedic project is made possible by a concerted envisioning of the true nature of the world as inherently theatrical. In arguing against a theatrical philosophy, Bacon draws attention to the seeming randomness of the natural world:

For if that great workmaster [God] had acted as an aedile [in building the heavens and arranging the stars], he would have cast the stars into some pleasant and beautiful order, like the frets in the roofs of palaces; whereas one can scarce find a posture in square or triangle or straight line amongst such an infinite number. Such is the discord of the harmony between the spirit of the human and the spirit of the world. (*De Augmentis* 5. 4, *Works*, I: 644f., IV: 433)

By denying God the role of a heavenly aedile – the official in charge of the games in the theatres of ancient Rome – Bacon explicitly rejects the idea that the sky's fretwork is the mark of one kind of *theatrum mundi*, because, spectacular though it is, it shows no signs of the orderly arrangement that human masques and entertainments do. Shakespeare's Hamlet, with the same idea of heavenly order, comes to exactly the opposite conclusion: "This most excellent canopy the air, look you, this brave o'erhanging firmament, this majestical roof fretted with golden fire – why, it appears no other thing to me than a foul and pestilent congregation of vapours."[28] While Hamlet finds his own skepticism vaguely incredible in light of the evidence of the majestical roof, what Bacon finds incredible is credulity like Hamlet's. To look for the direct sign of a divine aedile in the pattern of the stars is to give in to the Idols and see what is *not* there; it is to imagine a universe made to the measure of human desire. But Bacon's heaven is still theatrical in that it reveals its own discourse of things to one who can read it without prejudice. Not having terms at will like the Greeks, Bacon works with the linguistic heritage he has, here and in his description of the Idols coyly circling the term "theatre" by simultaneously invoking and dismissing it. In his plans for universal knowledge, Bacon seeks not the obvious frets of Hamlet's heaven, but a subtler ordering. Rejecting the possibility of a human order, he instead anticipates some other, inhuman organization. Whereas Hamlet speaks from within a theatre – both the Globe in which the actor performs and the globe of the *theatrum mundi* – Bacon's world, still theatrical in its doubleness, is one that hides its theatricality in self-absorption.[29] Bacon hopes to produce a middle ground, an order hidden within disorder, or a reality that includes the reality of appearance as appearance merely. One must both foresee this order and forget that one is waiting for it.

The relation of the verisimilar Idols to the truth is sketched out in this same pattern of indeterminate difference and identity, where a shared observation leads its viewers to opposite conclusions. As Bacon insists before outlining his doctrine of the Idols:

There is a great difference between the Idols of the human mind and the Ideas of the divine (*humanae mentis idola et divinae mentis ideas*). That is to say, between certain empty dogmas and the true signatures and marks set upon the works of creation as they are found in nature. (*Novum Organum* 1. 23, *Works*, I: 160, IV: 51)

But this actual "great difference" is complicated by the appearance of extreme likeness, of which the near homonymy of their names is a symptom. Bacon suggests that the fault is not in ourselves, but in our stars – the world presents us with almost identical displays that signify entirely different things. Hamlet doubts the fretwork of his Globe as Bacon does his, but Hamlet rejects the Idea of his Globe's builder in spite of what he perceives as clear evidence in the fretted sky above him, while Bacon rejects only the Idol of legible divinity erected by his world's inhabitants. To mistake an Idol for an Idea makes all the difference in the world, but it is as difficult to tell one from the other as it is to tell one philosophy from another in the philosophical theatre. In the *Advancement of Learning*, for example, Bacon notes that the geocentric astronomy of Ptolomy and Tycho Brahe saves the phenomena as well as the heliocentric astronomy of Copernicus, "and the calculations are indifferently agreeable to both; so the ordinary face and view of experience is many times satisfied by several theories and philosophies; whereas to find the real truth requireth another manner of severity and attention" (*Works*, III: 365). Experience and history, the raw facts of the case, outstrip in their multivalence the theories that purport to explain them.

Bacon's structure is not simply one of difficult interpretation and fine judgments. In Bacon, the divine Idea and the errant Idol actually coincide, occupying the same material ground. To reveal the truth, then, is a paradoxical process of edification that results in a universal leveling of all interpretations and a return to the bare phenomena. Ptolomy and Copernicus cannot both be offering true explanations of the movement of the heavens, but regardless of what the true explanation is, neither one is as close to it as Bacon, who makes no positive claim himself (although he admits elsewhere that he tends towards Brahe) but knows that there is something more to be said about the competing theories – namely, that the phenomena admit equally well of both, and no doubt of others also. Like the debate between geocentric and heliocentric astronomers, or the competing aphorisms contained and subsumed within the *Essays* or *The Colors of Good and Evil* (1597, *Works*, VII: 65–92), or Bacon's star-gazing and Hamlet's, what remains left over are the bare phenomena, the golden fretwork outside of their interpretation. This means that although the phenomena do speak for themselves, they must do so in many tongues, and error begins in choosing one or another of these speeches as definitive. Discourse is not something superadded to things, but, as in *The Alchemist*, the irreducible ground of understanding. It is for this reason that at the end of his life Bacon abandons his theorizing for the brute accumulation of data, like Pliny or Gessner: "my Organum, even if it were completed, would not without the Natural History much advance the Instauration of the Sciences, whereas the Natural History without the Organum would advance it not a little" (*Historia Naturalis et Experimentalis*, *Works*, V: 133–34). There is no ground for dismissing any of the meanings in things themselves; Bacon's nature knows no "no." Bacon's system is thus marked by an encyclopedic desire to accumulate knowledge without judging it, to defer, as Orpheus could not, the desire to decide. As with the conflict between Ptolomy and Copernicus, the narratives that purport to explain the facts are in fact superficial; what lies deepest and closest to truth is the mere accumulation of the phenomena – literally the appearances – themselves.

This relation of two seemingly opposed elements that turn out in fact to be bound together, even overlaid, at some supposedly deeper level of understanding that proves instead to be a flattening out of depth, occurs again and again in Bacon's work. Bacon's ambitious deferral of political ambition, Orpheus' successful failure in his descent, the paradox of the Idols and the Ideas – each rewrites an apparent opposition between two forms as an entailment of one by the other. Bacon opposes traditional forms of understanding in that what he looks for is not a deep unity of contraries, but the ability to simply see the things before one without interpretation, "simply as they are" (*Instauratio Magna*, *Works*, I: 145; IV: 32). This embrace of the language of things apart from their meanings – and the way in which things do have a discourse parallel to that of humans, their own theatre – can be seen in Bacon's approach to his cipher. In *De Augmentis* 6. 1, Bacon discusses a cipher that makes use of slightly different forms of individual letters to allow one message to be sent "inside" another, seemingly normal one. But "inside" is a metaphor to express the relation of one message to the other; in fact Bacon's cipher makes it impossible to apply any of the usual spatial or temporal metaphors to the relation between the two messages of Bacon's cipher. Bacon's cipher requires two separate encodings. First, each letter of a message is converted to a five-unit binary code, so that **A** becomes *aaaaa*, **B** becomes *aaaab*, **C** becomes *aaaba*, and so on. Another table provides an alphabet in two forms, so that every letter can be written in two different ways, or even two different hands,[30] so that one form of a letter signifies the *a* of the binary code, and the other the *b*. A second message longer than the first is then selected. The original binary-coded message is broken up into shorter segments of *a*'s and *b*'s corresponding to the length of the individual words of the second, so that the binary code can be mapped onto the letters of the second message. The second message is finally rewritten using the two different forms of the alphabet to signify the binary code of the first. In Bacon's first example, "Fly!" first becomes *aabab. ababa. babba.*, then a second message is selected and the encoded letters of the first message are redistributed to match the word breaks of the second, "Do not go till I come": *aa bab. ab aba.b a bba.* This becomes the guide for writing the second message in its two different hands (using italics for *a* and Roman for *b*) "*Do* n*o*t g*o ti*l\l *I* c*o*me" – a message with a meaning exactly opposite to the intended communication. Bacon's choice of an opposing message is a kind of bravura show, but the real strength of his cipher is not that it allows for one message to be conveyed by its opposite, but rather that the two levels of the message have no interdependence at all. The cipher is completely convertible and allows "the writing of anything by anything" (*omnia per omnia*, *Works*, I: 661, IV: 446). In the second of Bacon's examples, the message, "All is lost. Mindarus is killed. The soldiers want food. We can neither get hence, nor stay longer here," is concealed by the totally unrelated words of Cicero's first epistle (*Works*, I: 661, IV: 446–47).

Bacon's cipher does not rely on mere obfuscation, as a cipher that relied simply on altered letters or words might, or misdirection, as one in which meanings were altered would; as he warns in his essay "Of Simulation and Dissimulation," feigning something is much riskier than hiding it, and he notes of ciphers in particular that even if they are impossible to break they call attention to themselves unless they can be made to look absolutely ordinary. Bacon's cipher works in part by not calling attention to itself as a cipher; it is not hard to break as much as hard to *find*. It is like the order of the heavens; if we look at the arrangement of the stars, we may see either order or disorder, but in either case we look for the wrong thing, which is an order in human terms. The same phenomena have an order of their own, of a different kind. In Bacon's cipher, it is not possible to lift away a surface message to reveal a deeper, truer one. The cipher, for instance, cannot be recopied or repeated except by someone already knowing it, and so it is not a case of inside and outside. Rather, the two messages are inextricably interwoven in the material in which they are sent, and any alteration to either would change each. What Bacon demands is a reading of the full materiality of the object, in particular those qualities that a desiring gaze will overlook so as to subject the whole to an order. Every message can have two meanings, but not because one lies deeper than the other, or because a single sign is ambiguous or polyvalent. Instead of one message concealing another, Bacon's cipher instead requires that its signs be read, as it were, from varying angles, and that we read in one message the potentially significant marks and differences that are suppressed by the other message in order for it to mean. We must attend, for instance, not only to the words made by the letters and their meanings, but to the shapes of the letters, just as in the theatre we attend to both the part played and the actor playing it. In Bacon's cipher, Theodor Zwinger's observation that "diction... enters in place of actors for us" is quite actually the case (*Theatrum*, [1571], I, 26).

For all the inextricability of its messages in any given instance, though, Bacon's cipher – like the actor and the part – is also infinitely flexible. With the absolute convertibility that allows its user to represent *omnia per omnia* as the vanishing point of Baconian writing, it is easy to see how it is possible – although also possible to see that it not easy – to show that Bacon left clues of his authorship throughout Shakespeare's plays (the Earl of Oxford, Elizabeth, and their backers presumably did not have similar codebreaking resources at their disposal). A cipher in which it is possible to communicate *omnia per omnia*, however, raises several problems. Since any message can contain any message, what is most essential is the materiality of the message itself. Its meaning is inseparable from its means. In fact, in the last analysis, its meaning is nothing other than its infinitely flexible medium.

Because of the leveling of the phenomena and the predictability of desire in Bacon's thought, albeit the desire for a "harsh and unlikely" deferral of desire (*Historia Naturalis et Experimentalis*, *Works*, V: 131; see above, p. 17) that will, unlike Orpheus' harsh and unlikely descent, recognize its own complicity in its project and so emerge in the end with its own truth, Bacon finds that there is no available ground upon which to take on the theatrical shows of philosophy which reduce the phenomena into satisfyingly ordered explanations: "To attempt refutations in this case would be merely inconsistent with what I have already said: for since we agree neither upon principles nor upon demonstrations there is no place for argument" (*Novum Organum* 1. 61, *Works*, I: 172, IV: 62). With both Bacon and his opponents standing in judgment on each other, the result must end in a kind of stalemate, those who are capable of receiving Bacon's doctrine receiving it and the rest not (*Novum Organum* 1. 33, *Works*, I: 162, IV: 52). With no grounds of agreement upon which to base a truly philosophical disputation, the only way that Bacon can give his philosophical system any kind of priority over the other systems is through the same kind of appeal to the desires of his audience – this time for power over nature – that he decries in the idolatrous, theatrical systems he stands against. Bacon writes of nature as lying wholly outside the deceptive and theatrical realm of human interchange, unavailable except as a goal to yearn for. Bacon's rhetoric of reality and objectivity may mask it, but his shift of authority from written *auctores* to nature is not a transcendence of language, but a retreat in the face of language's unrecoverable ambiguity. Like Jonson, Bacon discovers a source for his authority in the shifting ground of human desire that initially seemed to be the danger of the Idols of the Theatre and the strength of Orpheus: "I am now therefore to speak touching Hope, especially as I am not a dealer in promises, and wish neither to force nor ensnare men's judgments, but to lead them by the hand with their good will" (*Novum Organum* 1.92, *Works*, I: 199, IV: 91). The distinction that Bacon establishes between speakers of hope and dealers in promises, and between ensnaring and leading by the hand, is an exceedingly nice one. Bacon's reliance on hope enables him to construct the similarities between his system and others as a temporary confusion, unavoidable now but soon to be dispelled. Charles Whitney notes that the "histories" into which Bacon collected his investigations on a single Form, or natural quality, follow this pattern, too. They are not constructed according to his theories of experiment, but by culling information from books. Bacon's histories are included in his work not as instances of his ideal history but as imitations of it in its (temporary) absence, simulacra of knowledge (using Bacon's term for Echo) that will stir the readers to desire the real thing. Only when his science is given the attention he seeks for it will it prove its superiority over the Idols that he rejects: "But as it is, it appears to me from what has been said, and also from what has been left unsaid, that there is hope enough and to spare, not only to make a bold man try, but also to make a soberminded and wise man believe" (*Novum Organum* 1. 114, *Works*, I: 210, IV: 102).

What anchors the pursuit of knowledge in Bacon's explanation is the belief in and hope for an authorized deliverer and a comparable receiver, bound not by a contract of error like those involved in Magistral teaching but by real shared knowledge. But the hope he requires is scarcely different from the contract of error he opposes – by what unexpressed miracle is the bold man's hope transformed into the wise man's secure belief? Bacon's attempt to touch hope in James seems like an intentional counterpart to the power by which Orpheus draws the desire of the animals while intent on something else:

Nay, the same Salomon the king, though he excelled in the glory of treasure, of shipping and navigation, of service and attendance, of fame and renown and the like, yet he maketh no claim to any of those glories, but only to the glory of the inquisition of truth; for so he saith expressly, *The glory of God is to conceal a thing, but the glory of the king is to find it out.* (*Advancement*, *Works*, III: 299)

Despite his promise of "some solid work, fixed memorial, and immortal monument" (*Advancement*, *Works*, III: 263), Bacon wants the king to sponsor not a static body of knowledge – not, in fact, the noiseless piling up of facts upon facts that characterized much encyclopedic writing up to Bacon – but a process of investigation that will produce those facts. Promising James an eventual mastery over the forces of nature, Bacon seeks to gain his own immediate goal of supporting his researches. This seems to be a shift from political or rhetorical power to practical power, or even from ideology to science. What has really been produced, though, is ideology, or, in Bacon's terms, hope. The reward will be a renewed rhetorical, civil, and moral power for James as Solomon's double and sponsor of Bacon's project rather than the hoped-for power of life and death – just as it was for Orpheus.

James' superiority to his subjects is in fact what moves his subjects to knowledge. Bacon makes James into an unchanging force of nature.[31] He gives a natural authority to James, whose speech "is indeed prince-like, flowing as from a fountain, and yet streaming and branching itself into nature's order, full of facility and felicity, imitating none, and inimitable by any" (*Advancement*, *Works*, III: 262). But the linguistic ability attributed to James does not trickle down to his subjects, since any speech less spontaneous than James', even one modeled on his, lacks his authority: "speech that savoreth of the affectation of art and precepts, or speech that is framed after the imitation of some pattern of eloquence, though never so excellent – all this has something servile, and holding of the subject" (*Advancement*, *Works*, III: 262). Although James' speech is a torrent, it is not the flood itself that Bacon wants, but rather the power it can provide to drive his investigations as a millwheel is driven by a stream. The elusive magnificence of the monarch provides a goal that leads the learner on. In contrast to the creative relation of power and knowledge that authorizes some meanings and dismisses others, and in doing so magnifies itself, outlined by Thomas Elyot, Bacon changes the king's power to an undirected force that can be tapped into by outsiders and turned to their purposes. The king provides another focus for hope and desire, along with the tempting power over nature, and Bacon sets up this moral and civil power as his way back to the natural-historical power lost by Orpheus. He proposes a literal backtracking, moving from the theatre this time and back to the infernal shades, this time equipped with the understanding of how human desire can be curbed and directed. Bacon writes to the king because his project is not possible for a subject, but "*opera basilica* [kingly work]; towards which the endeavors of a private man may be but as an image in a crossway, that may point at the way but cannot go it" (*Advancement*, *Works*, III: 328). For Bacon, king and subject do not authorize in the same way – Bacon's subject can only point at the road it cannot follow, not present the king with a mapped version of it. But the difference between them is that, as king, the king provides a source of unimpeachable hope for the subject. When the sovereign's actual power is analyzed, it looks like the subject's power – but what makes Bacon's doubles different from each other is the different investments in them of hope/desire/imagination, fields for which there is no science.[32] James' power is a product of the imagination. Such power is of course real, but it is grounded in a belief in its existence; it demands an acceptance, in this case a tacit one, of its premises by its audience. Bacon proposes a world in which knowledge creates power – but behind that knowledge is not, or not only, an objective, quiescent nature, but another, unknowable power, not a power over nature but one over men that seems to come from nature.

This principle of human authority, tautologically and frustratingly, is known only to those who already possess it; government, as Bacon calls it, "is a part of knowledge secret and retired ... We see all governments are obscure and invisible. *Totamque infusa per artus/ Mens agitat molem, et magno se corpore miscet.*"[33] Bacon borrows Vergil's lines on the soul to suggest that the relation of the government of things to the things themselves is, like that of the soul in the body, "inward and profound, and the passages thereof hardly to be reduced to demonstration." If for the subjects of power it is an omnipresent but invisible force, though, to rulers its workings are represented as transparent: "But contrariwise in the governors towards the governed all things ought, as far as the frailty of man permitteth, to be manifest and revealed" (*Advancement*, *Works*, III: 474). For Bacon, the king's power alone – as the lure of hope – escapes representation in scientific work. He pointedly refrains from discussing the secrets of governing, "considering that I write to a king that is a master of this science, and is so well assisted, I think it decent to pass over this part in silence" (*Advancement*, *Works*, III: 474). This instability of desire, though, is part of Bacon's project, although remaining outside it, much as money works for Jonson's encyclopedic theatre. In his essay "Of Empire," Bacon offers a brief psychology of princes that makes them uniquely useful to his project. Unlike other men, who lack certain things and desire to have them, princes, "being at the highest, want matter of desire, which makes their minds more languishing." This also makes them hard to read, "for multitude of jealousies, and lack of some predominant desire that should marshal and put in order all the rest, maketh any man's heart hard to find or sound." Left to their own, "princes many times make themselves desires, and set their hearts upon toys."[34] The prince, in other words, desires only to desire, and often picks trivial objects for himself, since the desire's focus is a matter of indifference to him. His subjects can make use of his wandering wants, though, which makes the ruler's desire the ultimate object of the subject's desire. This is a Foucauldian power bereft of a subject that can be tapped *by* its subject – by one subject *to* it, who can alter the course of the circulation of power and knowledge while necessarily remaining always within it.

The ruler is both the power that enables Bacon's project and its beneficiary, as he becomes the sole marvel that remains in a disenchanted world: "when all other miracles and wonders shall cease, by reason that you shall have discovered their natural causes," the Hermit of Bacon's play for Gray's Inn (1592) advises the Prince of Purpoole, "yourself shall be left the only miracle and wonder of the world" (*Gesta Grayorum*, in Nichols, *Progresses and Public Processions*, III: 290).

Real learning "taketh away vain admiration of any thing... Neither can any marvel at the play of puppets that goeth behind the curtain and adviseth of all the motion."[35] What remain wondrous are not theatrical displays of knowledge or power, but the truth of power behind the shows that creates the shows. There remains a residue of fascination even in the spectacle that is revealed as such. The negative power of debunking – the power to lay pretensions bare to knowledge through real power – becomes fascinating in its own right, whether it is Solomon's great gift of finding out the hidden mysteries of God or Bacon's own project of clearing the philosophical theatre of the Idols of earlier thinkers. When all the work of enlightening is over, a still-fascinating residue of ideology persists – how truth is produced and how it is exposed, as the unveiling not of a hidden meaning but rather of a process of veiling. Mystery fascinates and knowledge enlightens, but in the process all that fascinated while hidden becomes newly enchanting for the ways in which, ordinary as it was, it managed to fascinate. It is the fascination of doubleness that appears in his ciphers, in the organization of his project, and in the positioning of experiment between theatre and encyclopedia in Bacon's thought. The authority that Bacon seeks to establish in power over nature is something that can only be found by trusting in it before it exists. In the end, Bacon must make a kind of Pascal's wager, betting on the accuracy of his system and the hope that it will eventually prove itself without any possible ground: "For there is no comparison between that which we may lose by not trying and by not succeeding" (*Novum Organum* 1. 114, *Works*, I: 210, IV: 102).

For Bacon, a necessarily premature belief in the possibility of determining a real knowledge ensures the continuing viability of his ongoing encyclopedic project. Like Jonson's encyclopedia, then, Bacon's exists largely in the mind of its beholders as a desire. As Bacon says in the *Sylva Sylvarum* of an "Experiment solitary touching the force of imagination imitating that of sense":

Those effects which are wrought by the percussion of the sense and by things in fact, are produced likewise in some degree by the imagination... So if a man see another turn swiftly or long, or if he look upon wheels that turn, himself waxeth turn-sick. (*Sylva Sylvarum* 795, *Works*, II: 598)

In his world of speaking things, Bacon unambiguously acknowledges a shaping influence in the thoughts and dreams of the spectators of the world. Our attitudes to things appear in the things themselves; likewise, the conditions of the world manifest themselves in our feelings. For this reason, in a world of turning facts, even the Baconian investigator needs an imaginary still point that he can forget is imaginary long enough to secure himself against the turn-sickness of his own experiments:

For the mind of men is strangely eager to be relieved from suspense, and to have something fixed and immovable, upon which in its wanderings and disquisitions it may securely rest... so do men earnestly desire to have within them an Atlas or axletree of the thoughts, by which the fluctuations and giddiness (my transl., *vertigies*) of the understanding may be to some extent controlled; fearing belike that their heaven should fall. (*De Augmentis* 5. 4, *Works*, I: 640f., IV: 428–29)

"Certainly there be [some] that delight in giddiness and count it a bondage to fix a belief," allows Bacon at the beginning of "Of Truth" (*Works*, VI: 377). For most viewers, though, fixity is a relief; in both sorts alike, however, fixing a belief is an act of will, whether acknowledged or not.

One of the imaginary axletrees by which Bacon secures his vision of the world from giddiness is a realization of the structure of his cipher onto the world. Bacon calls the elementary natural phenomena uncovered in contemplation "Forms," which resemble not visual likenesses of things, but rather "the alphabet or simple letters."[36] This is not merely metaphorical. Just as combinations of letters make real words and sentences and not their imitations, so the various Forms are the real basis for all the particular things and phenomena of the world:

these forms of letters once known will lead us directly to the forms of words; so in like manner to inquire the form of a lion, of an oak, of gold, nay even of water or air, is a vain pursuit; but to inquire the form of dense, rare, hot, cold, heavy, light, tangible, pneumatic, volatile, fixed, and the like, as well configurations as motions, which in treating of Physic I have in great part enumerated (I call them *Forms of the First Class*), and which (like the letters of the alphabet) are not many and yet make up and sustain the essences and forms of all substances; – this, I say, it is which I am attempting, and which constitutes and defines that part of Metaphysic of which we are now inquiring. (*De Augmentis*, *Works*, I: 567, IV: 361)

Because Bacon's Forms combine like letters, they can be recorded just as easily as letters can, and no less safely with regard to accuracy. Unlike traditional books, which like other human interpretations are marked with fancy, Bacon's writing is meant to echo the world faithfully. Bacon's cipher teaches us how to read the facts Bacon compiles: they are not to be looked *through* to some meaning beyond or behind them that they imperfectly represent, but to be contemplated directly, with neither "calculations" nor "predictions" – that is, neither systems that reduce and explain phenomena that have already occurred, nor those that anticipate emergent phenomena. At first this appears like a step backwards, but as Bacon insists in *Advancement of Learning*, "The contemplation of nature and the observations of experience" are the two necessary foundations of true learning, while the theories that are built upon them change with time (*Works*, III: 292):

It may seem strange that I should wish to recall to their primitive rudeness and the simplicity of naked observations things so laboriously produced, advanced, and amended. But the truth is that, without meaning to throw away the benefit of former inventions, I am attempting a far greater work: for it is not merely calculations or predictions that I aim at, but philosophy ... (*Descriptio Globi Intellectualis*, *Works*, III: 734, V: 510f.)

Bacon understands the word philosophy in its etymological sense of the word, as the love of knowledge rather than knowledge itself; like his discourse of hope, philosophy is a potentially endless reaching after knowledge rather than its possession. The gathering of facts will present its own rewards – but these will not come in the form promised, or literally pretended, which is the mastery of natural essences.

Bacon's Forms bear a much closer relation to Aristotelian definitions than to Platonic Forms, with two important differences. First, Bacon's Forms are, so to speak, adjectival rather than nominal, distancing them from both Plato and Aristotle. To search for the Form of lion or gold is a vain task, but the Forms that compose the qualities that naturally belong to gold can be looked for. Bacon's emphasis is thus transferred, in terms of both the grammatical structure of its propositions and its reference to material reality, from the subject to the predicate, grounding his metaphysics securely in the physical world by leveling these two categories. Metaphysics collapses into physics, because there is nothing outside Nature that can be analyzed, no "lion" or "gold" apart from its phenomenal qualities. Redefined, Bacon's new metaphysics is left nothing "beyond nature; but of nature the most excellent part" (*De Augmentis* 3. 4, *Works*, I: 550, IV: 346). That is, there is no metaphysical substance in nature or subject in a sentence of which various properties can be predicated but which maintains an existence distinct from those properties. A subject is only the particular combination of its properties and nothing else. Bacon's definition of metaphysics must be understood in the atomistic context of his Forms – as a purely materialist conception that takes into account perceiver as well as perceived. In distinction to the alchemists, who seek to produce gold by a quasi-organic hastening of the internal maturing processes of other metals, Bacon's approach is both simpler and more forthrightly artificial:

> Gold hath these natures: greatness of weight, closeness of parts, fixation, pliantness or softness, immunity from rust, color or tincture of yellow. Therefore the sure way (though most about) to make gold, is to know the causes of the several natures before rehearsed, and the axioms concerning the same. For if a man can make a metal that hath all these properties, let men dispute whether it be gold or no.[37]

Bacon's understanding here of the properties of things is a literalization of the tradition of *imitatio naturae*, not the domination of nature as is often suggested. He elevates the appearance of things to the level of essence. What looks in every way like gold in fact is gold, not some clever simulacrum of it – or *even if* it is a clever simulacrum of it.[38] Second, the formal definition takes place equally in the world of language and the world of things. The description of a thing can be transcribed in words, because a thing and the properties that make it up are as convertible as the subject and predicate of a definition.[39]

This emphasis on the literal bookishness of the natural world also suggests, in a different way, its theatricality. With nothing but various kinds of seeming to make up the physical world and no underlying metaphysics to support the bare physics of elementary characteristics, the practicing philosopher strives for an *imitatio naturae* that is more theatrical than anything else, in which to seem to be a thing in every way is in fact to be the thing. Bacon is of course far from simply endorsing popular beliefs in appearances. As so often, though, Bacon understands theatre doubly. His anxiety about the Idols of the Theatre is with a theatre that gives its viewers what they want to see; opposed to it, though, is a theatre which will not, but which instead will display the Forms – not even as they are (since that still implies some metaphysical being behind their appearance), but merely display them like Bacon's facts. This "other theatre of things" is the theatre of experiment (*Parasceve* 1, *Works*, I: 395, IV: 253). Bacon has contempt for those who simply experiment blindly, as if they were producing a play (*leviter et tanquam per ludo experiantur, Novum Organum* 1. 70 *Works*, I: 180, IV: 70–71). To trust to mere empiricism is as foolish

as if some kingdom or state were to direct is counsels and affairs, not by letters and reports from ambassadors and trustworthy messengers, but by the gossip of the streets; such exactly is the system of management introduced into philosophy with relation to experience. (*Novum Organum* 1. 98, *Works*, I: 202, IV: 94)

To move beyond the uncertain opinions of surface seeming to the true physical properties of things requires a particular kind of reading – one that does not take in the letters of the Book of Nature in a haphazard way, but that first scrupulously gathers them as they appear, and then examines them in their own right to read the message hidden, cipher-like, within them.

It is this careful reading that experiment, properly carried out, supplies. Experiment is not precisely identical to ordinary experience[40] which can be deceptively led beyond itself by the influence of the Idols of the Mind: "by far the best demonstration is experience, if it go not beyond the actual experiment" (*Novum Organum* 1. 70, *Works*, I: 179–80, IV: 70). Contemplation and experience distinguish nature's regular productions and her extraordinary ones, but the centerpiece of Bacon's program of experiment is the compulsion of nature in artificial situations. Thus bound, nature can be tested and forced to demonstrate the characteristics of its forms in a way that neither undirected experience nor passive contemplation alone can uncover, "But by the help and ministry of man a new face of bodies, another universe or theatre of things (*rerum . . . theatrum alterum*) comes into view" (*Parasceve* 1, *Works*, I: 395, IV: 253). Experiment contrasts with the haphazard experience *per ludo*, but it too is represented as a form of theatre, this time a positive one. In the *Novum Organum*, Bacon defines the limits of this theatre of experience:

which, if taken as it comes, is called accident; if sought for, experiment. But this kind of experience is no better than a broom without its band, as the saying is; – a mere groping, as of men in the dark, that feel all around them for the chance of finding their way; when they had much better wait for daylight, or light a candle, and then go. (1. 82, *Works*, I: 189, IV: 81)

This candle-lighting is the systematic, controlled kind of experience called *experimentum*. Just as for Bacon Poesy is feigned History, tailored and adjusted to particular ends, experiment is a kind of feigned experience.[41] Like Poesy, it is non-accidental and autonomous, a real event that unfolds according to its own rules once it is set in motion, but which is carefully set up and delimited in advance. In the *Novum Organum*, Bacon sets up the relation of experience to experiment as a simple binary of blind groping versus clear sight, cursing the darkness versus lighting a candle. In the later *De Augmentis*, though, Bacon adds an intermediate term that reinstates the world's bookishness:

a man may proceed on his path in three ways: he may grope his way for himself in the dark; he may be led by the hand of another, without himself seeing anything; or lastly, he may get a light, and so direct his steps; in like manner when a man tries all kinds of experiments without order or method, this is but groping in the dark; but when he uses some direction and order in experimenting, it is as if he were led by the hand; and this is what I mean by Learned Experience (*Experientia Literata*). (*De Augmentis* 5. 1, *Works*, I: 623, IV: 413)

The Latin phrase *experientia literata* contains several related ideas that cannot be neatly disentangled. What Bacon's editor Spedding translates as Learned Experience is equally also a Learned Experiment, or Lettered Experience – experience broken down into its constitutive, letter-like elements – or a Literate Experience – an experience that can, in a sense, read other experiences. Its relation to the truth of the lit candle is that of the identical Other: *experientia literata* is meant to lead to certain knowledge, but as Bacon's metaphors suggest, there is no apparent link between being led by the hand through the dark and kindling a light to see by. Bacon also calls it "the Hunt of Pan" – Echo's pursuit of her coequal the universe.

Bacon's experiment is different from ordinary, accidental experience because it is active, not passive; it compels effects from an unwilling nature, surprising both the enterprising investigator and Nature itself with its displays. It is in this way, directed yet uncertain, that Bacon guarantees the vitality and continuing progress of his project: "The things based in nature grow and increase, but those [based] in opinion are changed, not increased."[42] If for Bacon the theatre and the encyclopedia are identical others, the "other theatre" of experiment offers a way of drawing on each, combining elements of both, and so rendering each obsolete. The goal of the Baconian experiment is an observable *factum* that can be sorted with other similar facts into an encyclopedic compendium of knowledge that will allow men to know the world completely and to work in it effectively. The means of producing the fact, though, and the mode of reading it, are both theatrical. The Baconian experiment is nothing other than the staging of natural phenomena. Like contemporary performances in public theatres, its primary characteristics are the pre-scription of a collision of different elements, enclosure of that collision to delimit it from the rest of the world, and recording and displaying the results so they can be reproduced. Unlike experience, it is cut off from the rest of the world by spatial and temporal boundaries predetermined by the experimenter.[43] Paradoxically, it gives an accurate impression of the world by insisting on the world's difference and distance from its observers as well as the experiment's self-aware presentation to them, just as the physical Elizabethan theatre aggressively demonstrated both the distance and the implication of the stage and the auditory. Bacon's experiment is a collision of Echo's writing and Orpheus' theatre, purged and distanced from the direct desire that thwarted Orpheus' ability to make use of his masterful knowledge.

One thing that ensures that Baconian experiment is not the sometimes stagy set of opinions bolstered by experience and by philosophical systems is the intervention of instruments and boundaries between the observer and the event. As Whitney has argued, these boundaries make of natural phenomena which include the viewer – nature being, after all, τὸ πᾶν – a spectacle which he views from the outside (*Bacon and Modernity*, 108). Bacon uses instruments not to extend the senses, as did Galileo and van Leeuewenhoek, but to alienate them from the immediacy of the phenomena:

the subtlety of experiments is far greater than that of the sense itself, even when assisted by exquisite instruments; . . . To the immediate and proper perception of the sense therefore I do not give much weight; but I contrive that the office of the sense shall be only to judge of the experiment, and the experiment itself shall judge of the thing. (*Instauratio Magna*, "Plan", *Works*, I: 138f., IV: 26)

In this sense *experientia literata* is Literate Experiment: in the space of the experiment, objects prove to have the capacity to read other objects.[44] While the experimenter brings the objects together for his own purposes, he has no role in their interpretation, since that is too liable to be shaped by his own desires. Held at a distance by the experiments in which the small spectacle of nature is framed, the investigator is forced to delay, to hold off his intervention, to watch – with the result that while he is powerless to halt or change the process of the experiment once he has set it in motion, his impotence then and there frees him to act in every context outside of the experimental one with the real knowledge of the world that he has gained from the experiment. Bacon calls attention to the etymological roots of the word *theatrum* in this philosophical vision by linking it to both idols and *theoria* when he says, "The Idols of the Theatre, or of theories, are many" (*Idola Theatri, sive theoriarum, multa sunt, Novum*

Organum 1. 62, *Works*, I: 173, IV: 63). Like Hamlet, hoping to learn to feel by watching the player king describe the death of Hecuba, the Baconian investigator learns to act by watching a controlled part of the world perform. Unlike Hamlet, though, or Jonson's gulls, he avoids projecting his own desires into what he sees, contemplating things non-judgmentally rather than focusing his vision, "for it is a speech of a lover and not for a wise man, *Satis magnum alter alteri theatrum sumus* [We are a theatre great enough for one another]" (*Advancement, Works*, III: 279).

What Bacon's program conspicuously lacks is a way of advancing from the collection of facts to judgment, from spectation to action. Bacon's own system means that he is never able to progress successfully from the theatre of his experiments to a theory which will enable him to evaluate the experiments of others. For instance, in experiment 791 of the *Sylvae Sylvarum*, Bacon cites an experiment of Galileo to refute the theory that Galileo derives from it.[45] Galileo filled a trough with water and moved it suddenly, causing the water to flow towards one end,

which he supposeth (holding confidently the motion of the earth,) to be the cause of the ebbing and flowing of the ocean; because the earth over-runneth the water. Which theory though it be false, yet the first experiment is true. (*Sylva Sylvarum* 791, *Works*, II: 596)

As the primary *datum*, the experiment could hardly be other than "true." Bacon's *Sylva Sylvarum* is filled with just such facts, observations of varied phenomena disjointed from their sources and from related issues and then strung together in loose aphoristic chains. In accordance with his ascetic commitment to "the simplicity of naked observations" (*Descriptio Globi Intellectualis, Works*, III: 734, V: 510), Bacon can and in fact must take Galileo's experiment as a pure *datum*; to do so, though, he must also separate it from Galileo's theory. What Bacon cannot do within his system is to contest Galileo's theory. He can suspend or deny it, but can neither produce a positive theory of his own as an alternative nor argue against Galileo's theory except to protest that Galileo has moved too quickly to a conclusion. Bacon wants to move easily from his experimental theatres to new theories as easily as he conflates their terms in his discussion of the Idols of the Theatre, but he cannot refute the theatre of Galileo's experiment. In spite of its claims, Bacon's project provides no way for passing from the collection of particular details like the *Sylva Sylvarum* to a universal theory that would explain and organize them definitively. It relies instead on an open-ended sequence of provisional organizations, each one of which must be superseded and each one of which is held temporarily in place by the force of hope and desire that Bacon wanted to dismiss in the theatre of philosophy. There is in this confusion, though, an accurate perception of the confusion in nature:

The universe to the eye of the human understanding is framed like a labyrinth; presenting as it does on every side so many ambiguities of way, such deceitful resemblances of objects and signs, natures so irregular in their lines, and so knotted and entangled. And then the way is still to be made by the uncertain light of sense, sometimes shining out, sometimes clouded over, through the woods of experience and particulars. (*Instauratio Magna*, Preface, *Works*, I: 129, IV: 18)

In spite of his protestations, Bacon's encyclopedia *is* the labyrinth, and the way out promised by the theatre is the way out found accidentally by Orpheus – by tapping into the contingent, human spheres of desire and moral philosophy, not by determining the truth of natural philosophy. Bacon's system requires the giddiness that it simultaneously rejects; in fact, it produces the giddiness, even *is* the giddiness in its inexhaustible appetite for data and its inability to move beyond its mere accumulation. Like the competing aphorisms contained and subsumed within the *Novum Organum*, the world sustains with its variety of phenomena various possible theories of its organization, potentially unjudgeable. This is the Initiative method raised to the level of the universe, in which Baconian writing offers an exact structural equivalent to the organization of the world.

In the end Bacon's duplicitous representation of the world as a theatre is authorized because the world itself is doubled, misleading, deceitful. Bacon discovers in nature the same ambiguity that he finds in the theatrical idols of philosophy. In the first of his *Essays*, "Of Truth," Bacon tries to establish the nature of truth by setting it against that of the theatre:

This same truth is a naked and open daylight that doth not show the masques and mummeries and triumphs of the world half so stately and daintily as candlelights. Truth may perhaps come to the price of a pearl that showeth best by day, but it will not rise to the price of a diamond or carbuncle that showeth best in varied lights. (*Works*, VI: 377)

Bacon's truth shifts even as he tries to hold it in view. At first it is defined in the familiar metaphorics of knowledge as clear vision, the "daylight" that reveals the seams and pins in the masque of life instead of the flickering "candlelights" that conceal them. In the next sentence, though, truth becomes, instead of the light itself, the variable object whose beauty depends on the type of light in which it is displayed, a pearl beautiful by day but less valued than the shimmering diamond in varied light. Rather than being the clear medium which shows pearls, diamonds, and masques all in their true states, Bacon's truth is also something inherent in the object, so that the diamonds may have one condition of truth – that they are valued more in varied light – and pearls another – that their value is separate from their appearance in varying lights. Truth is finally judged on its attractiveness like a gemstone, according to the rules of desire and display that govern the beautiful but unreal masque that it exposes in its appearance as daylight in the first sentence. The truth in Bacon's second metaphor is merely the right thing in the right context, a pearl by day and a diamond by night. "Certainly there be [those] that delight in giddiness,"

Bacon admits dismissively at the beginning of "Of Truth" (*Works*, VI: 377), "and count it a bondage to fix a belief." But taken together, Bacon's truth, like his scientific project, finds itself on both sides at once, and reveals that it may in reality be a bondage to fix a belief, if only because the reality of things themselves is that they remain unfixed and giddy. It is a congruence of perception and being, as it was also of writing and being in Bacon's lettered world. To make truth both the illumination and the object illuminated is to drive it back into the surfaces of things from the realm of metaphysics.

Truth is not only a material given for Bacon, but a moral necessity; mere reliance on the probable without a faith in the possibility of truth, like that of the skeptics of the Academy, cannot do otherwise than corrupt men (*Novum Organum* 1. 67, *Works*, I: 178–79, IV: 68–69). The second version of truth in Bacon's analogy can never be made determinate by any point of view, because the indeterminacy lies in the object itself; *must* lie in the object, in fact, because otherwise it becomes only probable indeterminacy. Any attempt to fix the object's meaning, then, cannot be cast as the proper authority that allows things to be themselves free from perverse interpretations, but as mere coercion. In keeping with his first image of truth as a light, however, Bacon also protests, "if behavior and outward carriage be intended too much, first it may pass into affection, and then *quid deformius quam scenam in vitam transferre*; [what is more distorted than] to act a man's life?"[46] In spite of its theatrical foundations, life cannot be lived as an act; because the world is not of a single piece, though, acting cannot be set aside as distinct from life either. What must be shunned is self-conscious, ironic acting; if we act, for Bacon, we must act in the name of truth, as if we did not know that we were acting. Bacon, in other words, counsels mystification about the performance of knowledge; to look too closely makes us turn-sick. We act like reflective Echo in order to have the capacity of creative Orpheus; we claim belief in the possibility of one project in order to secure the possibility of another, less grand one. The truth of the masque of life is not only that it is a masque, but that it must be understood as a masque is understood, under the obscurity of candlelight and not as if it were something else, either absolutely unreal or absolutely real. The giddiness of indeterminacy and unreality do not rest solely in an inappropriate attitude towards an object which can in some way or another be rectified, as Bacon at first suggests of "certain discursive wits" in "Of Truth," who take perverse pleasure in the confusion that new ways of looking at the world seem to produce. Indeterminacy and uncertainty are themselves the truth of things themselves, not only of human affairs but even of the natural ones in which Bacon hoped to find a final authority and a consistency outside the sphere of human influence. As Bacon admits in the final essay of his collection, "Of the Vicissitude of Things," "Certain it is, that the matter [of the world] is in a perpetual flux, and never at a stay" (*Works*, VI: 512). It is only the stability of the stars and the constancy of the sun's motion that allow men to exist at all. Giddiness, then, is a kind of radical misprision, a misprision without alternative because what it relies on for authority is itself in flux.

Bacon does not push his metaphor of the theatre and the world this far. To do so would, minimally, change his teaching from Initiative to Magistral. This unframed uncertainty, even if he admits it, is not one that Bacon will dwell on. The cause of the giddiness of the viewer in "Of Truth" shifts from the viewer to the object, as it does again in the concluding sentences of the last of the *Essays*, "Of the Vicissitude of Things": "But it is not good to look too long upon these turning wheels of vicissitude, lest we become giddy. As for the philology of them, that is but a circle of tales, and therefore not fit for this writing."[47] This allusion of the end to the beginning makes Bacon's *Essays* themselves a kind of wheel of vicissitude, an active circling different from the Magistral – and encyclopedic – circle of tales offered by philology. Such repetition is perhaps both the clue that leads one through the labyrinth of the *Essays* and the one that makes its literal circularity visible. Characteristically, Bacon turns away from the turning wheels his writing mimics, as he turns away with almost the same words but with no more of an explanation from another giddy, perverse, misprising object, the space for experiment that is the public stage: "But it is not good to stay too long in the theatre."[48]

With this conclusion, both the theatre – what we must not look too long on – and the encyclopedia – the philological Circle Learning of tales – are rejected for *experientia literata*, which combines their qualities. *Experienta literata* – the lettered world, the learned subjective experience of it, its recording in language that is duplicitous, metaphorical, ciphered, giving one clear and transparent account and at the same time showing the impossibility of such an account – like the encyclopedia whose project it inherits and transforms, is other than the world it represents. But Bacon's truth is itself Other to itself, and so only such an alienated account of it can capture it in its giddy whirl. "It is not good to stay too long in the theatre." It is not good, but it is where we live.

Notes

INTRODUCTION: CIRCLES OF LEARNING

1 Work on this aspect of the early modern period has tended to be more confined to special fields than studies of early modern theatricality, such as intellectual history and the history of science, in particular the work of Ann Blair, Paula Findlen, and Neil Kenny. Medieval literature has had a long engagement with its encyclopedic aspects, most recently and interestingly in Ann Astell's *Chaucer and the Universe of Learning* (Ithaca, NY: Cornell University Press, 1996) and Giuseppe Mazzotta's *Dante's Vision and the Circle of Knowledge* (Princeton University Press, 1993). See also C. S. Lewis' beautiful and prescient book, *The Discarded Image: An Introduction to Medieval and Renaissance Literature* (Cambridge University Press, 1964). Julie Stone Peters' magisterial *Theatre of the Book, 1480–1880: Print, Text, and Performance in Europe* (Oxford University Press, 2000) appeared too late for me to fully incorporate its arguments into this work.
2 Thomas Elyot, *The Image of Governaunce* (London: Thomas Berthelet, 1541), 41r.
3 Thomas Elyot, *Dictionary* (London: Thomas Berthelet, 1538).
4 A later discussion of the value of the theatre, Thomas Heywood's *An Apology for Actors* (London: 1612; facsimile reprint, New York: Garland Press, 1973), makes this connection more clearly, and at considerable length:

> Do not the Universities, the fountains and wellsprings of all good Arts, Learning and Documents, admit the like in their Colleges? . . . this is held necessary for the emboldening of their junior scholars, to arm them with audacity, against they come to be employed in any public exercise, as in the reading of the Dialectic, Rhetoric, Ethic, Mathematic, the Physic or Metaphysic Lectures. It teacheth audacity to the bashful Grammarian, being newly admitted into the private College, and after matriculated and entered as a member of the University, and makes him a bold Sophister, to argue *pro et contra*, to compose his Syllogisms, Categoric, or Hypothetic (simple or compound) to reason and frame a sufficient argument to prove his questions, or to defend any *axioma*, to distinguish of any Dilemma, & be able to moderate in any Argumentation whatsoever. To come to Rhetoric, it not only emboldens a scholar to speak, but instructs him to speak well . . . to keep a decorum in his countenance, neither to frown when he should smile, nor to make unseemly and dignified faces in the delivery of his words, . . . neither to buffet his desk like a madman, nor to stand in his place like a lifeless Image, demurely plodding, and without any smooth and formal motion. It instructs him to fit his phrases to his action, and his action to his phrase, and his pronunciation to them both ([C3v–C4r]).

5 Thomas Elyot, *The Boke Named the Governour* (London, 1546), 19r.

6 Elyot's theatre in *The Image of Governaunce*, though, seems more Horatian, and attending disputations was a popular Elizabethan pastime for those who knew Latin.
7 See, for example, Michel Serres, *Hermes – Literature, Science, Philosophy*, eds. Josué Harari and David F. Bell (Baltimore: Johns Hopkins University Press, 1981), 88: "In a culture with an oral tradition, story takes the place of schema, and theatre equals intuition. The diagram of a theorem can only be transmitted in written form, but in an oral culture, drama is the vehicular form of knowledge."
8 Plato, *Opera*, transl. Marselio Ficino (Paris: Ioanus Parvus et Iodocus Badius, 1518), 213v col. 2; Plato, *Opera Quae Extant Omnia*, ed. Ioanis Serranus, 3 vols. (Geneva: Henricus Stephanus, 1578), II, 475c, 475e.
9 Serranus, in Plato, *Opera* (1578), II, 955r, misnumbered as 950: "In tanto enim rei theatricae usu his de rebus cavere debuit Plato."
10 Serranus dedicated it to Queen Elizabeth I, and Philip Sidney consulted it in writing the *Defence of Poesy*. On this and Serranus' strategies for knowledge, see M. J. Doherty, *The Mistress-Knowledge: Sir Philip Sidney's* Defence of Poesie *and Literary Architectonics in the English Renaissance* (Nashville: Vanderbilt University Press, 1991), 149–67. The Stephanus edition which Serranus translated provides the division numeration for the Platonic corpus even today.
11 Serranus, in Plato, *Opera* (1578), I,**. iiii.r: "Denique ex his regulis, de omni genere doctrinae quae Philosophiae nomen dignitatémque profitetur, faciendum est iudicium: ut vera Philosophia à cothurno philosophico, verus Philosophiae usus ab abusu discriminetur."
12 "Inde illa tibi tuísque venit felicitas, qua tu, Elisabetha, totos novemdecim annos inter vicinorum & penè terrarum orbis horribiles ruinas, cumulatè frueris: partáque domi & foris pace, tu mulier fortissimis viris imperans, funestas vicinorum tuorum tragoedias veluti è specula conspexisti" (Ibid., I,*. iii.v).
13 "Nec vero eram nescius, dum in tam illustre theatrum prodirem, fore ut in varia incurrerem hominum iudicia . . ." (Serranus, in Plato, *Opera* (1578), I,**. iii.v). *Prodirem* as a semi-technical term for "appear on a stage" would no doubt have been familiar to Serranus from Cicero's *De Officiis* I, 129. Cf. *OLD* s.v. *prodeo*.
14 ". . . iuvat causas causarúmque effecta in hoc Universitatis theatro pervestigare" (Ibid., I**. iii.v).
15 "ne in re tanti momenti desint nobis solidae rationes, quibus constet nos minimè hac in re ludere operam, sed & Deo gratum & Ecclesia utilem laborem impendere . . . In hac instituti mei apologia, mihi propositum esse testor, satisfacere bonis & eruditis viris, non improbis momis: quibus quidem facile est μωμεισθαι, non aequè verò vel μιμεισθαι vel emandare ea quae reprehendunt" (Ibid., I,**. i.v).
16 Pliny the Elder, *Natural History*, transl. H. Rackham *et al.*, Loeb Classical Library (Cambridge, MA: Harvard University Press, 1938–62), XXXV, 36, 63.
17 Erasmus, *Moriae Encomium*, in *Opera Omnia* (Amsterdam: North Holland Publishing Company, 1969–), IV-3, 88. When Zeuxis could find no single model with all the features for an image of Helen, he combined the best features of the five most beautiful women he knew. See my fuller discussion of Zeuxis as a model for the encyclopedist in chapter 3.
18 Serranus could hardly use the word *mimesis* or any of its cognates without an oblique reference to the vast body of commentary that had accumulated around Aristotle's *Poetics* in the hundred years since their discovery.

19 "at docebit, Dei beneficio, certius & illustrius is Commentarius quem de doctrina Platonis conscripsimus, universae doctrinae suntagma ex ipsis Platonis verbis compositum atque contextum huiusmodi exhibens, ut ad perfectam absolutámque doctrinam desiderari nihil posse videatur" (Serranus, in Plato, *Opera* [1578], I,**. iiiiv and following recto [n.p.]). "Videatur" might also be translated as "will seem."

20 "Unum restat, nostro quidem iudicio pernecessarium, Ut universae doctrinae summam ex variis locis collectam atque in unum quasi corpus compositam, Aristotelis caeterorúmque autorum collatione, exemplorum vero appositione illustratam, tibi, lector, exhibeamus: ut quaecumque variè disiecta atque disseminata sunt, sub unum obtutum opportunè referantur, singulis ad suas familias revocatis, & usu ipsorum indicato" (Ibid., I,***. ii.v) On the image of the *disiecta membra* of the text and the scholar's task of collecting and rejoining them, see A. Bartlett Giamatti, "Hippolytus Among the Exiles," in *Exile and Change in Renaissance Literature* (New Haven: Yale University Press, 1984), 12–32.

21 For a careful working-out of the material circumstances surrounding the building of public theatres in England, see Douglas Bruster, *Drama and the Market in the Age of Shakespeare* (Cambridge University Press, 1992), 1–28.

22 The concepts I will examine here are not identical to the metaphor of *theatrum mundi*, which had a related but distinguishable development described by Ernst Curtius, *European Literature and the Latin Middle Ages*, transl. Willard Trask, Bollingen Series 36 (Princeton University Press, 1953) or Richard Bernheimer, "Theatrum Mundi," *Art Bulletin* 38 (1956), 225–47. The *theatrum mundi* expresses the insignificance of the present world beside the superior reality of the perspective of eternity outside it. This aspect of the metaphor has been extensively treated. Brian Vickers, "Bacon's Use of Theatrical Imagery," *Studies in the Literary Imagination* 4 (1971), 189–226, is a more narrowly focused collection of citations than Curtius', but perhaps even more useful for the study of this period, since he discusses the various uses of theatrical metaphors in general in addition to organizing Bacon's references to them. Jean Christophe Agnew, 57–100, traces the social changes that he argues led to the dominance of the *theatrum mundi* motif over images with similar meanings like the Dance of Death and the Ship of Fools in *Worlds Apart: The Market and the Theater in Anglo-American Thought* (Cambridge University Press, 1986). My point is that these readings do not exhaust the uses of the *theatrum* image in the late medieval and early Renaissance periods. See also Ann Blair, *The Theater of Nature: Jean Bodin and Renaissance Science* (Princeton University Press, 1997), chapter 5, "Theatrical Metaphors," 153–79, who makes a similar point – there are a number of metaphorical theatres in operation in sixteenth-century Europe.

23 Michel Foucault, "Space, Power and Knowledge," in *The Cultural Studies Reader*, ed. Simon During (London: Routledge and Kegan Paul, 1993), 161–69.

24 Kepler, *Apologia*, in *Gesammelte Werke* VI, 396; quoted in Frances Yates, *Theatre of the World* (London: Routledge and Kegan Paul, 1969), 443.

25 For a similar argument, see Paolo Rossi, *Clavis Universalis: Arti Mnemoniche e Logica Combinatoria da Lullo a Leibniz* (Milan: Riccardo Ricciardi, 1960), 108, where he notes that memory systems at some point cease to need to be practical because their mysticism and complexity becomes so seductive to their readers and writers that the promise of the possible outweighs any merely empirical results.

1 THE SPACE OF THE ENCYCLOPEDIA

1. "Il Sapienza . . . etiene un libro solo, dove stan tutte le scienze che fa leggere a tutto il populo. E questo ha fatto pingere in tutte le muraglie, su li rivellini, dentro é di fuori, tutte le scienze," *La Città del Sol: Dialogo Poetico/The City of the Sun: A Poetical Dialogue*, transl. and notes Daniel J. Donno (Berkeley: University of California Press, 1981). Translation modified, 32–33.
2. On the uncanniness of the encyclopedia that refuses to be derivative, see Jorge Luis Borges' "Tlön, Uqbar, Orbis Tertius," in *Ficciones*, ed., transl., and intro. Anthony Kerrigan (New York: Grove Press, 1962), 17–35, and his tale of an emperor who constructs a map equal in size and complexity to the territory it (literally) covers. Appropriately enough, I have not been able to locate this story in Borges' works.
3. Jacques Derrida, *Disseminations*, transl. Barbara Johnson (University of Chicago Press, 1981), 46–56, succinctly outlines the recurrent encyclopedic desire of philosophy – its reliance on the idea of its own singularity, its erasure of history, and, what is most interesting for my purposes, its recurrent connection to spectacle and display.
4. ". . . je vous puisse assuerer qu'il m'a ouvert le vray puys et abisme de l'encyclopédie," François Rabelais, *The Complete Works*, transl. Donald Frame (Berkeley: University of California Press, 1991), chapter 20, 298. I have slightly modified Frame's translation, 201.
5. As Franco Simone, "La Notion d'Encyclopédie: Elément Caractéristique de La Renaissance Français," in Peter Sharrat, ed. *French Renaissance Studies, 1540–1570: Humanism and the Encyclopedia* (Edinburg University Press, 1976), has pointed out, 236.
6. Jürgen Henningsen, "'Enzyklopädie' Zur Sprach und Bedeutungsgeschichte eines Pädogogischen Begriffs," *Archiv für Begriffsgeschichte* 10 (1966), 271–362 (276–83) finds the word "encyclopedia" entering Latin first in editions of Pliny and Quintilian, and then growing to wider use in the circle around Angelo Poliziano, in the 1480s, 276–83. See above p. 2, and especially n.8 below.
7. Randle Cotgrave's *A Dictionarie of the French and English Tongues* (London: 1611, facsimile reprint; intro. William S. Woods, Columbia, SC: University of South Carolina Press, 1950). None of the modern translations I consulted made use of the ambiguity within *puys*.
8. See Henningsen, "'Enzyklopädie,'" (276–84) on Poliziano and the origins of the word, with a reproduction of the printed page on which the word first appears, 357; also Ulrich Dierse, *Enzyklopädie: Zur Geschichte eines Philosophischen und Wissenschafts-theoretischen Begriffs*, Archiv für Begriffsgeschichte, Supplement 2 (Bonn: Bouvier Verlag Herbert Grundmann, 1977), 7–8. On humanism and the encyclopedia more generally, see Donald R. Kelley, *Renaissance Humanism* (Boston: Twayne Publishers, 1991) and "History and the Encyclopedia," in *The Shapes of Knowledge from the Renaissance to the Enlightenment*, International Archives of the History of Ideas 24, eds. Donald R. Kelley and R. H. Popkin (Dordrecht: Kluwer Academic Publishers, 1991), 7–22; Neil Kenny, *The Palace of Secrets: Beroalde de Verville and Renaissance Conceptions of Knowledge* (Oxford: Clarendon Press, 1991); Maurice Lebel, "Le Concept de l'Encyclopédie dans L'Oeuvre de Guillaume Bude," in *Acta Conventus Neo-Latini Torontonensis*, eds. Alexander Dalzell,

Charles Fantazzi, and Richard J. Schoeck (University of Toronto Press, 1991), 3–24; and A. H. T. Levi, "Ethics and the Encyclopedia in the Sixteenth Century," in Peter Sharrat, ed., *French Renaissance Studies 1540–1570: Humanism and the Encyclopedia* (Edinburgh University Press, 1976), 170–84.

9 Paul Skalich de Lika, *Encyclopaedia, seu Orbis disciplinarum, tam sacrarum quam prophanarum Epistemon* (Basel: Loannes Oporinus 1559), n.p., dedication to Emperor Ferdinand: "de tota Encyclopaedia tam sacrarum quam prophanarum disciplinarum: Philosophia nempe supernaturali, quae Metaphysica & prima Philosophia nuncupatur: Naturali, ex qua & Medicina, tum quae de Anima pertractat, & Mathematicae quatuor [sic], quas & doctrinales appellant, Arithmetica, Musica, Geometria, & Sphaerica (cum suis illis veluti pedissequis, Calculatoria, Geodesia, Canonica, Astrologia, Optica & Mechanica) nascuntur. Item de Morali, Oeconomica & Politica: de Rationali, unde Grammatica, Historia, Dialectica, Rhetorica, & Poetica emerserunt. Ultimò, de sancto illo & ineffabili symbolo sacrarum litterarum, quod Philosophiam symbolicam appellare soleo."

10 Pierre Gregoire, *Syntaxes Artis Mirabilis in Libros Septem Digestae* ..., 2 vols. in 1 (Lyons: Ant. Gryphius, 1578), I, 43: "Qua ratione & nos in hac arte magna ne quid deesset particularium finium, singularum scientiarum, veluti quddam epitome contexuimus, ut Dei beneficio & nostro medio, quicunque nostras habuerit lucubrationes, nullis aliis libris, vel certe paucissimis egeat ad scientiarum Encyclopediam addiscendam."

11 Not an ordinary one, as Henri Irénée Marrou points out; even for Plato it is an ideal rather than a description of an actual set of practices. See Marrou, "Les Arts Libéraux dans L'Antiquité Classique," in *Arts Libéraux et Philosophie au Moyen Age. Actes du Quatrième Congrès International de Philosophie Médiévale* (Montreal and Paris: Institute D'Etudes Médiévales/Librairie Philosophique J. Vrin 1969), 5–27 (16). See also L. M. DeRijk, "Ἐγκύκλιον παιδεία: A Study of its Original Meaning," *Vivarium* 3 (1965), 24–93 (29–38).

12 DeRijk, "Ἐγκύκλιον παιδεία," esp. 25–31, 85–87; Dierse, *Enzyklopädie*, 5–6. Marrou, "Les Arts Libéraux," 16f., rejects this history, arguing that in Greek, unlike in German, the root meanings of words do not persist on the surface, as it were, of their compounds and derivatives, and that usage alone determined meaning in Greek.

13 Quoted by Michel Simonin, "Faire des Encyclopédies à la Renaissance," in Annie Becq, ed. *L'Encyclopédisme: Actes du Colloque de Caen, 12–16 Janvier 1987* (Paris: Amateurs des Livres, 1991) 247.

14 Marrou, "Les Arts Libéraux," 17–18.

15 These examples are drawn from Henningsen's list of all the variant readings in early editions of Quintilian and Pliny; "Enzyklopädie," 279–81.

16 My claim is based on the list of variant readings and the analysis provided in Henningsen, "Enzyklopädie," 276–82. For a broad review of the symbolism of the circle in Renaissance and seventeenth-century poetry, see Georges Poulet, *Les Métamorphoses du Cercle* (Paris: Librairie Plon, 1961), chapters 1 and 2. Rudolph Arnheim, *The Power of the Center: A Study of Composition in the Visual Arts: The New Vision* (Berkeley: University of California Press, 1988), esp. vii–x and 1–12, provides a comprehensive survey of the symbolism of circles and centers from a psychologistic point of view that I find unsatisfactory; this does not affect the acuteness of his analysis of the meaning of circular shapes in various contexts. Mazzotta, *Dante's Vision*, and Kenny, *Palace of Secrets*, 1–21, review some medieval and Renaissance representations of encyclopedic texts as spatial.

17 Fritz Saxl, "Illustrated Medieval Encyclopedias," in *Lectures*, 2 vols. (London: Warburg Institute, 1957), I, 228–54 includes a plate of this and many similar circular representations of the liberal arts and encyclopedic texts, *passim*.
18 Erasmus, *Adagia*, quoted in J.-F. Maillard, "Fortunes de l'Encyclopédie à la Fin de la Renaissance," in Becq, *L'Encyclopédisme*, 319–25: "Circulum absolvere, est rem omnibus numeris omnibusque partibus perfectam reddere. Unde et cyclopaideia dicta, quae disciplinarum omnium velut orbem absolverit, et encyclopaideia. Metaphora sumpta a mathematicis, apud quos circularis figura perfectissima absolutissimaque judicatur . . ." (319–20).
19 *Contemplatio* as the appropriate reaction to the theatre of the world is a commonplace from Pliny the Elder onward. Cf. the complete title of Jean Bodin's work, *Universae Naturae Theatrum in quo Rerum Omnium effectrices causae, & fines contemplantur* . . . (Hanover: Typus Wechelianus, 1595), or Skalich de Lika's insistence on the importance of "ocium *contemplandi*." Its roots go back to Plato's Cave and Aristotle's contemplative life, but in this case the use of the Latin word has a particular importance.
20 Varro, *On the Latin Language* [*De Lingua Latina*] VII, 7–9, transl. Roland G. Kent, Loeb Classical Library (Cambridge, MA: Harvard University Press, 1971), translation slightly modified: "Quaqua in<tu>iti era<n>t oculi, a tuendo primo templum dictum . . . In terris dictum templum locus augurii aut auspicii causa quibusdam conceptis verbis finitus . . . In hoc templo faciundo arbores constitui fines apparet et intra eas regiones qua oculi conspiciant, id est tueamur, a quo templum dictum, et contemplare . . ."
21 Steven Mullaney, *The Place of the Stage: License, Play, and Power in Renaissance England* (University of Chicago Press, 1987), 62; cf. also the observations on museum objects in Robert Harbison, *Eccentric Spaces* (New York: Alfred A. Knopf, 1977), 144–45 and chapter 8, *passim*, to which I am indebted for his concept of "neutral space." Walter Benjamin's discussion of collecting in "Edward Fuchs: Collector and Historian," in *The Essential Frankfurt School Reader*, eds. Andrew Arato and Eike Gebhardt (New York: Continuum, 1993), 225–53, offers a more optimistic view of this decontextualization, seeing the objects as rescued from the circuit of commodity fetishism.
22 Excellent work has been done in recent years on the spaces in which knowledge is produced, influenced by Foucault's studies of the spaces of the hospital, the asylum, and the prison, but also diverging from them in methodology. Adi Ophir and Steven Shapin, "The Place of Knowledge: A Methodological Survey," *Science in Context* 4.1(1991), 3–21, provide a helpful survey. Roger Chartier, *The Order of Books*, transl. Lydia G. Cochrane (Stanford University Press, 1994), discusses the library as a space of information storage. As Foucault argued in "Space, Power and Knowledge," though, spatial organization alone cannot dictate discursive changes. Steven Shapin, *A Social History of Truth: Civility and Science in Seventeenth-Century England* (University of Chicago Press, 1994) links space and personal authority in the establishment of true facts, and Bruno Latour, *Science in Action: How to Follow Scientists and Engineers Through Society* (Cambridge, MA: Harvard University Press, 1987), provides a more theoretical account of the laboratory space as an area where textual and rhetorical conflicts are heightened by the appearance of the thing itself (chapters 2 and 6).
23 Gian Biagio Conte, *Generi e Lettori: Lucrezio, L'Elegia D'Amore, L'Enciclopedia di Plinio* (Milan: A. Mondadori 1991). Cf. also Saxl, "Illustrated Medieval

Encyclopedias," 228: "[Encyclopedias] are indicative of the fact that a period of learning is approaching its end . . ."

24 Cf. Saxl's observation that Isidore tells about things, but not about their uses or production – what a garden is, but not how to plant one, "Illustrated Medieval Encyclopedias," 232. See also Jacques Derrida, *Archive Fever: A Freudian Impression*, transl. Eric Prenowitz (University of Chicago Press, 1996). Michel Foucault, "Of Other Spaces," *Diacritics* 1b (1986), 22–27, is simply in error to claim that the library and the museum as attempts to gather all times and places together are nineteenth-century phenomena. To be sure, these two forms assumed a particular significance in that century of aggressive imperialism and scientism (cf. Thomas Richards, "Archive and Utopia," *Representations* 37 (1992), 1–32 on the British Museum), but the notion of the storage of information, even universal information, long predates them.

25 The analysis of "ready-made" science can be found in Latour, *Science in Action*, where he develops Thomas Kuhn's distinction between "normal" science, which fills in an existing paradigm, and original science, which challenges or disrupts existing paradigms (*The Structure of Scientific Revolutions*, International Encyclopedia of Unified Science 2.2 [University of Chicago Press, 1970]).

26 Hugh of St. Victor, *Didascalicon de Studio Legendi: A Critical Text*, ed. Charles Henry Buttimer (Washington, DC: Catholic University Press, 1939): "agriculturae ratio philosophi est, administratio rustici . . . vides iam qua ratione cogimur philosophiam in omnes actus hominum diffundere, ut iam necesse sit tot esse philosophiae partes quot sunt rerum diversitates ad quas ipsam pertinere constiterit" (I, iv).

27 Ong has discussed this in many of his works, beginning with and most extensively in *Ramus, Method, and the Decay of Dialogue: From the Art of Discourse to the Art of Reason* (Cambridge, MA: Harvard University Press, 1958). In *Knowledge, Discovery and Imagination in Early Modern Europe: The Rise of Aesthetic Rationalism* (Cambridge University Press, 1997), Timothy Reiss adopts a position similar to mine – what changes significantly in the course of the early modern period is less a mode of perception and representation than the discursive system within which perception is handled.

28 Conte, *Generi e Lettori*, 131. Wilhelm Schmidt-Biggemann, *Topica Universalis: Einie Modellgeschichte Humanisticher und Barocker Wissenschaft* (Hamburg: Felix Meiner Verlag, 1983), "Einleitung," xiii–xxiv, is an excellent reading of the encyclopedic self-consciously within the tradition of *Geistesgeschichte*.

29 Roland Barthes observed of the sociopathology of the reader: "Imagine someone . . . who abolishes within himself all barriers, all classes, all exclusions, not by syncretism but by simple discard of that old specter: *logical contradiction*; who mixes every language, even those said to be incompatible . . . Such a man would be the mockery of our society . . . he is the reader at the moment he takes his pleasure" (*The Pleasure of the Text*, transl. Richard Miller [New York: Hill and Wang, 1975], 3).

30 Richard Burton, *The Anatomy of Melancholy*, eds, Thomas C. Faulkner, Nicholas K. Kiessling, and Rhonda L. Blair, introd. J. B. Bamborough, 6 vols. (Oxford: Clarendon Press, 1989–94), I, 4.

31 Thomas Nagel, *The View from Nowhere* (New York: Oxford University Press, 1986). The logic of the encyclopedia is thus not magical, although there are certainly encyclopedic texts of magic as of many other disciplines in the Renaissance. The representation of the encyclopedia and the reality of the world are not linked by any

kind of sympathy; it is precisely the encyclopedia's detachment from the world that makes it useful. Michel Foucault's powerful description in *The Order of Things: An Archeology of the Human Sciences* (New York: Vintage Books, 1970) of the workings of analogy in Renaissance thought is over-generalized; cf. also Mary Thomas Crane, *Framing Authority: Sayings, Self, and Society in Sixteenth-Century England* (Princeton University Press, 1993), 20–21, which also suggests that similarities were by no means transparent. As Foucault points out in *The Archaeology of Knowledge and the Discourse on Language*, transl. A. M. Sheridan Smith (New York: Pantheon, 1972), the structures he delineates in the earlier book are dependent on the contingent choices of fields to study; had he chosen different fields and a different set of relations, the "underlying" structures also would have been different. A glance at his notes to "The Prose of the World" shows that his sense of a continuity between words and things derives from his heavy reliance on magical texts, which are remarkable precisely because they do suggest such a continuity. Even that continuity has been challenged as rhetorical and tactical in Ioan P. Coulianou, *Eros and Magic in the Renaissance*, transl. Margaret Cook (University of Chicago Press, 1987), which argues that the object of Renaissance magic was always the susceptible soul of the observer rather than things themselves.

32 Gregoire, *Syntaxes* I, Bk. III, 31: "cùm vita sit brevis, ars longa: & non solùm in medecina, ut aiebat Hippocrates, experientis periculosa, sed etiam fere in humanis omnibus actibus . . ." Donatus makes the same point about theatre; see my chapter 2, 76–77. Joel Altman, *The Tudor Play of Mind: Rhetorical Inquiry and the Development of Elizabethan Drama* (Berkeley: University of California Press, 1978), argues that that the Tudor theatre is a space free from the constraints of authority, and thus available for use in working out problems and experimenting with solutions that would be impossible under more directly practical circumstances. I differ from Altman in that he seems to see the theatre as somehow really free, while I would argue that it is *authorized* to act as a free space.

33 Gregor Reisch, *Margarita Philosophica, hoc est Habitum seu Disciplinarum Omnium . . .* (Basle: Sebastianum Henricpetri, [1535], first edition 1503). For the fullest account of Reisch's life and book, see Robert Ritter von Srbik, *Die Margarita Philosophica des Gregor Reisch: Ein Beitrag zur Geschichte der Naturwissenschaften in Deutschland* (Vienna: Hölder-Pichler-Tempsky, 1941). My thanks to Dr. Catrien Santing of the Rijksuniversiteit Groningen for sending me a copy of this very hard-to-find piece.

34 There are some flaws in Reisch's plan – for instance, the text of the book is in Latin, but the first lessons in Latin do not appear for some seventy pages, at which point Discipulus and Magister switch to German.

35 Srbik, *Die Margarita Philosophica*, 16–17, notes, as one example, that Aristotle and Seneca appear in both images as representatives of non-liberal disciplines.

36 On other manifestations of a similar image and a similar process, see Mazzotta, *Dante's Vision*, on Limbo, where the pilgrim encounters the historical bearers of allegorical meaning, and David Bevington, *From* Mankind *to* Marlowe: The Growth of Structure in Popular Drama of Tudor England (Cambridge, MA: Harvard University Press, 1962), on the theatre of John Skelton and John Bale, where moral allegory is taken over, as it were, by historical figures, anticipating the connection I will establish between theatre and encyclopedia.

37 Reisch, *Margarita Philosophica*, [introduction]: "Qui cum poëmata in scena agunt, saepe ut reges, vel ut potentes prodeunt, cum neque reges sint neque potentes, neque omnino forsitan liberi."

38 It was, in short, a device for developing the worldly virtue of *prudentia*, practical knowledge, a field linked historically to the arts of memory. The history of artificial memory systems from the ancient world to the Renaissance is a vast field. The best introductions to ancient, medieval, and Renaissance practices of artificial memory, especially its use of space and image to promote retention, are Frances Yates, *The Art of Memory* (University of Chicago Press, 1966), Mary Carruthers, *The Book of Memory: A Study of Memory in Medieval Culture* (Cambridge University Press, 1990), and Lina Bolzoni, *La Stanza Della Memoria: Modelli Letterari e Iconografic i dell'Età della Stampa* (Turin: G. Einaudi, 1995). On prudence proper, and for an understanding of how it might work, see Victoria Kahn, *Rhetoric, Prudence, and Skepticism in the Renaissance* (Ithaca, NY: Cornell University Press, 1985) and my chapter 5.

39 Skalich de Lika, *Encyclopaedia*, "Encyclopaedia," 8: "Non est alia causa... quam desiderium flagrans et contemplandi ocium [i.e., otium]." Skalich de Lika repeats the phrase "ocio contemplandi" from his "Prooemium", where it is what allows him to carry out the research that results in his book. On the significance of the word *contemplare*, see above.

40 Ibid., "Prooemium," [3]: "Quandoquidem natura omnes trahimur & ducimur, sapientissime Imperator, ad insitam, vel potius innatam nobis cognitionis & scientiae cupiditatem, ad congregationem, ad societatem, ad communitatémque generis humani: quorum amor in nobis tantus est, ut nemo dubitare possit, quin ad res nullo emolumento invitati rapimur: utique eius gratia avemus aliquid videre, audire, discere, cognitionémque rerum aut occultarum aut admirabilium. ad benè beatóque vivendum necessarium ducimus: ob id, Rex inclyte, ego ingenuis studiis atque artibus ita delector, ut etiam valetudinis posthabita ratione, ipsa cognitione & scientia captus, omnia perpeti cupiam, & cum maximis curis atque laboribus compensare eam quam discendo capio *voluptatem*." Voluptas, "sexual pleasure", is one of the gods in Martianus Capella who responds to the Liberal Arts with boredom.

41 Conte, *Generi e Lettori*, "la voluntà di stupire e la capacità di stupirsi," 135. On the role of wonder, see also Stephen Greenblatt, *Marvelous Possessions: The Wonder of the New World* (University of Chicago Press, 1991), 13–25.

42 *Natural History*, transl. H. Rackam *et al.*, Loeb Classical Library (Cambridge, MA: Harvard University Press, 1938–62). Cf. Christian versions of this idea, which see the arts and sciences as ways of compensating for the loss of human dominion over the world brought about by the Fall; e.g., Hugh of St. Victor, *Didascalicon* I, xi. This is not the Augustinian suspicion that makes *curiositas* a cause of fallenness; Hugh makes it the merciful response of God to humankind's post-lapsarian helplessness. On Pliny's "rediscovery" in the Renaissance, see Paula Findlen, "Jokes of Nature and Jokes of Knowledge: The Playfulness of Scientific Discourse in Early Modern Europe," *Renaissance Quarterly* 43 (1990), 292–331 (296–301).

43 Pliny, *Natural History* VII, 6: "aut quid non miraculo est cum primum in notitiam venit? quam multa fieri non posse priusquam sunt facta iudicatur? naturae vero rerum vis atque maiestas in omnibus momentis fide caret si quis modo partes eius ac non totam complectatur animo." My translation.

44 Aristotle, *Metaphysics* I, 2.9, 982b11: "διὰ γὰρ τὸ θαυμάζειν οἱ ἄνθρωποι καὶ νῦν καὶ τὸ πρῶτον ἤρξαντο φιλοσοφεῖν, . . ." I have used the Loeb edition (transl. Hugh Tredennick [London: William Heinemann, 1933]), translation modified as necessary.
45 "διὰ τὸ εἰδέναι τὸ ἐπίστασθαι ἐδίωκον καὶ οὐ χρήσεώς τινος ἕνεκεν," *Metaphysics* I, 2. 9–10, 982b11–23.
46 *Apologia Actoris*, in *Speculum Naturale*, 2 vols. (Strassburg: [Printer of the 1482 *Legenda Aurea*], c.1480), I, chapter 18: "verum etiam quibusdam aliis, qui forsitan curiositate quadam sciendi incognita laborantes talium noticia delectantur, satisfacere volui." Vincent's *Apologia* is also available in a modern edition edited by Anna-Dorothee van den Brincken, "Geschichtsbetrachtung bei Vincenz von Beauvais: Die Apologia Actoris zum Speculum Maius," *Deutsche Archiv für Enforschung des Mittelalters* 34 (1978), 410–99.
47 Bartholomaeus Anglicus, *De Proprietatibus Rerum*, ed. Wynkyn de Worde (London: Wynkyn de Worde, 1495), st. 7, Lines 1–4.
48 Greenblatt, *Marvelous Possessions*, 19–24.
49 The *exemplum* of Alexander and Aristotle is widespread in the Renaissance, and it appears as early as Pliny. Most interestingly for our topic, it is alluded to by Guillaume Budé, *Libri V De Asse* (Venice: Aldus Manutius, 1522), 61r; Philip Sidney, *Defence of Poesy*, in *Sir Philip Sydney: Oxford Authors*, ed. Katherine Duncan-Jones (Oxford University Press 1989), 212–50 (237–38); and Francis Bacon, letter to King James of *De Augmentis Scientiarum* 2, in *Works*, eds. James Spedding, Robert Leslie Ellis, and Douglas Denon Heath, 14 vols. (London: Longman and Co., 1857–74, facsimile reprint, Stuttgart: Friedrich Fromann Verlag, 1963), IV: 287ff. Budé records with disdain Aristotle's acceptance of a substantial sum to fund his research, but a marginal note marking this passage out in the Folger copy of the book suggests that at least one early reader was more in sympathy with Aristotle's grant-writing.
50 In his *Considerazioni sul Tasso*, Galileo compares reading the "stingy, poor, and wretched" Tasso to "entering the little study of some inquisitive little man (*qualche ometto curioso*)" in contrast to that of the "magnificent, rich, and admirable" Ariosto, whose work Galileo likens to a princely collection, a museum full of superb and representative pieces from all cultures and periods of history. For a further discussion of this passage, as well as Galileo's text and the translation that I borrow from, see Anthony Grafton, *Commerce with the Classics*, Jerome Lectures 20 (Ann Arbor: University of Michigan Press, 1997), 189–91.
51 Preface 33, "summa que cura ne legendos eos haberes operam dedi." My translation.
52 Pliny the Younger, *Fifty Letters of Pliny*, ed. A. F. Sherwin-White (Oxford University Press, 1969), Letter 3, 5: "Nihil enim legit quod non excerperet . . . nec minus varium quam ipsa natura."
53 Ibid., Letter 6, 16. Umberto Eco, in "A Portrait of the Elder as a Young Pliny," in *Limits of Interpretation* (Bloomington: Indiana University Press, 1990), 123–36, offers a fascinating reading of the younger Pliny's attempt to efface in his uncle's self-effacement his own ambition for fame.
54 Conrad Gessner, "Ad Lectorem," in *Historiae Animalium* (1551), 5 vols. in 4, I (Frankfurt: Bibliopolium Camberiano, 1603), B2r: "Quanquam, ut inquit Plinius, maius meritum esset, operis amore (quod ipsum non suae sed Romani nominis gloriae composuisse decuit) non animi causa perseverasse . . ." Hans H. Wellisch, *Conrad Gessner: A Bio-Bibliography* (Zug: IDC, 1984), xiii, explains the varying spellings of Conrad Gessner's name; Gesner is from the Latin form, Gesnerus, and

is usual in English and French, but not accurately German, where Gessner used the double *s*. In German or Latin, Gessner spelled Conrad always with a *C*; Konrad with a *K* is a late form. I treat Gessner's contributions to encyclopedism and theatricality at greater length in chapter 3.

55 Juan Luis Vives, *De Tradendis Disciplinis*, book II of *De Disciplinis* (Cologne: Ioannes Gymnicus, 1536), 338: "In quibus generalibus est doctrina, sicut in singularibus delectatio: illud enim est mentis, hoc sensus. Ideóque magis delectat Plinius, Aristoteles magis docet." My translation, although an English translation by Foster Watson of this book alone is available (*On Education* [Cambridge University Press, 1913]).

56 For Pliny's limited ability, *Natural History*, Preface, § 12: "nam nec ingenii sunt capaces [libri?], quod alioqui in nobis perquam mediocre erat." On the contents of the *Natural History*, Preface § 11: "viginti milia rerum dignarum cura... lectione voluminum circiter duorum milium... ex exquisitis auctoribus centum inclusimus triginta sex voluminibus." Pliny's ability to number his facts and sources and his use of "enclose" (*inclusimus*) to describe their presence in the work suggests how early knowledge began to be conceived as spatial and quantifiable.

57 My emphases. Pliny, *Natural History* XI, 4: "... quapropter quaeso ne nostra legentes, quoniam ex his spernunt multa, etiam relata fastidio damnent, cum in contemplatione naturae nihil possit videri supervacuum." *Fastidium* is also the reaction of the gods to the Arts in Martianus Capella.

58 In Bonaventure's influential definition, "aliquis scribit aliena addendo, sed non de suo; et iste compilator dicitur" (quoted in M. B. Parkes, "The Influence of the Concepts of *Ordinatio* and *Compilatio* on the Development of the Book," in *Medieval Learning and Literature: Essays Presented to Richard William Hunt*, eds. J. J. G. Alexander and M. T. Gibson (Oxford: Clarendon Press, 1976), 115–41 (127–28); Ivan Illich, *In the Vineyard of the Text: A commentary to Hugh's Didascalicon* (University of Chicago Press, 1993), translates this strikingly, though perhaps wrongly, as "those who write down other's words, and add something, however not their own additions" (106). On the role of the medieval compiler, see Parkes, "Influence of the Concepts"; Richard H. Rouse and Mary A. Rouse, "*Statim invenire*: Schools, Preachers, and New Attitudes to the Page," in *The Renaissance of the Twelfth Century*, eds. R. L. Benson and G. Constable (Cambridge, MA: Harvard University Press, 1982), 201–25, Neil Hathaway, "*Compilatio*: From Plagiarism to Compiling," *Viator* 20 (1989), 19–44 (35–44), covers both ancient and medieval attitudes; Conte, *Generi e Lettori*, 99, discusses "the spirit of the archive" in respect to Pliny; Crane, *Framing Authority*, looks at one aspect of Renaissance compilation, the commonplace book, in depth. In ancient Latin, the word *compilator* has the much more literal and negative senses of burglary or plagiarism, but William Harris Stahl's reference to it in Martianus Capella as "pillaging" and a bogus pretense to knowledge is vitiated by the anachronism of evaluating it in the light of a Romantic admiration of originality (*Martianus Capella and the Seven Liberal Arts*, transl. William Harris Stahl and Richard Johnson with F. L. Burge [New York: Columbia University Press, 1977], II). Isidore (*Etymologiae, Sive Origines*, ed. W. M. Lindsay [Oxford: Clarendon Press, 1911]) tells how Vergil was accused of "this crime" (*hoc scelere*) in imitating Homer, and defended himself by saying that he had wrestled the spear from Hercules ("Hoc scelere quondam accusabatur est Mantuanus ille vates, cum quosdam versus Homeri transferens suis

permiscuisset et compilator veterum ab aemulis diceretur. Ille respondit: Magnarum esse virium clavam Herculi extorquere de manu," X, 44); this suggests that the practice by the sixth century was by no means viewed entirely negatively. Interestingly, early plays are often described as "compiled"; George Gascoigne's *The Glasse of Governement* (1575), in *The Complete Works*, ed. John W. Cunliffe, 2 vols. (Cambridge University Press, 1910), II, 1–90 even provides a list of aphorisms after the Prologue, noting "This worke is compiled upon these sentences."

59 Vincent of Beavais, *Apologia Actoris*, in *Speculum Naturale* I, chapter 4; van den Brincken, "Geschichtsbetrachtung," 470: "presertim cum hoc ipsum opus utique meum simpliciter non sit, sed illorum potius, ex quorum dictis fere totum illud contexui, nam *ex meo pauca et quasi nulla addidi*. Ipsorum igitur est auctoritate, nostrum autem sola partium ordinatione" ("Above all since this work is not merely mine, but rather theirs, from whose writings I wove this whole thing, for of my own I have added little or virtually nothing"). Bartholomaeus, Prohemium, in *De Proprietatibus Rerum* [Cologne: William Caxton?, 1470], n.p.: "in quibus [libellis] *de meo pauca vel quasi nulla apposui*. Sed omnia dicentur de libris auctenticis sanctorum et philosophorum excipiens sub brevi hoc compendio compilavi."

60 Abraham Ortelius, *Theatrum Orbis Terrarum* (Antwerp: Coppenius Diesth, 1570), Aiiijr: "In Tabulis quae Auctorum nomina habent nihil (ut diximus) est à nobis immutatum [sic], exceptis duabus aut tribus Belgicarum Regionum maritimis oris, quas marè post, quam [sic; i.e., postquam] ab Auctoribus descriptiones earum editae sunt, multum mutavit . . ." According to the *OLD*, *immutatum* should mean "unchanged", but the context makes it clear that it does not; the text shows other errors in the Latin, suggesting perhaps a hasty or careless compositor. This is made more likely since the press of Christopher Plantin did not take over publishing Ortelius' works until later. Hathaway, "Compilatio," 26, also notes the use of *immutare* in medieval Latin as a negative synonym for correct, emend, or compile.

61 *Didascalicon* (transl. Taylor), 137. *Didscalicon* VI, iii: "omnia disce, videbis postea nihil esse superfluum. coartata scientia iucunda non est."

62 *Steganographia* (c.1499), quoted in Coulianou, *Eros and Magic in the Renaissance*, 173: "ET OMNIA, QUAE FIUNT IN MUNDO, CONSTELLATIONE OBSERVATA PER HANC ARTEM SCIRE POTERIS." Trithemius is discussing the use of astral magic to see other parts of the world, which is why there is a constellation to be observed.

63 "Posse animam per viam purgatoriam absque alio studio vel investigatione per solam modicam & facilem collationem & avertentiam superiam desuper habita intelligibilia perfectam omnium scibilium scientiam acquirere . . . habent concedere" (90). Pico's *Conclusiones DCCC*, in *Opere Omnia*, 2 vols. (Basel: Heinrich Petrina, 1572–73), I, 63–113, were published in Rome in 1486 but never, as he had intended, publicly disputed. See François Secret, "La Tradition du 'De Omni Scibile,' à la Renaissance: L'Oeuvre de Paul Scaliger" *Convivium* 24 (1955), 492–97 (492–93), for a compressed history of attempts to know everything.

64 Aristotle, *Metaphysics* I, 2. 2, 982a8–10: "ὑπολαμβάνομεν δὴ πρῶτον μὲν ἐπίστασθαι πάντα τὸν σοφὸν ὡς ἐνδέχεται, μὴ καθ' ἕκαστον ἔχοντα ἐπιστήμην αὐτῶν."

65 Gregoire, *Syntaxes* I, iii. 30, quoting *Epist. ad Atticum* 4: ". . . ut ait Cicero οὐδὲν γλυκύτερον ἦν εἰδέναι. nihil est dulcius quàm omnia scire." See also Jean Corbichon's preface (written in 1372) to his translation of Bartholomaeus Anglicus (*Le Proprietaire des Choses*): "Car selon le philosophe aristote il assiert au saige

de scavoir toutes choses." Corbichon cites Aristotle, but follows Cicero (Lyons: G. Le Roy, 1485).
66 Vives, *De Disciplinis*, 235 (transl. Watson, 17): "Nam quid prodest defatigare se hac solicitudine, si votis nihil paratur aliud, quam vota: si cupiditatis unius finis sequentis est gradus."
67 To cite several similar statements drawing on very different bodies of knowledge, the child psychologist and psychoanalyst D. W. Winnicott distinguishes play from other stimulating activities like masturbation that are inherently climactic. Play is endless, both its own object and potentially infinitely protractable. It excludes an external teleology like climax, although it is "inherently exciting and precarious," balanced between the poles of saturation and boredom (chapter 3, "Playing: A Theoretical Statement," esp. 52, in *Playing and Reality*, [New York: Basic Books, 1971]). J. Huizinga, *Homo Ludens: A Study of the Play-Element in Culture*, transl. R. F. C. Hull (London: Routledge and Kegan Paul, 1949), criticizes the idea that "play must serve something which is *not* play" (2) and stresses that play is essentially outside ordinary concerns of practicality, morality, and interest. Huizinga goes on to point out that play always occurs within a distinct space and time, although the connection I am making – that these limits are demanded by the autotelic, unbounded nature of play or *curiositas* – is my own. Finally, Gilles Deleuze and Felix Guattari base their *A Thousand Plateaus: Capitalism and Schizophrenia*, transl. Brian Massumi (Minneapolis: University of Minnesota Press, 1987) on the recognition of an alternative to the goal-oriented practices that they see as dominating official cultures – an idea of a pleasure that does not demand any release but can be indefinitely extended.
68 Carmen Codoñer, "De L'Antiquité au Moyen Age: Isidore de Seville," in Becq, *L'Encyclopédisme*, 19–35(21), suggests using these final purposes to categorize what we group together as encyclopedias, but this elides the other generic markers that let them be so grouped. I have been arguing that these purposes themselves are subordinate to a playful desire that requires the positing of purposes.
69 *Natural History* VII, 32: "ludibria sibi, nobis miracula, ingeniosa fecit natura."
70 Ibid. VIII, 34: "Quam quis aliam tantae discordiae causam attulerit nisi naturam spectaculam sibi ac paria conponentem?" D. C. Greetham, "Bartholomaeus Anglicus on Nature," *Journal of the History of Ideas* 41 (1980), 663–77 finds in nature a similar interest in balance.
71 Findlen, "Jokes of Nature," 293, also sees much ludic science as motivated by a need to avoid finding reasons. See Conte, *Generi e Lettori*, 105–18, on the emphasis in Pliny on meaning rather than causality; the emphasis on meaning in particular seems to me overstated, since what nature means in Pliny is not in any sense a communication to man, but an interpretation by him. This continues to be the case with surprising consistency in encyclopedic works into the Renaissance; even the encyclopedias of the preaching orders like Bartholomaeus Anglicus' show great restraint in assigning allegorical meanings to natural phenomena. Also see Pliny, *Natural History* XXXVII, 60: "reason is not to be looked for in every part of nature, but will!" (". . . nec quaerenda ratio in ulla parte naturae, sed voluntas!") *Voluntas* itself, though, is a kind of order. At XI, 8, Pliny declares that causes are for philosophers, not natural historians.
72 *Historiae Animalium*, I, "Epistola Nuncupatoria", a3v: "Hi tanquam ludi quidem naturae non contemnendi nobis sed spectandi proponuntur."
73 Other notable *adulteria* mentioned by Pliny are those of expensive spices (XII, 36), frankincense (XII, 65), and balsam (XII, 119). There are many others.

74 Pliny, *Natural History* XVI, 233: "Modo luxuria non fuerat contenta ligno, iam lignum et e testudine facit."
75 Ibid., VII, 32: ". . . quos Hermaphroditos vocamus, olim androgynos vocatos et in prodigiis habent, nunc vero in delicios."
76 Ibid., V, 12: "equidem minus miror inconperta quaedam esse equestris ordinis viris, iam vero et senatum inde intrantibus, quam luxuriae, cuius efficacissima vis sentitur atque maxima . . ." See also Budé, *De Asse*, who similarly contrasts virtuous *philologia* with its corrupt double, *philoplutia*, "love of wealth."
77 Jerome, *Opera*, Sections I, parts 1–3, *Epistylae*, ed. Isiderus Hilderberg, Corpus Scriptorum Ecclesiasticorum Latinum vols. 54–56 (Vienna: F. Tempsky, 1910–18), Letter 22, *Ad Eustachium* 30.
78 *Apologia Actoris*, in *Speculum Naturale*, chapter 1; Van den Brincken, "Geschichtsbetrachtung," 465: "ut et studio meo quasi modum quendam imponens curiositati mee: ceterorumque nonnullorum forsitan mei similium: quorum studium et labor est plurimos legere: eorumque flores excerpere: per hoc unum grande opus satisfacerem." In the translation I have followed the more logical punctuation of Van den Brincken, which connects *satisfacerem* to the following clause.
79 Vincent of Beauvais, *Apologia Actoris*, in *Speculum Naturale*, chapter 18, Van den Brincken, "Geschichtsbetrachtung," 495: "fateor ex magna parte: meo iudicio: professionis et intentionis mee modum excessi: in illis praecipue investigandis et describendis quorum nomina in divinis libris non repperi. Itaque dum curiosis morem gerere volui: vicium curiositatis incurri."
80 *Confessions*, ed. and annot. James J. O'Donnell, 3 vols. (Oxford: Clarendon Press, 1992), vol. I, I, 10 and X, 35. 54. In X, 35. 55, Augustine distinguishes *voluptas* and *curiositas*. Since *curiositas* is always of the new, whether pleasant or unpleasant, it is thus especially enmeshed with theatre, which fascinates even when it produces unpleasant emotions. The link between *curiositas* and novelty likewise makes *curiositas* much harder to control than *voluptas*. O'Donnell's commentary is helpful on this aspect of Augustine.
81 Ibid., II, 273. The encyclopedia, to which O'Donnell assimilates Augustine's sense of an education, thrown beyond its proper limits, is thus as likely to promote anti-Christian feeling as to be read as a faithful record of God's Book of the World; see "Excursus: The *Liberales Disciplinas*," II, 269–78.
82 In its self-conscious self-limiting as game, the encyclopedic project also precisely represents its object, the world. As Pliny suggests, the world is in a sense the game of Nature. The game of the encyclopedist is possible in part because nature plays along.
83 Pliny, *Natural History* VII, 34: "Pompeius Magnus in ornamentis theatri mirabiles fama posuit effigies od id diligentius magnorum artificium ingeniis elaboratas."
84 Conte, *Generi e Lettori*, 132–34, compares Aristotle's treatment of the sponge as a necessary intermediary between plant and animal with Pliny's emphasis on its strangeness and the good luck that that strangeness is so useful to humans.
85 Here, of course, the representation begins to sound less like Pantagruel and more like Pangloss.
86 *De Nuptiis Mercurii et Philologiae*, ed. Adolph Dick (Stuttgart: Teubner, 1925), § 68, transl. p. 26: "quae quidem sphaera imago quaedam videbatur ideaque mundi."
87 For a discussion of this combination in the eighteenth century, see Barbara Maria Stafford, *Artful Science: Enlightenment Entertainment and the Eclipse of Visual Education* (Cambridge, MA: MIT Press, 1994); Findlen, "Jokes of Nature."

88 Jorge Luis Borges, "An Examination of the Works of Herbert Quain," in *Ficciones*, ed., transl., and intro. Anthony Kerrigan (New York: Grove Press, 1962), 75.

2 THE IDEA OF A THEATRE

1 Quoted in E. K. Chambers, *The Elizabethan Stage*, 4 vols. (Oxford: Clarendon Press, 1923), II, 373; discussed by Andrew Gurr, *The Shakespearean Stage 1574–1642*, (Cambridge University Press, 1992), 121.
2 Claes Visscher's panoramic *View of London* of 1616, for instance, points out the theatres as unusual landmarks, and they are frequently commented on in the accounts of foreign visitors to London. On the Visscher drawing and its representation of the theatres, see John Orrell, *The Human Stage: English Theatre Design, 1567–1640* (Cambridge University Press, 1988). Other impressed tourists from Italy and Germany are quoted in Andrew Gurr, *Playgoing in Shakespeare's London* (Cambridge University Press, 1987); De Witt's drawing and a commentary are in R. A. Foakes, *Illustrations of the English Stage, 1580–1642*, (Stanford University Press, 1985), 52–55.
3 Marshall, "*Theatre* in the Middle Ages," scrupulously tracks the lexical and commentary tradition of the word *theatrum*.
4 Tertullian's images from *De Spectaculis* of a Hell filled with comedians no longer laughing, acrobats twisting as they never did in life in the torture of eternal flames, and actors weeping at their own tragedies (picked up by Kyd in *The Spanish Tragedy*) were venomous enough that Friedrich Nietzsche chose it as his central example of priestly *ressentiment* in *Genealogy of Morals*, in *Birth of Tragedy and Genealogy of Morals*, transl. Francis Golfing (New York: Doubleday, 1956). The story of Cicero and Roscius appears in Plutarch's *Life of Cicero* V, 3 (*Lives*, ed. and transl. Bernadotte Perin, Loeb Classical Library [London: William Heinemann, 1914–26]); see also Bruce R. Smith, *Ancient Scripts and Modern Experience on the English Stage, 1500–1700* (Princeton University Press, 1988), 14–16. On the importance of Terence and Plautus in humanist education, see Willi Flemming, "Formen der Humanistenbühne," *Maske und Kothurn: Vierteljahrschrift für Theaterwissenschaft* 6 (1960), 33–52, Howard B. Norland, *Drama in Early Tudor Britain 1485–1558* (Lincoln: University of Nebraska Press, 1995), and Smith, *Ancient Scripts and Modern Experience*.
5 Sebastian Münster, *Cosmographia* (Basel: Heinrichum Petri, 1550; facsimile reprint, Amsterdam: Theatrum Orbis Terrarum, 1968), ccxxiii: "Man findt zu Veron mere dann in keiner stat Italie/ausgenommen Rom/alt verfallen beüw [d.h., Gebaüde] und anzeignungen eins grossen wesens/das vor zeiten zü Veron ist gewesen."
6 Castiglione, *Opere*, ed. Giuseppe Prezzolini (Milan: Rizzoli, 1937):

> Superbi colli, e voi, sacre ruine,
> Che'l nome sole di Roma ancor tenete, . . .
> Colossi, archi, teatri, opre divine,
> Trionfal pompe gloriose e liete,
> In poco cener pur converse siete, . . . (Sonnet 6, 1–7)

Du Bellay, *Oeuvres Poetique*, ed. Geneviève Demerson, 8 vols. (Paris: Librairie Nizet, 1984):

> Ardua Pyramidum dicam, truncos Colossos,
> Maestaque nunc muta theatra sinu? (Elegy 2, 109f.)

Castiglione's poem is imitated by Du Bellay, *Antiquitez de Rome*, 7, who is in turn imitated by Spenser in Van der Noot's *Theatre for Voluptuous Worldlings*, but neither of the latter poets includes the word "theatre" in their versions.

7 "Ut parvi starent fondamina pontis,/ Ampla tuae quatinent amphitheatra manus?" Evangelista Maddaleni Capodiferro, writing c.1575, quoted and translated in Leonard Barkan, *Unearthing the Past: Archeology and Aesthetics in the Making of Renaissance Culture* (New Haven: Yale University Press, 1999), 36.

8 Van der Noot's *Theatre for Voluptuous Worldlings* (1569), which contains Spenser's first published poems, is the conceptual sibling of these titles.

9 For example, on the educational potential of the theatre and its universality, Philip Sidney mentions that although "naughty play-makers and stage-keepers have justly made [comedy] odious, . . . the right use of comedy will (I think) by nobody be blamed, and much less of the high and excellent tragedy" (*Defence of Poesy*, 229–30). Francis Bacon concurs: "And though in modern states play-acting is esteemed but as a toy . . . among the ancients it was used as a means of educating men's minds to virtue. Nay, it has been regarded by learned men and great philosophers as a kind of musician's bow by which men's minds may be played upon" (*De Augmentis, Works*, II, 13; see my chapter 6). Blair, *Theatre of Nature*, 166–79, provides a useful survey of the meaning of *theatre* when used as a book title.

10 This threefold definition of comedy is virtually universal in early modern writings, to the extent that even avowedly antitheatrical writers like John Northbrooke, in *A Treatise wherein Dicing, Dauncing, Vaine playes of Enterludes* . . . (London: H. Bynneman [1577]), make use of it. See Norland, *Drama in Early Tudor Britain*, 70–71, for the influence of this tag in Renaissance dramatic theory. This instance is from Terence, *Comoediae*, ed. Sebastian Brant (Strassburg: J. Grüninger, 1496), n.p.: "Comedia secundum grecos est & private civilisque fortune sine periculo vite comprehensio. Comedia secundum Ciceronem est imitatio vite speculum consuetudinis & imago veritatis." Not only is comedy an exact replica of life, it is also one that remains detached from it.

11 "homo sum: humani nil a me alienum puto." The extent to which this line was treated as a manifesto rather than a part of a playtext is suggested by the fact that it is underlined in the otherwise almost unmarked Newberry copy of the Lyons Terence.

12 See Norland, *Drama in Early Tudor Britain*, 84–94, on Erasmus' conviction of the value of Terence's texts for study; the educational program he designed for John Colet's St. Paul's School was based on reading principally Terence and other dramatists.

13 Joseph Webbe, ed., *The First Comedy of Pub. Terentius, called Andria* (London: Felix Kingston [1629]), ¶¶ 2v. For Webbe, see Martin Elsky, *Authorizing Words: Speech, Writing, and Print in the English Renaissance* (Ithaca, NY: Cornell University Press, 1989), 50–54; see also Robert C. Evans, *Jonson and the Contexts of His Time* (Lewisburg: Bucknell University Press, 1994), chapter 7. Webbe's method was a combinatory, which I will discuss more fully as it relates to encyclopedias and theatres in chapter 3 on the works of Giulio Camillo. According to Evans, Webbe had studied for many years in Italy, so it is not out of the question that he was familiar with Camillo's works.

14 For this and the Lydgate citation of the word *theatre* in Middle English, I am indebted to the editors of the *Middle English Dictionary* at the University of Michigan for allowing me to use their unpublished slips.

15 In the tradition of Hugh of St. Victor's *Didascalicon*, theatre was one of the mechanical, i.e. non-liberal, arts; Linne R. Mooney, "A Middle English Text on the Seven Liberal Arts," *Speculum* 68 (1993), 1027–52, provides an edition of the English text in which the confusion occurs.
16 John Rider, *Bibliotheca Scholastica* (Oxford: J. Barnes, 1589; facsimile reprint, Menston: Scolar Press, 1970).
17 Perhaps even longer. Gurr, *Playgoing*, 85–97, looks even-handedly at whether sixteenth- and seventeenth-century English spectatorship was thought of as more visual or aural and concludes that, first, the definition was very much a matter of current concern, and that, second, the eventual triumph of the word "audience" may have been a "Pyrrhic victory." In the seventeenth century, the faculty of hearing was elevated over that of seeing, to distinguish the learned ear of the reader from the ignorant eye of the mob. See my chapter 5 on this ideal "audience."
18 Vives continues, "thus the teacher of the people is both a painter and a poet" ("Venit in scenam poesis, populo ad spectandum congregato, et ibi sicut pictor tabulam proponit multitudini spectandam, ita poeta imaginem quandam vitae; ... ita magister est populi, et pictor, et poeta," Vives, *De Causis Corruptarum Artium* [1531], quoted in Chambers, *Elizabethan Stage*, IV, 186).
19 See previous note and also n.73. See also Flemming, "Humanistenbühne," 35, on the visual emphasis of early printed plays.
20 Shapin, *Social History of Truth*, 31, whose account is more nuanced than my shortened explanation. Properly speaking, these are not beliefs, but practices that make beliefs and disbeliefs possible (29–31).
21 For other selections of primary materials that show this misunderstanding, see Mary H. Marshall, "*Theatre* in the Middle Ages: Evidence from Dictionaries and Glosses," *Symposium* 4 (1950), 1–39, 366–89. It is possible that in "historial" Lydgate is also punning on, confusing, or connecting, *historia* and *histrio* ("actor"), as later writers do explicitly.
22 It is part of my later argument that these attempts to enact an encyclopedic control of the theatre failed, even that they failed necessarily. It is crucial to recognize in them, though, the desire (on the part of both early modern and modern critics) to subordinate performance to some kind of control. See my chapter 4.
23 *L'Idea del Theatro dell'Eccelente M. Giulio Camillo* (Florence: Lorenzo Torrentino, 1550). For backgrounds and interpretations to Camillo, see Lina Bolzoni's introduction to her edition of *L'Idea del Teatro* (Palermo: Sellerio, 1991) and to *Il Teatro della Memoria: Studi su Giulio Camillo* (Padua: Liviana, 1984); Yates, *Art of Memory*, 129–59; Jean-Claude Margolin, "Le *Théâtre de Memoire* de Giulio Camillo: Récapitulation des Connaissances Acquises, ou Instrument Heuristique de Connaissances Nonvelles?" in Becq, *L'Encyclopédisme*, 459–81; Douglas Radcliffe-Umstead, "Giulio Camillo's Emblems of Memory," *Yale French Studies* 47 (1972), 47–56; François Secret, "Les Cheminements de la Kabbala à la Renaissance: Le *Théâtre du Monde* de Giulio Camillo et son Influence," *Rivista di Storia della Filosophica* 14 (1959), 418–36.
24 I discuss Camillo's *Theatro* more fully in the following chapter.
25 "Et a voler bene intender queste cose inferiori è necessario di ascendere alle superiori è, di alto in giù guardando, di queste potremo più certa cognizione," Camillo, *Idea*, 62–63.

26 Theodore Zwingèr, *Theatrum Vitae Humanae* (Basel: I. Oporinus, 1565): "Supplementum: Hoc Est Titulorum & Exemplorum quorundam, in Dispositione totius Operis, seu casu, seu consilio, vel loco suo motorum, vel certe omissorum, SYLVA" (n.p.). Note the placement of *sylva* in the emphatic final position. What falls outside the theatre and is characterized by its very uncertainty, is a *silva*. Paolo Cherchi, *Enciclopedismo e Politicà della Riscrittura: Tommaso Garzoni* (Pisa: Pacini, 1980), 21–30, links the transformation of *silva* to *teatro* to the process of *rescrivere*: Tommaso Garzoni, for instance, makes the "irrepeatable anecdotes" of Montaigne iterable by setting them into an order; see also Walter Ong, "Commonplace Rhapsody: Ravisius Textor, Zwinger, and Shakespeare," in R. R. Bolgar, ed. *Classical Influences on European Culture*, A.D. 1500–1700 (Cambridge University Press, 1976), 91–126 (118–20).
27 On the hieroglyph, see Elsky, *Authorizing Words*.
28 As far as I know, the difference I am marking here is not made in the sixteenth century using these two terms. That is to say, while the term *theatre* is a significant one, it is not systematically or even regularly contrasted to *drama*. Instead, I will use these terms as a kind of shorthand for the historically important contrast between a neo-Aristotelian view of performance and the ideology of theatre that I am exploring.
29 *Contemplatio* as the appropriate reaction to the theatre of the world is a commonplace from Pliny the Elder onward. See my first chapter.
30 Blair, *Theatre of Nature*, gives an exhaustive and fascinating account of the intellectual position of Bodin's book in its time.
31 In Letter 2 of Bk. VI of the *Rerum Familiarum Libri I–VIII*, transl. Aldo S. Bernardo (Albany: SUNY Press, 1975), Petrarch and Giovanni Colonna visit the ruins of Rome. See Leonard Barkan, *Transuming Passion: Ganymede and the Erotics of Humanism* (Stanford University Press, 1991), 10–19, for the importance of the image of the ruined city as a place of discovery in the Renaissance.
32 Bodin, *Theatrum*,10: "eosque per civitatem circunducat, omnemque loci antiquitatem aperiat, templa, theatra, porticus, quaéque pulcherrima ac rarissima sciat, comiter explicet: ita me quoque in hac mundana civitate peregrinantem, de rebus omnibus abs te erudiri . . ."
33 On Agricola and his logic, see Crane, *Framing Authority*, 19–26; Ong, *Ramus*, 92–130; Schmidt-Biggemann, *Topica Universalis*, 2–15; on the metaphor of following a track for imitation, George Pigman, "Versions of Imitation in the Renaissance," *Renaissance Quarterly* 33 (1980), 1–32.
34 Bodin, *Theatrum*, 10: "quia non aliam ob causam in hoc mundi theatrum venimus, quam ut speciem universi, omniaque summi rerum omnium conditoris opera ac singula opificia contemplando . . . "
35 The first quote ends the volume, Bodin, *Theatrum*, 633: "Finis Theatri Natura [sic], quod IOAN. BODINUS Gallia tota bello civili flagrante conscripsit." The second nearly begins it, Bodin, 3r (before the page numberings commence): "At in natura nihil est incertum."
36 Bodin, *Theatrum*, 129: "explica, si placet universitatis tabulam, velut in teatro: ut quasi ob oculus [sic] rerum omnium distributione ad intuendum proposita, essentia cuiusque ac facultas planius intelligatur." A *tabula* could be a tablet for writing, a picture, or a game board; s.v. *OLD*. Bodin repeats the image of the *tabula* from his Dedication, 3v: "Et quidem Naturae Theatrum aliud nihil est, quam rerum ab immortali Deo conditarum quasi tabula quaedeam sub uniuscuiusque oculos subiecta."

37 Interestingly, this verbal emphasis on the analogies between Zwinger's book and a theatre seems to be the result of rewriting like Garzoni's. Most of these and other features that I will identify as theatrical appear in the greatly expanded edition of 1571 (4 vols. [Basel: Frobenius]) rather than in the first edition of 1565 (Basel: I. Oporinus), which is straightforwardly Ramist in organization.

38 Zwinger, *Theatrum* (1571), I, 27: "Nobis enim fortasse nec ocium nec vita suppetet, ut quod multa flagitant, et animus etiam iubet, Geometrarum [sic] imitatione, qui Vniversitatis machinam in exiguo globo describunt, magnum hocce Theatrum in Theatridij [sic, for Theatricalii?] formam contrahamus: nedum ut in dictione excolenda plus operae & studij collocemus."

39 For contemporary architectural book design, see Margery Corbett and Ronald Lightbown, *The Comely Frontispiece: The Emblematic Title-Page in England, 1550–1660* (London: Routledge and Kegan Paul, 1979). A. F. Johnson, ed., *One Hundred Title-Pages, 1500–1800* (London: Bodley Head, 1928), xi–xii, notes that "dispensing with ornament has always been common," but further observes that this "severe" classicizing is neither accidental nor semantically neutral.

40 Zwinger, *Theatrum* (1571), "De Inscriptione Operis," I, 32: "Nam sive rem ipsam consideres, τῶν ἀνϑρωπινῶν ϑεάματα continet, & ἀπὸ τὴν ϑεὰν Theatra olim, potius quàm ab ἀκροάσει Akroateria, dicere placuit."

41 Ibid., I, 11: "Historica igitur observatio vel nostro marte obitur, quam αὐτοψίαν à sensu principe vocare possumus: vel aliunde petitur ex aliorum scilicet narratione tum vocali, quae ἀκρόασις erit, tum scripta, quam ἀναγνῶσιν dicunt. αὐτοψίαν Historicis relinquimus: ἀκρόασιν parcé & raro adhibemus: ἀναγνώσει in primis utimur."

42 Lina Bolzoni, "L''invenzione' dello Stanzino di Francesco I," in *Le Arti del Principato Mediceo* (Florence: Studio Per Edizioni Scelte, 1980), 255–99 (287).

43 Here again we stand on well-traveled ground. On the possible cosmological significance of the Elizabethan stage, see John Gillies, *Shakespeare and the Geography of Difference* (Cambridge University Press, 1994), chapter 3; Kent van den Berg, *Playhouse and Cosmos: Shakespearean Theatre as Metaphor* (Newark: University of Delaware Press, 1985); Yates, *Theatre*.

44 See Mullaney, *Place of the Stage*, 10–15, on the policing of the structures of communal time and space in early modern London, and 47–55, on the stage's challenge to these orders by establishing its own, very different, boundaries at the margins of the larger communal ones. Bevington, *From* Mankind *to* Marlowe, long ago suggested that popular theatre effected a certain universality of topic because it was designed to be repeated in very different physical, emotional, and temporal settings. Greg Walker, *The Politics of Performance in Early Renaissance Drama* (Cambridge University Press, 1998), 34, stresses the importance that the "single physical environment" of most early plays had on their interpretation and performance.

45 In the definition he gave for the word *theatrum* in his *Thesaurus Linguae Romanae et Britannicae* (London: H. Wykes, 1565, facsimile reprint, Menston: Scolar Press, 1969), Thomas Cooper specified that the word meant "Sometime the multitude that beholdeth. Sometime the sight or play set forth in that place." See Charles Whitney, "Ante-Aesthetics: Towards a Theory of Early Modern Audience Response," in Hugh Grady, ed., *Shakespeare and Modernity: Early Modern to Millennium* (London: Routledge and Kegan Paul, 2000), 40–60 and Robert Weimann, *Popular Tradition in Theater: Studies in the Social Dimensions of Dramatic Form and Function*, ed.

Robert Schwartz (Baltimore: Johns Hopkins University Press, 1978), for a discussion of stage practice and the ways in which the audience and the actor in a sense interpenetrated. A variant of this position in recent criticism is Jean Howard, *The Stage and Social Struggle in Early Modern England* (New York: Routledge and Kegan Paul, 1994), whose argument is that the radical effectiveness of the Elizabethan theatre lay in the composition and behavior of its audience more than in what was presented on stage.

46 Vincent's work was reprinted in individual volumes several times in the fifteenth and sixteenth centuries, but only as a whole, and most recently, in 1591 and 1624, without the title changing from *Speculum* to *Theatrum*. I have not been able to find the 1591 Venice *editio princeps* of the collected set, cited in Parkes, "Concepts of *Ordinatio* and *Compilatio*," and several other secondary sources. Since I have not found it recorded in any of the library catalogues I have examined, I suspect it may be a ghost. Prior editions are only of individual volumes. Van den Brincken, "Geschichtsbetrachtung," gives an exhaustive account of the composition of the *Speculum Maius*.

47 This method of rubrication was also used occasionally to mark actors' lines in early editions of Terence and Plautus; the Folger copy of the Lyons Terence, for example.

48 *Apologia Actoris*, in *Speculum Naturale*, chapter 3; Van den Brincken, "Geschichtsbetrachtung," 468: "nomine meo id est actoris." The printed editions I used had taken the *lectio facilior* of *auctor*.

49 Vincent of Beauvais, *Speculum Naturale* XIX, xi, "De canis": "Actor. Canis ergo. ut legitur. cecus nascitur. lunaticus est: odoratu multum viget. Dentes habet acutos et os fissum. valde mordet: et lingit: non ruminat seu rodit. Ad vomitum redit: priusquam recubet lectum circuit. Bolissimum patitur id est rapidissimam famem."

50 M.-D. Chenu, "Auctor, Actor, Autor," *Bulletin du Cange – Archivium Latinitas Medii Aevi* 3 (1927), 81–86 (83). Chenu discusses the gradual individuation of the senses of the words *auctor*, *actor*, and *autor* in this period. Chenu does not discuss the possible echoes of the word *actor* in the sense of *histrio* in his article, nor does Abigail Ann Young include it in her article on medieval Latin terms for theatrical performers, "Plays and Players: The Latin Terms for Performance," *REED Newsletter* 9.2 (1984), 56–62; 10.1 (1985), 9–16. This has less to do with the word itself, though, than with the limits these two articles set themselves. Chenu is writing to correct an inadequate definition in Du Cange's dictionary of medieval Latin, which does not list *histrio* as a possible sense for *actor*. The use of *actor* to mean a stage player, though, was readily available to Vincent in authors such as Martianus Capella, Terence, and Cicero. E.g., Martianus Capella, *De Nuptiis* V, 543 (Dick 271. 14): "ad summam gestus non is oratori tenenda est, quo scaenae placere videntur actores" ("In sum, the orator should not use gesture to the extent that actors use it to please their audience"). See the *Thesaurus Linguae Latinae*, s.v. *actor*, for a fuller listing. Young specifically limits herself to those words that changed meanings or do not appear in classical texts. As she observes, Latin words continued to echo with their ancient meanings ("Plays and Players," 9).

51 At the International Medieval Conference in Leeds, England, July 10–13, 1995, Dr. J. B. Voorbij of Utrecht University informed me that to his knowledge, after examining the manuscripts of the *Speculum* from Vincent's period, the variant *actor* is not used for the author's part. I appreciate Dr. Voorbij's help on this vast subject.

52 For a collated edition of the manuscript texts of the *Apologia Actoris*, see Van den Brincken, "Geschichtsbetrachtung"; also see Parkes, "Concepts of *Ordinatio* and *Compilatio*," 128–29, for a discussion.
53 Vincent of Beauvais *Apologia Actoris*, in *Speculum Naturale*, chapter 3: "Interdum etiam ea que ipse vel a maioribus meis, sive modernis doctoribus didici: vel in quorundam scriptis notabilia repperi: nomine meo id est actoris intitulavi."
54 Ibid., chapter 4; Van den Brincken, "Geschichtsbetrachtung," 469–70: "Antiquum certe auctoritate et materia, Novum vero partium compilatione . . . Ipsorum igitur est auctoritate, meus autem sola partium ordinatione." The editions I used read *autoritate* in both places. Van den Brincken offers an analysis of Vincent's borrowed authority, 411–24; see also Monique Paulmier-Foucart, "Ordre Encyclopédique et Organisation de la Matiére dans la *Speculum Maius* de Vincent de Beauvais," in Becq, *L'Encyclopédisme*, 201–26 (201–05), for a reading of this passage.
55 Vincent of Beauvais *Apologia Actoris*, in *Speculum Naturale*, chapter 7; Van den Brincken, "Geschichtsbetrachtung," 474: "audiat iterum me non per modum autoris sed excerptoris ubique pro cedere [sic]. nec circum difficultates quarum libet artium enucliandas propositum meum instituisse." Van den Brincken gives "doctoris vel tractatoris" in her text, but cites one family of texts as having "auctoris." I have here, as usual, followed the texts I worked from.
56 Thomas Nashe, *Works*, eds. Ronald B. McKerrow and F. P. Wilson, 5 vols. (Oxford: Basil Blackwell, 1958), II, 235.
57 Varro, *De Lingua Latina* VI, 77: "Potest enim aliquid facere et non agere, ut poeta facit fabulam et non agit, contra actor agit et non facit." Cf. also VI, 58: "Ideo actores pronuntiare dicuntur, quod in proscaenio enuntiant poetae cogitata." Compare Nicolaus Perotti's definition in his *Cornucopiae sive Commentariorum Linguae Latinae* . . . (Venice: Augustinus Barbadicus, 1492/93): "Differtque Actor ab auctore: quod actor est qui recititat: Auctor qui opus facit" (172r).
58 Jody Enders, "The Theater of Scholastic Erudition," *Comparative Drama* 27(1993), 341–63. For two similar situations constructed very differently, see Avitall Ronell, *Dictations: On Haunted Writing* (Bloomington: Indiana University Press, 1986), on Goethe's amanuensis Eckermann, and Latour, *Science in Action*, on the scientist as "mouthpiece" for his laboratory, which in turn speaks for the world. Ronell and Latour stress the ways in which, in contrast to Vincent, the self-effacing speaker himself possesses the authority that he cedes to what he claims is the primary text, be it Goethe or Nature.
59 Robert M. Maniquis, "Encyclopedias and Society: Order, Disorder, and Textual Pleasure," in *The Encyclopédie and the Age of Revolution*, eds. Clorinda Donato and Robert M. Maniquis (Boston: G. K. Hall, 1992), 77–87 (80–81). Maniquis treats the *Encyclopédie* of Diderot and D'Alembert as a point of origin for encyclopedic writings and so does not consider earlier works.
60 Van den Brincken, "Geschichtsbetrachtung," 411.
61 The image is from Vaticanus Latinus 3305, 8v. On Calliopius as a judge, see Mary L. Richmond, *Terence Illustrated: An Exhibition in Honor of Karl Ephraim Weston*, forward, S. Lane Faison, Jr. (Williamstown, MA: Chapin Library, Williams College, 1955), 10–11.
62 "recognovi et censuram meam adhibui his scriptis coram recitatis," *Comoediae*, ed. Jodacus Badius Ascensius (Lyons: [Johannes] Wechsel, 1493), 51r. Once the link between the editor Calliopius and the actor-prologue is made, a number of other

"clues" to the inevitability of this relation appear in the text, e.g., *Heauton Timoroumenos*, Prologue: "He wants me to be an orator, not a prologue; he makes the judgment yours and offers me as a lawyer (*actorem*)."

63 Zwinger, *Theatrum* (1565), 186: "vel quod ιστορες quidam sint qui aliorum dicta factaqué quadam palingenesia in scenam producant."

64 *Batman uppon Bartholome, his Booke De Proprietatibus Rerum*, ed. Stephen Batman (London: Thomas East, 1582), facsimile reprint, intro. Jürgen Schäfer, Anglistica and Americana 161 (Hildesheim: Georg Olms Verlag, 1976).

65 E.g., Remigius Autissiodorensis, *Commentum in Martianum Capellam. Libri I–IV*, ed. and intro. Cora E. Lutz, 2 vols. (Leiden: E. J. Brill, 1962), I, 65: "Ergo ad illud quod interrogatur ΤΙΣ, id est quis, respondetur ΠΡΟΣΩΠΑ, id est persona auctoris, ut quis scripsit? Martianus." Isidore, *Etymologiae* XIII, 2, associates the trope *prosopopoeia* with tragedies.

66 This understanding of the meaning of *auctor* is becoming more widespread; two recent authoritative sources for it are Parkes, "Concepts of *Ordinatio* and *Compilatio*," and Carruthers, *Book of Memory*, 190–91. See also A. J. Minnis' magisterial work on authority, *Medieval Theory of Authorship: Scholastic Literary Attitudes in the Later Middle Ages* (Philadelphia: University of Pennsylvania Press, 1988), which takes this definition as a starting point.

67 This is of course one of Hamlet's concerns in his advice to the players. William Ingram, *The Business of Playing: The Beginnings of the Adult Professional Theater in Elizabethan London* (Ithaca, NY: Cornell University Press, 1992), 77–78 cites an incident in 1537,when the Duke of Suffolk complained to Thomas Cromwell that the player playing Husbandry in "A play which play was of a king how he should rule his Realm" wandered from "the book of the play" in order to abuse some of the gentlemen watching.

68 For more information on Webbe, see n.13, and also the following chapter.

69 For instance, the Venice edition of Terence (1496), which rendered the images in a more modern Italian style than the gothicism of the Lyons or Strassburg editions (Richmond, *Terence Illustrated*, 34), and the line of manuscripts represented by Figure 6 (Vaticanus Latinus 3305, 8v) in which "Calliopius is . . . in every way accorded the place of the author" (James Leslie Webber and C. R. Morey, *The Miniatures of the Manuscripts of Terence Prior to the Thirteenth Century*, 2 vols. (Princeton University Press, 1930–31), I, 165); Richmond, *Terence Illustrated*, 8.

70 Erasmus, *Epistola* 31 (1489?), quoted in Chambers, *Elizabethan Stage*, IV, 194: "Haec nobis in fabulis, *perinde atque in tabula*, proponuntur *depicta* . . ." ("These are displayed to us in fables, just as if they were painted in pictures"); Vives, *De Causis*, ii. 4, p. 89 (incorrectly cited in Chambers as 99): "Venit in scenam poesis . . . et ibi *sicut pictor tabulam proponit* multitudini spectandam, ita poeta imaginem quandam vitae" ("Poetry enters the scene . . . and there just as a painter displays a picture to be viewed by the crowd, so the poet shows a kind of image of life").

71 That the stage of *Andria* is the same stage as the one in the picture of the *Theatrum*, and not just a similar one, is confirmed by the shield-shaped ornaments above the stage houses. Flemming, "Humanistenbühne," 39, makes this observation as well.

72 More's association of the two was still remembered in Elizabethan England; Anthony Munday's much-revised *Sir Thomas More* (eds. Vittorio Gabrieli and Giorgio Melchiori, The Revels Plays [Manchester University Press, 1990]) has More muse

on his way to the block that "my offence to his highness makes me of a state pleader a stage player" (5. 4. 72–73). I am indebted to an anonymous reader from *Renaissance Drama* for bringing this to my attention.

73 More, *The History of Richard III*, (New Haven: Yale University Press, 1976), 80–81. Erasmus expresses similar sentiments in *Praise of Folly*, in *Collected Works of Erasmus*, multiple vols. (Toronto University Press, 1978–), XXVII, 77–153(103): "If anyone tries to take the masks off the actors when they're playing a scene on the stage and show their true, natural faces to the audience, he'll certainly spoil the whole play . . . To destroy the illusion is really to spoil the whole play, for it's really the illusion and make-up which hold the audience's eye."

74 Vives, *De Disciplinis*, 90–91: "Sic agunt fabulas, ut videantur agare, quod est indecorum: nam fabula non refert seipsam, sed rem gestam, aut quae gesta fingitur, ut rem pictura, non se." In *De Pintura*, Leon Battista Alberti concurs, but displays an unavoidable tension that surfaces in the works of writers equally concerned with advantageous presentation and decorous representation – he subordinates everything in the painting to its plot, or *istoria*, but allows, "I like to see someone who admonishes or points out what is happening there" (*On Painting*, transl. John R. Spencer [New Haven: Yale University Press, 1966], 78). In other words, the representation must acknowledge its onlookers, but in such a way that it seems to ignore them. Michael Fried brilliantly explores this phenomenon in the context of eighteenth- and nineteenth-century French painting, in *Absorption and Theatricality: Painting and Beholder in the Age of Diderot* (Berkeley: University of California Press, 1980).

75 For the unities as a mark of artistic skill in sixteenth-century German theatre, see Flemming, "Humanistenbühne," 46–47; Lodovico Castelvetro, a translator and commentator on Aristotle's *Poetics* whose work in formulating the doctrine of unities was highly influential, concludes that unity of time, place, and plot are rules "not of necessity but to show the excellence of the poet" (comments to *Poetics* VIII [318], in "A Commentary on the Poetics of Aristotle," selected and transl. Allan H. Gilbert, in *Literary Criticism: Plato to Dryden*, ed. Allan H. Gilbert [Detroit: Wayne State University Press, 1962], 304–57).

76 See Kathleen E. McLuskie, "The Poets' Royal Exchange: Patronage and Commerce in Early Modern Drama," *Yearbook of English Studies* 21 (1991), 53–62, and Jonathan Haynes, *The Social Relations of Jonson's Theater* (Cambridge University Press, 1992), on the theatre as a place of knowledge. While McLuskie concentrates on theatrical pretensions to knowledge, Haynes discusses the theatre as an actual source of the knowledge of fashion and social custom.

77 From *Francesco's Fortunes* (1590), quoted in Chambers, *Elizabethan Stage*, IV, 236.

78 Vives, *De Disciplinis*, 234 (transl. Watson, 16): "Tum quae adversus necessitatem fuerant quaesita, quibusque aliquid commoditatis accesserat, ferè vel ad delitias sunt traducta, vel ad superbiae acerbissimam tyrranidem pertracta, ut vel corpus oblectarent, vel oculis intentium tanquam in scena saltarent fabulam."

79 Vives wrote a commentary on *City of God* and was well aware of the anxiety over *curiositas* expressed by writers from Augustine onwards. For more on *curiositas* and the encyclopedia, see chapter 1. Cf. Mikkel Borch-Jacobsen, *Lacan: The Absolute Master*, transl. Douglas Brick (Stanford University Press, 1991), 70–71: "who says that the stakes for the actor are knowledge . . . Isn't his joy (or his anguish) above all to *play* his role, to move *inside* the pathetic scene that he incarnates?"

80 See Lorraine Daston, "Marvelous Facts and Miraculous Evidence in Early Modern Europe," in *Questions of Evidence: Proof, Practice, and Persuasion across the Disciplines*, eds. James Chandler, Arnold I. Davidson, and Harry Harootunian (University of Chicago Press, 1994), 243–74 (esp. 258–63), on the difficulty early science had with judging particulars, and the tendency to exclude them from the properly knowable.

81 Vives, *De Disciplinis*, 234 (transl. Watson, 16): "quin ad maiorem admirationem sui excitandam aucta est ostentandi cupido importuna. Adeo ut quidam universa vitae officia deseruerint, ut huic se scrutationi cunctos dederunt, ac velut manciparent."

82 For an excellent general treatment of the struggles and successes of humanist playwrights, see Kent Cartwright, *Theatre and Humanism: English Drama in the Sixteenth Century* (Cambridge University Press, 1999). This book came out too late for me to give it the attention it deserves. Ingram, *Business of Playing*, 78–82, quotes Richard Moryson, a gentleman of the chamber who some time after 1540 praised plays as politically useful, "specially when they declare either the abomination of the bishop of Rome and his adherents, or the benefits brought to this realm by your Grace's turning him and his out of it."

83 Mervyn James, "Ritual, Drama, and Social Body in the Late Medieval English Town," in *Society, Politics and Culture: Studies in Early Modern England* (Cambridge University Press, 1986), 16–47 acutely sketches the social divisions present in the civic mystery cycles, but also emphasizes that one significant function of these rituals was to identify and patch over such divisions.

84 Altman, *Tudor Play of Mind*, distinguishes two styles he calls *demonstrative* and *exploratory*, the first of which concludes an issue, while the second opens a question. I would add to these statements that even exploratory interludes frequently open their questions only within the frame of the drama that is safely closed, often by the presence of the patron at the performance, and frequently end with their question securely answered as well. Walker, *Politics of Performance*, 34–40, makes the similar point that the "single physical environment" and explicit political contents of early performed drama work against genuinely open-ended investigations of things. Sydney Anglo, *Spectacle, Pageantry, and Early Tudor Policy* (Oxford: Clarendon Press, 1969), 357–59, contrasts the superficiality of the advice offered in early Tudor pageants with the real and concerted appeals to Elizabeth in her coronation progress of 1558. See also Suzanne R. Westfall, *Patrons and Performance: Early Tudor Household Revels* (Oxford: Clarendon Press, 1990), 153–60, on the shift in performance style to one that emphasized the particular setting and encouraged the application of drama to the historical context rather than its reception and reproduction. On the disruptive potential in popular medieval theatre, by way of contrast, see Weimann, *Popular Tradition*.

85 Cynthia Pyle, "The Art and Science of Renaissance Natural History: Thomas of Cantimpre, Pier Candido Decembrio, Conrad Gessner, and Teodoro Ghisi in Vatican Library MS Urb. Lat. 276," *Viator* 27 (1996), 265–321 (266–67), rightly argues that the first of the scholarly disciplines to be based on careful observation and empirical induction was not natural history or science, but the humanist philology of the fifteenth century, and suggests that we understand its meticulous concern for details not as the opponent of early science, but as its ally.

86 Moeslein, Introduction to *Nature*, in *The Plays of Henry Medwall: A Critical Edition*, ed. M. E. Moeslein (New York: Garland Press, 1981) 256–57.

87 For the pageant, see Anglo, *Spectacle, Pageantry, and Early Tudor Policy*, 197 and Richard Axton, ed., *Three Rastell Plays: Four Elements, Calisto and Melebea, Gentleness and Nobility* (Cambridge: D. S. Brewer, 1979), 7. Walker, *Politics of Performance*, 8 n.4, states that the earliest printed play is probably either Rastell's edition of Medwall's *Fulgens and Lucrece* (c.1512–16) or Wynkyn de Worde's edition of *Hick Scorner* (1515–16). On Rastell more generally, including his theatre, see Axton, *Three Rastell Plays*, 1–14.

88 John Rastell, *The Nature of the Four Elements*, The Tudor Facsimile Texts, general ed. John S. Farmer (London, 1908, repr. New York: AMS Press, 1970), n.p.i; Messenger's speech.

89 The dominance of the "figure" is suggested by John Bale's recollection of the play as "a most ingenious but very lengthy comedy, with instruments and figures" (*ingeniossisimam ca longissimam comoediam . . . cum instrumentis et figuris*, quoted in Axton, *Three Rastell Plays*, 10–11). Axton, 6–7, links the figure to the *Carta Marina* of Martin Waldseemüller, printed in 1516, but without citing evidence.

90 For a similar relation of agency and authority, and the difference between seeing truth as adequation to a thing that already exists and as exploration which discovers and decides upon an object as author, see Robert Weimann, "Author-ity in Signification: Rabelais and Vernacular Renaissance Prose Fiction," in *Sprache und Literatur des Romania: Tradition und Wirkung: Festschrift für Horst Heintze zum 70, Geburtstag*, eds. Irmgard Osols-Wehden, Giuliano Staccioli, and Babette Hesse (Berlin Verlag, 1993), 87–99.

91 Title page. Bevington, *From* Mankind *to* Marlowe, also notes this alternative structure, but traces it to a class distinction. Weimann, *Popular Tradition*, notes the heavy investment of interludes in their festive, playful form, 103–05.

3 TRICKS OF VISION, TRUTHS OF DISCOURSE: ILLUSTRATION, *ARS COMBINATORIA*, AND AUTHORITY

1 Zwinger, *Theatrum* (1565), n.p.: "EHEUS TU Ò BONE/qui in hanc caveam non agendi, ut histrio, sed/spectandi causa descendisti . . ." For complete text, see Fig. 5.

2 I am suggesting, of course, that this randomness is not at all random, that instead it allows Elyot to introduce the idea of a single governor behind the back of the logic of his text. On the implications for metaphor generally of the shadowed motivation of another apparently randomly chosen metaphor, the sun, see Jacques Derrida, "White Mythology: Metaphor in the Text of Philosophy," in *Margins of Philosophy*, transl. Alan Bass (University of Chicago Press, 1982), 207–71.

3 Translation mine, *De Proprietatibus Rerum* (1470), II, 2, iiiir: "Angelus enim deiformem habet intellectum et ideo supra tempus est et totum intelligit †simpliciter† et non unum post aliud aut unum ex alio sicut ex premissis conclusionem sicut humanus intellectus qui est unius ex alio collativus. Unde qualis est compacio [sic; the text omits the abbreviation for *-par-* in *comparacio*] simplicis ad compositum. et puncti ad lineam in essendo. tali est comparacio angelici intellectus as humanum in intelligendo et iudicando." Illich, *In The Vineyard of the Text*, working with Hugh of St. Victor's *Didascalicon*, identifies a reconception of book as text in the twelfth century as the change that makes possible this particular idealization.

4 *On the Properties of Things*, Bartholomaeus Anglicus, transl. John of Trevisa, 2 vols. (1397/8), ed. M. C. Seymour (Oxford: Clarendon Press, 1975) II, 2.

De Worde's *De Proprietatibus Rerum* follows John in including this addition, but Batman omits it in his 1582 adaptation, *Batman uppon Bartholome*.

5 Pierre Boaistuau, *Theatrum Mundi: The Theatre or Rule of the World, Wherein may be seen the running race and course of every man's life . . . whereto is added a learned and pithy work of the excellency of man . . .* (London: Thomas East, 1581 [First French edition 1561]), 246–47. Boaistuau clearly felt this perfection to be of critical importance; Simonin, "Faire des Encyclopédies," 155–56, quotes a French version of the same sentiment, but from another of Boaistuau's works.

6 In so doing, it also stripped the text from authorial control. Perotti wonders in his introductory material of his *Cornucopiae*, one of the earliest printed lexical works, if the ease of copying a text by printing will increase the circulation of inferior texts, since readers and writers will no longer make their own copies of texts that they want. Worse, speculates Perotti, the press even risks making honest men into liars by circulating writings that have been corrupted by the conditions of printing (287r–v).

7 Many of the modern works that deal with Llull either presuppose a thorough understanding of his art or seem to lack it utterly themselves, and in either case are hardly clearer on Llull than Llull. The *Ars brevis* was the most popular of the versions of the art that Llull wrote and probably the most accessible; see Anthony Bonner's translations in Llull, *Selected Works*, 2 vols. (Princeton University Press, 1985), I, 579–625, with Bonner's useful introduction, I, 572–78. For explanations of Llull's project and the way in which it worked, see in the same work Bonner, 55–71; Bonner also gives a brief history of the later applications and understandings of Llullism. Mark D. Johnston's "Introduction" is a cogent initiation into the structural operations of Llullism, *The Spiritual Logic of Ramon Llull*, (Oxford: Clarendon Press, 1987), 1–27.

8 I discuss Bacon in more detail in my final chapter. Emil Wolff, *Francis Bacon und seine Quellen*, 2 vols. (Berlin: Emil Felber, 1913; repr. Liechtenstein: Kraus Reprint, 1977), I, 12–20, gives a list of ancient authors who make use of this trope, including Plato and Aristotle; see also Hans Blumenberg, *Die Lesbarkeit der Welt* (Frankfurt: Suhrkamp, 1981).

9 Gregoire, *Syntaxes* I, 112–13: "non secus ac qui rectè loquitur de omnibus, per easdem literas ratiocinatur . . . qui enim loquitur ex textura litteraturae alphabeti, & ex sonis quinque vocalium, tot libros variarum conceptionum implere potest." Note how Gregoire here conflates speech and writing.

10 Ramus, *Dialectici Commentarii Tres* (1546), quoted in Ong, *Ramus*, 245–46, with Latin 363–64 (Ong's translation); cf. Mario Carpo, *Alberti, Raffaello, Serlio e Camillo: Metodo ed Ordini nella Teoria Architettonica dei Primi Moderni*, Travanx d'Humanisme et Renaissance 271 (Geneva: Librairie Droz, 1993), 58–62, for an interpretation of this passage in the context of the development of a method in the Renaissance that was neither inductive nor deductive.

11 Radcliffe-Umstead, "Emblems of Memory," suggests that the structure was perhaps much smaller than Yates seems to believe, perhaps more of a filing cabinet than a theatre. The reasons for these confusions are the strange mix of too much evidence at too great a remove from eyewitness accounting; in the sixteenth century many more people seem to have *heard* of Camillo's theatre than *seen* it. Rossi, *Clavis Universalis*, for instance, calls it Camillo's "fumosa costruzione," both famous and fumous, 97–100. Secret, "Les Cheminements," includes many contemporary reactions to it. See also n.15 in this chapter.

12 The works of Lina Bolzoni on Camillo have been especially crucial. See her Introduction to *L'Idea*, 18–27, for an appraisal of the astrological and kabbalistic tendencies in Camillo.
13 Ibid., 28–33.
14 Ibid., 19, says that *L'Idea* was heavily edited by Lodovico Dolce; Margolin, "*Le Théâtre de Memoire*," 460, flatly states that it was written by Lodovico Domenichi after Camillo's death; even if this is excessive, Camillo certainly did not have much time to compose the work (although the physical Teatro is another case); the introductory material to *L'Idea* records that Camillo, at the request of the Marche del Vasto in Milan, "made in the space of a few days an Idea, or rather a model of its whole construction" ("fece in ispatio di pochi giorni una Idea, o vogliam dire modello di tutta la fabrica d'esso," Aiir).
15 Bolzoni, *L'Idea*, Introduction, 19–21. Camillo refers to the *volumine* hidden under the various images. Contemporary sources for Camillo's theatre include the letters of Zuichemus (in Erasmus, *Opus Epistolarum*, eds. P. S. Allen, H. M. Allen, and H. W. Garrod [Oxford: Clarendon Press, 1938], 9; 475–80 and 10; 28–30); also Zuichemus' Letter 2716 and Erasmus' Letter 3032 to Johann Choler; also *Ciceronianus*, in *Collected Works*, 609–615 (transl. and notes, Betty I. Knott [University of Toronto Press, 1986], XXVIII, 346–55). One eyewitness, Viglius Zuichemus, specifically likens Camillo's work in his theatre to the labors of Nosoponus, the character in *Ciceronianus* who has indexed all the works of Cicero minutely (Erasmus, *Opus Epistolarum*, Letters 2632 and 2657). Nosoponus boasts, "There isn't the smallest word in all the works of our divine author which I haven't classified and put into my alphabetical lexicon." See Jean-Claude Margolin, "Alberto Pio et les Cicéroniens Italiens," in *Società, Politica et Cultura a Carpi ai Tempi di Alberto Pio* (Padua: Antenore, 1981), 225–59, for Erasmus' views on Camillo. Such concordances existed: the tables accompanying Camillo's *Annotationi supra le Rime del Petrarca*, Tables by Lodovico Dolce (Venice: Gabriel Giolito, 1557) and Joseph Webbe's *Usus et Authoritas, Id Est, Liber Loquens . . . sub titulo Entheati Materialis Primi* (London: Felix Kingston, 1626).
16 In Giulio Camillo, *Tutte L'Opere* (Venice: Gabriel Giolito, 1567), 150–201 and 203–41 respectively.
17 See Reiss, *Knowledge, Discovery, and Imagination*, on the shift in the nature of linguistic invention during this century. Reiss sees a gradual loss of confidence in linguistic *inventio* that is eventually displaced by a reliance on mathematics. While Reiss is undoubtedly correct, efforts like Camillo's are attempts to purify and correct rhetorical invention, algebraicizations of it which are not abandonments of rhetoric for mathematics.
18 *Discorso*, in Giulio Camillo, *Tutte L'Opere* (Venice: Gabriel Giolito, 1597), 3–31: "Tutte le materie (si come io dissi in una delle mie orationi Latini) nelle mani dell'Oratore o del Poeta sono di necessitè qualificate da alcune delle passioni, che si dottamente ci insegna Arist. [sic]" (19). In general, see 19–21. See also *Discorso*, 17.
19 We might also add gender to this – and also note its elision from the problem as posed in the Renaissance. Bolzoni, *L'Idea*, Introduction, mentions some related manuscripts of Camillo's *Teatro della Sapienza*, in which quasi-Aristotelian categories seem to be superimposed on the Teatro described in *L'Idea*.

20 *Della Imitazione*, 239: "Ricordarmi gia in Bologna che uno eccellente anatomista chiuse un corpo humano in una cassa tutta pertugiata, & poi la espose ad un corrente d'un fiume, ilqual per que' pertugi nello spatio di pochi giorni consumò & portò via tutta la carne di quel corpo, che poi di se mostrava meravigliosi secreti della natura ne gli ossi soli, & i nervi rimasi. Cosi fatto corpo dalle ossa [sic] sostenuto io assomiglio al modello della eloquentia dalla materia, & dal disegno solo sostenuto."

21 *Discorso*, 16: "Ma quando la cosa non sarà honesta, o vero sarà povera, se lo scrittore la metterà dentro del centro di quella nostra artificiosa rota ... tirando, et assumendo dalla circonferentia al centro tutte quelle cose, che la possano aggrandire; potra senza dubbio farla parer quasi tale, quali sono le grandi." For *onesto* as "adorned, decorated," See *Dizionario dell'Accademia della Crusca*, s.v. *onestare*.

22 *Della Imitazione*, 212: "L'esempio daremo intorno al sospiro. Quando adunque dirò sospirare; piglierò il proprio, & queste parole accompagnate diranno il medesimo, ma haveranno traslatione quasi pura, mandar sospiri, gettar sospiri: ma se io dicessi, romper l'aere da presso co i sospiri, questa sarebbe figura topica tirata da loco necessario, cioè da conseguenti ..."

23 Ibid., 222. In this case one might want to admit that one's instincts of what makes a good figure correspond to the results of Camillo's more regulated process.

24 Carpo, *Metodo ed Ordini*, 53–55. See also Francis Bacon's desire to mechanize his method – to remove the burden of judgment from the human subject and to standardize it so that it would take no particular skill to reproduce results (*Novum Organum* 1. 122, *Works*, I: 217, IV: 109).

25 *Delle Materie*, 191–92: "ma volendo nella medesima lingua trattar le gia trattate materie da autor lodato; le circonstanze delle particolari materie, che alle nostre mani verrano, ci potranno far differenti."

26 *Discorso*, 30–31: "& 2[.]4. 5. del quale al presente non mi soccorre esempio. Ma se io haveßi meco il libro; dove sono state già per me ordinate queste fatiche ... farei vedere a V.[ostra] S.[ignoria] non solamente quante fiate habbia cantato il Petrarca in una medesima misura: ma quale egli, o piu tosto [sic] il suo buon orecchio ha cantato ..."

27 *Della Imitazione*, 231: "che io non credo, che la natura dall'autore possa esser giamai, ma solamente que' consigli, che da lei procedono."

28 On metaphors for the ineffability of imitation – as family resemblance, for instance – see Pigman, "Versions of Imitation."

29 *Discorso*, 31: "... tutta l'arte mia è governata dalla necessità & dall bastanza."

30 *Della Imitazione*, 223: "è stato mio consiglio di far di perfettissimi autori si minuta Anatomia ..." Devon Hodges, *Renaissance Fictions of Anatomy*, (Amherst: University of Massachusetts Press, 1985), offers a much fuller analysis of the burdens of symbolism carried by anatomy in the Renaissance. The anatomy theatres of Leiden and elsewhere are at this point still a generation or more in the future; the earliest accounts of anatomies in England are from around 1560, on which see Hodges and also Jonathan Sawday, *The Body Emblazoned: Dissection and the Human Body in Renaissance Culture* (London: Routledge and Kegan Paul, 1995), 54–84.

31 The claim varies in different sources from one month to three. Alciati is quoted as typical in Secret, "Les Cheminements," 419: "He claims in the short time of an hour a day for a month [to teach his students to express themselves] as fluently in conversation, in Greek and Latin, prose and verse ... as Demosthenes, Cicero, and

Vergil or Homer" ("'brevissimo tempore puta mense . . . horam diurnam' à s'exprimer 'tam illeganter, Graece et Latine, prosa et versu sermone . . . quam Demosthenes, Cicero, et Vergilius aut Homerus . . .'"). Accounts do not specify whether Francis or the illiterate would have represented the greater challenge. Margolin, "Le *Théâtre de Memoire*," 480, comments on how horrific Camillo's system must have seemed to a humanist like Erasmus, who was dedicated to the idea of individual skills and talents.

32 *Della Imitazione*, 207: ". . . è gia fermata ne' libri & noi che non siamo nati in lei, se la vogliamo havere convien, che la cogliamo da i libri, dove si è fermata . . ."

33 Ibid., 219: "eßi, quantumque non siam nati nella lingua Latina; ardiscono introdur non dico figure topiche, non dico lodevoli traslati; ma nuova proprietà da vocabuli . . ."

34 For this method in general, see Carpo, *Metodo ed Ordini*, 58–62; for the case of Camillo, 73–82.

35 Alciati is quoted in Secret, "Les Cheminements," 419; see n.31 above. Cf. Erasmus' objection to the Ciceronians that Cicero himself would speak differently now; a person is truly Ciceronian "only if he speaks as Cicero would be likely to speak if he were living today" (*Ciceronianus*, 643; discussion 637–44).

36 *Della Imitazione*, 227–28: "Adunque colui, che imita un perfetto, imita la perfettion di mille raunata [sic] in uno: & tanto meglio, quanto in quell'uno essa perfettione appar continuata, non in una sola parte della compositione composta . . . Ne dal giudicio di Zeusi debbiamo noi divenir presontuosi nel levar da molti le parti piu belle, si come fece Cicerone, o alcuno altro perfetto." Other Ciceronians take a similar position on the imitation of individual *perfetti*, but none to my knowledge codified it so completely. Zeuxis' story is given by Cicero as a model for good writing, *De Inventione* II, 1–3 and Pliny, *Natural History* XXXV, 36. 61–66.

37 *Dell'Imitazione*, 229: "Et se questi medesimi Scultori & Pittori, mentre voglion fare una figura; piu tosto si contentano di pigliar la imitation da una statua antica fatta di alcun grande artifice, che da molti individui fatti dalla natura, ne quai le bellezza non sono unite, & non è poco, quando in ciascun se non ritrovi una: percioche nella figura antica de perito artefice si veggon gia tutte le belle cose unite . . ." See Margolin, "Le *Théâtre De Memoire*," 475–79, and Carpo, *Metodo ed Ordini*, who both argue that the attempt to standardize and generalize the process of representation and to remove it from the vagaries of "genius" or even subjectivity was central to Camillo's project.

38 Hugh of St. Victor, *Didascalicon* (1939), I, ix: "disgregata coniugere vel coniuncta segregare." Translation mine.

39 This makes the reference to Nosoponus in Zuichemus' letter to Erasmus, one of the main sources of information on the Teatro, much more pointed, since the method Erasmus pillories as Nosoponus' in *Ciceronianus* is in fact none other than Camillo's.

40 Camillo, *L'Idea*, 84: "Et qui diro quattro parole della utilita della mia fatica, che proponendomi lo stato di questa età, & della nostra religione, ho cercato di accomodar molte cose al nostro costume, come per esempio. Quantunque Cicerone non habbia mai parlato di Christo, ne della Spirito Santo, considerando io il bisogno nostro del parlare, & dello scriver delle persone divine sotto la imagine della latitudine de gli enti, ho apparecchiato gran selva tratta da gli scritti di Cicerone, con la quale Ciceroniamente si potra vestire il nome del figliuolo & dello spirito santo." Camillo seems to have put this tactic of circumlocution into practice in his own

Latin speech. In the one place in *Ciceronianus* in which Camillo is named (637), Bulephorus reports having heard him give an oration in Rome in which he was careful never to use explicitly Christian terms for the pope, but always referred to him in classically defensible periphrases, describing Julius II as "Jupiter Optimus Maximus" (637). On English writers with similar Ciceronian views and practices, see Elsky, *Authorizing Words*, chapters 1 and 2.

41 *Dell'Imitazione*, 220: "Il perchè è da sapere, che nella gran fabrica del Theatro mio son per lochi & imagini disposti tutti quei luoghi, che posson bastare a tener collocati, & ministrar tutti gli humani concetti, tutte le cose, che sono in tutto il mondo, non pur quelle, che si appartengono alle scientie tutte, & alle arti nobili, & mechaniche."

42 Ibid., 224. Camillo, *L'Idea* gives the example of falconry as an instance of something for which there are no Ciceronian Latin terms, since the practice did not exist. But see the account of Camillo's only marginally successful solution in n.40 above.

43 Camillo, *L'Idea*, 10–11: "Or se gli antichi oratori volendo collocar di giorno in giorno le parti delle orationi che havevano à recitare, le affidevano à luoghi caduchi, come cose caduche, ragione è, che volendo noi raccomondar eternalmente gli eterni di tutte le cose, che possono esser vestiti di oratione con gli eterni di essa oratione, che troviamo à loro luoghi eterni."

44 Collections of examples like Zwinger's *Theatrum* or Ravisius Textor's *Officina*, were referred to as rhapsodic because they stitched together various *sententiae*; see Ong, "Commonplace Rhapsody," for a striking example of how such works could be used to create a passage in Shakespeare. Rhapsody, which here would certainly include products like those of Camillo's *artifici*, cultivates style *per se* and calls attention to words, while history strives for a highly personal style that defines its author's character.

45 Zwinger, *Theatrum* (1571) 26: "Superest Λέξις, sive dictionis genus, quod nobis histrionum loco inseruit, & interpretis munere fingitur."

46 Gessner *Historiae Animalium* I, "Ad lectorem," B2v: "Parentheses quoque (ut vocant grammatici) ad stilum pertinent, quae passim in toto Opere plurimae sunt."

47 Zwinger, *Theatrum* (1571), "Iam vero stylus ipse Theatri huius varius est: ut etiam scriptores, quorum authoritatem secuti sumus, diverso sunt usi charactere."

48 Gessner *Historiae Animalium* I, "Ad lectorem," B2v: "Quantum ad orthographicam, non semper eadem modo scripsi, sed secundum authores quorum verba recitabam nonnumquam variavi."

49 E.g., Gerald E. Se Boyar, "Bartholomaeus and his Encyclopedia," *Journal of English and German Philology* 19 (1920), 168–89 (184), claimed to be able to distinguish Bartholomaeus' own material from that of sources by his use of a distinctive rhythmical ending to his clauses.

50 Gessner, *Historiae Animalium* I, B2r: "Qui in arte grammatica proficere cupiunt, & alicuius linguae usum sibi comparare, illi ab optimis grammaticis qui methodo compositiva (ut vocant) artem tradunt, à literis & syllabis ad dictiones & octo sermones partes, & postremo sermonem ipsum, & syntaxin progressi, artis notitiam petunt, interim tamen Lexicorum (in quibus singulae dictiones locutionésque enumerantur longe aliter quam in praeceptis artis, ubi nec omnia singillatim nec eodem ordine recensebantur) utilitatem non negligit, non ut à principio ad finem perlegat, quod operiosus quàm utilius fieret, sed ut consulat ea per intervalla. Ita qui animalium historiam cogniturus est, & continua serie perlecturus, petat illam ab Aristotele, & si qui similiter scripserunt: nostro vero Volumine tanquam Onomastico aut Lexico utatur."

254   Notes to pages 99–102

51 From Sahagun's Spanish introduction to *Florentine Codex: General History of the Things of New Spain*, transl. Arthur J. O. Anderson and Charles E. Dibble, 13 vols. (Santa Fe: School of American Research, 1970–82), XIII, 50–51.
52 However, these fields were less distinct, or at least harder to distinguish, then than they are now. See Hans Widmann's afterword in the *Bibliotheca Universalis* und *Appendix*, Milliaria: Faksimiledrücke zur Dokumentation der Geistesentwicklung 5, 2 vols. (Osnabrücke: Otto Zeller Verlagsbuch handlung, 1966, repr. of Zurich: Christophorus Froscherus); also Chartier, *Order of Books*, 71–73.
53 The use of Latin as the language of composition and the master language of the tables of names is more likely a response to the practical conditions of scholarly communication in Renaissance Europe (and indeed much later).
54 *Historiae Animalium* I, "Ad lectorem", B1r: "Accedit praeterea quod natura à nimio stili cultu & omni affectione sim alienus, hac cura illis relicta, quibus verba magis quàm res sunt cordi."
55 Gessner's attitude is much like the one Foucault, *Order of Things*, 39–40, ascribes to the early modern collector Aldrovandi: "For Aldrovandi and his contemporaries, it was all *legenda* – things to be read." The third and final book of Raphael Volaterranus, *Commentariorum Urbanorum* [Rome: Ascanius, 1526], also entitled "Philologia," is similarly a catch-all, including plants, animals, virtues, and musical and optical instruments, among other topics.
56 See Hans Fischer, "Conrad Gessner (1516–1565) as Bibliographer and Encyclopedist," *The Library* 21 (5th series) (1966), 269–81 (277–80).
57 *Historiae Animalium* I, "Typographus Lectori, De Epitome Huius Operis," [a6r].
58 Ibid., I, "Epistola Nuncupatoria," a2r: "nec ullum egregium aut certe doctum medicum haberi, qui non altius primi methodi medendi rudimenta ex libris de natura tanquam fonte, coepi & ipse philosophorum qui de rebus naturalibus commentati sunt scripta cognoscere..."
59 Ibid., I, 563: "Picturam hanc Tiguri ad vivum fieri curavimus, cum agyrta quidam spectaculi gratia histricem circunducere."
60 Ibid., I, Cv: "Romani imperij principes olim adhuc maxime orbis terrarum partis domini, multa peregrina subinde animalia populo spectanda offerabant, ut ita illius animos devincirent... At qui illa non nisi brevi tempore, quo scilicet durabant spectacula, inspici & considerari potereant[?]. Nostrae vero icones, quas omnes ad vivum fieri aut ipse curavi, aut ab amicis fide dignis ita factas accepi (nisi aliter admonuerim, quod rarum est,) quovis tempore & perpetuò se spectandas volentibus, absque labore absque periculo, offerent." Cf. also I, a3v, a4r-v, on book and world as *theatra*.
61 In the Strassburg Terence [*Comoediae*] (1496) (n.p.),: "Comedy according to the Greeks is the epitome (*comprehensio*) of public and private fortune without peril of life" ("Comedia secundum grecos est & private civilisque fortune sine periculo vite comprehensio").
62 *Historiae Animalium* I, Cv: "Atqui eadem picta non modo sine terrore rerum & iucunde spectamus." But this terror differs from the pity and terror of tragedy, which according to Aristotle are functions of *muthos*, not *opsis*. For a discussion of the terrible made delightful by its representation in art, see Michael Baxandall, *Giotto and the Orators* (Oxford: Clarendon Press, 1971).
63 It is worth recalling the difference between the two woodcuts in Reisch's *Margarita Philosophica*, the first allegorical, the second historical – narrativized and mimetic.

64 Carruthers, *Book of Memory*, 256, as part of her larger discussion of diagrams, 247–56.
65 See in particular Shapin, *Social History of Truth*. This is not to suggest that any audience actually *is* unconstrained; the development Shapin points to is no doubt in part the result of the weakening of automatic exclusions of certain points of view and the heterogeneity of responses.
66 Walter Benjamin, *The Origin of German Tragic Drama*, transl. John Osborne (London: Verso, 1977) differentiates the allegorical from the symbolic on the basis of its legibility, and while the binary symbolic/allegorical itself is not especially applicable to Gessner or de Worde, this distinction is helpful in understanding the difference between images to be read and images to be seen. Jesse M. Gellrich discusses the importance of visual schematism in medieval books as a device for showing mastery and certainty of what is rendered in *The Idea of the Book in the Middle Ages: Language Theory, Mythology and Fiction* (Ithaca, NY: Cornell University Press, 1985), 55–59. Carruthers usefully points out that medieval diagrams are not iconographic, and so produce an effect rather than a single meaning: such an image "evokes (but does not explain)," *Book of Memory*, 221–29, 248–57. Nonetheless, Carruthers' diagrams also represent themselves as signs of things and not potential substitutes, and they are for meditation, not for examination as Gessner's naturalized images are.
67 Hans Fischer *et al.*, *Conrad Gessner, 1516–1565: Universalgelehrter, Naturforscher, Arzt* (Zurich: Orell Füssli Verlag, 1967), 277–79. Fischer includes two plates of drawings of plants annotated by Gessner but not drawn by him (plates V, VI). Wellisch, *Conrad Gessner*, mentions fieldwork anecdotally, and even a "museum" (9, 20), but does not try to substantiate it; Gessner himself in the introduction laments that he lacked "any Maecenas" (*Maecenas aliquis*) who might have funded travel for study (*Historiae Animalium* I, a2v). It is possible that Gessner, like many other natural historians, had a *Wunderkammer*, but this also ends up making an object into a kind of picture rather than being what a modern scientist would recognize as fieldwork.
68 Gessner, *Historiae Animalium* I, a2v: "Id quoniam non licebat, feci quod potui, aliquot in diversis Europae regionibus mihi comparavi amicos, qui benigne, candide, liberaliter, multas animantium omne genus effigies ad vivum reprasentatas, quarundam etiam nomina in diversis linguis & historias, mecum communicarent."
69 Ibid., II, 665: "Pelecanus ut vulgò a pictoribus effingitur"; II, 666: "Pelecani seu nostrae plateae figura."
70 Ibid., II, 666: "cum nulla talis, opinor, in rerum natura, avis sit."
71 Ibid., II, 666: ". . . nisi quis Aegyptios de vulture hoc verè tradere putet, quod Orus literis mandavit, cum ne fame pulli pereant, femori suo vulnus infligere, & emanentem sanguinem ab illis exorberi."
72 Ibid., I, 149, s.v. Camelopardis: "icon accuratior (quàm exhibita sit supra)."
73 Ibid., I, "De Picturis Animalium," C^v: "Optassem equidem cum suis coloribus excudi potuisse effigies: quod quoniam fieri non potuit, typographus pro ijs qui sumptum facere aliquanto maiorem non recusabant, exemplaria aliquot pictoris manu coloribus illustranda ad archetypum nostrum curavit. Minora animalia, inter aves, pisces et insecta praecipuè, ea qua vivunt magnitudine plerunque expressa sunt si libri vel charta spatium admittebant." Colored versions of the *Historiae Animalium* do survive; one colored leaf is reproduced in Fischer *et al. Conrad Gessner*, 137; see Roger Chartier, "General Introduction," in *The Culture of Print: Power and the*

Uses of Print in Early Modern Europe, ed. Roger Chartier transl. Lydia G. Cochrane (Cambridge: Polity Press, 1989), 1–10 and Tessa Watt, *Cheap Print and Popular Piety, 1550–1640* (Cambridge University Press, 1991), on the practice of coloring woodcut illustrations as a kind of personalization and reader response. The printer (*typographus*) is given an interesting note of his own, in which he advertises a shorter and cheaper version of the work, lacking the philological material that took so much space (Gessner *Historiae Animalium* I, [a6r]).

74 Gessner, *Historiae Animalium* I, 752–53: "haec figura bis ponitur, quoniam mustela alba solo colore ab altera differt."

75 I am grateful to Bettina Gockel for her help and suggestions on this problem.

76 Gessner, *Historiae Animalium* I, 677: "Figura haec lyncis est, sive lupi cervarij, ut Itali vocant, qualem habere potuimus. Audio probam esse excepto capite & naso [sic], quibus felem referre debet."

77 Ibid., I, 678: "Alia lyncis imago à Io. Caio mihi communicata quam probè expressam asserit."

78 Ibid., I, 678: "Alia adhuc lyncis effigies (ex tabula regionum Septentrionalium Olai Magni) felem sylvestrem persequentis." The image in the text of Olaus Magnus is found at *Historia de Gentibus Septentrionalibus* [Rome: Joannis Mari de Viottis, 1555], 610.)

79 Jonas Barish's monumental *The Antitheatrical Prejudice* (Berkeley: University of California Press, 1981) suggests the scope and variety of this anxiety; for a demonstration showing that the anxieties about the power of performance persist, see Worthen, "Disciplines of the Text/ Sites of Performance," *The Drama Review* 39 (1995), 13–28, which compares performative to textual approaches to drama, and the aggressive and even personal responses published with it.

4. HOLDING THE MIRROR UP TO NATURE?
THE HUMANIST THEATRE BESIDE ITSELF

1 Quoted in Gurr, *Playgoing*, 228–29. See also the discussion in Meredith Skura, *Shakespeare the Actor and the Purposes of Playing* (University of Chicago Press, 1993), 225ff., which approaches the significance of the circle that is drawn around the actor from a psychoanalytic perspective.

2 For this image, see Quentin Skinner, *Reason and Rhetoric in the Philosophy of Thomas Hobbes* (Cambridge University Press, 1996), 92–93. Hobbes himself derives an image of the delegation of power to the artificial sovereign from this image of the chained hearers: "But as men for the attaining of peace, and conservation of themselves thereby, have made an Artificial Man, which we call a Common-wealth; so also have they made Artificial Chains, called *Civil Laws*, which they themselves, by mutual covenants, have fastened at one end to the lips of that man, or Assembly, to who they have given the Sovereign Power; and at the other end to their own ears" (*Leviathan*, quoted in Skinner, *Reason and Rhetoric*, 389–90).

3 Tom Conley, "Pierre Boaistuau's Cosmographic Stage: Theater, Text and Map," *Renaissance Drama* n.s. 23 (1992), 59–86 and *The Self-Made Map: Cartographic Writing in Early Modern France* (Minneapolis: University of Minnesota Press, 1996). Similarly, Gillies, *Geography of Difference*, 86–88, suggests that in the "imaginary geography" of the Renaissance, near and far operate only slightly differently from high and low as conceptual tools, and that horizontal distance from Europe was regularly just as ideologically damning as vertical distance from God.

4 The horizontal *tabula* of the early modern, though, is not only Foucault's grid, but also the *tabulae* of the picture and of the game board.
5 Similarly, Stahl remarks in his notes on Martianus Capella how patently outdated much of the information contained in *De Nuptiis* was; this did not keep it from being a very popular source of information from the Middle Ages well into the sixteenth century. Elizabeth Eisenstein, *The Printing Press as an Agent of Change: Communications and Cultural Transformations in Early Modern Europe*, 2 vols. in 1 (Cambridge University Press, 1979), observes that one of the most important of early printed reference works was Isidore. Simonin, "Faire des Encyclopédies," argues that the insatiability of the press kept in circulation works that were out of date; it constantly required new material to print, but a great deal of the new material was in fact old material.
6 See Bevington, *From* Mankind *to Marlowe*, 50, for the categorical importance of the entrance to popular drama, and Weimann's analysis of this moment in *Popular Tradition*, 102–03.
7 On this folk etymology, see Axton, *Three Rastell Plays*, 2. Richard Schechner, "Towards a Poetics of Performance," in *Essays on Performance Theory, 1970–76* (New York: Drama Book Specialists [Publishers], 1977), suggests that the circle of theatre is a quasi-natural or physical negotiation of space produced by the movement of people past and around an event.
8 Encyclopedias usually authorize themselves as being the product of an *auctor*, like Pliny, or as being collected from various *auctores*, like Zwinger. In contrast, the title page of later printed plays stresses the particular moment of their production as a way of authorizing themselves, with phrases like, "As played before ... by ... on ..." Cf. Smith, *Ancient Scripts and Modern Experience*, 83: "Where does the dramatic event take place? Elizabethan audiences, tutored by Cicero and Horace, would have answered that question simply enough: 'Right here in front of us.' Later audiences, corrected by Aristotle, would have answered differently: 'On a public square in Thebes, on a street in Rome.'" I see these phenomena, though, as synchronic and ideological rather than historically serial.
9 Walker, *Politics of Performance*, 222–24, presents the first point as the burden of his book – that Tudor plays were direct interventions in court politics. The second point is Bevington's argument in *From* Mankind *to Marlowe*, that the direct audience interaction of the touring companies shaped a drama that was both completely immersed in its setting and generalized enough to be repeated in many different contexts.
10 See, for instance, the sermon delivered by John Stockwood at St. Paul's in 1578, which explicitly sets the theatre against the pulpit: "Will not a filthy play, with the blast of a trumpet, sooner call thither a thousand, than an hour's tolling of a bell bring to the Sermon a hundred?" (cited in Chambers, *Elizabethan Stage*, IV, 199). See Bryan Crockett, *The Play of Paradox: Stage and Sermon in Renaissance England* (Philadelphia: University of Pennsylvania Press, 1995), and Huston Diehl, *Staging Reform, Reforming the Stage: Protestantism and Popular Theater in Early Modern England* (Ithaca, NY: Cornell University Press, 1997), for the competition and similarities between playing and preaching. Theatre-going was restricted on Sundays and Thursdays to reserve those times for the more established but apparently less competitive church-going and bear-baiting. Likewise, a staple of antitheatricalist pamphlets is their discomfort with players dressing like nobility.

11 Nicholas Udall, *Respublica*, in *Recently Recovered 'Lost' Tudor Plays*, ed. John Stephen Farm (London: Early English Texts Society, 1907), Prologue, p. 179. See Walker, *Politics of Performance*, 163–72, for a discussion of this interlude.
12 *Ben Jonson*, eds. C. H. Herford and Percy Simpson, 12 vols. (Oxford: Clarendon Press, 1925–52), VII, 233ff.
13 Shapin, *Social History of Truth*, chapter 8, 355–403.
14 See Sawday, *Body Emblazoned*, 62–66, for a brief discussion of the Renaissance theatre of anatomy.
15 Lewis Wager, *The Life and Repentance of Marie Magdalen* (London: John Charlewood, 1566).
16 See, for instance, Andrew Gurr's chapter on "Auditorium behaviour," *Playgoing*, 44–48, and the repeated references to scuffles and arguments, in Chambers, *Elizabethan Stage*, IV, appendix D. On occasion, the audience demanded the staging of a different play from the one the actors had prepared; for one account, see Gurr, *Playgoing*, 227, 250f.
17 It is one of Cartwright's major claims in *Theatre and Humanism* that humanist drama in general was much more open than it is usually represented as being. See, e.g. 56, 75f., 166–69.
18 Richard Levin, "The Relation of External Evidence to the Allegorical and Thematic Interpretation of Shakespeare,"*Shakespeare Studies* 13 (1980), 1–29. This has been contested by Gurr, *Playgoing*, 105–11, and Harry Berger, *Imaginary Audition: Shakespeare on Stage and Page* (Berkeley: University of California Press, 1989), who argue convincingly that many other forms of evidence suggest more various and nuanced ways of watching plays; nonetheless, it is striking how slowly playgoers of all kinds developed a vocabulary for describing their complex reactions to the stage. As a consequence, I would argue, while Levin's view is not historically accurate, it does describe how people thought and felt they should understand theatre. As Gurr observes, "The normative way of describing a play need not have been particularly close to the normative response to it in performance" (*Playgoing*, 111).
19 Gurr, *Playgoing*, 108–09, briefly discusses Forman's records. They are also available in full in *The Norton Shakespeare Based on the Oxford Edition*, ed. Stephen Greenblatt *et al.* (New York: W. W. Norton & Co., 1997).
20 Howard, *Stage and Social Struggle*, 73; although Howard's entire chapters on "'Sathans Synagogue'" and "The Materiality of Ideology: Women as Spectators, Spectacles, and Paying Customers in the English Public Theatre" are indispensable in this context.
21 Stephen Gosson, *Plays Confuted in Five Actions* (London: Thomas Gosson, 1582), [C8v].
22 Philip Stubbes, *The Anatomy of Abuses* (London: Richard Jones, 1583), [lviiiv]. The same rant is repeated almost verbatim in John Greene's *A Refutation of the Apology for Actors* (London: W. White, 1615). Bryan Reynolds, "The Devil's House 'or worse': Transversal Power and Antitheatrical Discourse in Early Modern England," *Theatre Journal* 49 (1997), 142–67, suggests that this shows that the conditions of playing have not changed; it seems to me more likely that these are still largely imaginary theatres. See also Northbrooke, *A Treatise*, 67, for another list of the bad education theatregoers receive.
23 Marston, *Parasitaster, or, the Fawn*, ed. David Blostein, The Revels Plays (Manchester University Press, 1978), 70; see also his comment, "If any should wonder why I

print a comedy, whose life rests much in the actors' voice, let such know that it cannot avoid publishing . . ." (68).
24 John Webster, *Complete Works*, ed. F. L. Lucas, 4 vols. (New York: Oxford University Press, 1937), I, 107.
25 Francis Beaumont, *The Knight of the Burning Pestle*, ed. Michael Hattaway, New Mermaids Series (New York: W. W. Norton and Co., 1976), [Epistle Dedicatory], 519.
26 John Lyly, *The Complete Works*, ed. R. Warwick Bond, 3 vols. (Oxford: Clarendon Press, 1902), III, 115.
27 Heywood, *An Apology*, Gv–G2v; I learned that there are no cases brought upon these confessions in a conversation with Bill Ingram.
28 The dumbshow, and the king's (lack of) reaction to it, is a notorious crux. Harold Jenkins helpfully rehearses the main schools of thought in a lengthy note to the Arden edition of *Hamlet* (London: Methuen, 1982), 501–05, concluding that "To the curious spectator's eye, giving no more clue than the text does, [Claudius] must remain inscrutable." But dumbshows are frequently represented in Elizabethan and Jacobean plays as "inscrutable"; see my discussion of *The Spanish Tragedy* below.
29 This likeness occurs throughout the play – Hamlet and Claudius both have polished public personae, for instance, both seem to prefer court politics to old Hamlet's warlike activity, and their soliloquies represent them as strikingly similar. This scene offers a kind of key to these vaguer suggestions, which were expertly exploited in Kenneth Branagh's recent film production (1996).
30 Ingram, *Business of Playing*, 77–78.
31 This anxiety is present in the actual stage as well, most notably in Hamlet's advice to the players not to overstep their lines. Robert Weimann, "Memory, Fictionality, and the Issue of Authority: Author-function and Narrative Performance in *Beowulf*, Chrétien and Malory," in *Contexts of the Pre-Novel Narrative: The European Tradition*, ed. Roy Erickson, Approaches to Semiotics 114 (Berlin: Mouton de Gruyter, 1994), 83–100 (90–91), sees a shift around the time of Chrétien de Troyes from a performer as narrator of a text to an author as the fictional narrator, and any performer then as a mere mouthpiece, whose presence can only detract from the author's original message. See also Weimann, "Mimesis in *Hamlet*," in *Shakespeare and the Question of Theory*, eds. Patricia Parker and Geoffrey Hartman (London: Routledge and Kegan Paul, 1990), 275–91, and *Popular Tradition*, for the actor's self-display.
32 Katherine Eisaman Maus, *Inwardness and Theater in the English Renaissance* (University of Chicago Press, 1995), 67–71.
33 Thomas Kyd, *The Spanish Tragedy*, New Mermaids Series, ed. J. R. Mulryne (New York: W. W. Norton and Co., 1989), 4. 1. 172–78.
34 See Shadi Bartsch, *Actors in the Audience: Theatricality and Doublespeak from Nero to Hadrian* (Cambridge, MA: Harvard University Press, 1994), for a fascinating discussion of the historical basis of these lethal Roman plays. Bartsch begins from the assumption that the traditions are in fact historically accurate. See also Jody Enders' "Medieval Snuff Drama," *Exemplaria* 10 (1998), 171–206, which questions both the facticity of these traditions and finally the importance of that facticity. Factual or not, they present a set of anxieties and fantasies about theatre.
35 Since this play was produced only a year or two before the Armada, there is clearly another message being sent as well.
36 The logic of the murders was suggested to me by a student of mine, Neda Morrar.
37 John Webster plays on the necessarily feigned inimitability of death in *The White*

Devil, 5. 6. 120ff., when Vittoria shoots Flamineo. After he has fallen, Vittoria and her maid wonder whether he is still breathing. When he leaps up again after the scene unwounded, because he had removed the bullets from Vittoria's pistol, we recognize that both actor and character were still breathing. In the same way, King Lear is both right and wrong to notice Cordelia breathing at the end of the play.

38 In a penetrating analysis, Maus, *Inwardness*, has suggested that one reason for the kings' inability to understand Hieronimo's play is an inability to recognize the similar "experience of embodiment" (69) that both – indeed, that all humans – share and that puts all at risk for comparable forms of suffering: "that one dead child is very like another, that paternal love feels essentially the same for noble and commoner, that [Hieronimo's] suffering is worth as much as the suffering of princes" (68). See also Kay Stockholder, "'Yet can he write': Reading the Silences in *The Spanish Tragedy*," *American Imago* 47 (1990), 93–124 (119–20).

39 In a somewhat strained hypothetical frame tale, Stockholder, "Reading the Silences in *The Spanish Tragedy*," proposes that the play is (apparently literally) Hieronimo's dream and that its gaps can therefore be filled psychoanalytically, but this does not compromise the clarity of her delineation of the many silences, gaps, and unanswerable questions of this play.

40 James Shapiro, "'Tragedies Naturally Performed': Kyd's Representation of Violence," in *Staging the Renaissance: Reinterpretations of Elizabethan and Jacobean Drama*, eds. David Scott Kastan and Peter Stallybrass (New York: Routledge and Kegan Paul, 1991), 91–113 argues for a lingering uncertainty about the fictiveness of staged execution, but he seems to assume a connection between legally inflicted violence and staged violence which then "explains" why the two are never brought into contact. It seems easier to acknowledge that early modern audiences were fully aware that stage violence was not real.

41 I have used the documents compiled by Chambers, *Elizabethan Stage*, IV, 292ff., for the Paris Garden accident. A counter-example to the rationalism shown by these texts is Thomas Beard, *The Theatre of God's Judgements* (London: Adam Islip, 1597), who accounts the burning of the theatre to God's wrath. It is worth noting that problems connected to the cultural institutions of the theatres but not specifically with dramatic performance – plague in particular – were often tied to divine signs: "To play in plaguetime is to increase the plague by infection: to play out of plaguetime is to draw the plague by offendings of God upon occasion of such plays" (Corporation of London, 1574, quoted in Chambers, IV, 301). God does not like theatre, but apparently does not use its own tools to scourge the wicked.

42 Rather than see the permeability of reality and the theatre as a real anxiety of Elizabethan London, it may help to look at it as a displacement of another anxiety – that the percolation of the theatre through society would not be nearly so direct, and so easily limited, but that the theatre would instead provide a set of opportunities for license, interpretation, and fraternization for those social groups who rarely found other ones, among them women, apprentices, and the poor. See Howard, *Stage and Social Struggle*, 73–84; and Laura Levine, *Men in Women's Clothing: Antitheatricality and Effeminization, 1579–1642* (Cambridge University Press, 1994), 5–6, 10–25.

43 Barish gives this as the last instance of Heywood's "inept 'apology'": "There can be only the most accidental connection between the players' trade as players and their impact on the invading Spaniards" (*Antitheatrical Prejudice*, 120).

44 See Mullaney, *Place of the Stage*; Yates, *Theatre of the World*; Alvin Kernan, "Hamlet and the Nature of Drama," Yale conference on the Teaching of English (n.d.), 1–11; Weimann, *Popular Tradition*; Van den Berg, *Playhouse and Cosmos*.
45 Weimann, "Bifold Authority," 408–10; "*Hamlet*," 277–81.
46 Schechner treats such splits as fundamental to any theatrical production, the "*here and now performance of then and there events*" in "Towards a Poetics of Performance," 108–39, and includes in his analysis ancient Greek, Southeast Asian theatre, and European and American avant-garde theatres. See Paul Yachnin, *Stage-Wrights: Shakespeare, Jonson, Middleton and the Making of Theatrical Value* (Philadelphia: University of Pennsylvania Press, 1997), for a historically particular reading of theatre's (dis)engagement.
47 Weimann, "Bifold Authority," 415–17.
48 Schechner, "Towards a Poetics of Performance," 73–74, labels such a realm "aesthetic," although of course that is only one suggestion for appropriate terminology.

5 THE SHOW OF LEARNING AND THE PERFORMANCE OF KNOWLEDGE: HUMORS, *EPIGRAMS*, AND "AN UNIVERSAL STORE"

1 *The Complete Poems*, ed. George Parfitt (New Haven: Yale University Press, 1982), lines 92–104. Further quotations from Jonson's non-dramatic writing, except as noted, are from Parfitt's edition. Plays and masques are from the edition of Herford and Simpson (*HrS*).
2 For Jonson's difficult social position, see David Riggs, *Ben Jonson: A Life* (Cambridge, MA: Harvard University Press, 1989). Bruce Thomas Boehrer, *The Fury of Men's Gullets: Ben Jonson and the Digestive Canal* (Philadelphia: University of Pennsylvania Press, 1997), discusses how Jonson exceeds critical boundaries, his own as well as those of others, as a matter of necessity, and the ways in which Jonson's critics have tried to come to terms with this. See also Katherine Eisaman Maus, "Facts of the Matter: Satiric and Ideal Economics in the Jonsonian Imagination," in Jennifer Brady and W. H. Herendeen, eds., *Ben Jonson's 1616 Folio* (Newark: University of Delaware Press, 1991), 64–89, on the way Jonson's poems frustrate easy criticism because of their "mobility" – things play several roles or occupy several conceptual spaces at once; Marotti, "All About Ben Jonson's Poetry," *English Literary History* 39 (1972), 208–37, on how it attempts to be simultaneously stable and carnivalesque. Anne Barton, *Ben Jonson, Dramatist*, (Cambridge University Press, 1984), 323–25, notes that *The Tale of a Tub* "often reads like an anthology of Elizabethan public theatre humor," but that "there emerges something like the map of an entire countryside."
3 Even Jonson's most astute critics have found in him a half-hidden unity; it is only rarely that one is able to recognize how Jonson's fragments imply a (missing) whole by producing the desire for a whole in his readers. See Timothy Murray, *Theatrical Legitimation: Allegories of Genius in Seventeenth-Century England and France* (New York: Oxford University Press, 1987), on Jonson's construction of genius and Richard C. Newton, "Making Books from Leaves; Poets Become Editors," in *Print Culture in the Renaissance: Essays on the Advent of Printing in Europe*, eds. Gerald P. Tyson and Sylvia S. Wagonheim (Newark: University of Delaware Press, 1986), 246–64 (264), who observes that Jonson's works lack "the total inclusion of his

perfect or perfectible readers in the charmed circle of his perfective world," but "It is the action of succumbing to that temptation [to total inclusion and perfectibility], I believe, in the struggle to *know* what seems so knowable, that we do indeed come closest to knowledge of the figure who invites us to the knowing."
4 *Hymenaei*, Introduction, in *HrS*, VII, 209.
5 Van den Berg, *Playhouse and Cosmos*, 32, associates this Renaissance development especially with the public theatres. It is a constant concern of Jonson in every genre he takes up.
6 Even in plays that are not explicit revisitations of earlier genres: Edward Partridge, *The Broken Compass: A Study of the Major Comedies of Ben Jonson* (London: Chatto and Windus, 1958), finds the structure of a three-estates play in both *Every Man In His Humor* and *Every Man Out of His Humor*; William Blissett, "The Venter Tripartite in *The Alchemist*," in Harold Bloom, ed., *Modern Critical Views: Ben Jonson* (New York: Chelsea House Publishers 1987), 79–88, interprets Face, Dol, and Subtle as Jonson's modernized anti-Trinity of the World, the Flesh, and the Devil; Barton, *Ben Jonson, Dramatist*, 221–23, sees *The Devil is an Ass* as a nostalgic revision of the morality play in changed economic and cultural circumstances, so that the former Vice now finds himself the least corrupt and self-aware character on the stage.
7 The four identifications originate, respectively, with T. S. Eliot, "Ben Jonson," in Jonas Barish, ed., *Ben Jonson: A Collection of Critical Essays* (Englewood Cliffs, NJ: Prentice-Hall, Inc., 1963), 14–23; Edmund Wilson, "Morose Ben Jonson," (in Barish, *Critical Essays*, 60–74; L. C. Knights, *Drama and Society in the Age of Jonson*) London: Chatto and Windus, 1957, repr. from 1937); and Jonas Barish, "Jonson and the Loathèd Stage," in William Blissett, Julian Patrick and R. W. Van Fossen, eds., *A Celebration of Ben Jonson* (University of Toronto Press), 27–53. While nobody to my knowledge has discussed Jonson's encyclopedism before, there is a long critical tradition connecting Jonson with tropes and strategies that I have argued are encyclopedic. For a brief but penetrating discussion of Jonson's plays in the light of combinatory mechanisms and Bakhtin's theory of the novelistic, see Robert Watson, "*The Alchemist* and Jonson's Conversion of Comedy," in Barbara Kiefer Lewalski, ed. *Renaissance Genres: Essays in Theory, History and Interpretation* (Cambridge, MA: Harvard University Press, 1986), 332–65 (332–37). On language as a possession, see John Hollander, "Ben Jonson and the Modality of Verse," in Bloom, *Modern Critical Views*, 205–22 (219–20); Joseph Loewenstein, "The Script in Marketplace," *Representations* 12 (1985), 101–14 (104–09), gives a more material reading of how language could be owned.
8 James P. Bednarz's "Representing Jonson: Histriomastix and the Origin of the Poet's War," *Huntington Library Quarterly* 54 (1991), 1–30, and *Shakespeare and the Poets' War* (New York: Columbia University Press, 2001) offer a fuller account of the conflict.
9 Thomas Dekker, *The Dramatic Works*, ed. Fredson Bowers (Cambridge University Press, 1962), *Satiromastix*, 1. 2. 8–14.
10 See chapter 3. Joseph Webbe wrote to Jonson for support in his project of editing Terence into easily recombinable sections; see Evans, *Contexts of His Time*, 132–46.
11 The dates I give for *Every Man In* and *Every Man Out* are those of their early quarto editions and thus closer to their original dates of production. Both plays were substantially revised for Jonson's folio *Works* (1616), and it is from this text, unless otherwise noted, that I quote.

12 Harry Levin, "An Introduction to Ben Jonson," in Barish, *Critical Essays*, 40–59, notes that "Each [character] has only his characteristic move, as in chess, and the object of the game is to see what new combinations have been brought about" (56); editors Herford and Simpson describe *Every Man Out of His Humor* as "a collection of pathological specimens, labeled and classified" (I, 378). See John J. Enck, *Jonson and the Comic Truth* (Madison: University of Wisconsin Press, 1957), especially 34, 142. See also L. A. Beaurline, "Ben Jonson and the Illusion of Completeness," *Papers of the Modern Language Association* 84 (1969), 51–59; Jonas Barish, *Jonson and the Language of Prose Comedy* (Cambridge, MA: Harvard University Press, 1960), 79, 118–21; Maus, "Facts of the Matter," 70, notes that in *The Alchemist* and other plays, elements are rearranged without altering their "original, unassimilable characteristics." In the poems, for instance, Van den Berg, *Action of Jonson's Poetry*, 89, calls the *Epigrams* "a 'compact series,' a set of possibilities developed within a carefully defined framework." To define the *Epigrams* this way is on some level to ally them with Jonson's theatre, another carefully defined space in which possibilities were systematically exhausted.

13 Samuel Taylor Coleridge, *Specimens of the Table-Talk*, 2 vols. (London: John Murray, 1835), II, 339 (July 15, 1834) and 426 (February 17, 1835).

14 *Marginalia 1*, in *Collected Works*, ed. Kathleen Coburn, Bollingen Series 75, 13 vols. (Princeton University Press, 1969–), XII, 3, 182: "Jonson's [characters] are either a man with a huge *Wen*, having a circulation of its own, & which we might [have] conceived amputated, and the Patient thereby losing all his *character*, or they are mere Wens instead of Men, Wens personified, or with eyes, nose & mouth, cut out, mandrake-fashion."

15 Like me, Enck, *Comic Truth*, sees the physiological explanation as incorrect. By pleading humors, he believes, the characters are freed from moral responsibility for their actions. While we both lean away from physiology and towards a more socially constructed view of Jonson's humors, Enck is more confident than I am that they are a willful deviation from a socially established norm, and that their persistence is in conflict with what the characters really are and what they know themselves to be. Enck is also deeply uncomfortable with plays that do not make clear a better avenue of behavior, the "comic truth" of his title. This includes notably *The Alchemist*. As will become apparent, I want to avoid a contrast between humoral behavior and an underlying code that produces it. Cf. Terence Dunford, "Consumption of the World: Reading, Eating, and Imitation in *Every Man Out of His Humor*," *English Literary History* 14 (1984), 131–47, who links the humors to obsessive and unswerving reliance on a master text to provide a conceptual framework for the world, much like Don Quixote's ailment (144–46).

16 Other humors not easily linked to a physiological imbalance are Puntarvolo's excessive solicitousness towards his dog; the almanac that Sordido consults obsessively, and which in fact may more accurately be called his humor than his greed; and, in *Epicoene*, Captain Otter's compulsive references to his three drinking glasses, the horse, the bull, and the bear.

17 Enck, *Comic Truth*, 73–75; Dunford, "Consumption of the World."

18 Enck, *Comic Truth*, 57, notes that Clove and Orange emphasize and symbolize the general disjointedness of the play.

19 J. L. Austin, *How to Do Things with Words*, eds. J. O. Ormison and Marina Sbisà (Cambridge, MA: Harvard University Press, 1962). McLuskie, "Poets'

Royal Exchange," 55–56, fascinatingly connects the spread of publicly available theatre – as early as 1573 – with an anxiety that it "afforded an opportunity for the unlearned to appear learned, removing the controls on the trade in learning which a closed patronage system would have imposed."

20 Dunford, "Consumption of the World," suggests that the connection with such master texts may in *Every Man Out of his Humor* be much closer; he argues that the humors characters have each selected a particular text or genre through which to organize his or her life, and their inability to vary their behavior comes from an excessive desire to elevate one kind of discourse above every other: "Each character speaks the script of his own author; Jonson merely collects" (144).

21 Richard Dutton, *Ben Jonson: To the First Folio* (Cambridge University Press, 1983), 35–37, comments on the fashionableness of melancholy in this period. See also Haynes, *Social Relations*, 40–51, on the stage as a source of information on fashions and social types.

22 Vives, *De Disciplinis* II, i, 253: "Usus vitae, exempla maiorum, cognitio praesentium facit eum, qui Graes voce polyhistor dicitur, quasi multiscius: nobis sit sanè honestiore nuncupatione prudens: & eius tractatis prudentia."

23 See Volaterranus, *Commentariorum Urbanorum*, preface to book III, *Philologia*; Lebel, "Le Concept de l'Encyclopaedia," and Levi, "Ethics and the Encyclopedia."

24 Vives, *De Disciplinis* II, iv, 359: "Quae sunt omnia της εγκυκλοπαιδειας: de quibus carptim attigere Plinius, Athenaeus, Aelianus, Macrobius, meliusque dissererunt de his senes in circulis suis, & exhedris, sicut Cicero inquit, quam homines eruditissimi in gymnasiis, quod Plinius in praefatione sua conqueritur." See n.33 for the conclusion of this passage. Vives' placement of "meliusque" allows the sentence to be read alternatively as, "it is better for old men to discuss these things... than learned men..."; I will discuss the possibility of irony below.

25 Ibid., II, i, 253: "Everything is to be learned from books, for without books, who could hope to be able to follow the knowledge of great things?" ("Cognoscenda sunt ex libris omnia: nam sine libris quis spereret se magnarum rerum scientiam consecuturum?") Cf. Lebel, "Le Concept de l'Encyclopaedia," 16, on humanist culture as encyclopedic because omnivorous.

26 Ibid., II, iv, 360: "... hominis non perinde literati, ut boni; nec illi ingenium aut diligentia defuit, sed locus & tempora: ..." I was unaware that Virulus was more than a mere exemplum until alerted to his real existence by Professor Catrien Santing of the University of Groeningen. Typically enough, this awareness reveals complications in Vives' attitude towards encyclopedic learning; although Virulus was held in high esteem in Louvain at the end of the fifteenth century, his reputation dropped among the younger humanists of the early sixteenth, including Vives' friend Erasmus. See Pieter Bietenholz, ed., *Contemporaries of Erasmus*, 3 vols. (University of Toronto Press, 1987), s.v.

27 Ibid., II, iv, 360: "audirétque brevissima hora, quae ille usu multorum annorum vix esset assecutus: ita discedebat de colloquio & conviva laetior, & convivator prudentior, ac peritior."

28 Elsky, *Authorizing Words*, 36–47, on Vives' interest in ordinary rather than specialized language as authoritatively knowledgeable; see also Kahn, *Rhetoric, Prudence, and Skepticism*, 20–24, 39–41.

29 Kahn's *Rhetoric, Prudence and Skepticism* is the fullest discussion of the place of prudence in humanist thought, in particular its reliance on contingency and context; see especially the introduction.

30 Bacon, *Works*, I:12.
31 Edward Partridge, "Jonson's *Epigrammes*: The Named and the Nameless," *Studies in the Literary Imagination* 6 (1973), 153–98 (164); most other commentators, following Herford and Simpson, prefer Camden, if any historical figure is to be assumed. See Joseph Loewenstein, "The Jonsonian Corpulence or The Poet as Mouthpiece," *English Literary History* 53 (1986), 491–518, for the most astute reading of this poem.
32 Jonas Barish, "Feasting and Judging in Jonsonian Comedy," *Renaissance Drama* n.s. 5 (1972), 3–35, provides several instances of this topos. Haynes, *Social Relations*, 47–51, acutely distinguishes Jonson's private party from a Bakhtinian public riot; he also discusses the fantasy of communal feasting restoring a lost social order, 129–35.
33 Vives, *De Disciplinis* II, iv, 359: "Hinc quae ad convehendum, in quo est equus, mulus, bos & omne genus vehiculi, cui navigatio est finitione, nempe etiam vectio: haec omnia persequetur qua ratione ac modo sint inventa, quaesita, aucta, conservata, applicata usui, & emolumentis nostris. Iam quae ad oblectamenta sunt per sensus omnes reperta, quae sit societas domi privata viri, uxoris, liberorum, consanguineorum, affinium, asseclarum, servorum, quae in civitate publica, quae ad eam per hominum ingenia excogitata, & inventa, quae per stultitiam conficta nomine atque opinione sine re omnino ulla. Quae sunt omnia της εγκυκλοπαιδειας: . . ." This passage immediately precedes the one in n.24.
34 My reading of Vives draws heavily on the overview of his position given in Elsky, *Authorizing Words*, 36–47, and the more detailed treatment of Richard Waswo, *Language and Meaning in the Renaissance* (Princeton University Press, 1987).
35 The phrase "centered self" is originally Thomas M. Greene's, "Ben Jonson and the Centered Self," in Bloom, *Modern Critical Views*, 89–110; it has subsequently become hugely influential in criticism of Jonson's lyrics.
36 Numerous critics have remarked on this, although never to my knowledge in the context of encyclopedic writing: Thomas Greene, "The Centered Self"; see also W. H. Herendeen, "Like a Circle Bounded in Itself: Jonson, Camden, and the Strategies of Praise," *Journal of Medieval and Renaissance Studies* 11 (1981), 137–67; Illona Bell, "Circular Strategies and Structures in Jonson and Herbert," in Claude J. Summers and Ted-Larry Pebworth, eds., *Classic and Cavalier: Essays on Jonson and the Sons of Ben* (University of Pittsburgh Press, 1987), 157–70; earliest of all, Enck, *Comic Truth*, 31, for whom the circle is Jonson's general "symbol of approbation," regardless of context.
37 In addition, Jonson seems to see description as outside the epigram's scope; he told Drummond that Harington's epigrams were "narrations and not epigrams" (*Conversations with Drummond*, in *Complete Poems*, lines 44f.).
38 Cf. his poem to Burlase, *Underwoods* 52; to surpass the painter's portrait of him in the "black and white" of writing, Jonson needs, he claims, only a single word:

> Yet when of friendship I would draw the face,
> A lettered mind, and a large heart would place
> To all posterity; I will write *Burlase*.

39 "Epigrammatum autem genera tot sunt, quot rerum" (*Poetices* III, 125; my translation. Quoted in Wesley Trimpi, *Ben Jonson's Poems: A Study of the Plain Style* [Stanford University Press, 1962], 85 n.25).

40 *Underwoods* 14, 36, two lines after Jonson has mentioned Selden's "circle . . ./ Of general knowledge"; it is his first answer to his question, "Which grace shall I make love to first?" as he begins to look at each chord of Selden's circle separately. Of Camden, Jonson simply exclaims ". . . what faith thou hast in things!" (*Epigrams* 14, 7).

41 Alastair Fowler, "The *Silva* Tradition in Jonson's *The Forrest*," in *Poetic Traditions of the English Renaissance*, eds. Maynard Mack and George deForest Lord (New Haven: Yale University Press, 1982), 163–80, rightly connects Jonson's titles with ancient collections of varied poems called *silvae*. I would argue that these collections too are working within the tradition of *silva* as manifold.

42 Perotti, *Cornucopiae*, 286v: "Interpretationem primi libri quod est universi operis & totius fere latinae linguae dimidium . . ."

43 Ibid.: "Diligentius lectoris officium erit aliorum scripta cum nostris conferre."

44 Martial, *Epigrammata*, ed. and transl. D. R. Shackleton Bailey, Loeb Classical Library (Cambridge, MA: Harvard University Press, 1993). *Epistles* I, my translation. "cur in theatrum, Cato severe, venisti?/ an ideo tantum veneras, ut exires?"

45 Partridge, "*Epigrammes*" cites Martial on this passage but dismisses the theatre's significance, 156–57. The complexity of the antitheatrical theatre is precisely what Jonson is seeking. On Jonson's antitheatricality, see Barish, "Loathèd Stage" and his *Antitheatrical Prejudice*. See also my discussion of poetry as theatre in chapter 2.

46 Mary Thomas Crane, "*Intret Cato*: Authority and the Epigram in Sixteenth-Century England," in Lewalski, *Renaissance Genres*, 158–86 (165–69), on the ideology of the epigram in Renaissance England.

47 I am particularly indebted to the reading of this poem in Stanley Fish, "Authors-Readers: Jonson's Community of the Same," *Representations* 7 (1984), 26–58; see also Trimpi, *Ben Jonson's Poems*, 142–46.

48 See Richard C. Newton, "'*Ben./ Jonson*': The Poet in the Poems," in *Two Renaissance Mythmakers: Christopher Marlowe and Ben Jonson: Selected Papers from the English Institute, 1975–76* (Baltimore: Johns Hopkins University Press, 1977), 191–93, on the melancholy of this loss.

49 *Conversations with Drummond*, in *Complete Poems*, 598f.

50 *Underwoods* 70, 9–10. Richard S. Peterson, *Imitation and Praise in the Poems of Ben Jonson* (New Haven: Yale University Press, 1981), 202–06, sees (incorrectly, to my mind) the infant's progress as "a grotesquely inadequate extreme." Although an extreme, the infant's course is the minimal model of perfection.

51 William Kerrigan's powerful reading of this poem ("Ben Jonson Full of Shame and Scorn," in Bloom, *Modern Critical Views*, 111–28) suppresses the question mark at the next stanza's end, even printing the line without it, and so treats the sentence "could they but life's miseries foresee/ No doubt all infants would return like thee?" as a statement when in the second folio it is punctuated as a question. It is true that Renaissance punctuation conventions were not as standardized as modern ones, and also that question marks and exclamation points were easily confused; see Steven Booth, ed., *Shakespeare's Sonnets* (New Haven: Yale University Press, 1977), 314. Given the care that Jonson habitually (and unusually, in this period) took in punctuating his works, though, it seems a hazardous step to assume that a question mark means a period. The poem is from *Underwoods*, in the inferior second folio finally assembled by Kenelm Digby, but we know that Jonson was collecting his later works for

publication in a folio, and we cannot assume that the punctuation is not Jonson's own. See most recently Michael McCanles, *Jonsonian Discriminations: The Humanist Poet and the Praise of True Nobility* (University of Toronto Press, 1992), 5–10.

52 Kerrigan,"Full of Shame and Scorn," 125, refers to his "meaninglessly repetitive circles"; see also Peterson, *Imitation and Praise*, 208–10, who contrasts the stirrer's circularity to that of figures like Selden or Roe.

53 Fish, "Authors-Readers," 39–40.

54 Riggs, *Life*, 309–10.

55 "Second Sounding," 266–70. Jonson's commitment to an enduring and singular Comedy that manifests itself in many forms of course makes this argument possible.

56 See Joseph Loewenstein, "Printing and 'The Multitudinous Presse': The Contentious Texts of Jonson's Masques," in Brady and Herendeen, *1616 Folio*, 168–91 (181–82), on how Jonson's masques and playtexts in general privilege *reading* over *watching* by emphasizing the need for invisible knowledge.

57 Similarly, in the "Epistle to Katherine, Lady Aubigny," the poem Jonson offers is a mirror of her in which she will be able to see herself unchanged "as long years do pass" (*Forrest* 13, 121–24).

58 *HrS*, IX, 396. On circular reading, Bell argues that Jonson and Herbert require a reading that is "circular rather than dramatic, progressively retrospective rather than developmental" ("Circular Strategies," 158). Jonson's translation of these lines of the *Ars Poetica* reads: "Some man's hand/ Will take you more, the nearer that you stand; . . . this, ten times over will delight."

59 *Every Man Out of His Humor* was Jonson's first printed work, which may explain some of the urgency with which he foregrounds its textuality. It is also the longest play printed during the English Renaissance, Dunford, "Consumption of the World," 132. The play went through three editions in quarto, a number unprecedented since Lyly's publication in 1578. On the ways in which the printed quarto reminds its reader that it is not a playscript, see also Loewenstein, "Script in the Marketplace"; Murray, *Theatrical Legitimation*, 23–38.

60 Walker, *Politics of Performance*, 30f.

61 Barish, "Loathèd Stage," 32, was the first to make this argument.

62 Seneca, *Epistles* 7, 11, records that Epicurus wrote to one of his students, "Thus not to many, but to you, for we are theatre enough for each other" (*'Haec,' inquit, ego non multis, sed tibi: satis magnum alter alteri theatrum sumu*). Bacon explicitly rejects this conceit, "for it is a speech of a lover and not for a wise man, *Satis magnum alter alteri theatrum sumus*" (*Advancement of Learning*, in *Works*, III: 279). See chapter 6.

63 See, for instance, Ernest William Talbert, "Current Scholarly Works and the 'Erudition' of Jonson's *Masque of Augurs*," *Studies in Philology* 44 (1947), 605–24.

64 The citations are Herodotus II, 68, Pliny VIII, 25, and Bartholomaeus VII, 25 and XVIII, 33, given in Lucas's edition of the play. Lucas' use of entry numbers of Bartholomaeus shows that he is referring to *Batman uppon Bartolome*, but it is not clear if this is for his own convenience or because Webster used it as well. Mythili Kaul, "A Possible Source for Flamineo's 'Tale' in Webster's *The White Devil*," *Notes and Queries*, n.s. 39 (1992), 360–61, reviews other suggested sources and adds Leo Africanus; while he usefully assembles earlier treatments of the issue, he treats the encyclopedias as collections of equivalent data about the world and so fails to distinguish the different versions given in each source.

65 References are to *Doctor Faustus: A- and B-Texts (1604, 1616)*, eds. David Bevington and Eric Rasmussen (Manchester University Press, 1993) except as noted.
66 On Faustus' selective memory, see, e.g., *Faustus: A- and B-Texts*, Bevington and Rasmussen, 14–17; *The Complete Works of Christopher Marlowe*, ed. Roma Gill, 5 vols., II, *Doctor Faustus*, 56.
67 1. 1. 52f. I read A's "sceanes" literally as "scenes" rather than Bevington and Rasmussen's "signs" and Gill's "schemes," "which B (and many modern editors) dismisses as apparently unintelligible" (Gill). I remain uncertain why "sceanes" should be unintelligible in the first place. Faustus may well be scanning a *theatrum*.
68 I quote the stage direction, 3. 2. 28, from Gill. Bevington and Rasmussen omit it. The clowns here may even be exhibiting a more skillful application of knowledge than Faustus does; in this scene Mephistopheles is forced to appear, "vexèd with these villains' charms . . . Only for the pleasure of these damnèd slaves" (3. 2. 32, 34). When he first appears to Faustus, though, Mephistopheles insists that the spell that Faustus has just pronounced has not compelled him to come. Faustus' conjuring was but the cause "*per accidens,/* For when we hear one rack the name of God,/ Abjure the scriptures, and his Savior Christ,/ We fly, in hope to get his glorious soul . . ." (1. 3. 46–49).
69 Vives, *De Disciplinis* II, iv, 360.
70 See Ben Jonson, *The Alchemist*, in *Drama of the English Renaissance* vol. 2. *The Stuart Period*, eds. Russell A. Fraser and Norman Rabkin (New York: Macmillan Publishing Co., 1976), 143–90, esp. notes to 2. 3 and 4. 5.
71 See Dunford, "Consumption of the World," on the humors characters as inhabited by particular discourses; Watson, "Conversion of Comedy," 339, diagnoses the gulls in *The Alchemist* as being similarly obsessed with contemporary discourses.
72 Robert Weimann, *Authority and Representation in Early Modern Discourse*, ed. David Hillman (Baltimore: Johns Hopkins University Press, 1996), makes the argument that this is a significant change in early modern discourse, most prominently theatrical but also religious and fictional.
73 Robert Greene, *A Notable Discovery of Cozenage* (1591), quoted in A. V. Judges, ed., *The Elizabethan Underworld* (London: George Routledge and Sons, 1930), 118–48, (121). I owe the reference to this work to Haynes, *Social Relations*, 113–14. Greene himself apparently seemed to Gabriel Harvey to have a similarly encyclopedic tendency, who called him, "a scholar, a discourser, a courtier, a ruffian, a gamester, a lover, a soldier, a traveller, . . . a cozener, a railer, a beggar, an omnigatherum, a gay nothing!" (Judges, *Elizabethan Underworld*, 498–99). Or everything . . .
74 On this idea of language and learning among humanists generally, and particularly for Vives, see Waswo, *Language and Meaning*, 14–16; Elsky, *Authorizing Words*, esp. chapter 1 on the primacy of speech and rhetoric to humanist theories of language.
75 R. L. Smallwood, "'Here, In the Friars': Immediacy and Theatricality in *The Alchemist*," *Review of English Studies* 32 (1981), 142–60.
76 George Hibbard, "Ben Jonson and Human Nature," in Blissett *et al.*, *Celebration*, 55–81 (64–68), calls the discovery of how desire can create a *deceptio visus*, in the tradition of Isaiah Berlin's hedgehog, Jonson's "one great thing."
77 See Haynes, *Social Relations*, 63–73, on the theatre as the place in which fashion was both made and critiqued; 113–14 on the conversion of knowledge to social capital.

78 Jonson Induction, *Bartholomew Fair*. Also at issue here is Jonson's well-documented interest in shifting the authority for the performance to himself as author.
79 For the importance of treating the actions of the spectators as part of the theatrical experience, Schechner, "Towards a Poetics of Performance," 122–26.
80 On the full range of the meaning of "preposterous," see Patricia A. Parker, *Shakespeare from the Margins: Language, Culture, Context* (University of Chicago Press, 1996), chapter 1.

6 FRANCIS BACON'S THEATRE OF ORPHEUS: "LITERATE EXPERIENCE" AND EXPERIMENTAL SCIENCE

1 Harry Levin, "Bacon's Poetics," in *Renaissance Rereadings: Intertext and Content*, eds. Maryanne Cline Horowitz, Anne J. Cruz, and Wendy A. Furman (Urbana: University of Illinois Press, 1988), 3–17 for instance, seems to me to misread when he links Bacon's rejection of the so-called Idols of the Theatre with a rejection of the actual theatre. See also Vickers, "Bacon's Use of Theatrical Imagery," on Bacon's complex and variegated interest in theatre.
2 Bacon, *Works*, VIII: 108–09. Julian Martin, *Francis Bacon, the State, and the Reform of Natural Philosophy* (Cambridge University Press, 1992), 6–22, links this letter to a growing sense in the sixteenth century that "problems of knowledge were a proper part of a statesman's concerns" (45).
3 B. H. G. Wormald, *Francis Bacon: History, Politics, and Science*, 1561–1626 (Cambridge University Press, 1993), 1–5, suggests that Bacon "pre-enacted his subsequent reputation" and had a "grand strategy" in politics "analogous to and comparable with his *Great Instauration*." Unless otherwise noted, Bacon's works are cited in the edition of Spedding *et al.*, with volume in Roman numerals and then page number. Bacon's chapter and section divisions in the works themselves, when they exist, are given in Arabic numerals. I cite *Novum Organum* by aphorism number. Elsewhere I give references to Bacon's works in the text, citing first Bacon's original division, then the volume and page of Spedding's edition and finally his translation, where applicable. I have sometimes silently modified the translations.
4 Martin, *The State and the Reform of Natural Philosophy*, 60–62, gives an interesting reading of this letter as a metaphorization of knowledge as exploration and colonialism.
5 *Instauratio Magna*, Preface, *Works*, IV: 14. See also *Redargutio Philosophiae*, *Works*, III: 579: "Philosophia autem et scientiae intellectus statuarum more adorantur et celebrantur, sed non moventur."
6 When Bacon failed to get the Solicitorship, he sent a letter to Essex saying that "with this disgrace of my fortune . . . [he would] retire myself with a couple of men to Cambridge, and there spend my life in my studies and contemplations, without looking back" (Lambeth MSS. 650, f. 62, quoted in Jean Overton Fuller, *Sir Francis Bacon: A Biography* (London: East-West Publications, 1981), 65). When he lost the Chancellorship much more palpably disgraced, Bacon wrote a prayer in which, alluding to his gift for philosophical thought, he confessed that "I am a debtor to thee for the gracious talent of gifts and graces . . . but misspent it in things for which I was least fit; so as I may truly say, my soul hath been a stranger in the course of my pilgrimage" (British Museum, Birch MSS. f. 110, quoted in Fuller, *A Biography*, 284). On Bacon's self-presentation in 1621, see Lisa Jardine and Alan Stewart,

Hostage to Fortune: The Troubled Life of Francis Bacon (London: Victor Gollancz, 1998), 473–78. I have also made use of Fulton H. Anderson, *Francis Bacon: His Career and His Thought*, The Arensberg Lectures, 2nd series ([Los Angeles]: University of Southern California Press, 1962), and the introductions to Spedding's and Pitcher's editions of Bacon's works. Perez Zagorin's intellectual survey is also extremely helpful in approaching Bacon (*Francis Bacon* [Princeton University Press, 1998]). Fuller's *A Biography* includes a good selection of quoted materials, but has an occult bias that makes her conclusions both amusing and practically worthless.

7 I am grateful to Elizabeth Allen for helping me work out some of these relationships.

8 *Instauratio Magna*, Plan (*Works*, I: 144, IV: 32): "Itaque intentiones geminae illae, humanae scilicet *Scientiae* et *Potentiae*, vere in idem coincidunt . . ." See also *Novum Organum* 1. 3. Bacon discusses the relationship of Aristotle and Alexander at length in the introductory letter to King James of *De Augmentis* 2, *Works*, IV: 287ff.

9 Ronald Levao, "Francis Bacon and the Mobility of Science," *Representations* 40 (1992), 1–32, discusses Bacon's crossing of boundaries, and indeed of both these boundaries and their crossings as constitutive of Bacon's project. As an example, I would add that the motto Bacon gives to the frontispiece of the *Instauratio Magna*, "*Plus ultra*," requires both a limit and a beyond into which it can be transgressed. Wormald, *History, Politics, and Science*, argues that Bacon's most important contributions are to the human rather than to the natural sciences. John C. Briggs, too, argues for an emphasis on Bacon's approaches to securing human action rather than to the "encyclopedic and esoteric" contents of his work, in *Francis Bacon and the Rhetoric of Nature* (Cambridge, MA: Harvard University Press, 1989), 3.

10 Spedding, in his notes to the *Filum Labyrinthi* (c.1607, *Works*, III: 493–504), observes that Bacon was able to fool himself through his discursive ability into believing that his science was more filled up than it was. He certainly argued that it was more possible than it proved; he wrote (and perhaps believed) the accumulation of experimental data that would allow investigation of the Forms of nature would be the work of a few years. I will suggest below one way in which Bacon's faith is a kind of rhetorical persuasion.

11 *Novum Organum* 1. 124: "Etenim verum exemplar mundi in intellecto humano fundamus; quale invenitur, non quale cuipiam sua propria ratio dictaverit. Hoc autem perfici non potest, nisi facta mundi dissectione atque anatomia diligentissima" (*Works*, I: 218, IV: 110).

12 Cf. the discussion on this trope in Alvin Snider, *Origin and Authority in Seventeenth-Century England: Bacon, Milton, Butler* (University of Toronto Press, 1994), 37–38.

13 John Nichols, ed., *The Progresses and Public Processions of Queen Elizabeth*, Research and Source Works Series 117, 3 vols. (New York: Burt Franklin, 1964, repr. of 1823), III, 373.

14 "sed instauratio facienda est ab imis fundamentis; nisi libeat perpetuo circumvolui in orbem, cum exili et quasi contemnendo progressu" (*Novum Organum* 1. 31, *Works*, I: 162, IV: 52).

15 Charles Whitney, *Francis Bacon and Modernity* (New Haven: Yale University Press, 1986), 23–28, 94–95.

16 *Descriptio Globi Intellectualis*, *Works*, III: 734, V: 510–11. Cf. Mary Hesse, "Francis Bacon's Philosophy of Science," in Brian Vickers, ed., (127). *Essential Articles for the Study of Francis Bacon* (Hamden, CT: Archon Books, 1968), 114–39.

17 On the scientist as hero, including Orpheus, in Renaissance literature, see John Steadman, "Beyond Hercules: Bacon and the Scientist as Hero," *Studies in the Literary Imagination* 4 (1971), 3–47.
18 On the ascetic drive of the Baconian scientist, see Briggs, *Rhetoric of Nature*, 13–16, and Whitney, *Bacon and Modernity*, 84–85, for what he calls Bacon's "titanic modesty."
19 The idea of knowledge as a sort of Eleusinian mystery into which a beginner was inducted is central to Bacon's ideas of pedagogy. This is in contrast to the more usual encyclopedic conception of knowledge as an object that can be possessed, traded, acquired, and so on. Bacon thus treats knowledge as an experience – Orpheus lives all of life twice, even going into the land of the dead twice; so also knowledge lets us mirror the truth of our own history.
20 Coulianou, *Eros and Magic in the Renaissance*, looks at the connections between desire and Renaissance magic, and argues that Renaissance magic, far from being an attempt to control the physical world, is much more of a science of manipulating and refiguring human desires.
21 *De Augmentis* 6. 4, *Works*, IV: 496; for further praise of Jesuit use of educational theatre, see *Advancement, Works*, III: 276f.
22 *De Augmentis* 3. 4, *Works*, I: 567, IV: 361: "Sunt enim Scientiae instar pyramidum, quibus Historia et Experientia tamquam basis unica substernuntur; ac proinde basis Naturalis Philosophiae est Historia Naturalis."
23 Ibid., 5. 4; *Works*, I: 643, IV: 431. The Idols have received many and varied analyses in several secondary sources, but rarely are they examined in much depth. Lisa Jardine, *Francis Bacon's Discovery and the Art of Discourse* (Cambridge University Press, 1974), 80–83, suggests that within Bacon's process of induction they are analogous to the *elenchi* given by Aristotle for syllogistic, warning readers of regularly occurring or predictable errors in their thinking.
24 *Valerius Terminus, Works*, III: 241–42 and 245; the Idols are also discussed in two separate précis of chapter 16 of *Novum Organum*. Only three types are mentioned in the later *De Augmentis* (1623), which I discuss below. See also Spedding's long note C on the development of Bacon's doctrine of the Idols (*Works*, I: 113–17).
25 Snider, *Origin and Authority*, 47, also notes this difference between the Idols of the Theatre and the other types.
26 Aristotle and Paracelsus respectively, in *Redargutio Philosophiae, Works*, III: 577, and *Masculine Birth of Time [Temporis Partus Masculus], Works*, III: 532.
27 This emphasizes the "Maker's knowledge" of Antonio Pérez-Ramos' title, *Francis Bacon's Idea of Science and the Maker's Tradition of Knowledge* (Oxford: Clarendon Press, 1988). Levao notes that while Bacon continually contrasts the products of the scientific imagination with those of the poetic, Sidneian one, in the end the two come together on pragmatic grounds – each affirms its truth on the basis of its usefulness ("Mobility of Science," 19–20). I want to explore how not only their end points but their processes may be seen to be homologous.
28 *Hamlet*, 2. 2. 301–05. Anne Righter, "Francis Bacon," in Vickers, *Essential Articles*, 300–21 (320–21), notes this similarity in observation between Hamlet and Bacon and also their opposition in meaning.
29 In the sense given *theatricality* by Michael Fried in *Absorption and Theatricality* – self-presentation before an implied onlooker. Its opposite for Fried is *absorption*, the sense of indifference to the viewer – but as Fried points out in his study of

eighteenth-century French paintings, *absorption* is the pose of atheatricality, a careful demonstration to its audience that the work does not require an audience. D. G. James, *The Dream of Learning: An Essay on* The Advancement of Learning, Hamlet, *and* King Lear (Oxford: Clarendon Press, 1951), has an idiosyncratic but suggestive reading of *Lear*, *Hamlet*, and the *Advancement of Learning* that treats each of them as explorations of the ways the mind can bow, or bow to, the world.

30 Learned or professional seventeenth-century writers often wrote in several hands, so the effect of this might be much less pronounced than it would seem to a twentieth-century reader. Jonson's masques, for instance, in manuscript show a combination of several hands, even within words; see the introduction to the *Masque of Blackness* in *HrS*. On the practices and significances of Renaissance handwriting, see Jonathan Goldberg, *Writing Matter: From the Hands of the English Renaissance* (Stanford University Press, 1990).

31 More generally on Bacon and James, see Robert E. Stillman, "The Jacobean Discourse of Power: James I and Francis Bacon," *Renaissance Papers* (1989), 89–99.

32 In his discussion of the faculty of the imagination Bacon states that, unlike reason or memory, the imagination has no scientific discipline connected to it and in fact cannot be subjected to scientific analysis: "imagination hardly produces sciences: poesy (which in the beginning was referred to imagination) being to be accounted rather as a pleasure or play of wit than a science" (*De Augmentis* 5. 1, *Works*, I: 615, IV: 406) In a reading of *Leviathan*, Christopher Pye argues that the desire in the subject to lay bare what provides the prince with his power is in fact the source of the prince's power, which is only the alienated power of the subject (*The Regal Phantasm: Shakespeare and the Politics of Spectacle* [London: Routledge and Kegan Paul, 1990], 44–45). Hobbes, not coincidentally, was Bacon's secretary for a period of time.

33 *Advancement, Works*, III: 474. Bacon quotes Vergil, *Aeneid* VI, 727f., "poured through the whole and the parts/ The mind moves the mass, and mingles itself with the great body."

34 Bacon, *Essays*, "Of Empire," in *Works*, VI: 419.

35 *Advancement, Works*, III: 314. On the process of learning natural history in the seventeenth century as a disenchanting of the world and the uses of wonder in this same period, see Mark Schneider, *Culture and Enchantment* (University of Chicago Press, 1993).

36 *Valerius Terminus, Works*, III: 243. This idea of nature as scripted, however, appears throughout Bacon's work; see also *Advancement* 2; *Novum Organum* 1. 121, *Works*, IV: 107; *Instauratio Magna, Works*, IV: 29–30. The fragment of the *Abecedarium Naturae* gives a very small set of coded graphemes for writing the properties of the world in a perfectly descriptive, perfectly non-magical, language, a tendency that will reach its apogee perhaps in the work of John Wilkins later in the seventeenth century. See also Timothy Reiss, *The Discourse of Modernism* (Ithaca, NY: Cornell University Press, 1982), "Introduction," on "analytico-referential discourse," a mode of reference characterized by a "self-possessed" analyst who by means of some abstracting instrument breaks down an object into its elements in order to come to know it. I take this to be more typical of the genre of encyclopedic writing than of a particular historical period. See my discussion of this trope in chapter 3.

37 *Sylva Sylvarum* 328, *Works*, II: 450; cf. also *Novum Organum* 2. 5, *Works*, IV: 122.
38 On Bacon's project as a kind of *imitatio naturae,* see J. Peter Zetterberg, "Echoes of Nature in Salomon's House," *Journal of the History of Ideas* 43 (1982), 179–94 191–92; Whitney, *Bacon and Modernity,* 10–28; Hesse, "Philosophy of Science," 123. On the naming of things as "primal baptism," so that essence is less important than history and accident, see Slavoj Žižek, *The Sublime Object of Ideology* (London: Verso, 1989), on Saul Kripke.
39 Hesse, "Philosophy of Science," 124. See also James J. Bono, *The Word of God and the Language of Man: Interpreting Nature in Early Modern Science and Medicine* (Madison: University of Wisconsin Press, 1995), 231–36, on Bacon's treatment of the language of nature as consisting entirely of things themselves, rather than seeing things in nature as signs of other things.
40 *Experientia* and *experimentum* not yet being regularly distinguished, although Bacon himself often does distinguish them; on the relation of these terms, see Charles B. Schmitt, "Experience and Experiment: A Comparison of Zabarella's View with Galileo's *De Motu,*" *Studies in the Renaissance* 16 (1969), 80–138.
41 Pérez-Ramos, *Bacon's Idea of Science*, notes that Bacon's experiments work "by *creating* new experience," 130, n.30. In this, as Levao notes in "Mobility of Science," Bacon is following Sidney's neo-Aristotelian theory of poetry's usefulness, that it teaches by simulating an experience.
42 My translation, *Novum Organum* 1. 74, *Works*, I: 183, IV: 74: "Quae enim in natura fundata sunt crescunt et augentur: quae autem in opinione, variantur non augentur."
43 See Briggs, *Rhetoric of Nature*, who stresses the importance of the experiment being "sealed," 143ff.
44 *Sylva Sylvarum* 9, introduction, *Works*, II: 602–03, discusses the possibility that all objects have perception, although not all have sense, and that making use of these more sensitive perceptions, such as loadstones or water-glasses, allows a person to borrow the ability of these objects to perceive conditions that are not humanly perceptible. See also *De Augmentis* 4. 3, *Works*, IV: 402f.
45 Bacon had been following Galileo's work on tides since at least 1619, even sending Galileo his own studies of tides; Jardine and Stewart, *Hostage*, 306f.
46 *Advancement, Works*, III: 44; Bacon does not translate the bracketed section, and that part of the translation is mine.
47 *Works*, VI: 517. Pitcher notes this repetition of "giddiness" in the introduction to his edition of the *Essays* (Harmondsworth: Penguin, 1985).
48 *Advancement, Works*, III: 346; cf. *De Augmentis* 2. 13, *Works*, I: 538, IV: 335, for the same sentiment, "Verum in theatro nimis diu moramur," with explicit connection to the use of stories such as those of Pan and Echo.

Bibliography

Agnew, Jean Christophe. *Worlds Apart: The Market and the Theatre in Anglo-American Thought*. Cambridge: Cambridge University Press, 1986.
Alberti, Leon Battista. *On Painting* [*De Pintura*]. Transl. John R. Spencer. New Haven: Yale University Press, 1966.
Alighieri, Dante. *Convivio*. Ed. Franca Brambilla Ageno. 2 vols. in 3. Florence: Casa Editrice di Lettere, 1995.
　The Banquet. Transl. Christopher Ryan. Stanford French and Italian Studies 61. Saratoga, CA: Anma Libri, 1989.
Altman, Joel B. *The Tudor Play of Mind: Rhetorical Inquiry and the Development of Elizabethan Drama*. Berkeley: University of California Press, 1978.
Anderson, Fulton H. *Francis Bacon: His Career and His Thought*. The Arensberg Lectures, 2nd series. [Los Angeles]: University of Southern California Press, 1962.
Anglo, Sydney. *Spectacle, Pageantry, and Early Tudor Policy*. Oxford: Clarendon Press, 1969.
Aristotle. *Metaphysics*. Transl. Hugh Tredennick. Loeb Classical Library. London: William Heinemann, 1933.
Arnheim, Rudolph. *The Power of the Center: A Study of Composition in the Visual Arts: The New Version*. Berkeley: University of California Press, 1988.
Astell, Ann. *Chaucer and the Universe of Learning*. Ithaca, NY: Cornell University Press, 1996.
Augustinus, Aurelius. *Confessions*. Ed. and annot. James J. O'Donnell. 3 vols. Oxford: Clarendon Press, 1992.
　Confessions. Transl. R. S. Pine-Coffin. Harmondsworth: Penguin, 1961.
Austin, J. L. *How to Do Things with Words*. Eds. J. O. Ormison and Marina Sbisà. Cambridge, MA: Harvard University Press, 1962.
Axton, Richard, ed. *Three Rastell Plays: Four Elements, Calisto and Melebea, Gentleness and Nobility*. Cambridge: D. S. Brewer, 1979.
Bacon, Francis. *Essays*. Ed. and intro. John Pitcher. Harmondsworth: Penguin, 1985.
　Works. Eds. James Spedding, Robert Leslie Ellis, and Douglas Denon Heath. 14 vols. London: Longman and Co., 1857–74. [Facsimile Reprint. Stuttgart: Friedrich Fromann Verlag, 1963.]
Barish, Jonas. *The Antitheatrical Prejudice*. Berkeley: University of California Press, 1981.
　"Jonson and the Loathèd Stage." In Blissett *et al.*, *Celebration* (1973): 27–53.
　"Feasting and Judging in Jonsonian Comedy." *Renaissance Drama* n.s. 5 (1972): 3–35.

Jonson and the Language of Prose Comedy. Cambridge, MA: Harvard University Press, 1960.

Barish, Jonas, ed. *Ben Jonson: A Collection of Critical Essays.* Englewood Cliffs, NJ: Prentice-Hall, Inc., 1963.

Barkan, Leonard. *Unearthing the Past: Archeology and Aesthetics in the Making of Renaissance Culture.* New Haven: Yale University Press, 1999.

Transuming Passion: Ganymede and the Erotics of Humanism. Stanford: Stanford University Press, 1991.

Barthes, Roland. *The Pleasure of the Text.* Transl. Richard Miller. New York: Hill and Wang, 1975.

Bartholomaeus Anglicus. *On the Properties of Things.* Transl. John of Trevisa 2 vols. (1397/8). Ed. M. C. Seymour. Oxford: Clarendon Press, 1975.

Batman uppon Bartholome, his Booke De Proprietatibus Rerum. Ed. Stephen Batman. London: Thomas East, 1582. [Facsimile Reprint. Intro. Jürgen Schäfer. Anglistica and Americana 161. Hildesheim: Georg Olms Verlag, 1976.]

De Proprietatibus Rerum. Ed. Wynkyn de Worde. London: Wynkyn de Worde, 1495.

Le Proprietaire des Choses [Livre des propriétés des choses]. Transl. Jean Corbichon. Lyons: G. Le Roy, 1485.

De Proprietatibus Rerum. [Cologne: William Caxton?, 1470.]

Barton, Anne. *Ben Jonson, Dramatist.* Cambridge: Cambridge University Press, 1984.

Bartsch, Shadi. *Actors in the Audience: Theatricality and Doublespeak from Nero to Hadrian.* Cambridge, MA: Harvard University Press, 1994.

Baxandall, Michael. *Giotto and the Orators.* Oxford: Clarendon Press, 1971.

Beard, Thomas. *The Theatre of God's Judgements.* London: Adam Islip, 1597.

Beaumont, Francis. *The Knight of the Burning Pestle.* Ed. Michael Hattaway. New Mermaids Series. New York: W. W. Norton and Co., 1976.

Beaurline, L. A. "Ben Jonson and the Illusion of Completeness." *Papers of the Modern Language Association* 84 (1969): 51–59.

Becq, Annie, ed. *L'Encyclopédisme: Actes du Colloque de Caen, 12–16 Janvier 1987.* Paris: Amateurs des livres, 1991.

Bednarz, James P. *Shakespeare and the Poets' War.* New York: Columbia University Press, 2001.

"Representing Jonson: *Histriomastix* and the Origin of the Poets' War." *Huntington Library Quarterly* 54 (1991): 1–30.

Bell, Ilona. "Circular Strategies and Structures in Jonson and Herbert." In Summers and Pebworth, *Classic and Cavalier* (1982): 157–70.

Bellay, Joachim du. *Antiquitez de Rome.* Transl. Edmund Spenser. Ed. and annot. Malcolm C. Smith. Binghamton: Medieval and Renaissance Texts and Studies, 1994.

Oeuvres Poetiques. Ed. Geneviève Demerson. 8 vols. Paris: Librairie Nizet, 1984.

Benjamin, Walter. "Edward Fuchs: Collector and Historian." In *The Essential Frankfurt School Reader.* Eds. Andrew Arato and Eike Gebhardt. New York: Continuum, 1993 (repr. of 1978): 225–53.

The Origin of German Tragic Drama. Transl. John Osborne. London: Verso, 1977.

Berger, Harry. *Imaginary Audition: Shakespeare on Stage and Page.* Berkeley: University of California Press, 1989.

Berlin, Isaiah. *The Crooked Timber of Humanity: Chapters in the History of Ideas.* Ed. Henry Hardy. New York: Alfred A. Knopf, 1991.

Bernheimer, Richard. "Theatrum Mundi." *Art Bulletin* 38 (1956): 225–47.

Bevington, David. *From* Mankind *to* Marlowe: *The Growth of Structure in Popular Drama of Tudor England*. Cambridge, MA: Harvard University Press, 1962.
Bietenholz, Pieter, ed. *Contemporaries of Erasmus*. 3 vols. Toronto: University of Toronto Press, 1987.
Blair, Ann. *The Theatre of Nature: Jean Bodin and Renaissance Science*. Princeton: Princeton University Press, 1997.
Blissett, William. "The Venter Tripartite in *The Alchemist*." In Bloom, *Modern Critical Views* (1987): 79–88.
Blissett, William, Julian Patrick, and R. W. van Fossen, eds. *A Celebration of Ben Jonson*. Toronto: University of Toronto Press, 1973.
Bloom, Harold, ed. *Modern Critical Views: Ben Jonson*. New York: Chelsea House Publishers, 1987.
Blumenberg, Hans. *Die Lesbarkeit der Welt*. Frankfurt: Suhrkamp, 1981.
Boaistuau, Pierre. *Theatrum Mundi: The Theatre or Rule of the World, wherein may be seene the running race and course of every man's life . . . whereto is added a learned and pithy worke of the excellency of man . . .* London: Thomas East, 1581 [first French edition 1561].
Bodin, Jean. *Universae Naturae Theatrum in quo Rerum Omnium effectrices causae, & fines contemplantur . . .* Hanover: Typus Wechelianus, 1595.
Boehrer, Bruce Thomas. *The Fury of Men's Gullets: Ben Jonson and the Digestive Canal*. Philadelphia: University of Pennsylvania Press, 1997.
Bolzoni, Lina. *La Stanza della Memoria: Modelli Letterari e Iconografici dell'Età della Stampa*. Turin: G. Einaudi, 1995.
—. Introduction to Giulio Camillo, *L'Idea del Theatro*. Palermo: Sellerio, 1991.
—. *Il Teatro della Memoria: Studi su Giulio Camillo*. Padua: Liviana, 1984.
—. "L' 'invenzione' dello Stanzino di Francesco I." In *Le Arti del Principato Mediceo*. Florence: Studio per Edizioni Scelte, 1980: 255–99.
Bono, James J. *The Word of God and the Language of Man: Interpreting Nature in Early Modern Science and Medicine*. Madison: University of Wisconsin Press, 1995.
Booth, Steven, ed. *Shakespeare's Sonnets*. New Haven: Yale University Press, 1977.
Borch-Jacobsen, Mikkel. *Lacan: The Absolute Master*. Transl. Douglas Brick. Stanford: Stanford University Press, 1991.
Borges, Jorge Luis. "An Examination of the Works of Herbert Quain." In *Ficciones*. Ed., transl., and intro. Anthony Kerrigan. New York: Grove Press, 1962.
—. "Tlön, Uqbar, Orbis Tertius." In *Ficciones*. Ed., transl., and intro. Anthony Kerrigan. New York: Grove Press, 1962.
Brady, Jennifer and W. H. Herendeen, eds. *Ben Jonson's 1616 Folio*. Newark: University of Delaware Press, 1991.
Briggs, John C. *Francis Bacon and the Rhetoric of Nature*. Cambridge, MA: Harvard University Press, 1989.
Bruster, Douglas. *Drama and the Market in the Age of Shakespeare*. Cambridge: Cambridge University Press, 1992.
Budé, Guillaume. *Libri V De Asse*. Venice: Aldus Manutius, 1522.
Budra, Paul. "*Doctor Faustus*: Death of a Bibliophile." *Connotations* 1 (1991): 1–11.
Burton, Robert. *The Anatomy of Melancholy*. Eds. Thomas C. Faulkner, Nicolas K. Kiessling, and Rhonda L. Blair. Introd. J. B. Bamborough. 6 vols. Oxford: Clarendon Press, 1989–94.

Camillo Delminio, Giulio. *Tutte L'Opere*. Venice: Gabriel Giolito, 1567.
Annotationi Supra le Rime del Petrarca. Tables by Lodovico Dolce. Venice: Gabriel Giolito, 1557.
L'Idea del Theatro dell 'Eccelente M. Giulio Camillo. Florence: Lorenzo Torrentino, 1550.
Campanella, Tommaso. *La Città del Sol: Dialogo Poetico/ The City of the Sun: A Poetical Dialogue*. Trans. and notes Daniel J. Donno. Berkeley: University of California Press, 1981.
Carpo, Mario. *Alberti, Raffaello, Serlio e Camillo: Metodo ed Ordini nella Teoria Architettonica dei Primi Moderni*. Travaux d'Humanisme et Renaissance 271. Geneva: Librairie Droz, 1993.
Carruthers, Mary. *The Book of Memory: A Study of Memory in Medieval Culture*. Cambridge: Cambridge University Press, 1990.
Cartwright, Kent. *Theatre and Humanism: English Drama in the Sixteenth Century*. Cambridge: Cambridge University Press, 1999.
Cassirer, Ernst, Paul Oskar Kristeller, and John Herman Randall, Jr., eds. *Renaissance Philosophy of Man*. Chicago: University of Chicago Press, 1948.
Castelvetro, Lodovico. "A Commentary on the Poetics of Aristotle." Selected and transl. Allan H. Gilbert. In *Literary Criticism: Plato to Dryden*. Ed. Allan H. Gilbert. Detroit: Wayne State University Press, 1962: 304–57.
Castiglione, Baldessar. *Opere*. Ed. Giuseppe Prezzolini. Milan: Rizzoli, 1937.
Chambers, E. K. *The Elizabethan Stage*. 4 vols. Oxford: Clarendon Press, 1923.
Chartier, Roger. *The Order of Books*. Transl. Lydia G. Cochrane. Stanford: Stanford University Press, 1994.
"General Introduction." In *The Culture of Print: Power and the Uses of Print in Early Modern Europe*. Ed. Roger Chartier. Transl. Lydia G. Cochrane. Cambridge: Polity Press, 1989: 1–10.
Chenu, M.-D. "Auctor, Actor, Autor." *Bulletin du Cange – Archivium Latinitas Medii Aevi* 3 (1927): 81–86.
Cherchi, Paolo. *Enciclopedismo e Politica della Riscrittura: Tommaso Garzoni*. Pisa: Pacini, 1980.
[pseudo-]Cicero, Marcus Tullius. *Ad C. Herennium de Ratione Dicendi (Rhetorica ad Herennium)*. Ed. and transl. Harry Caplan. Loeb Classical Library. Cambridge, MA: Harvard University Press, 1954.
Codoñer, Carmen. "De l'Antiquité au Moyen Age: Isidore de Seville." In Becq, *L'Encyclopédisme* (1991): 19–35.
Coleridge, Samuel Taylor. *Marginalia 1*. Vol. XII no. 3 of *Collected Works*. Ed. Kathleen Coburn. 13 vols. Bollingen Series 75. Princeton: Princeton University Press, 1969–.
Specimens of the Table-Talk. 2 vols. London: John Murray, 1835.
Conley, Tom. *The Self-Made Map: Cartographic Writing in Early Modern France*. Minneapolis: University of Minnesota Press, 1996.
"Pierre Boaistuau's Cosmographic Stage: Theatre, Text, and Map." *Renaissance Drama* n.s. 23 (1992): 59–86.
Conte, Gian Biagio. *Generi e Lettori: Lucrezio, L'Elegia D'Amore, L'Enciclopedia di Plinio*. Milan: A. Mondadori, 1991.
Cooper, Thomas. *Thesaurus Linguae Romanae et Britannicae*. London: H. Wykes, 1565. [Facsimile Reprint. Menston: Scolar Press, 1969.]

Corbett, Margery and Ronald Lightbown. *The Comely Frontispiece: The Emblematic Title-Page in England, 1550–1660*. London: Routledge and Kegan Paul, 1979.
Cotgrave, Randle. *A Dictionarie of the French and English Tongues*. London, 1611. [Facsimile Reprint. Intro. William S. Woods. Columbia, SC: University of South Carolina Press, 1950.]
Coulianou, Ioan P. *Eros and Magic in the Renaissance*. Transl. Margaret Cook. Chicago: University of Chicago Press, 1987.
Crane, Mary Thomas. *Framing Authority: Sayings, Self, and Society in Sixteenth-Century England*. Princeton: Princeton University Press, 1993.
"*Intret Cato*: Authority and the Epigram in Sixteenth-Century England." In Lewalski, *Renaissance Genres* (1986): 158–86.
Crockett, Bryan. *The Play of Paradox: Stage and Sermon in Renaissance England*. Philadelphia: University of Pennsylvania Press, 1995.
Curtius, E. R. *European Literature and the Latin Middle Ages*. Transl. Willard Trask. Bollingen Series 36. Princeton: Princeton University Press, 1953.
D'Alembert, Jean le Rond. *Preliminary Discourse to the Encyclopedia of Diderot*. Transl. Richard N. Schwab. Indianapolis: Bobbs-Merrill, 1963.
Daston, Lorraine. "Marvelous Facts and Miraculous Evidence in Early Modern Europe." In *Questions of Evidence: Proof, Practice, and Persuasion across the Disciplines*. Eds. James Chandler, Arnold I. Davidson, and Harry Harootunian. Chicago: University of Chicago Press, 1994: 243–74.
Deleuze, Gilles and Felix Guattari. *A Thousand Plateaus: Capitalism and Schizophrenia*. Transl. Brian Massumi. Minneapolis: University of Minnesota Press, 1987.
Dekker, Thomas. *The Dramatic Works of Thomas Dekker*. Ed. Fredson Bowers. Cambridge: Cambridge University Press, 1962.
DeRijk, L. M. "Ἐγκύκλιον παιδεία: A Study of its Original Meaning." *Vivarium* 3 (1965): 24–93.
Derrida, Jacques. *Archive Fever: A Freudian Impression*. Transl. Eric Prenowitz. Chicago: University of Chicago Press, 1996.
"White Mythology: Metaphor in the Text of Philosophy." In *Margins of Philosophy*. Transl. Alan Bass. Chicago: University of Chicago Press, 1982: 207–71.
Disseminations. Transl. Barbara Johnson. Chicago: University of Chicago Press, 1981.
Diehl, Huston. *Staging Reform, Reforming the Stage: Protestantism and Popular Theatre in Early Modern England*. Ithaca, NY: Cornell University Press, 1997.
Dierse, Ulrich. *Enzyklopädie: Zur Geschichte eines Philosophischen und Wissenschafts-theoretischen Begriffs*. Archiv für Begriffsgeschichte, Supplement 2. Bonn: Bouvier Verlag Herbert Grundmann, 1977.
Doherty, M. J. *The Mistress-Knowledge: Sir Philip Sidney's* Defence of Poesie *and Literary Architectonics in the English Renaissance*. Nashville: Vanderbilt University Press, 1991.
Dunford, Terrance. "Consumption of the World: Reading, Eating, and Imitation in *Every Man Out of His Humor*." *English Literary History* 14 (1984): 131–47.
Dutton, Richard. *Ben Jonson: To the First Folio*. Cambridge: Cambridge University Press, 1983.
Eco, Umberto. "A Portrait of the Elder as a Young Pliny." In *Limits of Interpretation*. Bloomington: Indiana University Press, 1990: 123–36.

Eisenstein, Elizabeth. *The Printing Press as an Agent of Change: Communications and Cultural Transformations in Early-Modern Europe*. 2 vols. in 1. Cambridge: Cambridge University Press, 1979.
Eliot, T. S. "Ben Jonson." In Barish, *Critical Essays* (1963): 14–23.
Elsky, Martin. *Authorizing Words: Speech, Writing, and Print in the English Renaissance*. Ithaca, NY: Cornell University Press, 1989.
Elyot, Thomas. *The Boke Named the Governour*. London, 1546.
  The Image of Governaunce. London: Thomas Berthelet, 1541.
  Dictionary. London: Thomas Berthelet, 1538.
Enck, John J. *Jonson and the Comic Truth*. Madison: University of Wisconsin Press, 1957.
Enders, Jody. "Medieval Snuff Drama." *Exemplaria* 10 (1998): 171–206.
  "The Theatre of Scholastic Erudition." *Comparative Drama* 27 (1993): 341–63.
Erasmus, Desiderius. *Collected Works of Erasmus*, multiple vols. Toronto: University of Toronto Press, 1978–.
  Opera Omnia. Amsterdam: North-Holland Publishing Company, 1969–.
  The Ciceronian [Ciceronianus]. In *Collected Works*, vol. XXVIII (1986). Transl. and notes Betty I. Knott.
  Praise of Folly [Moriae Encomium]. In *Collected Works*, vol. XXVII: 77–153 (1986). Transl. and notes Betty Radice.
  Moriae Encomium. In *Opera Omnia* IV–3. 1979.
  Ciceronianus. In *Opera Omnia* I–2. 1971: 581–710.
  Opus Epistolarum Desiderii Erasmi Roterodami. Eds. P.S. Allen, H.M. Allen, and H.W. Garrod. Oxford: Clarendon Press, 1938.
Evans, Robert C. *Jonson and the Contexts of His Time*. Lewisburg: Bucknell University Press, 1994.
Ficino, Marsilio. See Plato.
Findlen, Paula. *Possessing Nature: Museums, Collecting, and Scientific Culture in Early Modern Italy*. Berkeley: University of California Press, 1994.
  "Jokes of Nature and Jokes of Knowledge: The Playfulness of Scientific Discourse in Early Modern Europe." *Renaissance Quarterly* 43 (1990): 292–331.
  "The Museum: Its Classical Etymology and Renaissance Genealogy." *Journal of the History of Collections* 1.1 (1989): 59–78.
Fischer, Hans. "Conrad Gessner (1516–1565) as Bibliographer and Encyclopedist." *The Library* 21 (5th series) (1966): 269–81.
Fischer, Hans *et al*. *Conrad Gessner, 1516–1565: Universalgelehrter, Naturforscher, Arzt*. Zurich: Orell Füssli Verlag, 1967.
Fish, Stanley. "Authors-Readers: Jonson's Community of the Same." *Representations* 7 (1984): 26–58.
Flemming, Willi. "Formen der Humanistenbühne." *Maske und Kothurn: Vierteljahrschrift für Theaterwissenschaft* 6 (1960): 33–52.
Foakes, R. A. *Illustrations of the English Stage, 1580–1642*. Stanford: Stanford University Press, 1985.
Foucault, Michel. "Space, Power and Knowledge." In *The Cultural Studies Reader*. Ed. Simon During. London: Routledge and Kegan Paul, 1993: 161–69.
  "Of Other Spaces." *Diacritics* 16 (1986): 22–27.
  The Archaeology of Knowledge and the Discourse on Language. Transl. A. M. Sheridan Smith. New York: Pantheon, 1972.

The Order of Things: An Archeology of the Human Sciences. New York: Vintage Books, 1970.

Fowler, Alastair. "The *Silva* Tradition in Jonson's *The Forrest*." In *Poetic Traditions of the English Renaissance*. Eds. Maynard Mack and George deForest Lord. New Haven: Yale University Press, 1982: 163–80.

Fried, Michael. *Absorption and Theatricality: Painting and Beholder in the Age of Diderot*. Berkeley: University of California Press, 1980.

Fuller, Jean Overton. *Sir Francis Bacon: A Biography*. London: East-West Publications, 1981.

Gascoigne, George. *The Glasse of Governement* [1575]. In *The Complete Works*. Ed. John W. Cunliffe. 2 vols. Cambridge: Cambridge University Press, 1910: II, 1–90.

Gellrich, Jesse M. *The Idea of the Book in the Middle Ages: Language Theory, Mythology, and Fiction*. Ithaca, NY: Cornell University Press, 1985.

Gessner, Conrad. *Historiae Animalium* (1551). 5 vols. in 4. Vol. I Frankfurt: Bibliopolium Camberiano, 1603; vol. II Frankfurt: Robert Camberius, 1586; vol. III Frankfurt: Robert Camberius, 1585; vol. IV Zurich: Christophoros Froscherus, 1558; vol. V Zurich: Christophoros Froscherus, 1587.

Bibliotheca Universalis und *Appendix*. Afterword by Hans Widmann. 2 vols. Milliaria: Faksimiledrücke zur Dokumentation der Geistesentwicklung 5. Osnabrücke: Otto Zeller Verlagsbuchhandlung, 1966 (repr. of Zurich: Christophorus Froscherus).

Giamatti, A. Bartlett. "Hippolytus Among the Exiles." In *Exile and Change in Renaissance Literature*. New Haven: Yale University Press, 1984: 12–32.

Gillies, John. *Shakespeare and the Geography of Difference*. Cambridge: Cambridge University Press, 1994.

Goldberg, Jonathan. *Writing Matter: From the Hands of the English Renaissance*. Stanford: Stanford University Press, 1990.

Gosson, Stephen. *Playes Confuted in Five Actions*. London: Thomas Gosson, 1582.

Grafton, Anthony. *Commerce with the Classics*. Jerome Lectures 20. Ann Arbor: University of Michigan Press, 1997.

Greenblatt, Stephen. *Marvelous Possessions: The Wonder of the New World*. Chicago: University of Chicago Press, 1991.

G[reene], I[ohn]. *A Refutation of the Apology for Actors*. London: W. White, 1615.

Greene, Robert. *A Notable Discovery of Cozenage*. [1591]. In Judges, *Elizabethan Underworld* (1930): 118–48.

Greene, Thomas M. "Ben Jonson and the Centered Self." In Bloom, *Modern Critical Views* (1987): 89–110.

Greetham, D. C. "Bartholomaeus Anglicus on Nature." *Journal of the History of Ideas* 41 (1980): 663–77.

Gregoire, Pierre. [Petrus Gregorius]. *Syntaxes Artis Mirabilis in Libros Septem Digestae. Per quas de omni re proposita, multis & propè infinitis rationibus disputari aut tractari, omniumqué summaria cognitio haberi potest . . .* and *Commentarius in Prolegomena Syntaxewn mirabilis artis*. 2 vols. in 1. Lyons: Ant. Gryphius, 1578.

Gurr, Andrew. *The Shakespearean Stage 1574–1642*. Cambridge: Cambridge University Press, 1992.

Playgoing in Shakespeare's London. Cambridge: Cambridge University Press, 1987.

Harbison, Robert. *Eccentric Spaces*. New York: Alfred A. Knopf, 1977.

Hathaway, Neil. "*Compilatio*: From Plagiarism to Compiling." *Viator* 20 (1989): 19–44.
Haynes, Jonathan. *The Social Relations of Jonson's Theatre*. Cambridge: Cambridge University Press, 1992.
Henningsen, Jürgen. "'Enzyklopädie': zur Sprach- und Bedeutungsgeschichte eines pädogogischen Begriffs." *Archiv für Begriffsgeschichte* 10 (1966): 271–362.
Herendeen, W. H. "'Like a Circle Bounded in Itself': Jonson, Camden, and the Strategies of Praise." *Journal of Medieval and Renaissance Studies* 11 (1981): 137–67.
Hesse, Mary. "Francis Bacon's Philosophy of Science." In Vickers, *Essential Articles* (1968): 114–39.
Heywood, Thomas. *An Apology for Actors*. London: 1612. [Facsimile Reprint. New York: Garland Press, 1973.]
Hibbard, George. "Ben Jonson and Human Nature." In Blissett *et al.*, *Celebration* (1973): 55–81.
Hodges, Devon. *Renaissance Fictions of Anatomy*. Amherst: University of Massachusetts Press, 1985.
Hollander, John. "Ben Jonson and the Modality of Verse." In Bloom, *Modern Critical Views* (1987): 205–22.
Howard, Jean. *The Stage and Social Struggle in Early Modern England*. New York: Routledge and Kegan Paul, 1994.
Hugh of St. Victor. *Didascalicon*. Transl. Jerome Taylor. New York: Columbia University Press, 1961.
   Didascalicon de Studio Legendi: A Critical Text. Ed. Charles Henry Buttimer. Washington, DC: Catholic University Press, 1939.
Huizinga, J. *Homo Ludens: A Study of the Play-Element in Culture*. Transl. R. F. C. Hull. London: Routledge and Kegan Paul, 1949.
Illich, Ivan. *In the Vineyard of the Text: A Commentary to Hugh's Didascalicon*. Chicago: University of Chicago Press, 1993.
Ingram, William. *The Business of Playing: The Beginnings of the Adult Professional Theatre in Elizabethan London*. Ithaca, NY: Cornell University Press, 1992.
Isidore. *Etymologiae, sive Origines*. Ed. W. M. Lindsay. Oxford: Clarendon Press, 1911.
James, D. G. *The Dream of Learning: An Essay on* The Advancement of Learning, Hamlet, *and* King Lear. Oxford: Clarendon Press, 1951.
James, Mervyn. "Ritual, Drama, and Social Body in the Late Medieval English Town." In *Society, Politics and Culture: Studies in Early Modern England*. Cambridge: Cambridge University Press, 1986: 16–47.
Jardine, Lisa. *Francis Bacon: Discovery and the Art of Discourse*. Cambridge: Cambridge University Press, 1974.
Jardine, Lisa and Alan Stewart. *Hostage to Fortune: The Troubled Life of Francis Bacon*. London: Victor Gollancz, 1998.
Jerome, Saint. *Opera*. Section I, parts 1–3. *Epistylae*. Ed. Isiderus Hilderberg. Corpus Scriptorum Ecclesiasticorum Latinum vols. 54–56. Vienna: F. Tempsky, 1910–18.
Johnson, A. F., ed. *One Hundred Title-Pages, 1500–1800*. London: Bodley Head, 1928.
Johnston, Mark D. *The Spiritual Logic of Ramon Llull*. Oxford: Clarendon Press, 1987.
Jonson, Ben. *The Complete Poems*. Ed. George Parfitt. New Haven: Yale University Press, 1982.
   The Alchemist. In *Drama of the English Renaissance*. Vol. II, *The Stuart Period*. Eds. Russell A. Fraser and Norman Rabkin. New York: Macmillan Publishing Co., 1976: 143–90.

Ben Jonson. 12 vols. Eds. C. H. Herford and Percy Simpson. Oxford: Clarendon Press, 1925–52.
Judges, A. V., ed. *The Elizabethan Underworld*. London: George Routledge and Sons, 1930.
Kahn, Victoria. *Rhetoric, Prudence, and Skepticism in the Renaissance*. Ithaca, NY: Cornell University Press, 1985.
Kaul, Mythili. "A Possible Source for Flamineo's 'Tale' in Webster's *The White Devil*." *Notes and Queries* n.s. 39 (1992): 360–61.
Kelley, Donald R. *Renaissance Humanism*. Boston: Twayne Publishers, 1991.
——. "History and the Encyclopedia." In *The Shapes of Knowledge from the Renaissance to the Enlightenment*. International Archives of the History of Ideas 24. Eds. Donald R. Kelley and R. H. Popkin. Dordrecht: Kluwer Academic Publishers, 1991: 7–22.
Kenny, Neil. *The Palace of Secrets: Beroalde de Verville and Renaissance Conceptions of Knowledge*. Oxford: Clarendon Press, 1991.
Kernan, Alvin. "Hamlet and the Nature of Drama." In *Yale Conference on the Teaching of English* (n.d.): 1–11.
Kerrigan, William. "Ben Jonson Full of Shame and Scorn." In Bloom, *Modern Critical Views* (1987): 111–28.
Knights, L. C. *Drama and Society in the Age of Jonson*. London: Chatto and Windus, 1957 (repr. from 1937).
Kuhn, Thomas. *The Structure of Scientific Revolutions*. International Encyclopedia of Unified Science 2.2. Chicago: University of Chicago Press, 1970 (first ed. 1962).
Kyd, Thomas. *The Spanish Tragedy*. New Mermaids Series. Ed. J. R. Mulryne. New York: W. W. Norton, 1989.
Latour, Bruno. *Science in Action: How to Follow Scientists and Engineers Through Society*. Cambridge, MA: Harvard University Press, 1987.
Lebel, Maurice. "Le Concept de l'Encyclopaedia dans l'Oeuvre de Guillaume Budé." In *Acta Conventus Neo-Latini Torontonensis*. Eds. Alexander Dalzell, Charles Fantazzi, and Richard J. Schoeck. Toronto: University of Toronto Press, 1991: 3–24.
Levao, Ronald. "Francis Bacon and the Mobility of Science." *Representations* 40 (1992):1–32.
Levi, A. H. T. "Ethics and the Encyclopedia in the Sixteenth Century." In Sharrat, *French Renaissance Studies* (1976): 170–84.
Levin, Harry. "Bacon's Poetics." In *Renaissance Rereadings: Intertext and Context*. Eds. Maryanne Cline Horowitz, Anne J. Cruz, and Wendy A. Furman. Urbana: University of Illinois Press, 1988: 3–17.
——. "An Introduction to Ben Jonson." In Barish, *Critical Essays* (1963): 40–59.
Levin, Richard. "The Relation of External Evidence to the Allegorical and Thematic Interpretation of Shakespeare." *Shakespeare Studies* 13 (1980): 1–29.
Levine, Laura. *Men in Women's Clothing: Anti-theatricality and Effeminization, 1579–1642*. Cambridge: Cambridge University Press, 1994.
Lewalski, Barbara Kiefer, ed. *Renaissance Genres: Essays in Theory, History, and Interpretation*. Cambridge, MA: Harvard University Press, 1986.
Lewis, C. S. *The Discarded Image: An Introduction to Medieval and Renaissance Literature*. Cambridge: Cambridge University Press, 1964.
Llull, Ramon. *Selected Works*. Transl. and ed. Anthony Bonner. 2 vols. Princeton: Princeton University Press, 1985.

Loewenstein, Joseph. "Printing and 'The Multitudinous Presse': The Contentious Texts of Jonson's Masques." In Brady and Herendeen, *1616 Folio* (1991): 168–91.

"The Jonsonian Corpulence, or The Poet as Mouthpiece." *English Literary History* 53 (1986): 491–518.

"The Script in the Marketplace." *Representations* 12 (1985): 101–14.

Lyly, John. *The Complete Works*. Ed. R. Warwick Bond. 3 vols. Oxford: Clarendon Press, 1902.

Magnus, Olaus. *Historia de Gentibus Septentrionalibus*. Rome: Joannis Mari de Viottis, 1555.

Maillard, J.-F. "Fortunes de l'Encyclopédie à la Fin de la Renaissance." In Becq, *L'Encyclopédisme* (1991): 319–25.

Maniquis, Robert M. "Encyclopedias and Society: Order, Disorder, and Textual Pleasure." In *The Encyclopédie and the Age of Revolution*. Eds. Clorinda Donato and Robert M. Maniquis. Catalogue of an exhibition at the UCLA Library, 1989. Boston: G. K. Hall, 1992: 77–87.

Margolin, Jean-Claude. "Le *Théâtre de Memoire* de Giulio Camillo: Récapitulation des Connaissances Acquises, ou Instrument Heuristique de Connaissances Nouvelles?" In Becq, *L'Encyclopédisme* (1991): 459–81.

"Alberto Pio et les Cicéroniens Italiens." In *Società, Politica e Cultura a Carpi ai Tempi di Alberto Pio*. Padua: Antenore, 1981: 225–59.

Marlowe, Christopher. *The Complete Works of Christopher Marlowe*. Ed. Roma Gill. 5 Vols. Vol. II, *Doctor Faustus*. Oxford: Clarendon Press, 1990.

Marlowe, Christopher, his Collaborators and Revisers. *Doctor Faustus: A- and B-Texts (1604, 1616)*. Eds. David Bevington and Eric Rasmussen. Manchester: Manchester University Press, 1993.

Marotti, Arthur. "All About Ben Jonson's Poetry." *English Literary History* 39 (1972): 208–37.

Marrou, Henri Irénée. "Les Arts Libéraux dans L'Antiquité Classique." In *Arts Libéraux et Philosophie au Moyen Age. Actes du Quatrième Congrès International de Philosophie Médiévale*. Montreal and Paris: Institute D'Etudes Médiévales/Librairie Philosophique J. Vrin, 1969: 5–27.

Marshall, Mary H. "*Theatre* in the Middle Ages: Evidence from Dictionaries and Glosses." *Symposium* 4 (1950): 1–39; 366–89.

Marston, John. *Parasitaster, or, The Fawn*. Ed. David Blostein. The Revels Plays. Manchester: Manchester University Press, 1978.

The Plays of John Marston. Ed. H. Harvey Wood. 3 vols. Edinburgh: Oliver and Boyd, 1934–39.

Martial. *Epigrammata*. Ed. and transl. D. R. Shackleton Bailey. Loeb Classical Library. Cambridge, MA: Harvard University Press, 1993.

Martianus Capella. *Martianus Capella and the Seven Liberal Arts*. Vol. II. Transl. William Harris Stahl and Richard Johnson with E. L. Burge. New York: Columbia University Press, 1977.

De Nuptiis Mercurii et Philologiae. Ed. Adolph Dick. Stuttgart: Teubner, 1925.

Martin, Julian. *Francis Bacon, the State, and the Reform of Natural Philosophy*. Cambridge: Cambridge University Press, 1992.

Maus, Katharine Eisaman. *Inwardness and Theatre in the English Renaissance*. Chicago: University of Chicago Press, 1995.

"Facts of the Matter: Satiric and Ideal Economies in the Jonsonian Imagination." In Brady and Herendeen, *1616 Folio* (1991): 64–89.

Mazzotta, Giuseppe. *Dante's Vision and the Circle of Knowledge*. Princeton: Princeton University Press, 1993.

McCanles, Michael. *Jonsonian Discriminations: The Humanist Poet and the Praise of True Nobility*. Toronto: University of Toronto Press, 1992.

McLuskie, Kathleen E. "The Poets' Royal Exchange: Patronage and Commerce in Early Modern Drama." *Yearbook of English Studies* 21 (1991): 53–62.

Medwall, Henry. *The Plays of Henry Medwall: A Critical Edition*. Ed. M. E. Moeslein. New York: Garland Press, 1981.

Minnis, A. J. *Medieval Theory of Authorship: Scholastic Literary Attitudes in the Later Middle Ages*. Philadelphia: University of Pennsylvania Press, 1988.

Mooney, Linne R. "A Middle English Text on the Seven Liberal Arts." *Speculum* 68 (1993): 1027–52.

More, Thomas. *The History of Richard III*. New Haven: Yale University Press, 1976.

Mullaney, Steven. *The Place of the Stage: License, Play, and Power in Renaissance England*. Chicago: University of Chicago Press, 1987.

Münster, Sebastian. *Cosmographei*. Basel: Henrichum Petri, 1550. [Facsimile Reprint. Amsterdam: Theatrum Orbis Terrarum, 1968.]

Munday, Anthony et al. *Sir Thomas More*. Eds. Vittorio Gabrieli and Giorgio Melchiori. The Revels Plays. Manchester: Manchester University Press, 1990.

Murray, Timothy. *Theatrical Legitimation: Allegories of Genius in Seventeenth-Century England and France*. New York: Oxford University Press, 1987.

Nagel, Thomas. *The View from Nowhere*. New York: Oxford University Press, 1986.

Nashe, Thomas. *Works*. Eds. Ronald B. McKerrow and F. P. Wilson. 5 vols. Oxford: Basil Blackwell, 1958.

Newton, Richard C. "'Ben./ Jonson': The Poet in the Poems." In *Two Renaissance Mythmakers: Christopher Marlowe and Ben Jonson: Selected Papers from the English Institute, 1975–76*. Baltimore: Johns Hopkins University Press, 1977: 165–95.

———. "Making Books from Leaves: Poets Become Editors." In *Print Culture in the Renaissance: Essays on the Advent of Printing in Europe*. Eds. Gerald P. Tyson and Sylvia S. Wagonhein. Newark: University of Delaware Press, 1986: 246–64.

Nietzsche, Friedrich. *Birth of Tragedy and Genealogy of Morals*. Transl. Francis Golfing. New York: Doubleday, 1956.

Nichols, John, ed. *The Progresses and Public Processions of Queen Elizabeth*. Research and Source Works Series 117. 3 vols. New York: Burt Franklin, 1964 (repr. of 1823).

Norland, Howard B. *Drama in Early Tudor Britain, 1485–1558*. Lincoln: University of Nebraska Press, 1995.

Northbrooke, John. *A Treatise wherein Dicing, Dauncing, Vaine playes of Enterludes* . . . London: H. Bynneman, [1577].

Ong, Walter, S.J. "Commonplace Rhapsody: Ravisius Textor, Zwinger and Shakespeare." In *Classical Influences on European Culture, A.D. 1500–1700*. Ed. R.R. Bolgar: 91–126. Cambridge: Cambridge University Press, 1976.

———. *Ramus, Method, and the Decay of Dialogue: From the Art of Discourse to the Art of Reason*. Cambridge, MA: Harvard University Press, 1958.

Ophir, Adi and Steven Shapin. "The Place of Knowledge: A Methodological Survey." *Science in Context* 4.1 (1991): 3–21.
Orrell, John. *The Human Stage: English Theatre Design, 1567–1640*. Cambridge: Cambridge University Press, 1988.
Ortelius, Abraham. *Theatrum Orbis Terrarum*. Antwerp: Coppenius Diesth, 1570.
Parker, Patricia A. *Shakespeare from the Margins: Language, Culture, Context*. Chicago: University of Chicago Press, 1996.
Parker, Patricia and Geoffrey Hartman, eds. *Shakespeare and the Question of Theory*. London: Routledge and Kegan Paul, 1990.
Parkes, M. B. "The Influence of the Concepts of *Ordinatio* and *Compilatio* on the Development of the Book." In *Medieval Learning and Literature: Essays Presented to Richard William Hunt*. Eds. J. J. G. Alexander and M. T. Gibson. Oxford: Clarendon Press, 1976:115–41.
Partridge, Edward. "Jonson's *Epigrammes*: The Named and the Nameless." *Studies in the Literary Imagination* 6 (1973): 153–98.
The Broken Compass: A Study of the Major Comedies of Ben Jonson. London: Chatto and Windus, 1958.
Paulmier-Foucart, Monique. "Ordre Encyclopédique et Organisation de la Matiére dans la *Speculum Maius* de Vincent de Beauvais." In Becq, *L' Encyclopédisme* (1991): 201–26.
Pérez-Ramos, Antonio. *Francis Bacon's Idea of Science and the Maker's Tradition of Knowledge*. Oxford: Clarendon Press, 1988.
Perotti, Nicolaus. *Cornucopiae sive Commentariorum Linguae Latinae* . . . Venice: Augustinus Bardadicus, 1492/93.
Peters, Julie Stone. *Theatre of the Book, 1480–1880: Print, Text, and Performance in Europe*. Oxford: Oxford University Press, 2000.
Peterson, Richard S. *Imitation and Praise in the Poems of Ben Jonson*. New Haven: Yale University Press, 1981.
Petrarca, Francesco. *Rerum Familiarum Libri I–VIII*. Transl. Aldo S. Bernardo. Albany: SUNY Press, 1975.
Pico della Mirandola, Giovanni. *Oration on the Dignity of Man*. In *Renaissance Philosophy of Man*. Transl. Elizabeth Livermore Forbes. Ed. Cassirer *et al.* (1948): 223–54.
Opera Omnia. 2 vols. Basel: Heinrich Petrina, 1572–73.
Conclusiones DCCC. In *Opera Omnia*, I: 63–113.
De Hominis Dignitate . . . Oratio. In *Opera Omnia*, I: 313–31.
Pigman, George. "Versions of Imitation in the Renaissance." *Renaissance Quarterly* 33 (1980): 1–32.
Plat, Hugh. *Jewell House of Art and Nature*. London: Peter Short, 1594. [Facsimile Reprint. Amsterdam: Theatrum Orbis Terrarum, 1979.]
Plato. *Republic*. Transl. G. M. A. Grube. Indianapolis: Hackett Publishing Co., 1992.
Opera Quae Extant Omnia. Ed. and transl. Io. Serranus. 3 vols. Geneva: Henricus Stephanus, 1578.
Opera. Transl. Marsilio Ficino. Paris: Ioanus Parvus et Iodocus Badius, 1518.
Plinius Caecilius, Gaius. [Pliny the Elder]. *Natural History*. Transl. H. Rackham *et al*. Loeb Classical Library. Cambridge, MA: Harvard University Press, 1938–62.
Plinius Caecilius Secundus, Gaius. [Pliny the Younger.] *Fifty Letters of Pliny*. Ed. A. F. Sherwin-White. Oxford: Oxford University Press, 1969.

Plutarch. *Lives*. Ed. and transl. Bernadotte Perin. Loeb Classical Library. London: William Heinemann, 1914–26.
Poulet, Georges. *Les Métamorphoses du Cercle*. Paris: Librairie Plon, 1961.
Pye, Christopher. *The Regal Phantasm: Shakespeare and the Politics of Spectacle*. London: Routledge and Kegan Paul, 1990.
Pyle, Cynthia. "The Art and Science of Renaissance Natural History: Thomas of Cantimpre, Pier Candido Decembrio, Conrad Gessner, and Teodoro Ghisi in Vatican Library MS Urb. Lat. 276." *Viator* 27 (1996): 265–321.
Rabelais, François. *The Complete Works*. Transl. Donald Frame. Berkeley: University of California Press, 1991.
Oeuvres Complètes. Ed. Guy Demerson. Paris: Editions du Seuil, 1973.
Radcliffe-Umstead, Douglas. "Giulio Camillo's Emblems of Memory." *Yale French Studies* 47 (1972): 47–56.
[Rastell, John.] *The Nature of the Four Elements*. The Tudor Facsimile Texts. General Ed. John S. Farmer. London, 1908. Repr. New York: AMS Press, 1970.
Reisch, Gregor. *Margarita Philosophica, hoc est Habitum seu Disciplinarum Omnium, quotquot philosophiae syncerioris ambitu continentur, perfectissima* κυκλωπαιδεια. Basle: Sebastianum Henricpetri, [1535] (first edition 1503, lacked *kuklopaideia* in the title).
Margarita Philosophica noua, cui sunt sequentia epigrammata in commendationem operis. [Ex Argentoraco veteri, J. Gruningerus, 1508].
Reiss, Timothy. *Knowledge, Discovery, and Imagination in Early Modern Europe: The Rise of Aesthetic Rationalism*. Cambridge: Cambridge University Press, 1997.
The Discourse of Modernism. Ithaca, NY: Cornell University Press, 1982.
Remigius Autissiodorensis. *Commentum in Martianum Capellam. Libri I–IV*. Ed. and intro. Cora E. Lutz. 2 vols. Leiden: E. J. Brill, 1962.
Reynolds, Bryan. "The Devil's House, 'or worse': Transversal Power and Antitheatrical Discourse in Early Modern England." *Theatre Journal* 49 (1997): 142–67.
Richards, Thomas. "Archive and Utopia." *Representations* 37 (1992): 1–32.
Richmond, Mary L. *Terence Illustrated: An Exhibition in Honor of Karl Ephraim Weston*. Foreword, S. Lane Faison, Jr. Williamstown, MA: Chapin Library, Williams College, 1955.
Rider, John. *Bibliotheca Scholastica*. Oxford: J. Barnes, 1589. [Facsimile Reprint. Menston: Scolar Press, 1970.]
Riggs, David. *Ben Jonson: A Life*. Cambridge, MA: Harvard University Press, 1989.
Righter, Anne. "Francis Bacon." In Vickers, *Essential Articles* (1968): 300–21.
Ronell, Avital. *Dictations: On Haunted Writing*. Bloomington: Indiana University Press, 1986.
Rossi, Paolo. *Clavis Universalis: Arti Mnemoniche e Logica Combinatoria da Lullo a Leibniz*. Milan: Riccardo Ricciardi, 1960.
Rouse, Richard H. and Mary A. Rouse. "*Statim invenire*: Schools, Preachers, and New Attitudes to the Page." In *The Renaissance of the Twelfth Century*. Eds. R. L. Benson and G. Constable. Cambridge, MA: Harvard University Press, 1982: 201–225.
Sahagun, Fray Bernardino de. *Florentine Codex: General History of the Things of New Spain*. Transl. Arthur J. O. Anderson and Charles E. Dibble. 13 vols. Santa Fe: School of American Research, 1970–82.
Sawday, Jonathan. *The Body Emblazoned: Dissection and the Human Body In Renaissance Culture*. London: Routledge and Kegan Paul, 1995.

Saxl, Fritz. "Illustrated Medieval Encyclopedias." In *Lectures*. 2 vols. London: Warburg Institute, 1957: I, 228–54.
Seneca, Lucius Annaeus. *Epistolae ad Lucilium*. Transl. Richard M. Grummere. Loeb Classical Library. 3 vols. London: William Heinemann, 1925.
Schechner, Richard. "Towards a Poetics of Performance." In *Essays on Performance Theory, 1970–76*. New York: Drama Book Specialists (Publishers), 1977: 108–39.
Schmidt-Biggemann, Wilhelm. *Topica Universalis: Eine Modellgeschichte Humanistischer und Barocker Wissenschaft*. Hamburg: Felix Meiner Verlag, 1983.
Schmitt, Charles B. "Experience and Experiment: A Comparison of Zabarella's View with Galileo's *De Motu*." *Studies in the Renaissance* 16 (1969): 80–138.
Schneider, Mark. *Culture and Enchantment*. Chicago: University of Chicago Press, 1993.
Se Boyar, Gerald E. "Bartholomaeus Anglicus and his Encyclopedia." *Journal of English and German Philology* 19 (1920): 168–89.
Secret, François. "Les Cheminements de la Kabbala à la Renaissance: *Le Théâtre du Monde* de Giulio Camillo et son Influence." *Rivista di Storia della Filosophica* 14 (1959): 418–36.
"La Tradition du 'De Omni Scibili' à la Renaissance: L'Oeuvre de Paul Scaliger." *Convivium* 24 (1955): 492–97.
Selden, John. *Table-Talk: Being the Discourses of John Selden Esq; or his Sence of Various Matters of Weight and High Consequence Relating especially to Religion and State*. London: for E. Smith, 1689.
Serranus, Ioannes. See Plato.
Serres, Michel. *Hermes–Literature, Science, Philosophy*. Eds. Josué Harari and David F. Bell. Baltimore: Johns Hopkins University Press, 1981.
Shakespeare, William. *The Norton Shakespeare Based on the Oxford Edition*. Eds. Stephen Greenblatt *et al*. New York: W. W. Norton & Co., 1997.
Hamlet. Ed. Harold Jenkins. Arden Shakespeare Series. London: Methuen, 1982.
Shapin, Steven. *A Social History of Truth: Civility and Science in Seventeenth-Century England*. Chicago: University of Chicago Press, 1994.
Shapiro, James "'Tragedies Naturally Performed': Kyd's Representation of Violence." In *Staging the Renaissance: Reinterpretations of Elizabethan and Jacobean Drama*. Eds. David Scott Kastan and Peter Stallybrass. New York: Routledge and Kegan Paul, (1991): 99–113.
Sharrat, Peter, ed. *French Renaissance Studies, 1540–1570: Humanism and the Encyclopedia*. Edinburgh: Edinburgh University Press, 1976.
Sidney, Philip. *Defence of Poesy*. In *Sir Philip Sidney: Oxford Authors*. Ed. Katherine Duncan-Jones. Oxford: Oxford University Press, 1989: 212–50.
Simone, Franco. "La Notion d'Encyclopédie: Elément Caractéristique de la Renaissance Française." In Sharrat, *French Renaissance Studies* (1976): 234–62.
Simonin, Michel. "Faire des Encyclopédies à la Renaissance." In Becq, *L'Encyclopédisme* (1991): 153–60.
Skalich de Lika [Scalichius, Scaliger], Paul. *Encyclopaedia, seu Orbis disciplinarum, tam sacrarum quam prophanarum Epistemon*. Basel: Ioannes Oporinus, 1559.
Skinner, Quentin. *Reason and Rhetoric in the Philosophy of Thomas Hobbes*. Cambridge: Cambridge University Press, 1996.
Skura, Meredith. *Shakespeare the Actor and the Purposes of Playing*. Chicago: University of Chicago Press, 1993.

Smallwood, R. L. "'Here, In the Friars': Immediacy and Theatricality in *The Alchemist*." *Review of English Studies* 32 (1981): 142–60.
Smith, Bruce R. *Ancient Scripts and Modern Experience on the English Stage, 1500–1700.* Princeton: Princeton University Press, 1988.
Snider, Alvin. *Origin and Authority in Seventeenth-Century England: Bacon, Milton, Butler.* Toronto: University of Toronto Press, 1994.
Srbik, Robert Ritter von. *Die Margarita Philosophica des Gregor Reisch: ein Beitrag zur Geschichte der Naturwissenschaften in Deutschland.* Vienna: Hölder-Pichler-Tempsky, 1941.
Stafford, Barbara Maria. *Artful Science: Enlightenment Entertainment and the Eclipse of Visual Education.* Cambridge, MA: MIT Press, 1994.
Steadman, John. "Beyond Hercules: Bacon and the Scientist as Hero." *Studies in the Literary Imagination* 4 (1971): 3–47.
Stillman, Robert E. "The Jacobean Discourse of Power: James I and Francis Bacon." *Renaissance Papers* (1989): 89–99.
Stockholder, Kay. "'Yet can he write': Reading the Silences in *The Spanish Tragedy*." *American Imago* 47 (1990): 93–124.
Stubbes, Philip. *The Anatomy of Abuses.* London: Richard Jones, 1583.
Summers, Claude J. and Ted-Larry Pebworth, eds. *Classic and Cavalier: Essays on Jonson and the Sons of Ben.* Pittsburgh: University of Pittsburgh Press, 1982.
Talbert, Ernest William. "Current Scholarly Works and the 'Erudition' of Jonson's *Masque of Augurs*." *Studies in Philology* 44 (1947): 605–24.
Terentius, Afer, P: [*Comoediae*]. Ed. Sebastian Brant. Strassburg: J. Grüninger, 1496.
  Comoediae. Venice: Simon Bevilacqua, 1496.
  Comoediae. Ed. Jodocus Badius Ascensius. Lyons: [Johannes] Wechsel, 1493.
Trimpi, Wesley. *Ben Jonson's Poems: A Study of the Plain Style.* Stanford: Stanford University Press, 1962.
Udall, Nicholas. *Respublica*. In *Recently Recovered 'Lost' Tudor Plays*. Ed. John Stephen Farmer. London: Early English Texts Society, 1907.
Van den Berg, Kent. *Playhouse and Cosmos: Shakespearean Theatre as Metaphor.* Newark: University of Delaware Press, 1985.
Van den Berg, Sara. *The Action of Ben Jonson's Poetry.* Newark: University of Delaware Press, 1987.
Van den Brincken, Anna-Dorothee. See Vincent of Beauvais.
Varro, Marcus Terentius. *On the Latin Language* [*De Lingua Latina*]. Transl. Roland G. Kent. Loeb Classical Library. Cambridge, MA: Harvard University Press, 1977 (repr. of. 1938).
Vergilius Maro, P. *Opera*. Ed. Sebastian Brant. Strassburg: Iohannis Grieninger, 1502.
Vickers, Brian. "Bacon's Use of Theatrical Imagery." *Studies in the Literary Imagination* 4 (1971): 189–226.
Vickers, Brian, ed. *Essential Articles for the Study of Francis Bacon.* Hamden, CT: Archon Books, 1968.
Vincent of Beauvais. *Speculum Historiale*. 4 vols. in 2. Strassburg: [The R-printer], 1473.
  Speculum Naturale. 2 vols. Strassburg: [Printer of the 1482 *Legenda Aurea*], c. 1480.
  "Geschichtsbetrachtung bei Vincenz von Beauvais: Die Apologia Actoris zum Speculum Maivs." Ed. Anna-Dorothee Van den Brincken. *Deutsche Archiv für Erforschung des Mittelatters* 34 (1978): 410–99.

Vives, Ioannes Lodovicus [Juan Luis]. *A Fable about Man*. In *Renaissance Philosophy of Man*. Transl. Nancy Lenkeith. Eds. Cassirer *et al.* (1948): 387–93.
   On Education: A Translation of De tradendis disciplinis [book II of *De Disciplinis*]. Transl. Foster Watson. Cambridge: Cambridge University Press, 1913.
   Fabula de Homine. In *Opera Omnia* Ed. Gregorius Majansio. 8 vols. Benedict Montfort: Valencia, 1783: IV, 3–8.
   De Disciplinis. Cologne: Ioannes Gymnicus, 1536.
Volaterranus, Raphael. *Commentariorum Urbanorum Libri III*. [Rome: Ascanius, 1526.]
Wager, Lewis. *The Life and Repentance of Marie Magdalene*. London: John Charlewood, 1566.
Walker, Greg. *The Politics of Performance in Early Renaissance Drama*. Cambridge: Cambridge University Press, 1998.
Wapull, George. *The Tide Taryeth No Man*. Ed. Ernst Rühl. *Jahrbuch der Deutschen Shakespeare-Gesellschaft* 43 (1907): 1–52.
Waswo, Richard. *Language and Meaning in the Renaissance*. Princeton: Princeton University Press, 1987.
Watson, Robert. "*The Alchemist* and Jonson's Conversion of Comedy." In Lewalski, *Renaissance Genres* (1986): 332–65.
Watt, Tessa. *Cheap Print and Popular Piety, 1550–1640*. Cambridge: Cambridge University Press, 1991.
Webbe, Joseph, ed. *The First Comedy of Pub. Terentius, called Andria*. London: Felix Kingston, 1629.
   Usus et Authoritas, Id Est, Liber Loquens . . . sub titulo Entheati Materialis Primi. London: Felix Kingston, 1626.
Webber, James Leslie and C. R. Morey. *The Miniatures of the Manuscripts of Terence Prior to the Thirteenth Century*. 2 vols. Princeton: Princeton University Press, 1930–31.
Webster, John. *Complete Works of John Webster*. Ed. F. L. Lucas. 4 vols. New York: Oxford University Press, 1937.
Weimann, Robert. *Authority and Representation in Early Modern Discourse*. Ed. David Hillman. Baltimore: Johns Hopkins University Press, 1996.
   "Memory, Fictionality, and the Issue of Authority: Author-function and Narrative Performance in *Beowulf*, Chrétien and Malory." In *Contexts of the Pre-Novel Narrative: The European Tradition*. Ed. Roy Erickson. Approaches to Semiotics 114. Berlin: Mouton de Gruyter, 1994: 83–100.
   "Author-ity in Signification: Rabelais and Vernacular Renaissance Prose Fiction." In *Sprache und Literatur der Romania: Tradition und Wirkung: Festschrift für Horst Heintze zum 70. Geburtstag*. Eds. Irmgard Osols-Wehden, Giuliano Staccioli, and Babette Hesse. Berlin: Berlin Verlag, 1993: 87–99.
   "Mimesis in *Hamlet*." In Parker and Hartman, *Question of Theory* (1990): 275–91.
   "Bifold Authority in Shakespeare's Theatre." *Shakespeare Quarterly* 39 (1988): 401–17.
   Shakespeare and the Popular Tradition in Theatre: Studies in the Social Dimension of Dramatic Form and Function. Ed. Robert Schwartz. Baltimore: Johns Hopkins University Press, 1978.
Wellisch, Hans H. *Conrad Gessner: A Bio-Bibliography*. Zug: IDC, 1984.
Westfall, Suzanne R. *Patrons and Performance: Early Tudor Household Revels*. Oxford: Clarendon Press, 1990.

Whitney, Charles. "Ante-Aesthetics: Towards a Theory of Early Modern Audience Response." In *Shakespeare and Modernity: Early Modern to Millennium*. Ed. Hugh Grady. London: Routledge and Kegan Paul, 2000: 40–60.
— *Francis Bacon and Modernity*. New Haven: Yale University Press, 1986.
Wilson, Edmund. "Morose Ben Jonson." In Barish, *Critical Essays* (1963): 60–74.
Winnicott, D. W. *Playing and Reality*. New York: Basic Books, 1971.
Wolff, Emil. *Francis Bacon und seine Quellen*, 2 vols. Berlin: Emil Felber, 1913; repr. Liechtenstein: Kraus Reprint, 1977.
Worthen, W. B. "Disciplines of the Text/ Sites of Performance." *The Drama Review* 39 (1995): 13–28.
Wormald, B. H. G. *Francis Bacon: History, Politics and Science, 1561–1626*. Cambridge: Cambridge University Press, 1993.
Yachnin, Paul. *Stage-Wrights: Shakespeare, Jonson, Middleton, and the Making of Theatrical Value*. Philadelphia: University of Pennsylvania Press, 1997.
Yates, Frances. *Theatre of the World*. London: Routledge and Kegan Paul, 1969.
— *The Art of Memory*. Chicago: University of Chicago Press, 1966.
Young, Abigail Ann. "Plays and Players: The Latin Terms for Performance." *REED Newsletter* 9.2 (1984): 56 – 62; 10.1 (1985): 9–16.
Zagorin, Perez. *Francis Bacon*. Princeton: Princeton University Press, 1998.
Zetterberg, J. Peter. "Echoes of Nature in Salomon's House." *Journal of the History of Ideas* 43 (1982): 179–94.
Žižek, Slavoj. *The Sublime Object of Ideology*. London: Verso, 1989.
Zwinger, Theodor. *Theatrum Vitae Humanae*. 4 vols. Basel: Frobenius, 1571.
— *Theatrum Vitae Humanae*. Basel: I. Oporinus, 1565.

Index

actor, 56–60, 63f., 69–71, 96, 128f.
  etymology, 57
    Varro's definition, 58f., 63
    Webster's definition, 111f.
  Cicero as, 43, 172f.
  Roman emperors as, 4, 130, 132, 137
  scholar as, 3, 27f., 39, 63, 71, 98, 171, 224n.4
Aristotle and Aristotelianism, 6, 9, 17, 24–26, 29, 32, 35, 49, 87, 170, 180, 194, 204f., 216, 229n.19, 231n.35, 254n.62, 271n.26, 273n.41
  dramatic unities, 71, 151, 246n.75,
  and Alexander, as image of knowledge and power, 30f., 35, 195f., 233n.49
audience, 23–27, 40f., 46–48, 64, 67, 70f., 111, 113f., 116–21, 124f., 173f., 176, 179, 190, 198, 213, 242n.45
  behavior of, 119f., 128f., 139f., 190f.
  in relation to readers, 69, 98, 119, 128, 144, 170, 172–75
Augustine, 24, 38, 43, 232n.42, 246n.79
authority, 3f., 57–69, 79–81, 127–29, 142, 176, 211–14, 257n.8
  etymology, 57
  author as actor, 31, 59–67, 93, 98, 158

Bacon, Francis, 84, 143f., 158f., 193–95, 226n.22, 233n.49
  Abecedarium Naturae, 272n.36
  Advancement of Learning (1605), 201, 207, 211–15, 220, 222f., 271n.21
  De Augmentis Scientiarum (1623), 193, 197f., 201–06, 208f., 214–16, 218
  De Sapientia Veterum (1609), 198–201, 218
  Descriptio Globi Intellectualis (c.1612), 198, 215, 220
  dramatic works, 197, 203, 213f.
  Echo, as figure for philosopher, 198–200, 211, 218f., 222
  Essays, 196, 208f., 213, 215, 221–23
  Historia Naturalis et Experimentalis (1622), 204f., 208, 210
  Historia Vitae et Mortis, 200
  Historia Ventorum, 198
  Idols of the Mind, 203–07, 219f.
  Instauratio Magna, 194f., 197, 205, 208, 219–21
    definition of *instauratio*, 197f.
  Novum Organum (1620), 195f., 199, 204f., 207, 210f., 214, 217–22
  Orpheus, as figure for philosopher, 199–202, 205f., 208, 210–12, 219, 222
  pedagogy, 202f., 271n.19
  Redargutio Philosophiae, 269n.5, 271n.26
  Sylva Sylvarum, 214, 216, 220
  Valerius Terminus (1603), 197, 204, 215
Bartholomaeus Anglicus, 30, 34, 81f., 103f., 175
Batman, Stephen, 63, 175
Beaumont, Francis, *Knight of the Burning Pestle*, 121f., 137
Bodin, Jean, 50–52, 70, 226n.22
Budé, Guillaume, 17, 156, 159, 233n.49

Camillo, Giulio, 50, 83–102, 110, 147, 154, 160
Chapman, George, dedicatory poem for *Sejanus*, 166
Cicero, Marcus Tullius, 27, 35, 209
  as an actor, 43, 172
  as a figure for Jonson, 172
  Ciceronianism, 38, 85, 94–96, 250n.15, 252n.35; *see also* Erasmus, *Ciceronianus*
combinatory, 81f., 84, 97, 145, 147f., 151, 154f., 173, 177f.
  defined, 83f., 90f., 93–95, 147
  as a theatrical technique, 147f., 171, 176; *see also* Jonson's critique of
  elements
    facts as, 33f., 83, 96, 146f., 176f.; *see also silva*
    letters as, 84, 215
  Jonson's critique of, 149–51, 153–55
  See also Camillo, grammar, Llull, print, Ramus, *silva*

291

contemplatio, 18–22, 28, 30, 33, 51, 215, 217; see also *templum*, Varro
curiositas, 29f., 34, 37–39, 74–78, 83, 86, 164, 232n.42, 236n.67; see also desire

Dekker, Thomas, *Satiromastix*, 146f.
desire, 29f., 32f., 35–41, 165f., 179f., 196, 200–03, 210–13, 219f; see also *curiositas*, *superbia* .
  cupiditas, 28, 36f.
  negation in *fastidium*, 32f., 41f., 159, 234n.57
  luxuria, 37f.
  voluptas, 42, 237n.80
Diderot and D'Alembert, *Encyclopédie*, 28, 59, 196
Donatus, definition of comedy, 45f., 170

Elyot, Thomas, 3f., 15, 17, 79–81, 90, 116, 162f., 212
Encyclopedia, etymology of, 14–18; see also Pliny the Elder, Quintilian, spatiality (Circle of Learning)
  Bacon's definition, 197f.
  Elyot's definition, 3, 15, 17
  Jonson's definition, 146, 188f.
    as projection, 165f.; see also desire
  Vives' definition, 156f.
  ethical encyclopedia, 155, 158, 160f., 165–67, 174
  dinner party as, 158f.
  poet or orator as, 14, 152
epigram, as a genre, 160, 163–65; see also *theatrum* (books as; collections of poems as)
Erasmus, Desiderius, 8, 18, 46, 69, 246n.73, 250n.15, 251n.31
  Ciceronianus, 91, 250n.15, 252n.35

Forman, Simon, 118
Fried, Michael, on "theatricality" and "absorption," 246n.74, 271n.29

Galilei, Galileo, 31, 219f.
Garzoni, Tommaso, 241n.26
Gessner, Conrad, *Historiae Animalium*, 32, 37, 83, 96–110, 256.n54
  Bibliotheca Universalis, 99
Gosson, Stephen, 119f.
grammar, 27, 215f.
  as metaphor, 81–83
Greene, John, author of *Refutation of an Apology for Actors?*, 130
Greene, Robert, 71, 186
Gregoire, Pierre, 16, 24, 35, 82, 84

Heywood, Thomas, 119, 124–26, 130f., 138–42
Hobbes, Thomas, 256n.2, 272n.32
Horace, *Epistles*, 173f.
  as a figure for Jonson, 145–47, 174
Hugh of St. Victor, 22, 34, 42, 94

index, as exemplar of comprehensiveness, compression, and order, 161–63, 291ff.

Jonson, Ben
  alternative identities; see Cicero, Horace, and Vergil
  masques:
    Hymenaei, 115, 144f.
    Pleasure Reconciled to Virtue, 172
  plays:
    The Alchemist, 151, 158, 179–92, 208, 220
    Bartholomew Fair, 140, 151, 155, 158, 190f.
    Catiline, 172–74
    Every Man In His Humor, 147, 153f., 157, 171, 262n.11
    Every Man Out of His Humor, 147–55, 170f., 173f., 179–82, 190, 262n.11
    The New Inn, 151, 170
    Poetaster, 145f., 173–75
    Sejanus, 166, 174
    Volpone, 151
  poems, 160–63, 167, 169f., 172f., 178
    Cary–Morison Ode, 167–70, 173, 175; see also Selden, John
  Timber, 143, 145f., 152, 171, 186, 188–90
  Conversations with Drummond, 166, 265n.37, 266n.49
  See also combinatory, Johnson's critique of

Kyd, Thomas, *The Spanish Tragedy*, 130–37

Llull, Ramon, 83f.
  Llullism, see combinatory
Lyly, John, 121, 267n.59

Marlowe, Christopher, *Doctor Faustus*, 31, 177–79, 181–83, 185f., 189f.
Marston, John, *The Fawn*, 120
  target of Jonson, 145f.
Martial, 163–65, 266n.45
Martianus Capella, 18, 41f., 159, 234n.57, 234n.58, 257n.5
metalanguage/metatheatre, defined, 132–34, 136f., 139–43, 186–88
  humanist discomfort with, 70–72, 122f., 132–34, 138
  referentiality, 14f., 22–24, 124f., 161–63, 182
More, Thomas, 70, 72f., 121f., 129; see also Vives

Index

Nashe, Thomas, 58, 117–19, 124, 130
Nero, 4, 37, 130, 137; *see also* actor, (Roman emperors as)

Ortelius, Abraham, 34, 45, 52, 112

Perotti, Nicolaus, *Cornucopiae*, 163f., 246n.6
Petrarch, Francesco, 50, 89–92, 250n.15
Pico della Mirandola, Giovanni, 35, 43
picture, 14, 47, 101–10, 241n.36, 257n.4
 as opposed to diagram, 24–27, 103f.
Plato, vii, 6–9, 16f., 158, 216, 229n.19
 Platonism and Neoplatonism, 7f., 35, 181, 186, 216
 as author of *Histriomastix*, 154
playfulness, 2, 9, 36f., 42, 159, 196, 213, 217–19, 236n.67, 257n.4
 irony, 15, 23, 41, 85–87, 137, 139f., 155
Pliny the Elder, 8, 22, 29, 32–41, 83, 100, 175
 as origin of word "encyclopedia," 2, 15, 17
 as model encyclopedist, 29, 31f., 96, 198, 203
Pliny the Younger, 31f.
print, 173, 257n.5
 as metaphor for combinatory, 82f.
prudentia, 23, 156–58, 160f., 163, 171f., 178f., 186

Quintilian, as origin of word "encyclopedia," 2, 15, 17

Rabelais, François, 14f., 42
Ramus, Petrus, and Ramism, 84, 156, 190, 202, 242n.37
Rastell, John, 72f.
 The Nature of the Four Elements, 73–78, 114–16, 139, 143
Reisch, Gregor, *Margarita Philosophica*, 16, 24–28, 113

Selden, John, 158
 Jonson's poems on, 160, 162f., 165f., 171
Shakespeare, William
 Hamlet, 111, 122–31, 134, 136, 138, 141f., 206f., 220
 Henry V, 112
 King Lear, 259n.37
 A Midsummer Night's Dream, 123, 128, 136f., 140
 A Winter's Tale, 118
Sidney, Philip, 63, 71, 117, 171, 233n.49, 273n.41
silva (also *sylva* and *selva*), 48, 57, 95, 98f., 145, 154f., 157, 163, 266n.41
Skalich de Lika, Paul, 16, 28
spatiality, 14, 16–18, 21–24, 26f., 48–56 111–14; *see also* visuality

Circle of Learning, 15–18, 27, 196–98, 201f.
 circle of tales, 223
 circular space, 18, 24–27, 42, 111–13, 196f.
 rejection or failure of, 45, 52–54, 214f., 221–23
 theatre as space, 43, 46
Stubbes, Philip, 120
superbia, 71f., 83; *see also* desire

templum, 18–22, 28, 39, 50f.
 as *theatrum*, 19
Terence, 43, 46, 59–62, 64–69, 148–50, 152, 170f.
theatrum
 books as, 45, 52f., 67–69, 204f., 216f.
 collections of poems as, 117, 164f., 170, 172f.
 educational potential of, 2–4, 49, 171–73, 179, 201
 etymology, 46–48
 opposed to *drama*, 49, 74, 76f.
 physical theatres and performance, 43–45, 49, 55f., 70f., 73, 78, 102, 111–14, 120, 133, 140–42, 202, 206f.
 ruins of, 44, 50
 See also actor, audience, *templum*

Udall, Nicholas, *Respublica*, 114f.

Varro, 18f., 49–51, 58f., 63; *see also* *contemplatio*
Vergil, 89, 91, 213, 272n.33
 as a figure for Jonson, 174
Vincent of Beauvais, 30, 34, 38f., 56–59, 96, 98, 129, 158
visuality, 18f., 23–26, 47–50, 56, 80f., 101f., 104–06, 114f., 125, 127f., 202, 207, 214, 217–21
 as knowledge, 46f., 51, 83, 101, 181f., 189, 214
 deceptio visus [optical illusion], 181–84, 187, 204
 rejection or failure of, 52f., 104–06, 172, 181f.
 See also audience, picture, spatiality, *theatrum*
Vives, Juan Luis, 32, 35, 43, 47, 51, 69–72, 121f., 129, 156–60
 as source for Jonson's *Timber*, 146

Webbe, Joseph, 46, 64, 147, 250n.15, 262n.10
Webster, John
 "An Excellent Actor," 111f.
 The White Devil, 120f., 129f., 175–77, 259n.37

Zeuxis, 8, 93, 101f.
Zwinger, Theodor, 45, 48, 52–55, 57, 63, 71, 95f., 98, 158, 210

Cambridge Studies in Renaissance Literature and Culture

General editor
STEPHEN ORGEL
Jackson Eli Reynolds Professor of Humanities, Stanford University

1. Douglas Bruster, *Drama and the market in the age of Shakespeare*
2. Virginia Cox, *The Renaissance dialogue: literary dialogue in its social and political contexts, Castiglione to Galileo*
3. Richard Rambuss, *Spenser's secret career*
4. John Gillies, *Shakespeare and the geography of difference*
5. Laura Levine, *Men in women's clothing: anti-theatricality and effeminization, 1579–1642*
6. Linda Gregerson, *The reformation of the subject: Spenser, Milton, and the English Protestant epic*
7. Mary C. Fuller, *Voyages in print: English travel to America, 1576–1624*
8. Margreta de Grazia, Maureen Quilligan, Peter Stallybrass (eds.), *Subject and object in Renaissance culture*
9. T. G. Bishop, *Shakespeare and the theatre of wonder*
10. Mark Breitenberg, *Anxious masculinity in early modern England*
11. Frank Whigham, *Seizures of the will in early modern English drama*
12. Kevin Pask, *The emergence of the English author: scripting the life of the poet in early modern England*
13. Claire McEachern, *The poetics of English nationhood, 1590–1612*
14. Jeffrey Masten, *Textual intercourse: collaboration, authorship, and sexualities in Renaissance drama*
15. Timothy J. Reiss, *Knowledge, discovery and imagination in early modern Europe: the rise of aesthetic rationalism*
16. Elizabeth Fowler and Roland Greene (eds.), *The project of prose in early modern Europe and the New World*
17. Alexandra Halasz, *The marketplace of print: pamphlets and the public sphere in early modern England*
18. Seth Lerer, *Courtly letters in the age of Henry VIII: literary culture and the arts of deceit*
19. M. Lindsay Kaplan, *The culture of slander in early modern England*
20. Howard Marchitello, *Narrative and meaning in early modern England: Browne's skull and other histories*

21. Mario DiGangi, *The homoerotics of early modern drama*
22. Heather James, *Shakespeare's Troy: drama, politics, and the translation of empire*
23. Christopher Highley, *Shakespeare, Spenser, and the crisis in Ireland*
24. Elizabeth Hanson, *Discovering the subject in Renaissance England*
25. Jonathan Gil Harris, *Foreign bodies and the body politic: discourses of social pathology in early modern England*
26. Megan Matchinske, *Writing, gender and state in early modern England: identity formation and the female subject*
27. Joan Pong Linton, *The romance of the New World: gender and the literary formations of English colonialism*
28. Eve Rachele Sanders, *Gender and literacy on stage in early modern England*
29. Dorothy Stephens, *The limits of eroticism in post-Petrarchan narrative: conditional pleasure from Spenser to Marvell*
30. Celia R. Daileader, *Eroticism on the Renaissance stage: transcendence, desire, and the limits of the visible*
31. Theodore B. Leinwand, *Theatre, finance, and society in early modern England*
32. Heather Dubrow, *Shakespeare and domestic loss: forms of deprivation, mourning, and recuperation*
33. David Posner, *The performance of nobility in early modern European literature*
34. Michael C. Schoenfeldt, *Bodies and selves in early modern England: physiology and inwardness in Spenser, Shakespeare, Herbert, and Milton*
35. Lynn Enterline, *Rhetoric of the Body from Ovid to Shakespeare*
36. Douglas A. Brooks, *From Playhouse to Printing House: Drama and Authorship in Early Modern England*
37. Robert Matz, *Defending Literature in Early Modern England: Renaissance Literary Theory in Social Context*
38. Ann Jones and Peter Stallybrass, *Renaissance Clothing and the Materials of Memory*
39. Robert Weimann, *Author's Pen and Actor's Voice: Playing and Writing in Shakespeare's Theatre*
40. Barbara Fuchs, *Mimesis and Empire: The New World, Islam, and European Identities*
41. Wendy Wall, *Staging Domesticity: Household Works and English Identity in Early Modern Drama*
42. Valerie Traub, *The Renaissance of Lesbianism in Early Modern England*
43. Joe Loewenstein, *Ben Jonson and Possessive Authorship*
44. William N. West, *Theatres and Encyclopedias in Early Modern Europe*